W9-CFB-091

The Silent Brotherhood

The Chilling Inside Story of America's Violent Anti-Government Militia Movement

———— ∞∞∞ ————

Kevin Flynn
and
Gary Gerhardt

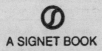

A SIGNET BOOK

SIGNET
Published by the Penguin Group
Penguin Books USA Inc., 375 Hudson Street,
New York, New York 10014, U.S.A.
Penguin Books Ltd, 27 Wrights Lane,
London W8 5TZ, England
Penguin Books Australia Ltd, Ringwood,
Victoria, Australia
Penguin Books Canada Ltd, 10 Alcorn Avenue.
Toronto, Ontario, Canada M4V 3B2
Penguin Books (N.Z.) Ltd, 182–190 Wairau Road,
Auckland 10, New Zealand

Penguin Books Ltd, Registered Offices:
Harmondsworth, Middlesex, England

Published by Signet, an imprint of Dutton Signet,
a division of Penguin Books USA Inc.

This is an authorized reprint of a hardcover edition published by The Free Press,
a division of Macmillan, Inc. and in Canada by Collier Macmillan Canada, Inc.

First Signet Printing, November, 1990
10 9 8 7 6 5 4 3

🄢 REGISTERED TRADEMARK—MARCA REGISTRADA

Printed in the United States of America

We dedicate this book
and all the effort that went behind it to
Kathy and Nancy, our wives;
and to our children and families,
because families are what matter

Contents

Preface

Comfortably secure Americans are used to thinking of terrorism as something that carries a foreign dateline. But the bombing of the federal office building in Oklahoma City in April 1995—and the suspicion that an army veteran of the Persian Gulf War may be the perpetrator of that deadliest act of terrorism on U.S. soil—will erase forever the false notion that this threat comes from beyond our shores.

Home-grown terrorists have long scarred America's landscape with guns and bombs. From our biggest metropolises to the heartland cities, these true believers have struck. When they surface, their acts give us a glimpse into a shadowy world of fear. Often with political aims, they target their weapons at individuals and institutions they believe are conspiring against the true America and its sacred Constitution.

To prepare for possible battle with a government they see as their enemy, seemingly ordinary citizens have enlisted themselves in paramilitary training. Such a group was the Silent Brotherhood, a private guerrilla army with the goal of launching a terror and sabotage campaign against what they called the Zionist Occupation Government. In the shorthand of the American media, the gang later became known as The Order. In the mid-1980s, it launched a campaign of robberies, assassination, sabotage, and terrorism that brought nearly $4 million in stolen loot into their treasury. Its members gunned down Jewish talk show host Alan Berg in Denver in 1984 to silence his over-the-air railings against their cause. They amassed an impressive arsenal of weaponry, set up a salary system for their soldiers, and purchased land in the Idaho forest for establishment of a military boot camp to train America.

After an intensive manhunt by the Federal Bureau of Investigation, the Silent Brotherhood's conspiracy was eventually broken. But after all the courtrooms emptied and the prison cells slammed shut, one striking gap remained, one nagging question no one yet had addressed.

Who was Robert Jay Mathew; the man who founded the Silent Brotherhood?

The FBI didn't know him. The media never heard of him until after his death. The only thing obvious about him was that he defied the stereotype of an American racist. His story bore witness to something more pervasive, more threatening to the nation's way of life, as most Americans understand it, than is generally believed. With the potential to be a successful family man had he chosen that course, he nevertheless formed a terrorist underground, crossing a line that the radical right had been toeing for years.

So at a time when race relations in America continue to spark conflict and outrage, when the radical right rises up with guns and bombs as the radical left had done in the 1960s and 1970s, the authors set out to look at the Silent Brotherhood as a microcosm of the extremist movement.

What we found was an intricately woven web where lines are blurred, and distinctions are matters not always of difference but merely of deree.

—Kevin Flynn and Gary Gerhart
April, 1995

List of Main Characters and Organizations

Aryan Nations: A Hayden Lake, Idaho, organization that is one of the preeminent racist groups in the nation, preaching the anti-Semitic Identity religion.

Andrew Barnhill: An intelligent young man with a good-paying job in Florida, he becomes steeped in survivalist religion and the ultraconservative cause.

Richard G. Butler: The Aryan Nations' leader whose goal is to unify the radical right, he loses younger followers to the more militant Robert Mathews.

Christian Identity: This race-based theology, one of the far right's fastest-growing segments, claims white Christians are the true biblical Israelites.

Jean Craig: A Wyoming grandmother and Identity believer who assists the Silent Brotherhood with tasks ranging from soothsaying to surveillance.

Zillah Craig: Jean's estranged daughter and believer in Identity, she becomes Robert Mathews's lover and confidante.

CSA: Started in 1976 as a fundamentalist Christian commune deep in the Ozarks woods, the *Covenant, the Sword, and the Arm of the Lord* grows into a military encampment of survivalists waiting for Armageddon.

Randy Duey: A studious, conservative bachelor, he progresses deeper into the movement until he finds himself carrying an Uzi machine gun for the cause.

James Dye: A Marine Corps veteran of Vietnam with a shrapnel wound in his head, the scorn he receives upon his return drives him into the racist movement.

Richard Kemp: A high school basketball star from Salinas, California, he is drawn at a young age to the neo-Nazi National Alliance and is impressed by Mathews.

David Lane: A Klansman from Denver, he leaves his

real estate and title insurance jobs after a divorce and deepens his involvement in the radical right.

Ken Loff: Robert Mathews's closest friend, he is a farmer and family man who follows Mathews devotedly and becomes the banker of the white revolution.

Wayne Manis: The veteran FBI agent whose intuition leads to busting one of the biggest cases of domestic terrorism in history.

Thomas Martinez: A Philadelphia janitor and racist who, when backed into a corner between Robert Mathews and the FBI, decides he cannot join the underground and still remain true to his family's love.

Robert Jay Mathews: Founder of the Silent Brotherhood who yearns to lead a white underground to, in his words, "remove the Jew forever from this world."

Ardie McBrearty: A congenial man from a big family, he becomes involved in the tax protest movement because of what he considers unfair taxation.

Robert and Sharon Merki: A middle-aged husband and wife who make mnoney in their basement when their finances fall apart, then set up a counterfeiting and spying operation for Mathews with help from their children.

Robert Miles: One of the leading racist figures in the country, his remarks at rallies motivate Mathews to embark on armored car robberies.

National Alliance: A neo-Nazi group based at the time in Arlington, Virginia, it gives Mathews his principal motivation for forming the white underground.

Charles Ostrout: He blames his lack of advancement at the Brink's Company on its affirmative action program and helps set up a multimillion-dollar robbery.

Denver Parmenter: In two years he goes from working for Ronald Reagan's election to wearing a neo-Nazi uniform at a congress of racists, losing his marriage and child in the process.

Bruce Carroll Pierce: A Kentuckian enthralled with the Western mystique, he moves to Montana where, in less than a year, he discovers the race-based theology of Pastor Butler and joins Mathews as his top lieutenant.

Randall Rader: A backwoods boy and rock musician turned Christian survivalist, he becomes the Rommel of the Radical Right by running Mathews's guerrilla camp.

Richard Scutari: A martial-arts expert and ultra-conservative religious man, he gives up a secure job and family to become Mathews's chief of security.

David Tate: His parents, ardent followers of Pastor Butler, rear him in the church and school at Aryan Nations, where he meets Mathews.

Gary Lee Yarbrough: A convicted burglar, he finds his religious roots at Aryan Nations and later joins the Silent Brotherhood, becoming the only member of the gang who had ever been in prison.

ZOG: The *Zionist Occupation Government,* a euphemism among far right activists for what they feel is a Jewish-dominated government and culture in the United States.

Richard Starns. A martini and cigar and then remove the glasses item by item and a game it, in fact, isn't it Paying Make a name at activity.

What have. The universe patent litovets of Baby they act: me: into it in... chrysler and senior in Anvil we ok here: he Reinee Mad.

Take our. University. A kommunal letters (or first, but in our from an Astael tainin. and here, plus the deep it them in we have, in the the structure of the pain text: bid ever from a group.

Equi.a.B - is a far. Oct.edet, and tainen in a subit may in a/t.oo but in at stuffer: his plus the looking. but in cathology about man ... magating in the frienal Nevs.

Prologue
The Underground

Wayne Manis shifted his automatic rifle to his shoulder as he heard the front door opening. Pressing against the damp bark of a tall fir tree, he peered at the isolated house through the milky haze cast by a set of powerful spotlights.

"Get ready!" he heard Danny Colson whisper sharply as a young man stepped out on the front porch.

The young man squinted into the glare of the lights, then nervously turned his head away. His hands were clasped tightly around an olive drab duffel bag. He hesitated before continuing to walk slowly off the porch.

An agent dressed in fatigues and face paint triggered a bullhorn.

"Hold your hands out where we can see them at all times," the amplified voice reverberated through the darkness. The man turned sharply to his left, facing the direction of the voice. Clutching the duffel bag in his left hand, he opened the palm of the right to show it was empty.

"Now, slowly, walk directly forward between the garage and the shed," the voice ordered. The young man appeared terrified. Manis was aware that he probably believed he was about to be assassinated.

The lights carved through the mist blowing in from Puget Sound and reflected off the tiny droplets, setting off the young man with a luminous, surreal glow.

The house, a two-story vacation chalet, faced west on a cliff overlooking the water. There was 50 feet of clearing on either side and twice that much in the back, where the curving driveway disappeared into a stand of immense pine trees. The forest dwarfed the garage and shed, tucked into the southern edge of the clearing. To the west was a

15

commanding view over Admiralty Inlet, the line of sight impeded only by three small pines on the left side. About 20 feet from the front of the house there was a sharp drop, and from this bluff a wooden staircase descended 100 feet through steep bramble to a slender thread of beach.

"Continue walking forward until you are out of the light," the agent with the bullhorn barked. The man stepped into the darkness. "Stop right there and put down that bag, slowly," the voice commanded.

The bag landed with a muffled thud on the wet ground.

"Now lower yourself face down, putting your arms straight out to both sides," the voice ordered.

The young man hugged the soggy ground. Several men rushed forward. They twisted his arms behind him and snapped ice-cold handcuffs around his wrists. Hands slid roughly down his legs, into his boots, back up to his crotch, then over his back and down his arms. Two men grabbed his arms and lifted him to his feet, and a third ran his hands over the front of the prisoner. Satisfied he wasn't armed, the man stepped back.

Manis and Colson hustled their prisoner behind the garage, out of sight of the house. They played their flashlights over his face.

"Know him?" Colson asked, figuring Manis was the expert.

"Nope," answered a puzzled Manis.

"What's your name, boy?" Colson said stiffly to the prisoner.

The man offered no answer. In the darkness behind them, another team member blurted out: "Hey, get a load of this! This bag's filled with money! There's about $40,000 here!"

"It's mine!" the young man shouted, trying to twist and look over his shoulder. "That's my money!"

Manis knew better. He didn't know who the man was, but the money represented less than 1 percent of the millions his buddies had liberated from the backs of armored trucks over the last nine months. Manis wanted the other 99 percent.

"Who's that we've been talking to on the field phone?" Manis asked the prisoner. "Is it Mathews? Bob Mathews?"

The young man hesitated, then nodded.

"Who else is in there?" Colson asked.

Silence.

"Listen," Manis tried. "Are there women and kids in there?"

Silence.

"Look, kid," Manis tried again. "We're trying to do everything we can to make sure nobody gets hurt. What can we offer Mathews so he'll surrender?"

The young man stiffened. "He told you on the phone. He wants a place for an Aryan homeland."

It would be laughable if it weren't such a deadly situation. Whidbey Island was crawling with FBI agents, and Mathews was trapped. He was hardly in a position to demand anything.

"Isn't there anything else we might . . . ?"

"No," the young man cut Manis short. "He has enough ammunition in there to hold you off forever. Bob will never surrender."

"Take him to the CP," Colson said, stepping back.

Two agents took the man's arms and led him off, reaching for the rope that had been strung through the dense growth to the command post several hundred feet away in a small opening among the trees. The main command center, 8 miles up the island at the Whidbey Naval Air Station, was in charge of 150 agents plus local police, some involved at two other arrest sites nearby.

Resuming their positions in the woods on the south side of the house, Manis and Colson tried to find a comfortable seat in the wet ferns. The quiet watch resumed. It was impossible to know what was happening in the house, because Mathews had refused to talk since he told them the young man was coming out.

Something moved behind Colson and Manis, and they turned to see an agent bringing sandwiches and hot coffee. Manis couldn't remember when he'd been so cold. Night comes early this far north in December, and the spray from the sound reinforced the dampness, saturating his jacket. He welcomed the coffee as much to warm his hands with the cup as to warm his stomach.

Manis tilted his head upward and glanced toward the fog-shrouded treetops. Nine months of a tedious cat-and-mouse game went fast-forward through his mind. As the Coeur d'Alene, Idaho, FBI agent who was instrumental in breaking this case, his work had been pointing toward Mathews for months. Now, this close to his prey, his primary goal was to interrogate him.

Inside the fashionable vacation home in the clearing was Robert Jay Mathews, who had taken a group of people, most of whom had never committed a crime before in their lives, and turned them into armored car robbers and killers.

Erstwhile squire of a little spread in Metaline Falls, Washington, population 285, Mathews was robust and handsome, born with a quick, disarming smile. His wife spent her days rearing their adopted three-year-old son, and his widowed mother lived next door on the land. Until Mathews quit his job a year earlier, he worked at a cement plant all day, then busted his butt pulling calves, cutting hay or doing other chores around his small cattle ranch. By all accounts, he was a hard-working family man dedicated to making it on his own.

There was just one blotch on that all-American image. He wanted to rid the world of Jews.

The townspeople knew it, of course, but Metaline Falls is a live-and-let-live place. He never forced any of his beliefs on them, and they accepted him in their midst. As far as they were concerned, Bob Mathews was just another fugitive from the rat race of the cities, one more guy who wanted to be left alone.

But something happened to Bob over the years that no one yet understood. His family thought he had settled down after a stormy youth to make a fruitful life on the land. But inside, he never let go of his deep resentment for the government harassment that had driven him from Arizona into isolation.

So after several years, he began to yearn for a whites-only nation in his adopted Pacific Northwest. Part of his meager paycheck went into newspaper ads and brochures promoting the "White American Bastion," a relocation service for the white race. It met with failure—only one couple moved there because of him.

Mathews then sought out men who thought like him, nearly all of them law-abiding, and convinced them they could form a white underground. Manis thought it was absurd when he stumbled across it. But he quickly came to realize that Mathews had no misconceptions at all about overthrowing the government. He didn't think he was going to win the war. He only wanted to start it.

The fog continued to build, making it difficult to see the house clearly. It was quiet except for occasional routine radio checks, and the snapping of twigs as the assault teams shifted to get comfortable. About a half-hour had elapsed since the prisoner was taken to the command post, and agents kept trying to raise Mathews on the field phone with no success.

Suddenly, they were startled by a loud gunshot inside the house, followed by a long, mournful, anguished wail. Then the woods fell silent again.

"Jesus! He killed himself!" Colson bolted upright.

The radio snapped on as the CP asked the various posts to report whether they saw anything. Each team reported negative.

Manis looked toward the house. Did the bastard do it? Or was it a sucker play? Was he trying to pull the agents into his field of fire? Staring at an upstairs window, Manis thought to himself: You better not have done it, damn you. Not after all this, you don't get off that easy.

THE UNITED STATES of America.

The words evoke strong images of freedom, liberty, opportunity; their venues are such places as Yorktown, Plymouth Rock, and Philadelphia. It is a nation built not around one national identity but around many. Wave after wave of foreigners, starting with the Spanish, Dutch, French, and English, came to this New World, overwhelmed the sparse native tribes, and claimed it as their own.

Swells of immigrants shaped the spirit of the new land, integrating into society after a period of ghettoizing. Slavs moved among Saxons; Catholics among Protestants; Jews among Gentiles. The process was not without struggle, and it isn't yet finished as the newest wave, the Indochinese, seeks the same.

The classic picture of America is as a melting pot, the land where people seeking personal freedom came from their oppressive homelands to join a nation built around common humanity, not ethnicity. Anybody can be an American.

But beneath the surface there are a significant number of people to whom it's not a melting pot at all. To them, it's a boiling cauldron; not beautiful, spacious skies, but acid rain destroying the land; not amber waves of grain, but the fallow fields of a foreclosed family farmer. It's no longer a land of opportunity, but one of stifling regulation that robs the common folk and is headed toward a centralized economic, if not political, dictatorship.

That's what America was to Robert Jay Mathews, a product of its heartland and its hard-working immigrant stock. As his view of America was honed sharper, he lost sight of the hope, dreams, and compassion that form the popular image. In their stead he saw greed, despair, and conspiracy. It was a conspiracy he believed was aimed at his white race. And he blamed it on the Jews.

In September 1983, in a barnlike shed on his farm in the northeast corner of Washington state, Mathews formed a group he later named the Silent Brotherhood. Over fifteen months, it became the most dangerous right-wing underground group since the Ku Klux Klan first rode more than a century earlier. Mathews was not content, as were other extremists, to play soldier in the woods or cheerleader from the sidelines. Nor was the random, unorganized racial violence that often bubbles to the surface of American society to be his hallmark.

Amid a resurgence of white racial activism in America since the late 1970s, he saw the line racist leaders wouldn't cross, and he vaulted over it. He had no use for white sheets, burning crosses, or other anachronisms in his new Order. His was a white underground with an ambitious plan: funding the far right's victory through robberies, battling its enemies with assassinations, and establishing its presence through a guerrilla force bent on domestic terrorism and sabotage.

Its aim: a separate white nation on U.S. soil.

Mathews didn't fit the stereotype of a racist. He never smoked and didn't curse or swill beer at the taverns night after night. He was a generous, hard-working man with an ingratiating smile and a penchant for physical fitness who emerged from an ordinary American family where a person's race was never raised as a topic of concern. He did not come from a Klan family, wasn't abused as a youngster, and didn't grow up around guns. Racism wasn't drummed into his head.

Yet he went on to stir among his friends a militant hunger for something elders of the radical right merely preached from the safety of their pulpits: a white homeland. Their hidden anger became a horrifying reality.

Most of Mathews's followers were not unlike him. Few possessed the emotional characteristics outsiders attribute to racists. There was a drifter here, an embittered loner filled with hate there. But they were outnumbered by people who abandoned careers, families, and lives filled with promise to follow the cause. Only one of Mathews's followers had done prison time. Most of the others were law-abiding folk who, as their frustration with America's course grew harder to handle, gradually, almost casually, slipped into the world of extremism.

They met informally and talked of family, their hopes for the future, the struggle to make a better and happier life. Then, inflamed by Mathews's call to arms and inspired by his fervor, they joined him in a conspiracy they believed, with stupefying confidence, would deliver Armageddon to America's doorstep.

Mathews once proudly announced to an assembly that he wished to rewrite Ralph Waldo Emerson's stirring poem about the rude bridge at Concord and "the shot heard 'round the world":

> Out of the valleys, out of the fields pour the Aryan yeoman horde, their flag to April's breeze unfurled;
> Thence the Aryan farmers came and removed the Jew forever, forever from this world.

Instead, the Silent Brotherhood became the object of one of the most massive and expensive criminal investigations since the Patty Hearst-Symbionese Liberation Army case. In this and offshoot cases between 1983 and 1987, there were more than seventy-five arrests. In the Silent Brotherhood case, five people were killed. Counting the related cases, five more deaths occurred. Authorities were alarmed at the harrowing plans the group laid—sabotage against dams, water supplies, utility and communications lines—all designed to transform American cities into Beirut. They stopped Mathews only four months short of attempting the shutdown of a major U.S. city through terrorism.

Mathews followed the lead of leftist gangs of the 1960s and 1970s, snubbing the old right's predilection for goosestepping, nifty uniforms, and fancy weaponry. Mathews substituted stealth, the secret bomb, and the bullet. He wanted to become the Robin Hood of the radical right. In his Sherwood Forest, filled with destitute "racialist groups," as he called them, he would rob from the Jews and give to the Aryans. He wanted to cement the fragmented right wing, with stolen money as mortar, and link Klansmen, neo-Nazis, survivalists, tax protesters, militant farmers, Identity churches, and other groups whose unifying characteristic is distrust of the government.

In a culture that craves labels so that complicated issues can be conveyed in a "news nugget," the Silent Brotherhood has been tagged as neo-Nazi and racist. But it wasn't that simple. Not all of the dozens of people swept into Mathews's vortex fit that neatly. The unifying thread binding them together was their own brand of superpatriotism, based on their vision of America's meaning. They loved their country, but they hated its government. They were the new "red, white, and blue"— red neck, white skin, and blue collar.

The Silent Brotherhood was an inevitable outgrowth of the increasingly angry level of rhetoric and accompanying frustration on the far right, both of which had been building over the last decade. While official membership in the numerous Klan factions dwindled to between seven thousand and ten thousand after peaking at around twelve thousand in 1982, other less structured and less visible groups have sprouted with no census-taking. Christian Identity churches preaching white racial theology minister to believers across rural America. Posse Comitatus groups, stockpiling their sophisticated weapons, have replaced the Minutemen of the 1960s.

The Center for Democratic Renewal, which monitors right-wing organizations from its base in Atlanta, estimated in 1988 that there were fifteen thousand to twenty thousand right-wing activists in the nation, backed by 150,000 supporters who show up at rallies, patriots' group meetings, and church services.

Yet even these numbers fail to account for the deep reservoir of racial hostility existing in a far larger population that Mathews, and the rest of the extreme right wing, sought to tap. America found more to fear in the impromptu act of white teenagers in Howard Beach, New York, who chased a black man from their neighborhood to his death, than in Mathews's deliberate moves to foment an outright race war. Yet it is the latent racism in a great mass of the white middle class that the right wing wishes to radicalize.

How many people joined the dozens of right-wing groups that have operated in the United States over the last twenty years is only a matter of speculation since their membership rolls aren't public record. Some only attract a handful, others number in the thousands. Aryan Nations head Richard Butler preached Christian Identity, that Christian whites and not Jews are the true Israelites of the covenant, from his compound in northern Idaho, and maintained a mailing list of six thousand names.

Aryan Nations' clarion call for a great white migration to the Pacific Northwest—the "10 percent solution" of creating a white homeland in five of the fifty states—is largely ignored by Southern racists, who would never entertain the thought of leaving Dixie. Mathews felt such self-centered activism would get the right wing nowhere. It angered him to see the divisions. Promising action that the elder Butler wouldn't deliver, Mathews drew about one-fourth of the Silent Brotherhood's recruits from Aryan Nations.

THOSE WHO HAVE been part of the emergence of survivalist ideology on the right have smoldered with feelings of powerlessness and disfranchisement. These white males saw themselves as targets of all other empowerment movements, from women's liberation to black power to gay pride. Watching while everyone else's consciousness was raised in the 1960s and 1970s, their values remained the same. They didn't want communists teaching in schools, criminals being slapped on the wrists, or government taxing them onto the endangered species list.

They watched society's moral decline, reflected in the slide from Paul Anka's "Put Your Head On My Shoulder" to the Beatles' "I Want to Hold Your Hand" to George Michael's "I Want Your Sex." They saw manufacturing jobs go overseas. It became more economical to assemble products in Korea and ship them to their neighborhood stores than to have their own neighbors earn that livelihood. They saw the growth of minimum-wage service jobs that widened the gap between haves and have-nots. And they stared squarely into the prospect of being the first generation of Americans not to be economically better off than its parents.

It was just such observations Mathews used to radicalize those around him. When he spoke of affirmative action programs that reduced white children to second-class status, it enraged the fathers. While legitimate groups condemned discrimination against women, blacks, homosexuals, and others, there was no acceptable similar group a working man could join simply because he was white.

Mathews first proposed a peaceful plan for whites to migrate to the Pacific Northwest, which he called the White American Bastion. It is no accident that the Silent Brotherhood was spawned in the American West. It is a land of huge proportions, its vast emptiness alluring to the frontier spirit. In the West, the right to carry a gun not only is unquestioned, it's universally revered in the rear window racks of pickup trucks lumbering down its dusty highways.

It is that frontier spirit that produced the Posse Comitatus, American Agriculture Movement, Sagebrush Rebellion, Aryan Nations, and other far-right groups. It also produced individuals steeped in the mountain man mystique of individualism and survivalism, such men as Claude Dallas, killer of two Idaho game wardens who dared to question his taking game out of season. Dallas became something of a folk hero among inhabitants of the Great Basin, who sympathized with his plea of self-defense against the intractable government bureaucracy.

It is impossible to calculate how much Old West mythology truly survives in the late twentieth century. But the West's frontier roots still make it hostile to anything smelling of central authority, and the federal government reeks of it.

OVER THE LAST two decades, America's backwoods became dotted with survivalist training camps. A Klan-run camp at Anahuac, Texas, taught guerrilla warfare techniques. A Christian survival school deep in the Arkansas Ozarks taught urban warfare in a silhouette city constructed Hollywood set-style in the forest. The leader of the Carolina Knights of the KKK, Frazier Glenn Miller, claimed a thousand men would answer his trumpet call at Angier, North Carolina, and that they'd be dressed not in white sheets but in combat fatigues, ready for race war.

And farmers, the veritable salt of America's earth, put a "face" on their plight by blaming Jewish bankers for bringing them to the brink of economic collapse. In March 1982 they toted rifles to a paramilitary camp in Weskan, Kansas, to hear a right-wing religious guru, William Potter Gale, discuss the theological foundation for racism. They then moved over to where Posse Comitatus members held a small-cell guerrilla warfare training class.

The Christian Identity theology gives the blessing of God to the racist cause, turning right-wing organizing into a holy war. This anti-Semitic creed preaches that Jews literally are the children of Satan, while North European whites are the true descendants of the lost tribes of Israel.

Armed with Bibles and .308-caliber carbines, these soldiers had been content to paint their faces, sleep in the woods, shoot paper targets featuring Menachem Begin's picture, and swear to protect the kinfolk fom the rabble in these, the last days before Christ's reign on earth. The armed camps of the right were well prepared for war, but they weren't inclined to instigate it.

Mathews changed that. Let the elders play Moses the prophet, he came to believe. He would be Joshua the warrior.

Robert Miles, one of the central racist figures in the nation, wrote obliquely of Mathews and his group in late 1984 on the Aryan Nations *Liberty Net,* a computer bulletin board that could be dialed from anywhere in the country. Headed "From the Mountain," the message that could be downloaded by anyone with a computer modem read:

We, the older and less active spokesmen for the folk and faith, are being replaced by the young lions. These dragons of God have no time for pamphlets, for speeches, for gatherings. They know their role. They know their duty. They are the armed party which is being born out of the inability of white male youths to be heard. They are the products of the failure of this satanic, anti-white federal monstrosity to listen to more peaceful voices, such as our own. We called for the dog federals to let our people go! We called for the government in Le Cesspool Grande to let us be apart from their social experiments and their mongrelism, but to no avail.

And now, as we had warned, now come the Icemen! Out of the north, out of the frozen lands, once again the giants gather.

Chapter 1

Robbie, the All-American Boy

The morning sun doesn't take long to heat the desert floor once it climbs over the Superstition Mountains east of Phoenix. The chill of the desert night quickly dissipates into the thin air and high altitude as the sun's biting rays begin to bake the dry dirt surrounding the city.

But the Phoenix area, set amid thousands of square miles of scorched earth, is an oasis of green. Tall, graceful palms wave their fronds in the hot, dry breeze. Expensive desert-style homes on neatly landscaped lots bump up against the manicured fairways of the resorts. Saguaro cactus provides landscaping for stucco homes with tile roofs, typical of the Southwest.

Only a few formidable obstacles have withstood the march of development. Camelback Mountain and Squaw Peak stick their ragged, treeless spines 1,500 feet above the flat terrain, forcing the city to lap around their edges. Their toasted, craggy faces testify to the earlier, primitive conditions.

But aided by water storage projects and, more importantly, indoor cooling, Phoenix boomed in the 1950s, as did many Western cities after World War II.

Despite Phoenix's oppressive summer highs well over 100 degrees, people kept coming. The Valley of the Sun became Eden, a paradise set adrift in the otherwise barren desert Southwest.

In the fall of 1964, things were restive in paradise.

A newsboy tossed his papers early Sunday morning at the houses along West Lawrence Lane, a quiet street near Phoenix's border with the northwest suburb of Glendale. Una Mathews opened her front door after she heard the thud, and as she bent over to pick up the paper, she could feel the sun scorching her arms already.

It would be another pleasant fall day, high in the 80s again. She loved Southwest living, sharing this tract house with her husband, Johnny, their three boys and Norah Grant, Una's mother.

The Mathews clan were not churchgoers. Johnny, Una, Norah, and the boys lounged around the house instead of worshiping at the Methodist church. They didn't give organized religion much thought in the hectic scheme of their lives. Johnny had his office job at the Graham Paper Company, and in his off hours he studied his War College correspondence courses to increase his rank in the Air Force Reserve. He had already made major and had his eye on lieutenant colonel.

Una had been working outside the home for five years now, a necessity of the times that tore at her. Her natural instinct was to be at home to rear the boys. But with Norah to keep house for her, the decision was made easier.

The *Arizona Republic* was Phoenix's only Sunday newspaper, and Robbie Mathews, going on twelve, enjoyed reading it. It was one of the positive influences his mother had on him. Una Mathews encouraged her boys to read and learn more about the world, starting back when they were three little tykes in Marfa, a forsaken dot on the west Texas map. She didn't want them to think the quiet life they knew there was all that went on in the world.

On October 25, 1964, there was a lot going on, and some of the biggest news swirled around Arizona itself.

In world news, anxiety was at fever pitch in the West over the sudden ouster of Soviet Premier Nikita Khrushchev and what it meant for relations with the United States. The players and the strategies had changed radically from two Octobers ago, when President Kennedy and Khrushchev faced each other down over nuclear missiles in Cuba. It was a confrontation of inestimable consequence, defused by two rational men. Now both leaders were gone from the stage, each intentionally removed by forces the average American couldn't hope to understand. It was unnerving to see a Soviet leader ousted for being too accommodating to the West.

For Arizonans, however, the big story was the presidential campaign. Barry Goldwater, the hard-line conservative who represented the Grand Canyon state in the U.S. Senate, was nine days away from what looked certain to be a humiliating defeat by President Lyndon Johnson. Goldwater, the self-proclaimed "Conscience of the Conservative," was being portrayed as a warmonger, a man who couldn't be trusted to act rationally in a crisis with the communists. The implication was clear: Goldwater would tolerate a nuclear exchange with the Soviets.

To Robbie, the idea of people called communists who wanted to lob nuclear missiles over the polar ice cap from Siberia was terrifying. He saw black and yellow fallout shelter signs spring up overnight on public buildings. He sensed the international uneasiness, reflected in everything from Khrushchev's sudden ouster to the bone-chilling drone of air raid sirens that sent him and his classmates diving under their desks. Despite his age, he could feel there were more sinister things in life than what he could see on West Lawrence Lane.

So it was natural that Robbie would turn his head when his mom mentioned a special section in that Sunday's paper. Rising from the floor, he walked to her chair and looked at the cover of a sixteen-page tabloid, dominated by a portrait of an army officer in dress uniform. The unsmiling man had dark, penetrating eyes focused on something well beyond the lens. Along the bottom of the cover he was identified as "Captain John Birch, U.S. Army." A title in large type down the right side of the page read: "The John Birch Society: A Report." Una flipped through the magazine's pages, each marked "Advertisement" at the top.

"Boy, will you look at this," Una exclaimed as her family listened. "This John Birch Society really has quite an organization for fighting communist influence." The article described how the society was composed of local chapters with ten to twenty members, usually formed by someone in the neighborhood who was concerned about communism. A full-time coordinator gave assistance and direction to the chapters. Then Una read one of the Birch Society's favorite analogies. "Do you remember that poor girl in New York who was stabbed to death on the streets and no one lifted a finger to help?" Una related to her family. "Kitty Genovese? Thirty some people watched or listened to it for a half-hour and no one so much as called the police. They just closed their curtains and ignored it." Una then read aloud:

How are we reacting to the realities of our world? What do we think of the steady gain of communism —of the millions killed, tortured and enslaved by this criminal conspiracy? Do we still laugh at Khrushchev's claim that our children will live under communism? Do we shrug off Cuba? Will we shrug off Mexico? Do we watch with curiosity?

Do we pull down the curtain on these disturbing thoughts? Do we draw the warm covers of apathy around our necks?

She stopped reading and took in those frightening thoughts.

"This group really wants to do something about it," Una remarked.

Intrigued, Robbie later carried the magazine into his room, closed the door, and studied it thoroughly. He didn't understand everything, but he comprehended enough to become increasingly alarmed. These people he'd been hearing about, these Russian communists, wanted to take over the world. It frightened him when he imagined what that would mean for his family.

He read in the Birch magazine about Lenin's three-step strategy for spreading communism:

• Take Eastern Europe. "Except for Greece and the city of Istanbul, this was completed by 1950," the report stated.
• Gain control of the mass and masses of Asia. "Today this is more than 80 percent accomplished."
• Encircle and infiltrate the United States. "Now more than 50 percent accomplished," was the dread assessment from the Birch Society.

By the time Robbie made it to page 15, his mind was made up. He clipped the coupon to send to San Marino, California, for more information including, for $5, founder

Robert Welch's manifesto for the society, *The Blue Book*. No more would the world be just what he could see up and down West Lawrence Lane.

THE MATHEWS FAMILY was the prototypical all-American clan of the 1950s. They came from hard-working, idealistic stock. In the early 1950s, Johnny not only was Mayor of Marfa, but Chamber of Commerce president, upstanding businessman, and scout leader. Una, his charming, loving wife, was the town's den mother and matriarch of her brood—three boys, spaced four years apart.

By 1964, the paint on this Norman Rockwell portrait was peeling.

Johnny Mathews's ancestors left the Scottish Highlands to settle in North Carolina. Johnny was born in 1915 in Atoka, Oklahoma, while his father ran a store there. But the business failed and the family went back to North Carolina before finally moving to Detroit when Johnny was nine. His dad got a job running the dining room at the Ford Motor Company training school.

In 1930, at age fifteen, Johnny ran away to Arizona, where he found work on a ranch near Red Rock, in the hot stretches of saguaro halfway between Phoenix and Tucson. There, he was awestruck at the wide open spaces of the Arizona desert. The scrubby hills and blistering sun were distinctively different from the humid Blue Ridge of western North Carolina. The desert horizon took in hundreds of square miles in a single glance, and the sky was an unspoiled azure, which he'd never seen in smoggy Detroit.

Johnny's family begged him for three years before he returned to finish at Western High School. But his independent nature guaranteed he wouldn't be tied down to Detroit for long. It seemed to him a person could make his own way in the West and not face a lifetime on the assembly lines, the future of most working people who remained in Detroit. He went off to Dallas in fruitless pursuit of a football scholarship at Southern Methodist University and ended up working for the Graham Paper Company there. But he found himself again in Detroit, transferring to Graham's office there when he learned his dad was dying of a brain tumor.

Although they went to Western High together, Johnny didn't meet Una Grant until years later, when her family happened to rent an apartment above Johnny's sister's on West Grand Boulevard north of downtown Detroit. Una's dad, Bob Grant, had lost the family's home in Lincoln Park to foreclosure in the Depression.

Grant, a native of York, England, came with his bride Norah to Detroit to work as a painter at Ford. Though he excelled at it, his dream—never fulfilled—was to be an operatic tenor. He had a Sunday morning radio show in the early 1930s on which he sang requests. But when he tried to push Una into a show business career, she decided life with Johnny was a more attainable dream.

While they were dating, the United States entered World War II. Johnny decided if he had to fight, he'd rather do it as an officer. In early 1942, Johnny and Una became engaged just before he left for training at Marana, Arizona, and Thunderbird in California. He was transferred to bomber school at Fort D. A. Russell in Marfa and after graduation stayed as an instructor. Then, in April 1943, he returned to Detroit, where he and Una exchanged vows in the Presbyterian church on West Grand Boulevard.

A year after they were married, when Johnny was stationed at Fort Russell, on the lonely plains of West Texas, Una became pregnant. About the fifth month she got a serious case of the flu, and she was miserable so far away from family. She returned to Detroit in 1945 to deliver a baby boy. She named him Grant after her father. Grant Mathews was christened in the church where Una and Johnny were married.

V-J Day came just as Johnny was preparing for a Pacific assignment. He quickly mustered out and returned with his family to Detroit. The city was depressing, and Johnny and Una talked about moving. He persuaded Una to give Marfa another try. Una had never lived in a small town before and was astounded that people in Marfa didn't lock their doors.

Marfa is the seat of vast Presidio County, which takes in thousands of square miles but only a half-dozen towns. Larger than Rhode Island, which has a million inhabitants, Presidio County is home to only five thousand people.

It was ranching country, rolling high plains covered with grama grass and white-faced herefords. The Davis Mountains cut across the northern horizon. To the east, the Del Norte Mountains gave birth to the unexplained phenomenon of the Marfa Lights, an ethereal phosphorescence visible at night. Discovered by a cowboy on a cattle drive in the 1880s, some believed the ghost lights were Indian spirits, while others held them to be swamp gas, despite the area's dryness.

Marfa was a crossroads on the Alamito Creek for two highways that went nowhere else important. Sixty miles south was the town of Presidio, on the Rio Grande, and the road continued into the Mexican state of Chihuahua. El Paso was 194 twisting miles west across barely inhabited plains and hill country. Pecos was north by nearly 100 miles. East of Marfa, there was nothing much in the way of habitation. Over the Del Nortes, it was 239 miles to Del Rio by way of Judge Roy Bean's saloon in Langtry. Marfa was a place where trips to civilization were measured not in miles but in tankfuls of gasoline.

It was a place where a man looking for a quiet place to raise his family would look no farther. When night fell in Presidio County, there was no glare of city lights, only the ghost lights reflecting off the hills under a sky saturated with more stars than ever existed on West Grand Boulevard.

The young couple, with baby Grant and Una's parents, moved to Marfa in 1947. Marfa couldn't have been better for Johnny Mathews. He was a natural-born salesman, short in stature but long in personality. If any stranger could weave his way into the close-knit social fabric of Marfa, it was Johnny.

Johnny found an old Spanish-style home in the middle of town. It was a roomy single-story adobe that was so large, the family didn't occupy the front portion. They used it later for scout troop meetings when Johnny was the only scoutmaster in town, and Una the only den mother.

The house was close to the railroad track that literally divided the haves and the have-nots in Marfa. Just around the bend was Mexican Town, where young Grant made his first friends. The Mathews family got along well with the *señores y señoritas,* although a Mexican Town soldier on leave once stole Johnny's new Chevrolet and wrapped it around a pole.

Johnny was managing a wool warehouse when the General Electric appliance store went up for sale. He scrounged up financing and bought it.

The Mathews clan quickly won status in the community. Most of their friends were Methodists, so they joined a Methodist church, where Johnny became a steward. He joined the Chamber of Commerce and became its president in short order, as well as president of the Marfa Lions Club, commander of the local American Legion post, and a member of the Masonic Lodge.

Within two years, the thirty-three-year-old newcomer was asked by some of the locals to run for mayor. Una didn't like it. Normally the mayor of Marfa was a rancher. For a businessman to stick out his neck, Una argued, was just too risky. "A rancher can be independent," she told Johnny. "His cows don't care what he does. If people don't like the way he carries on town business, his cows aren't affected and the people can't get back at him." But the lure of office was powerful. Johnny disregarded her advice, and Una backed his decision.

Johnny was elected in 1949. Their second son was born on January 16 of that year. Una wanted to name him Lee, because she felt any family with a son named Grant should also have a Lee. The doctor who delivered the baby berated her. Every father, he said, wants a son named after him. So the second boy was named John Lee Mathews. The family, however, always called him Lee.

In the demobilization after 1945, Marfa lost the bomber school where Johnny had taught. The pullout crippled the town. There was no real industry to support a sizable Mexican population when ranching was slow. So Mayor Mathews set out to rectify the problem. A Lebanese friend was an uncle to the Farrahs, El Paso clothing manufacturers. Mathews and his friend persuaded the Farrahs to move a factory to Marfa. When it opened, it provided work for many of the Mexicans.

But this didn't set well with the ranchers. The factory decimated their dirt-cheap Mexican labor pool. As a result, the Farrahs got a cold reception from a substantial part of the population. The factory didn't last long before Farrah pulled its machinery out and went back to El Paso.

Mayor Mathews made a few other impolitic moves, such as equalizing tax assessments and instituting the town's first garbage fee to balance the municipal budget. After that, Johnny found out that small towns aren't always as friendly as they appear. His political career ended after four short years.

As it did, on January 16, 1953, his third son was born, sharing a birthday with Lee. They named him Robert Jay and christened him at the Methodist church. The nickname "Robbie" immediately caught on. Even into adulthood, he answered to "Robbie" among his close friends. It reminded him of his Scottish ancestry.

Una couldn't imagine God giving her a nicer family. The boys seldom got into trouble although once, when Robbie was three and Lee seven, Robbie swung a baseball bat and whacked his brother in the head. It was an accident, and Lee was barely hurt, but Robbie was so frightened he ran home and hid under his grandmother's bed, where he fell asleep. Una and Johnny had called in the county sheriff before finally discovering the youngster snoring under the bed.

One of Una's greatest pleasures was reading to the boys. A favorite source were the booklets she received from the Unitarian Church in Boston, to which she turned as part of her personal religious growth. At bedtime she read to all three about Indian traditions, African cultures, and other topics foreign to their lives in Marfa. She hoped to instill in them a larger view of the world. There was a danger, she thought, of becoming too provincial when living in a small town.

Johnny operated the appliance store on a shoestring, and the lustre went out of his rapport with the town after his term at City Hall. By the time Robbie was four, in 1957, business was too thin at Mathews Appliances to support the family. Johnny sold out to the town's undertaker and set off for Presidio to pursue an import-export venture with a friend. When that didn't work, Johnny took a job in an insurance office in Midland.

But soon a familiar name resurfaced: Graham Paper

Company. After sixteen years, Johnny's old employer was willing to rehire him. The home office in St. Louis offered him a position in Phoenix, where he and Una had spent a short time at Luke Field, west of Phoenix, during the war. The family was so broke, Una had to sell some personal belongings so they could afford to move what they needed. It was just days before Christmas 1958 when the family settled into Phoenix's Encanto Park neighborhood, near downtown, determined to start over.

Leaving Marfa was crushing. Una's father had died there earlier that year. Bob Grant had been a caretaker at the Marfa Masonic Hall. When he died, the Masons donated a four-grave plot in the local cemetery for the Grants and the Mathewses, and Bob Grant was buried there.

But underlying their other emotions was the feeling they were driven from Marfa in defeat. They had come with the best of intentions and had risen to prominent stature, but were beaten down. They wanted to raise their boys in a wholesome environment, but because of some backbiting and meanness they had to retreat and build anew. With a bitter taste, they left Marfa behind. They would never be that happy again.

AT THE TIME Johnny Mathews was looking to rebuild his life in Phoenix, two other men embarked on separate paths that would influence his youngest boy.

The first was Robert Welch, a retired candy manufacturer from Massachusetts. In 1958, he elevated John Birch to martyrdom as "the first American casualty of World War III." Birch was a Baptist missionary in China when World War II washed over the Orient. For two years he bird-dogged Japanese troop positions for the American Volunteers. Birch was executed by Chinese communists in the closing days of the war, and Welch blamed "communism's powerful friends in Washington" for covering it up. In Indianapolis, Welch organized the John Birch Society as a grassroots American campaign against communist infiltration and takeover.

Welch quickly attracted thousands of upstanding citizens who agreed with the theme "less government and more individual responsibility." They were business leaders, conservative politicians, and America-first activists who believed America was becoming soft, growing undisciplined, and creeping toward socialism.

A Phoenix chapter was organized in 1960, and within two years a half-dozen units had formed. The rallying points attracting those who joined were support for local police, whose authority was being weakened by liberals; spreading the truth about communist influence in the civil rights movement; and pulling the United States out of the United Nations.

But what helped most was a man who, although not a Bircher, embodied many of the causes the society held dearly. He was Barry Goldwater. He began his quest for the White House as the standard-bearer of the farthest right corner of the Republican Party, a balance to New York's Governor Nelson Rockefeller in a party that was trying to accommodate a wider range of political sentiments than at any time since.

Within five years of arriving in the Grand Canyon State, the John Birch Society had one hundred chapters and two thousand members. Most of them were in Maricopa County around Phoenix, where Goldwater first ran for the city council in 1949. But there were fifteen chapters in Tucson and Pima County, and organized units in the smaller towns of Prescott, Flagstaff, and Douglas. Most members were Republicans.

The influence carried both ways. As growing numbers of Republicans joined Birch chapters, Birchers also rose in the Republican hierarchy. When Goldwater's presidential campaign was launched, 10 percent of Maricopa County's Republican committeemen, including the chairman, were Birchers. For a short time before the campaign, Goldwater's campaign manager, Denison Kitchel, was a Bircher.

Kitchel dropped out of the Birch Society after finding some of its positions too extreme, its leaders irresponsible, and its stridency a liability with the public. Yet party insiders said Goldwater won the presidential nomination at San Francisco with the help of Birchers, who got delegates into the Cow Palace despite the strong efforts of Goldwater's staff to minimize their impact. After Goldwater's devastating loss to Johnson, some party faithful felt the Birchers' overeagerness had hurt Goldwater in the public eye.

Controversy over the society began in 1961 with an attack the Birchers called the "Big Smear" by the San Francisco communist newspaper *People's World*. The society was painted as fascist, racist, and anti-Semitic. The secrecy Welch built into it backfired, making it appear to be a clandestine organization of extremists. Welch didn't help with public statements accusing President Eisenhower of aiding the communist cause.

A California Senate committee made its own study and found the John Birch Society to be "a Right, anti-Communist, fundamentalist organization." There was no evidence it was anything more than a community-based group organizing to spread the "truth about the Communist menace," the committee concluded.

But in an assessment of the John Birch Society in the *Arizona Republic* in 1965, a Republican leader in Tucson characterized the people he knew as Birchers: "Eighty percent are dedicated, patriotic and frightened Americans; more than 19 percent are nuts whose brains and judgment are warped; and the remaining people frighten me to death." Indeed, the paper reported one applicant for the society volunteered to parachute into Cuba to assassinate Fidel Castro.

The second man who would influence Robbie Mathews was Robert Bolivar DePugh, who founded a group in Independence, Missouri, in 1961 that became one of the most feared right-wing movements of the time. It was defiant, self-righteous, and brazenly militant. It had the weaponry, secret cell structure, and paranoiac world view that misinformed critics had attributed to the John Birch Society. But, by comparison, the Birchers were benign. After all, a person could contact the Birch Society by thumbing through the telephone book.

The Minutemen, however, could be contacted only if a person knew what pay phone to call at what time of the week.

DePugh, thirty-eight at the time, owned a veterinary pharmaceutical firm. Believing up to 500,000 communist infiltrators were working in the United States, Minutemen prepared for a last-ditch military defense against the communist takeover. Its members belonged to secret numbered networks. They held survivalist camps for weapons and explosives training. They kept intelligence folders on activities in their areas, clipping newspapers for items containing names of potential enemies, such as members of the United Nations Association or the American Friends Service Committee. They filed intelligence cards on friend and foe on every contact.

DePugh made his headquarters in Norborne, Missouri, a small town northeast of Independence. He claimed his Minutemen were not planning insurrection; the organization was a strictly defensive instrument against communism in America. But authorities didn't buy that. In 1966, twenty Minutemen were arrested in New York after an investigation showed they had obtained tons of guns, ammo, rockets, and bombs for attacks on three socialist camps in New York, New Jersey, and Connecticut.

The next year, DePugh was prosecuted twice for weapons violations in federal courts in Kansas City and Joplin. He disappeared while on an appeal bond, after he was indicted for conspiracy in a bank robbery scheme centered in Seattle. Seven people were charged in that plot in February 1968. Police said they planned to blow up a suburban Seattle police station and a power plant to provide diversion for four bank robberies.

After all his trials and appeals, DePugh served four years of a ten-year prison term for firearms violations. He later was a leader of an ultra-conservative umbrella group called the Committee of 10 Million.

JOHNNY AND UNA found life bearable in a neighborhood of professionals northwest of downtown Phoenix. Robbie entered first grade in September 1959 in the Encanto School. But they yearned for enough money once again to own their home, so Una took a job at the First National Bank of Arizona. Soon the closeness the family knew in Marfa had irretrievably vanished.

The year after moving to Phoenix, Grant, fifteen, was diagnosed as a schizophrenic. Grant's behavior required that Johnny and Una devote an inordinate amount of time to him. They often felt they were neglecting Lee and Robbie. Several times they had to rush Grant to the hospital after he tried to kill himself, deepening their sense of guilt over his condition.

Lee and Robbie naturally gravitated toward one another while their parents spent time with Grant. They shared the same birthday, four years apart, and formed a strong bond that quietly compensated for the lack of parental attention.

Johnny and Una looked to the suburbs for their next home, selecting a standard floor plan for a house they had built on West Lawrence Lane in 1961. Ironically, families seeking more room in the suburbs ended up with overcrowded schools on split sessions because there had been inadequate planning for growth.

The boys were enrolled in a school they didn't like at all. With Grant's problems, both parents working, and the overall hectic pace of life, the family couldn't recapture the slow-town pace of Marfa.

The best times came during their camping vacations in the White Mountains near the New Mexico border. Robbie loved the cabin and often told his parents, "Mom and dad, when I grow up I'm going to buy you a place in the mountains."

An average student in school, Robbie could excel if he liked the subject. And he happened to love history, especially the Civil War. In all, for a boy of eleven, he had a pretty fair grasp of the subject.

Yet it floored Johnny and Una when, after Robbie read the John Birch supplement that Sunday in October 1964, he came to them and said he was joining.

Johnny Mathews erupted. He argued it was moronic for Robbie to get involved in such politics before he was old enough to shave. It was the beginning of a battle royal between father and son over political issues that would grow considerably more complex in time.

Una jumped in to defend her son. After all, it was the 1960s, a pretty precarious time in terms of the Soviet threat. It was popular for true-blue Americans to look for reds behind the bushes. If this is what Robbie heard on the news and talked about in school, they shouldn't stifle his interest. She thought it was a healthy sign that Robbie was taking an interest in world events.

Johnny relented, and Robbie became a young member of the John Birch Society as the group was peaking in Arizona during the Goldwater campaign. In many ways, Una thought as her son went through his teens, it was a good influence on Robbie. At a time when the hippie culture was blooming, he kept his hair cut short. He never touched drugs, never even took a drag from a cigarette. He didn't get into trouble with girls. In fact, he didn't even date until after high school.

Soon, Robbie went on a health kick. He took up wrestling and weightlifting in an earnest effort to shed his perpetual chubbiness. He stopped eating hot dogs after reading the ingredients that went into them. And when her teenage son got to be overbearing while expressing his beliefs, Una consoled herself by deciding she was lucky.

"Here he is," she told Johnny after one father-son row, "such a clean-living boy. These other kids are taking dope, scrounging around the streets, while our boy is trying to live a good and clean life. We ought to be proud."

Johnny wavered between bewilderment and frustration. Robbie liked to argue. Even when he was right he would be so insufferable that Johnny resisted. When Robbie tried to get his dad to quit smoking, he started leaving little notes around the house, in Johnny's sock drawer or on his pillow, saying, "For your health's sake, don't smoke." Johnny resented having anyone tell him what to do, and he finally told Robbie flatly to lay off.

Una's mother died in 1967 and was buried in Marfa Cemetery next to her husband. By that time, the Mathews boys were old enough to be on their own. Lee graduated from high school in June and was accepted at Arizona State University in Tempe, a southern suburb.

With the kids' schedules, Johnny's office job and studies, and Una's duties at the bank, there was precious little time for family talks, even if they hadn't developed habits that kept them apart. The parents took pride in their lawn and spent most weekends defending it against the brutal Arizona sun. Conversation at dinner gave way to the din of a nearby television, left on while they ate.

During his Birch Society years, Robbie began to assert

his independence from the family. Society members took an interest in him and saw that the teenager made his meetings. The older men burst with pride when Robbie, still a boy, spoke of patriotism, fighting communism, and defending the Constitution. In time, Robbie tried to influence his parents. When Robert Welch came to Phoenix for a society dinner, Robbie persuaded them to come see the man whose anticommunist message he had taken to heart. They went, but begged off from any other society functions.

In 1969, Johnny and Una sold their home so Lee could attend Arizona State without a crosstown drive. They got a three-bedroom apartment on Jen Tilly Lane, across Apache Boulevard from the campus. With Grant in an institution, both Lee and Robbie had their own bedrooms. That marked the emotional as well as the physical separation of the brothers. Lee was studying to be a teacher and wanted nothing to do with the ultra-right philosophy his younger brother was espousing.

Robbie started at McClintock High School as a junior. Many of the students were Mormons, and Robbie quickly began to admire them as model teenagers, industrious, clean-living kids with whom he shared a conservative life-style and philosophy. The city of Mesa, adjacent to Tempe, was founded by Mormons in 1877. It was the site of one of Mormonism's most beautiful temples. The more he learned of Mormons, the more Robbie liked them. Their bodies were temples of the spirit. It was a religion that fitted the way of life Robbie had chosen.

Mormons regard the family as one of the most sacred earthly institutions because it represents the path to exaltation in the afterlife. The purpose of marriage is procreation, to provide physical bodies for God's spiritual children. Motherhood is the noblest calling for women, and it is a serious sin for Mormon women to refuse to bear children.

Mormons also believe the second coming of Christ is near, bringing on the period of the millennium, the thousand-year rule of Christ on earth when Jesus, along with other saints, will return to earth to help run temporal matters. Many signs of Jesus' return already are fulfilled, Mormons believe. As a result, many of them stockpile food and other provisions in preparation for the calamities that will precede the Second Coming.

Robbie returned to the apartment after school one day and told his folks he was becoming a Mormon. True to form, Johnny flew off the handle, saying no son of his was going to join *that* church. But Una was concerned that if they forbade Robbie to join, it would only make the boy more determined. Una convinced Johnny that this would be a passing phase.

Reluctantly, Johnny sat down with his seventeen-year-old son.

"All right, Robbie," he said. "Go ahead and become a Mormon. But I'm telling you one thing. Don't come preaching to us about the Mormons. It's not for us."

Robbie's parents accompanied him to the Temple the night he was baptized by immersion. While they liked the people from the local Mormon stake, Robbie's conversion was strictly his own doing.

After they returned from the stake, Johnny joined his wife in bed. Just as they were dozing off, the door popped open. In marched Robbie with the Book of Mormon opened in one hand and a finger pointing skyward on his other hand, like a preacher preparing to deliver a truckload of brimstone. Before five words left his mouth, Johnny interrupted with just one word of his own.

"Robbie!" he bellowed, leaning up on his elbow.

"Okay, all right," the boy said in a suddenly apologetic tone. He backed out of his parents' room, taking his proselytizing with him. "Sorry."

In the years since he had joined the John Birch Society, Robbie had moved beyond simple anticommunism. He was forming a more complete conservative philosophy and now had a religion to go with it. Una still had justifiable pride in her son. He once took her to a meeting on the detrimental effects of rock 'n' roll on youth. She figured that of all the things to worry her about her boys, being rebellious anti-establishment types wouldn't be one of them.

BOTH PARENTS SOON saw a change in Robbie. Now Una felt she had to put her foot down. Robbie still was seventeen when he told her he was going to a seminar in

Mesa where a fellow Mormon, Marvin Cooley, was teaching tax resistance. Una had heard of Cooley, a Mesa melon farmer who was jerked around once in an IRS audit. His specialty was invoking the Fifth Amendment on blank tax returns. It seemed to Una that Cooley's teaching teetered on the edge of the law.

Johnny was more blunt. The United States is the best country in the world, despite its problems, he told Robbie. He believed in supporting the government, not in fringe groups Johnny thought had more on their agendas than protesting taxes. Una argued with Robbie until she was exhausted, but he went anyway.

The antitax activism he heard was like a call to action. The very act of paying income taxes, which he was taught were illegal, was aiding the communist cause. Enthralled with Cooley, the dynamic Robbie was singled out after a while to act as sergeant-at-arms for some of Cooley's meetings.

Una and Johnny now began to worry that their youngest son was turning into a revolutionary. Somehow his hatred of the Russians was turning around into anger at his own country, and it frightened his parents. By the time Robbie was a senior at McClintock, true to his nature, he was putting his beliefs into practice.

He had an economics course that covered the Keynesian theory of government intervention in the economy. Robbie had learned from the Birch Society that Lord Keynes's thoughts and Franklin Roosevelt's embrace of them signaled the start of creeping socialism in America. When it appeared to Robbie that his teacher was defending Keynes, he entered into spirited debate with him. But it went beyond that for Robbie. So convinced was he that the teacher was promoting dangerous philosophy, Robbie stopped going to the class entirely.

When the school office notified his parents, they tried to lecture him. "Do you have to agree with what's being taught, for heaven's sake?" Una argued.

But Robbie was adamant. And when they pointed out it could hurt his chances of good placement in college, Robbie stunned them with another of his periodic pronouncements. He wasn't going to college. Colleges were "hotbeds of communism."

But, Robbie said, there was one institution that was perfect for him. He now dreamed of going to the U.S. Military Academy at West Point.

Johnny Mathews was an Arizona recruiter for the U.S. Air Force Academy in Colorado Springs. He tried to talk Robbie into going there instead. But Robbie insisted on West Point. So for months Johnny Mathews worked to get his son an appointment to the academy. He wrote to Goldwater, who had returned to the Senate in 1968. He wrote to his congressman, the powerful Mesa Republican leader John Rhodes, who, like Johnny, was an Army Air Corps veteran. Finally he got his son scheduled for an exam to be given at Fort Huachuca near Sierra Vista, south of Tucson.

But as the date for the test approached, Robbie again changed his mind, prompted by an incident that caused an uproar across the nation and soured Robbie on any thoughts of becoming a U.S. soldier.

It was called My Lai.

On March 31, 1971, Lieutenant William Calley was convicted at Fort Benning, Georgia, after a lengthy court-martial, of murdering twenty-two Vietnamese civilians. About four hundred had been killed during the raid by Calley's troops on the village of My Lai in 1968, the darkest period of the Vietnam War. The verdict evoked outrage from the war's supporters as well as many who opposed it. Calley was a scapegoat, they felt. American soldiers were fighting a no-win war in a hostile land with lessening support at home. Politicians, not military strategists, were leading the war, and a large number of boys were getting chewed up in a meat grinder as a result.

Robbie believed Calley was punished for following orders, so he wanted no part of the Army. Shortly before they were to drive to Fort Huachuca, Robbie told his dad of his latest decision.

Johnny was perplexed. He didn't believe the country was as bad off as his son made it appear. This was still the finest place in the world to live, he told Robbie, and it's worth defending. Robbie agreed to take the test, if only to satisfy his dad. But he failed to make the cut, scoring too low on math, his weakest subject. Johnny never knew whether Robbie blew it on purpose.

Early in 1971, Johnny and Una moved into the Meadows mobile home park in Tempe, a new development with a nice golf course and clubhouse at the junction of the Pima and Superstition freeways. Robbie tagged along, but as 1971 wore on, Robbie talked less and less with his parents. When June arrived, they learned from McClintock High that Robbie would not be allowed to graduate because of that incomplete grade in the economics course he refused to attend.

But by then the Mathewses' youngest son was beyond their control.

TED KNIGHT WAS used to such phone calls. The young man didn't want to give his name, but only to pass on a good tip to the veteran television reporter. It was June 1972, the end of a very hot day in Phoenix. The man was very nervous, and from his story it was easy to see why.

"Mr. Knight, you're known around town as a conservative. That's pretty rare in the media, you know," the man said haltingly.

It was true. Knight was well known as a conservative, and a hard-nosed investigative reporter for KOOL-TV, Channel 10 news. "What can I do for you, Mister . . . ?" Knight said with an anticipatory pause, fishing for a name.

"No names, please. I'm just a middleman. I don't really want to do this, but a friend asked me to call you."

"Okay, no names. Go ahead."

"My friend believes this nation is headed for imminent disaster," said the man. "Communists already control most of the government. We're falling apart from within. My friend's preparing for it. He'd like you to meet his little army."

"What are they doing?" Knight asked.

"They're training for guerrilla war, Mr. Knight, out in the desert. You're invited to the next maneuvers. Are you interested?"

"Yeah, I'm interested," Knight said apprehensively. "How do we set it up?"

The caller directed him to a downtown pay phone at a certain time. From there he'd receive further directions, if he wasn't being followed.

After checking with Bill Close, his news director, Knight grabbed cameraman Chuck Hawley and headed out. Over the next two days they played a game of tag with four different phone booths until finally the last call came late in the evening at a phone booth near the Paradise Valley golf course.

"Mr. Knight," said the final caller, "drive east on Bell Road to Scottsdale Road and turn left. Go three miles to a dirt road on the right and pull off. Flash your headlights three times, wait five minutes, then flash them twice more. Got it?" Knight got back in the car with Hawley. He looked down on the seat at the loaded .22-caliber pistol they had brought along. Knight placed it on the floor at his feet and pulled out toward Bell Road.

When they arrived at the spot, Knight stopped and flicked the headlights three times, as instructed. After five minutes he flashed them two more times.

He and Hawley waited ten minutes, unsure if they were at the right spot. But then they heard a crunch, crunch, crunching noise. It was the sound of military boots hitting the desert sand in lockstep, double-time. In the darkness, Knight made out a phalanx of men in camouflage uniforms marching toward the car. They were carrying semi-automatic assault rifles at port arms. Across their chests were bandoliers of ammunition, hand grenades strapped to them. The men wore steel helmets, and most frightening were the camouflage hoods that hid their faces.

Knight counted about thirty soldiers, an ungodly sight. With his foot, he nudged the .22 pistol deep under his car seat.

The men stopped, and one came to the car. Silently, he opened the door and got in with the two newsmen. The platoon leader signaled the car to follow the men, who marched down into an arroyo where a small camp was assembled. The light from the lanterns couldn't be seen up on ground level. Six of the men stayed in the camp; the other desert rats patrolled the perimeter outside the gulch.

One man did the talking. From his voice, Knight judged him to be young, maybe not even into his twenties. Some of the others were in their thirties.

"We are the Sons of Liberty," the youngster said. Behind the face mask, Knight could make out a vibrant pair of deep brown eyes. The voice was the essence of confidence, the speech articulate. Knight conducted his interview on a tape recorder while Hawley shot film of the men doing maneuvers.

The young man told Knight that these soldiers, many of them army veterans, believed society was facing imminent collapse under communist infiltrators in government, especially in the Internal Revenue Service.

"They even have effective control of the media, which makes it hard for us to get our concerns out to the people," the hooded stranger said. "The way this country is headed, there must be changes or people will die. Can't they see? The people of Arizona, of the whole country, are woefully prepared for this chaos. We must return to the constitutional, organic law of the land." Despite his cause, the young man impressed Knight as dedicated and very intelligent.

"Those you see here are only a part of our army. There are other kinsmen who stand ready. When it's time, we will act. Before that, you have no way of knowing who we are. We could be the policeman you see on the beat, your postman, your friendly bartender. Even we don't know the identities of all of the men here. We are organized in cells of three, and only one has contact with the mother group.

"You must know we're serious," the young man continued. "I have a family back home and I'd rather be with them under any other circumstance."

"Oh, I can see you're serious," Knight said, glancing up the ravine to see Hawley photographing the men firing their Ml carbines. "I can see that."

The next morning at KOOL, four men from the FBI and the Secret Service were waiting in Bill Close's office when Knight arrived for work. They asked that the station refrain from showing the footage of the Sons of Liberty. Knight was puzzled that they even knew he'd been out there until one of them flashed a grin. Then Knight realized there had been an informant in the group.

"Mr. Knight," one agent said, "these people aren't a big group, and you can't take them seriously. We would prefer the people of Phoenix not see your story until we can identify just who all of them are."

Knight was getting angry. The phrase "control of the media" coursed through his mind. After the group left, Close called CBS News in New York—KOOL was a CBS affilliate—and was advised to run the story. After all, if it were a gang of leftists out in the desert, there'd be no hesitation about airing it.

KOOL ran the story, causing a stir in the community for a few days.

The morning after the newscast, Charles Middleton came to his desk at the FBI office in Phoenix and found a case ticket on it. The Sons of Liberty had to be cracked open, and Middleton, who specialized in investigating right-wing groups, got the assignment. Knight soon found himself at the center of a storm. His audio tape was subpoenaed and Hawley's film carted away, along with some strident, threatening literature the hooded man had given Knight. Under authority of a federal grand jury, Middleton applied pressure to his snitches to come up with the identity of the young man behind the camouflage hood.

Knight began to fear for his life, thinking the Sons would conclude he'd betrayed them. He didn't breathe easily until two months later, when an antitax brochure, printed by the Sons of Liberty, came addressed to him at KOOL.

On the brochure someone had scribbled in pen: "Thanks for a job well done." It was a relief to learn the group didn't hold grudges.

Several months later, in November 1972, he answered the newsroom phone to hear a familiar voice. It was clear, very articulate, and highly confident.

"Mr. Knight?" the man on the phone asked. "Do you remember the Sons of Liberty story you did back in June?"

Did he remember, indeed! How the hell could he forget?

"We have another invitation for you," the man said. "How would you like to go with us on a raid into Cuba?"

Knight's blood chilled. Were they serious or just trying to get a rise out of him? Knight relayed the invitation to

Close, who immediately replied that KOOL would play no part in Bay of Pigs II.

THE YEAR AFTER he failed to graduate from McClintock High, Robbie made a lot of new friends. Through Cooley's group, he met several young men with an intense fascination with firearms. Those friendships, plus events on the world stage that were troubling to Robbie, convinced him he should prepare for the endtime struggle.

Robbie formed the Sons of Liberty, a group dominated by fellow Mormons and survivalists. He'd met some of them hanging around gun shops and motorcycle shops in south Phoenix. Robbie was easily the most intelligent one in the group, but he was fascinated with the netherworld. He was acting out a fantasy, imagining he was the last bulwark between decent society and communistic chaos.

Johnny and Una were bothered by some of these people Robbie brought around to the trailer. They seemed like losers, and his parents refused to believe Robbie had stooped so low. Yet Robbie picked up their gun lust. It seemed so unlikely for a young man whose job was making ice cream at the Carnation plant.

There was one man who particularly upset Johnny. Gregory Thorpe had a cocky and impulsive mien, a bad combination when guns are handy. He was a lieutenant in the Sons of Liberty but was hard to control. During one argument with Robbie, Thorpe whacked him on the head with a Luger.

Robbie still went to his Birch Society meetings in Tempe, his orator's gift impressing the older members with his fervent patriotism. Robbie also remained active in the Young Republicans and once took them beyond the bounds of typical GOP decorum. The occasion was an international event that became a turning point for many anticommunists, especially for Robbie.

Richard Nixon, the staunch anticommunist of the 1950s, was pursuing ties with Red China. While the administration held out for Nationalist China in the United Nations, it was clear the world body was intent on seating Mao Tse-tung's regime and ousting Chiang Kai-shek. On October 25, 1971, seven years to the day after Robbie first read the Birch Society's warning about the communists' plan for world domination, the U.N. voted overwhelmingly to seat Peking and reject the United States' two-China compromise. Pro-Peking delegates cheered the U.S. defeat. The Tanzanian ambassador, wearing a Mao jacket, danced an African version of an Irish jig at the rostrum. It was a day of great fear among conservatives. For Robbie it meant the communist plan had gained steam. The circle was closing.

Una Mathews opened her paper one morning at the bank shortly after the China vote and was shocked to find a picture of Robbie among some Young Republicans, burning a Red Chinese flag outside the Phoenix City Hall to protest the vote. The paper got his name wrong, thank heavens, and she folded it away before her co-workers could see it.

Shortly after Channel 10's film and tapes were seized by Middleton, Robbie ran off to California to let the situation cool down. On August 26, 1972, he wrote to his dad, enclosing the key to his Jeep and asking his dad to sell it. He was happier than he'd ever been, he wrote, but he also had a dire warning:

> If you have any money left over after the payoff, you and mother keep it and buy some long-lasting food items for yourselves. Will you please keep on consant alert for any unusual national happening and have a plan worked out in case of an emergency. From all the information I have obtained I feel that Phoenix along with all other major cities or towns would be a death trap in case of civil war, famine, a depression or any other calamity. The White Mountain area, and northeastern Arizona along with the general Four Corners area would be the safest place in this country in the face of a disaster.
>
> Don't worry about me, I am doing fine and I have learned a secret of life that very few people have discovered. I hope that I am wrong about an upcoming depression and famine, but if I am not I have everything worked out so that you and mother and Grant and Lee will be taken care of. I already have several places arranged for the family to stay.

I love you both dearly. Your son, Robert

Robbie was nineteen. His parents were curious as to why he felt civil strife was about to break out. Was he planning something to cause it? They felt powerless. For anyone that young to be so serious about life was such a waste, they thought. Robbie's youth seemed to have passed so quickly. All of a sudden, Una wasn't so happy that her son was more interested in politics than in the things that normally interest teenagers. Maybe soon, she prayed, he'd start chasing girls instead of commies and tax collectors.

By the fall of 1972, Middleton finally found someone who could identify the person speaking on Knight's taped interview. It was Robbie Mathews, the informant told him, a Mormon tax protester who was in Marvin Cooley's entourage.

Johnny Mathews answered his door one night that fall to two grave-looking FBI agents who said a few things about his son and some radical literature. They wanted to check the family's typewriter. It was a mortifying experience for the parents. The agents typed a sample from the typewriter and left. The bureau never was able to match that sample with the threatening brochure the desert commandos had given Knight during the interview. Robbie Mathews, though, became a central figure in Middleton's investigation.

Robbie returned before the end of the year. Instead of staying with his parents, he took a room at a strip motel on West Southern Avenue in Tempe, a mile from McClintock High and a few blocks from the Tempe Irrigation Canal, which marked the Mesa city limits. He found a job at a copper mine in Superior, in the Superstition Mountains about 50 miles east on U.S. 60. The road passed through Apache Junction, a desert town where some of the Sons of Liberty lived. A few also worked at the mine with Robbie. He persuaded some of them to join the desert rescue team of the Maricopa County Sheriff's Posse. That way they could get legitimate training and, if necessary, also could flash a deputy's badge.

But it wasn't long before Robbie's fantasy world crashed around him with a vengeance. His violent friend, Gregory Thorpe, snapped.

Thorpe was twenty-two. He married Inez Allen on

November 11, 1972, when their baby was four months old. Inez was eighteen, a student at Glendale Community College. Greg had been president of the Young Republicans and chairman of Young Americans for Freedom at Mesa Community College. He worked for a time on the successful campaign of Maricopa County Sheriff Paul Blubaum. Besides Robbie's Sons of Liberty, Greg was in another paramilitary group called the Secret Army Organization.

Five days before Christmas 1972, the Thorpes were moving into an apartment with another couple, Alan and Willa Bremer, near 44th Street and McDowell Road, a dozen blocks north of Sky Harbor International Airport. Alan was twenty, his wife nineteen. They had moved a month earlier from Illinois looking for work and met Greg.

Shortly after midnight on December 20, Greg and Inez got into an argument. Quick-tempered, he slugged Inez, knocking her to the floor, then kicked her in the face. As the yelling continued, Alan chased Greg to a back bedroom, and Willa Bremer phoned for the police from the kitchen.

"We've had some trouble over here and need an ambulance," she said. The dispatch tape recorded the horrifying events that followed.

As Alan walked toward the bedroom, Greg emerged with a shotgun and a 9mm pistol. He raised the shotgun toward Alan and fired squarely into his chest. The force of the blast blew Alan against a wall. He crumpled dead to the floor as the women began screaming.

Greg moved next into the kitchen and fired at Willa. The pellets slammed her against the sink, and she rolled on the floor dead. A friend who was helping Greg move ran out a back door, barely escaping a blast aimed in his direction.

Then Greg turned toward Inez. By now he was beyond hesitation. He ended her life with a single squeeze of the shotgun's trigger. There was a minute of silence on the police tape. Then, with cops hot on the way, Greg took his pistol and fired once into Alan's back, twice into Inez's head.

The final shot heard on the tape was when Greg placed

the muzzle of the 9mm against the side of his own head and fired, killing himself.

Police found the gory scene one minute later. Inside the Bremers' apartment, several motorcycles were parked, and engine parts were scattered around the rooms. A small Christmas tree with carefully wrapped presents around it stood on a small table. A swastika flag was hanging on a wall, and a smaller Nazi flag was draped over an inert aircraft bomb.

The Phoenix police, as they began their grim work, had no idea that a crazy scheme for a terrorist raid into Cuba had died along with these four young people.

Robbie withdrew into a deep depression over the deaths, and his Sons of Liberty foundered. He believed they were a team, a crack fighting unit that would spill its blood for the cause, not over a petty domestic squabble. What happened to the clean-cut, clean-living conservative folk he thought were his friends?

While he was trying to sort it all out, Mathews met Donald Edward Clarke.

Clarke introduced himself to Mathews at one of Cooley's sessions in early 1973. Clarke reminded Mathews a lot of Thorpe, but without the bitter edge. Clarke was wrapped up in the paramilitary aspect of the survivalist fringe. He loved guns. He had a survival room in his house with most of his equipment, and at least one gun in every room in case he needed it.

But Clarke wasn't impulsive. He had acquired his methodical nature in childhood. The woman who lived across the street from him when he was seven constantly had to chase him out of her flower bed, where he busily dug foxholes.

Clarke talked Robbie into reviving the Sons of Liberty in 1973. Some members had lost their enthusiasm, but the group was able to find new recruits. Some were on Middleton's snitch list. This time Robbie was under close surveillance by federal agents, even though he hadn't yet committed a crime. The surveillance only fed Robbie's paranoia and persecution complex, and filled him with righteous indignation.

"Is that fair?" he often asked his perplexed parents. Well, maybe it wasn't fair, but he was quickly learning there is the way the world should be, and there is the way the world is.

IT WASN'T VIOLENCE that finally got Robbie in trouble with the law. It was tax resistance. When he filled out his W-4 form for his employer's federal tax withholding files in 1973, he listed ten dependents. The effect was to reduce his withholding, since he had no intention of filing a 1040 return.

But Mathews listed his correct age, twenty, and stated that he was unmarried. Putting down ten dependents was bound to draw attention. The IRS opened a case as soon as it saw the form. The agency already was aware of Mathews since he often wrote to complain that the federal income tax was unconstitutional. Now that he was trying to get out of paying it, the agents figured he'd gone beyond free speech.

The U.S. attorney's office drew up a misdemeanor complaint, and a federal judge issued a bench warrant for Mathews's arrest on Friday, July 20, 1973. Agents brought their guns, because they knew the proclivities of the Sons of Liberty.

They spotted Robbie at a friend's home that evening and followed him to a nearby 7-Eleven store. When Robbie saw them, he dashed to his pickup. A loud crack resounded, and Robbie was convinced one of the agents had fired a gun at him. He had no idea why they were after him as he sped south toward the desert. During the chase, Robbie swerved off the road and rolled his truck. He managed to crawl away behind some brush, his adrenalin pumping madly, before the agents pulled up and started to search for him. It took a while to find him, but when they did, he was hustled away to a federal holding cell for the weekend.

Robbie went for legal help to the American Civil Liberties Union, which agreed to represent him. The irony of their son's going to the ACLU wasn't lost on Johnny and Una. It took nearly six months for the case to be resolved. In the meantime he went back to work at the mines as a maintenance worker at Mimi Inc. in Miami, Arizona, a short way up the road from Superior.

Before the court date, Johnny loaned an old suit to

Robbie, who didn't own any dress clothes of his own. Una took a day off from the bank, and Bruce Rogers, an elderly gentleman who drove Robbie to his Birch Society meetings, came along as a character witness. Aside from the magistrate and the attorneys, they were the only ones in the courtroom.

Magistrate Richard Gormley sentenced Robbie to six months of probation. After the threats, the guns, and the chase, all he got was probation. Robbie sighed with relief. It was January 16, 1974, his twenty-first birthday.

He got a new job that month as a crusher operator at the Magma copper mine in Superior and held it all through probation. But he resolved to get out of Arizona as soon as he was free. He was disgusted and forlorn.

People were pouring into Phoenix by the thousands, materialistic people who Robbie felt were unaware of the struggle going on under their noses. They were satisfied with government getting fatter, taking care of all their needs. Their greatest conflict after coming home from mundane jobs was whether to go out for fast food or stay home to watch the latest brainless sitcom on television.

But more than that, Robbie was disgusted with the people he thought were his friends. He put into practice what he'd been taught about tax protest, was chased into the desert by IRS agents, sat in jail, and went to court without any of his associates standing up for him, save the gallant Dr. Rogers.

None of his erstwhile friends would even help raise the money to get his truck out of police impound. Robbie made plans to leave even as he helped Don Clarke reorganize the Sons of Liberty.

Mathews made a list of weapons each recruit should have: 9mm pistol, .308 assault rifle, and 12-gauge shotgun. Then Clarke went to each recruit's apartment and selected items they should pawn to buy those guns. Televisions, stereos, and other mass culture distractions would have to go. When Clarke brought the recruits to Mathews, he had an awesome-looking electronic box he called an E-Meter. It was supposed to determine whether a man was lying, but everyone passed it, including three of Middleton's informants.

When Middleton heard of the E-Meter, he wondered if

Robbie had found the Church of Scientology while in California. The E-Meter is the galvanic skin-tester used by Scientologists. Maybe that was the "secret of life" of which Robbie wrote.

Toward the end of his probation, Robbie bought an old pickup truck. One of his friends, Chuck Gelisse, came by, and the two planned a trip to the Pacific Northwest. Robbie was fascinated by his Scottish ancestry and imagined the area around Oregon and Washington would be similar to the Scottish Highlands. They searched a road atlas for areas where they thought they'd find mines to work.

On a Friday night in July 1974, Clarke brought a recruit to a Scottsdale office where Mathews had the E-Meter set up. The recruit passed, as usual, and Robbie told Don to start his training. As the two left, Mathews said quietly, "See you later, Don." The next day, Robbie and Chuck set out for Oregon in the pickup.

When the two men saw the natural beauty of the Northwest, they were beside themselves. Swinging up the coast, then across the Cascades, they saw snow on Mount Hood in July. The land around the treeless peaks was the deepest green they'd ever seen. The valleys were wet and fertile. Turning inland, they crossed the high desert of Oregon and Washington, headed for the Rocky Mountain chains.

On the Washington state map, Robbie and Chuck saw a road that wound north out of Spokane along the eastern edge of the state, leading into Canada. They drove along the picturesque, two-lane Highway 31, which followed the wide, slow-moving Pend Oreille River. It went past old farms, ranches, and small towns, through meadows and thick pine forests. The Selkirk Mountains rose on either side of the river valley, which narrowed into a canyon several times.

About 12 miles south of the border, Highway 31 coursed down a hillside on the river's west bank. At the bottom, it made a graceful curve over a spindly, steel-trussed bridge to the east bank, where the town of Metaline Falls was nestled on a flat piece of ground at the base of the mountains. The Pend Oreille flowed on into Canada to meet the mighty Columbia River.

It's easy in Metaline Falls to get the feeling of being backed up against the edge of the country. Fewer than three hundred people live there, with Canada breathing down their necks. It is easier to go to Nelson, British Columbia, for shopping than to make the two-hour drive to Spokane. Isolated at the northern end of Pend Oreille County, Metaline Falls and the smaller town of Metaline on the west bank are tiny outposts where outside influences are few. There is no K-mart, Penney's or Sears, no McDonald's or Burger King, just a few greasy-spoon places with names like Buster's and Heidi's. The only movie theater, the NuVu, is now boarded up. It is an uncomplicated town of few streets, dominated by the concrete silos, towers, and railyards of the Portland Lehigh Cement Company.

It is a perfect place to begin anew.

Robbie fell in love with the area as soon as he saw it. When he asked around town about jobs, he discovered there were only three places for newcomers to get work: the cement plant, the Bunker Hill lead and zinc mine, and Boundary Dam a mile south of the border. With his experience in mining, Robbie was hired on the spot at Bunker Hill, along the river a mile north of town.

Pointing the beat-up truck south, Robbie and Chuck made it to Phoenix in two days. It was Saturday, July 27, a day Robbie normally would head out with Don Clarke to Cave Creek, a primitive desert area north of Phoenix, for military maneuvers. He startled his parents with news of his move as he begged them to help gather his belongings. It had been so long since they'd seen their youngest son devoid of the anger and bitterness he usually harbored.

They scoured the mobile home wildly looking for things Robbie would need. He was in a rush, he told them, because he had to get back to Metaline Falls by Monday morning to start work at the mine. Robbie took off Saturday evening, heading back to the deep Washington woods.

In Metaline Falls, Robbie rented an apartment in an old brick hotel on Grand View Street. But his goal was to find a sizable piece of ground for a farm. He had dreamed of owning a place in the mountains since he was a kid on vacation with his family in the White Mountains of Ari-

zona. He remembered what he told his parents then:
"Mom and dad, when I grow up I'm going to buy you a
place in the mountains."

Within a month, Johnny and Una came to visit. They
were elated with the change they saw in Robbie. But
Una felt a touch of maternal sorrow for him, living in an
old hotel with his two dogs. He prepared dinners in a
blender, and the oatmeal he made for breakfast had a
consistency similar to what was being manufactured at
Portland Lehigh. He had very few friends, none of them
female. But it was worth it, she realized, because Robbie
finally was away from the craziness in Phoenix. Maybe it
had been just a phase he went through after all, Una told
Johnny. They prayed that their personal nightmare was
over.

Robbie told his parents about his dream of the family
living together in the mountains, and he had already
scouted some properties for sale. He showed them a
60-acre tract off Boundary Dam Road, west of the river
on the mountainside, 480 feet above the town. It was
thickly wooded, with a 60-foot drop on the north side to
Beaver Creek, which cascaded down to the river. It was
almost directly across the river from Bunker Hill Mine.
To the west, an odd-shaped mountain with a treeless
summit named Hooknose dominated the skyline. Robbie
wanted to buy the land, and Johnny agreed to help him
with some earnest money.

Early in November, Johnny got a letter from Robbie.
It was a refreshing change from the dread letter he'd sent
two years earlier. It was full of hope instead of cynicism.
In fact, the letter was remarkably childlike. Robbie drew
pictures in place of some of the words, like a rebus. At
the top was a drawing of a log cabin with flowers in front,
a pine tree in back and a smiling sun overhead. A sign in
front said "Mathews Acres."

"Hello loved ones," he wrote.

> *I've enclosed the [drawing of dollar bills] for the
> [drawing of a motorcycle] payment. It has occurred
> to me that I was sort of rude to you the last time I
> [drawing of stick man in a phone booth] you. I've
> been feeling [drawing of a sad face with tears] about it.*

Please forgive me.

*There's still no snow here in town, but there's about
5 inches on our land. Lucien and his family saw two
cow elk and two partridges on our land. . . .*

*I'm going to build the most comfortable cabins for
us that you've ever seen. Lucien has told me how easy
it is to build a full basement, so I'm going to build one
for us. When I showed Lucien that little pond on our
creek, across from the meadow, we saw 3 or 4 pan size
trout in it.*

*I love you two more than you'll probably ever know,
and I want you to know that my friends are fine, but
my family is what I really care about. My dream in life
is that someday soon the whole Mathews clan will be
living together on Mathews Acres.*

At Christmas, Robbie flew back to Phoenix to spend
the holidays with his family. Johnny was ready to give his
son an answer about moving up, but there was something
in the air that had to be cleared. Johnny called Robbie
into the living room while Una and Lee were there to
listen. An unspoken tension filled the room, and Una,
unaware of what Johnny wanted, could feel it was a
solemn moment.

"Now Robbie," his dad finally said in firm, measured
tones, "before we go up there with all that trouble and
expense, I want you to make me a promise. I want you to
give me your word that you're through with all this
radical involvement and with these crazy people who put
you in this spot."

"Oh!" Robbie said, somewhat startled.

Una was surprised as well and shot up straight when
she heard her husband. Una knew how disappointed
Robbie had been when his friends abandoned him when
he was arrested. Una believed Robbie wanted nothing
more to do with them.

"Oh, Johnny, that's not necessary," she protested to
her husband. "You don't have to ask that of Robbie.
Surely after his experience, he's grown up now. Can't
you see he's a man?"

But Robbie extended his hand to hush her. He knew
what his dad wanted. It wasn't enough for Johnny to

sense the change, he needed his son to articulate it.

"Dad," Robbie said, "it's all over. I give you my word. I'm satisfied just to get in my little corner of the world and watch the rest of it go by. And I want my family with me."

It was what Johnny wanted to hear. That Christmas was a celebration such as the family hadn't had in a long time. It was the tenth anniversary of Robbie's membership in the John Birch Society, the end of a decade in which Robbie had lived half a lifetime. It was the end of a path that began innocently that day in 1964 when Una fetched the Sunday paper from her porch. And now, finally, there was the promise that it was over.

Johnny wouldn't retire for another two and a half years, but he sent money to Robbie for the land and helped each summer clearing it of timber. In the spring of 1975, Una even talked Robbie into writing the principal at McClintock High about completing the course work for his diploma. The school allowed Robbie to take a history course by mail rather than the economics course he had deserted.

He didn't backslide on his vow either, and he told his parents when temptation rose. In May 1975, he wrote home again.

It is wonderfully beautiful up here right now. Everything is extremely lush and green, and all the fruit trees are in bloom. Yesterday I cut a path down to the creek, and made a little park out of a grassy area that borders the water. I made a little log bench to sit on and planted a bunch of irises down there. Today I went exploring down the road that we walked along last year. I found a golden eagle's nest at the very top of a big dead pine tree. There was only one eagle by the nest, and it kept making a "weeeeweee" sound. I also found a little spring and a little hidden cleared area where a small herd of elk is apparently bedding down at night.

Then he reported the serious matter.

Don Clarke has found out where I'm at and there's a remote possibility that he might come up here to visit

*me, but don't worry about anything because I can han-
dle him without any difficulty. He apparently has just
left the fight and is in the same place where I was not
too long back so I can sympathize with him.*

*It's true that his personality leaves a lot to be desired,
but he is facing the same problems that I faced just
recently. If he comes up it will just be for a short time,
but I doubt if he will come up at all. He's finding
out that there are very few people who a patriot can trust,
but I guess he must trust me.*

*Don't worry about me getting involved again. The
only goal I have right now is to finish building that
house. I hope to move onto the land by September.*

                    Your son for all eternity, Robbie XXXX

Clarke had a good reason to track down his former
friend. There was a grand jury subpoena out for him in
May 1975.

After Robbie abandoned the Sons of Liberty, it took
Clarke a few weeks to realize what happened. Here he
was, left out at Cave Creek teaching low-crawl and weapons assembly to a bunch of recruits every Saturday. He
didn't learn Robbie had left until August 24. After that
the Sons developed a deep schism between the Mormon
and non-Mormon members, and it became moribund.

Clarke joined a splinter group called Concord II, emu-
lating the Minutemen. Two friends, one a janitor and the
other a successful accountant, joined him. Unfortunately
for Clarke, Middleton's informants were admitted as well.
Just two weeks after Robbie disappeared, Middleton
started to bear down on Clarke. As Concord II pro-
gressed to bomb-making, the FBI became more concerned.

By May, Middleton had used the information from his
snitches to secure subpoenas for the leaders. Clarke was
nervous. The first night he hid out in Apache Junction
while he put out word among his contacts to locate Robbie
Mathews. He then went to his mother's house in Phoenix, where he learned that a friend in Mesa knew where
Mathews was. The friend was a survivalist who had a
concrete and steel bunker in his yard. Clarke spent the
night there and then called Metaline Falls, prompting
Mathews to write his parents the letter.

Don immediately set out for Washington. True to his word, Robbie handled him well. Robbie got Don a job at Bunker Hill but made plans for his quick exit. That was fine with Don, who sold his car to Robbie and used the money the next month to get a phony passport in Seattle. Don Clarke soon departed for Rhodesia, where he joined a white mercenary group fighting the black nationalists. It took British Intelligence four years to locate him for the FBI.

In the meantime, Robbie had more unwelcome visitors. Two FBI agents drove up from Spokane to Metaline Falls to visit the Bunker Hill Mine office after learning Clarke had worked there. They spoke with a secretary about the backgrounds of Mathews and Clarke. Fortunately for Robbie, it wasn't the mine manager they met, because he probably would have been fired. Instead, the secretary spoke to Mathews's foreman in the electrical department, who didn't like federal agents any more than Robbie. That was as far as the inquiries went.

Middleton also phoned Mathews to talk about Clarke. It was a brief conversation, and Mathews wasn't very cooperative. Don was gone, Robbie told him, and everything was cool. He was buying some land and thinking of getting married. The fact that Clarke had found him seemed to upset Robbie. Middleton had heard the last from Robbie Mathews, he said.

When Middleton hung up, he concluded Robbie was sincere about leaving the movement. Middleton believed Robbie was a cut above the typical right-winger, with too much on the ball to spend his life crawling around arroyos waiting for communist invaders.

In October 1975, Clarke and two other Concord II members—the janitor and the accountant—were indicted for conspiring to kill Middleton.

But no explanation could placate Mathews, who was angry that the FBI had tracked him and almost cost him his job. He sent a letter of warning to the FBI's Seattle office. He would take no more of it, he wrote.

"Leave me alone, or I will respond in such a way that could be very painful to certain agents."

Chapter 2

Gathering Aryans, the Covenant People

On a bright April day in 1974, Richard Girnt Butler stood in the center of a clearing, studying the dense forest. The stand of Douglas fir and lodgepole pine formed a natural screen, encasing the property from the outside world.

A tight smile creased his craggy, leathery face as he drew on one of his endless supply of Pall Malls and turned slowly to study a two-story wood frame farmhouse. It was 100 yards up a winding, tree-lined drive off Rimrock Road, the nearest access into this 20-acre cul-de-sac. And, Butler noted with satisfaction, it was on high ground, defensible if necessary.

Butler's love for the north Idaho panhandle began years earlier, when he and his wife, Betty, would pack his single-engine airplane with fishing gear and fly from Southern California to Coeur d'Alene on vacations. They were particularly fond of boating on Coeur d'Alene Lake and mighty Lake Pend Oreille. The property was between the two large lakes and near the smaller Hayden Lake, which appeared from the air as a glittering starfish floating in the dense, dark-green forest.

The property was a couple of miles from the exclusive Hayden Lake community where 2,500 well-to-do residents lived around the lakeshore. It was incorporated in the 1940s as an expedient way of acquiring a liquor license for the Hayden Lake Country Club. Its most famous part-time resident, the crooner Bing Crosby, often was seen on the links with some of Hollywood's brightest stars.

The property that interested Butler was on the western edge of Coeur d'Alene National Forest in the Bitterroot mountain range, where elk, whitetail deer, and bobcats were common sights. A short walk into the back country might bring him upon the huge shovel antlers of a bull moose along a willow-clogged drainage or a grizzly sow and her cubs digging on the mountain slopes for tubers and mites.

While this country stirred images of Butler's ancestral Scottish Highlands, its real appeal was that it was white man's land. Minorities were practically nonexistent, which was important to Butler. He reveled in being among "his own people," those among whom his faith, Christian Identity, compelled him to live.

Richard Girnt Butler proudly categorized himself a racist—"one who loves his race." He thought of himself not as antiblack or anti-Jewish, but as a white nationalist. Each race should have its own homeland, and the Pacific Northwest, with its strong Nordic ambience, was his. The Inland Empire, as the Idaho panhandle, eastern Washington, and western Montana is called, has nearly 1.1 million residents. Fewer than 3 percent are Hispanic, less than 2 percent Native Americans, not quite 1 percent black, and even fewer Jews.

The cornerstone of any society is faith, and the practice of that faith requires a church. Once a man believes his fight is for God and country, he becomes invincible. It's impossible to limit what he can accomplish if he believes his quest is righteous and his death a martyrdom.

Placing his arm around Betty, Butler felt the Lord had led them to this place. It was here they'd build the Church of Jesus Christ Christian, a monument to the preservation of the white race.

RICHARD GIRNT BUTLER was born Feb. 23, 1918, in Bennett, Colorado, a small community on the high plains 20 miles east of Denver. His parents, Clarence and Winfred, moved with their son to a nice residential area of south-central Denver in the early 1920s and opened a machine shop. The Butlers were Presbyterians and, while not regular worshipers, understood morality and kept to the straight path.

Spending hours at his father's side, Butler often heard his dad denounce communism as a Jewish conspiracy, conceived and financed in New York and London, and transported to Russia. Those beliefs, ingrained in Richard's mind, eventually formed the basis of his lifelong conviction that communism, controlled by the Jews, was the instrument of the anti-Christ, the "red dragon" of the Apocalypse.

A love of history prompted the young Butler to read, which in turn heightened his aversion to communism. He found horror stories in which soldiers of the U.S. Occupational Forces returning from Russia after World War I testified that the Jews were with the Bolsheviks, murdering White Russians in every conceivable manner.

The idea of a Jewish conspiracy was further entrenched when Butler heard his dad say that billions of dollars were being shoveled to the revolutionary government through such Jewish investment firms as Kuhn, Loeb & Company.

But it was fiction, not fact, that solidified Butler's dread of communism. It came when he was a lad of eleven earning spending money with a weekend job delivering *Liberty Magazine* in his neighborhood. In one issue, he read a serialization of *The Red Napoleon* by Floyd Gibbons of the *Chicago Tribune*. The war correspondent's work, published in 1929, was a futuristic account of an invasion of Europe and North America by Bolshevik raiders from the Soviet Union, led by the Mongol dictator Karakhan of Kazan, who was bent on miscegenating all races into one.

The Red Napoleon raised the hackles on Butler's neck. It told of America's life-and-death battle against communist enslavement, uncannily foretelling the rise of the Third World against capitalism and white colonialism.

When Butler was thirteen, his family moved to east Los Angeles. He attended City College there for two years, studying science and aeronautical engineering. While in college, Butler got a part-time job with the Consolidated Vultee Air Craft Company, a private contractor building the B-11 bomber.

In 1941, Vultee sent Butler to Bangalore, India, on a contract to overhaul P-25s, P-24s, and PBYs for the Royal Indian Air Force. He was given the honorary rank of captain, which entitled him to a valet. The man he hired was named Jeroum, a Hindu who proudly wore a red dot in the center of his forehead.

At night, while he polished Butler's boots or did other work around his hut, the two men often discussed India's caste system. Jeroum described it as a way of maintaining racial purity. He extolled the virtues taught in the ancient Sanskrit hymns of the Rig Veda. According to Brahmanism, precursor to Hinduism, blond-haired, blue-eyed Indo-Europeans, the Aryans, conquered the Indus Valley 1,500 years before Christ. In time they married with the dark-skinned people, and a caste system was instituted to save what few pure-blooded Aryans were left.

"Sahib, I have Aryan blood," Jeroum said one warm evening in the hut.

"Now, Jeroum, you can't say that," Butler gently chided the man. "You're as black as the ace of spades."

But Jeroum insisted: "Yes, Sahib, I have Aryan blood. I've traced it back. The reason I'm where I am is that the caste system didn't hold." That started Butler thinking. If this Indian servant knew more about his own race than Butler did about his, he'd better start studying. He was so impressed by Jeroum's insight that the study of the history of the races became his lifelong passion.

Butler returned to the United States after Japan attacked Pearl Harbor and enlisted in the Army Air Corps. Putting his aeronautics experience to good use, he spent the war years stateside teaching hydraulics. After V-J Day, Butler returned to Vultee, married his sweetheart, Betty, and had a daughter they named Cindy. It was the beginning of what could have been a normal, sedate life.

Butler's staunch anticommunist attitudes increased, as did many Americans', in the Cold War of the 1950s. His interest was perked when Wisconsin's Senator Joseph McCarthy targeted communists in government as a springboard to national attention in 1954. Bent on exposing Bolsheviks in the Army and the Defense Department, McCarthy waved a laundry list he said contained "hundreds of names of communists" under the noses of congressmen and reporters alike, while taking care that no one actually read the list. The paranoia of Americans about anything "Red" was fueled mightily as McCarthy fired the first barrages in his campaign.

Several years after McCarthy mustered a subcommittee to expose the alleged communists, the American Broadcasting Company made a bold decision to provide live daytime coverage of the Army-McCarthy hearings. Butler and millions of other Americans had ringside seats in the comfort of their homes to watch their authentic American hero at work. The Army-McCarthy hearings began a five-week run and Butler watched with rapt attention. The Senator's critics began to charge that he criss-crossed the lines of ethics and legality while trying to prove the existence of subversives. Butler saw no such waffling. So certain was he that McCarthy was a righteous, God-fearing American that Butler sent money to enable the senator to continue.

When public sentiment turned against McCarthy, particularly following Edward R. Murrow's three-part *See It Now* TV documentary on the Senator, Butler was sure he was seeing another conspiracy engineered by the communists. McCarthy's Senate colleagues formally censured him by a vote of 67–22 in December 1954. That only increased Butler's distrust and fear of the federal government.

Then, when George Lincoln Rockwell's American Nazi Party was formed, Butler followed it with interest. Many years after Rockwell's assassination, Butler reminisced about the neo-Nazi in an interview in the Boise *Idaho Statesman:* "Sure I knew Rockwell. I'm proud of it. He was 100 percent m-a-n. He loved his race and he wanted to do something about it."

The stage was set for Butler in 1962 when he heard an anticommunist California lawmaker named Louis Francis give a speech on a proposed state constitutional amendment to bar communists from state jobs, political office, and property tax exemptions, Butler decided it was time to become active. He'd heard there were about 10,000 communist teachers in California public schools. He joined the California Committee to Combat Communism and helped organize seven hundred people who gathered signatures on petitions to get the issue on the ballot. Butler became the group's Los Angeles leader on his first foray into politics.

Among the places Butler looked for support were veterans' groups. When the Signal Hill American Legion Post in Los Angeles invited him to speak, Butler accepted nervously. Although he cut an imposing figure at 6 feet and 185 pounds, he had a slightly nasal, hollow speech delivery that was uninspiring. Nevertheless, he easily persuaded the old guard to sign petitions. The group eventually gathered 400,000 signatures to put the issue on the ballot, but it was solidly defeated in the 1962 general election.

For Butler, however, the gain at Signal Hill was far greater than a few signatures, for that night altered the course of his life. In the audience was retired Army Colonel William Potter Gale, a Douglas MacArthur staff member who had directed guerrilla operations in the Philippines during World War II. Like Butler, Gale had gone to work in the expanding aircraft industry in California.

In 1958, Gale ran for governor on the Constitution Party ticket, calling in part for the impeachment of President Eisenhower and all nine justices of the Supreme Court for their efforts to desegregate Southern schools. He later lost in the Republican primary for governor, and in 1964 and 1968 he ran in the Republican primary for the House of Representatives and failed again.

Then, in 1969, a loosely structured band of armed vigilantes and survivalists named the Posse Comitatus (Latin for "Power of the County") was formed in Portland, Oregon. It proclaimed that all governmental power was rooted at the county level and that the federal government had usurped it. Gale immediately organized his own chapter, called the U. S. Christian Posse Association, and later wrote several handbooks for the Posse, plus a number of manuals on guerrilla warfare.

In 1962 Gale was well respected among his peers at Signal Hill. After listening to Butler's pitch for a communist-free school system, Gale pulled him aside and told him there was someone Butler needed to hear, someone who really knew what communism was about—Dr. Wesley Swift of Lancaster, California, the founder of the Anglo-Saxon Christian Congregation.

Swift, an ordained Methodist minister, was one of the best-known advocates in the United States of the doctrine known as Christian Identity. He was anti-Jew and anti-Catholic, which was consistent with his past history as a KKK organizer. He was a follower of Gerald L. K. Smith, a well-known racist who had inspired George Lincoln Rockwell. Swift was Smith's advance man until he broke with him in the late 1950s and moved to California to form the Anglo-Saxon Christian Congregation, a fusion of Smith's racism and Christian Identity doctrine.

At the time Butler gave the Signal Hill speech, he wasn't too fond of religion at all. He and Betty tried going to the Presbyterian church where they were married in Los Angeles, but to Butler the new preacher was talking communism, pure and simple. Butler tried a number of Christian denominations in Southern California before concluding that life's answers weren't found in a church.

But when Gale told him Swift's church would appeal to him as a white man, he was intrigued. He felt everything had gone against the United States since the war. The communists were gobbling up Eastern Europe. Every compromise in the newly created United Nations was being resolved in the communists' favor. Then Harry Truman announced the armed forces would be integrated forcibly, at bayonet point if necessary. And in 1957, the Army was brought in to Little Rock, Arkansas, to enforce integration of the city high schools.

"My God," Butler eventually concluded. "This is war against the white race."

On the Sunday morning he went to Swift's church, Butler felt as out of place as he did in any church. For one thing, the building was located at Hollywood and Vine, dead center of the entertainment world. He sat listening half-heartedly among the congregants as Swift began his sermon.

Who are the true Israelites? Swift asked rhetorically before going through the heraldry of race, the symbols and tribal signs. Swift discussed the 48th and 49th chapters of Genesis, the prophesies of Jacob for his twelve sons, and how the tribes they founded came down to this day to form the Aryan nations of Europe. Swift told his congregation there was no evidence of white man on earth before 7,200 years ago. Yet wherever the white man went after that, there was a sudden explosion of civilization. Butler felt like Paul on the road to Damascus. What he heard neatly answered all his nagging questions about life.

Butler immediately researched Christian Identity. It was founded by Edward Hine, an Englishman, who outlined his theory in an 1871 book, *Identification of the British Nation with Lost Israel*. For its time, it was a runaway best-seller. The crux of the doctrine is that European Jews are not descended from ancient Hebrew stock at all but from Khazars, residents of a warlike nation of southern Russia who converted to Judaism in the eighth or ninth century. They cannot claim lineage from Abraham, Isaac, and Jacob and are not the covenant people, according to Identity's genealogists. On the contrary, today's Nordic–Anglo-Saxon–Teuton whites are the descendants of the lost tribes of the Biblical Israelites, making white Christians the true people of the covenant.

To support this, Hine reinterpreted the book of Genesis with a "two-seed theory." Eve was seduced by the serpent and bore a son by him, Cain, who slew his brother Abel. After that Adam, the first white man, passed on his seed to another son, Seth, who became the father of the white race, God's Chosen People. Cain's descendants, Identity says, are the Jews. They literally are the seed of Satan.

Other races, or "mud people" to racists, descend from others cursed by God.

Secular history gives a different story. The ten tribes of Israel, the northern kingdom after the death of Solomon, were deported in 722 B.C. by the conquering Assyrians and were assimilated by intermarriage into other groups. Judah, the southern kingdom of two tribes, remained racially intact.

But Identity doctrine claims the lost tribes crossed the Caucasus Mountains and settled in the Scandinavian and West European countries. Descendants of those tribes ultimately sailed on the Mayflower. After settling the New World, the true Promised Land, America's founding fathers were inspired by God to write the sacred documents we know as the Declaration of Independence, the Constitution, and the Bill of Rights. The amendments that followed, according to Identity, are Satanic additions dictated through today's Jews to undermine the white race.

Christian Identity followers tend to think in apocalyptic terms. Many believe the era of the beast is fast approaching; some think the field of Armageddon is in Nebraska or Kansas. Some see in our current system of banking and commerce the very signs foretold in the Book of Revelation. To many on the fringe, this trend represents the dreaded mark of the beast, without which in Apostle John's nightmarish vision, "no one could get a job or even buy in any store" (Rev. 13:17).

The capability already exists for a cashless society, thanks to computer technology. To the extreme right, that means an inevitable march to world government. The banking system is increasingly multinational, and the managing of the world's wealth, with private banks issuing currency upon the debts of nations instead of nations issuing currency backed by its peoples' productivity, delivers the real power into the hands of internationalists, a euphemism for Jews.

With such endtime convictions, Christian Identity churches sprang up in small communities across the heartland.

"You cannot avoid the reality of the fact that the Consummation of an Age is upon us!" warned the *Zion's Watchman* newsletter of Nevada, Missouri, in 1979. "It is extremely important that all White Christian People take immediate steps to prepare themselves and their families for these forthcoming conditions."

FROM THE FIRST service, Richard Butler became a regular at the Anglo-Saxon Christian Congregation. After a few Sundays, he mustered enough confidence to introduce himself to Swift, and almost instantly the two became close and trusted friends. Swift chose Butler to lead his newly formed Christian Defense League.

Butler threw himself into the league's activities. His first CDL project was to counter a move by Jewish groups to ban Christian crosses in military cemeteries. His next campaign was to defend the Christmas practice of light-

ing the windows on all four sides of Los Angeles City
Hall in the pattern of a cross.

In the late 1960s Butler was hired as a manufacturing
engineer by Lockheed to help set up the assembly lines
for the company's jumbo jet, the L-1011, at the Palmdale,
California, plant. While at Lockheed, Butler's commitment to Identity grew. Swift's home was in Lancaster, 7
miles down the highway from the plant. Butler met a
number of people there who were in the movement.
After taking a correspondence course from the American
Institute of Theology, he became an ordained minister in
the Christian Identity church.

Swift, who suffered from diabetes, died in 1970. Butler
fell heir to his throne, although there is some debate as
to how readily William Potter Gale agreed to that. Some
former church members said Butler assumed the pulpit
on his own initiative. Butler says the church board appointed him. Either way, Butler lacked Swift's dynamic
oratory style. Before long, the pews began to empty,
and, in the end, all that were left were Butler's hard-core
friends.

In 1973 there was a falling out between Gale and
Butler, and they went their separate ways. Gale went to
Mariposa, California, 140 miles east of San Francisco,
where he established the Ministry of Christ Church in a
fifty-seven-seat, triple-width mobile home. Butler left for
the Pacific Northwest the next year.

Butler called a friend who owned a realty company in
the Coeur d'Alene area, and soon word came that there
was a parcel near Hayden Lake that was perfect.

On that April day in 1974 when Butler stood in the
center of the pine grove near Hayden Lake, he had
already formulated the basis of a plan to consolidate the
fragmented segments of the right wing under the umbrella of religion. With a dozen or so followers from
California who came with him to Kootenai County, he
started to construct a church and meeting hall that would
dominate the property.

All they had at the start was the farmhouse, a pleasant,
two-story, white woodframe. Modestly furnished, the living room contained a couple of television sets, a video
recorder, overstuffed furniture, and walls covered with

framed pictures of Butler and his relatives. Over the fireplace was a large portrait of the riderless Four Horses of the Apocalypse, snorting the premillennial fates of War, Famine, Pestilence, and Death.

The congregation built a chapel large enough to accommodate one hundred chairs in comfort. Butler's lectern was in front of the altar that featured a sword mounted upright with a swastika on its hilt. Candles and Aryan flags flanked it. The focal point on the wall behind the altar was a 9-square-foot stained glass window, which framed Butler's head while he preached. The window depicted the symbol of his Church of Jesus Christ Christian, a red, white, blue, and gold logo of which Butler was enormously proud. It is a deep blue shield in the center of a brilliant red background. On the shield is a white sword with a gold crown on its handle. Traversing the blade is a white cross-member, an elongated "N." The stylized swastika is a sacred symbol of the cross of the risen Christ. Twelve beams of blue and white radiate from the shield to the four corners.

Once the chapel was completed, the congregation built Aryan Hall, a meeting place that doubled as the chapel's vestibule and dining room, forming the bottom leg of the L-shaped structure. Paneled in waxed knotty pine, the hall was both a large dining room and a work space for Butler's mailing operations. It was also called the Hall of Flags, with flags from the twelve Aryan countries of Western Europe, the British Commonwealth, and Scandinavia, as well as Canada and South Africa, hanging in two rows where the vaulted ceiling met the walls. Two flags dominated: a hand-knit "Betsy Ross" American flag with a circle of thirteen stars on the blue background, and the swastika of the Third Reich.

The building was capped by a steepled bell tower, topped with a cross.

Next to be built was the office, including a room for a printing press and plenty of storage for the reams of paper Butler used to print his literature. A trailer was brought in to be used as a school. Several cabins were constructed under the canopy of tall pines west of the farmhouse. Butler alloted the cabins to transplanted believers, some of whom lived on the compound for several years, while others quickly found homes among the many small panhandle towns.

Although more than a dozen families followed Butler to Idaho from Southern California, he hoped to attract local converts. He understood Kootenai County's conservative politics. These were honest people trying to scratch out a living in an economy devastated by the ups and downs of the mining and timber industries.

Hoping to make a quick impression, Butler set out in 1974 to establish a chapter of Posse Comitatus with himself as marshal. He figured those who joined would be potential converts to his church. But two years later, Butler was ousted by members who felt he was trying to run the Posse like a private army. Stunned at first by their decision, Butler briefly aligned his church with the Louisiana-based National Emancipation of the White Seed. But the alliance was short-lived, because Butler by this time was formulating powerful plans of his own.

Butler had come to Idaho to be with white people like himself. "Race" to Butler meant "nation," and he told his followers that no race of people could survive without a territory of its own. Other races and ethnic groups had nations in which to propagate. In Japan, one could not be a citizen without being born Japanese. Yet he felt whites were prevented from having a racial nation in America because civil rights laws had obliterated racial differences in the eyes of the law. In Europe as well, white nations were being overrun with people of color. Butler didn't believe mixed races could live together without conflict. He aspired to a nation-state for whites.

The Inland Empire was the perfect place. Its cold, wet winters gave it a Nordic texture, and it contained so few minorities that it wouldn't be difficult to alienate those who attempted to remain.

Hayden Lake townsfolk had no qualms about Butler. They called him "Reverend" or "Dick" and chatted with him whenever he stopped by the Owl Café. Around these people, he felt he could promote his all-white nation. He spent many hours in his study mapping out strategy. Always within arm's reach was the Bible, to which he referred constantly. Beside it were *Mein Kampf* and a framed picture of Adolf Hitler.

In time, Butler formulated the goal of Aryan Nations: to establish a state representing the voice and will of the white Aryan race as a divinely ordained, sovereign, independent people, separate from all alien, mongrel people in every sphere of their individual and national life. One sunny morning in June 1978, Butler strolled down the drive to Rimrock Road and nailed up a sign proclaiming the land "ARYAN NATIONS," the political arm of the Church of Jesus Christ Christian.

Butler began to sell family memberships in Aryan Nations for $15 a year, and members were encouraged to tithe. Usually, thirty-five to fifty people showed up for Sunday services. By the early 1980s, Butler claimed six thousand members in all fifty states and Canada, and three hundred local members. Butler also taped his sermons and sold them to four hundred subscribers weekly at $2.50 per tape. It cost him 80 cents a tape and was one of his chief money-raisers. He also sold a wide assortment of memorabilia, including flags from the Aryan nations of the world, belt buckles, shoulder patches, coffee mugs, and T-shirts with the Aryan Nations symbols or Klan/Nazi motifs. One popular item was a ceramic Klansman with his "hand raised in Sacred salute" for $5.

There was also a wide assortment of books on the Christian Kingdom Identity movement, including a Holy Bible in modern English, hardbound for $22.50. Less expensive books included *To Heal the Nation,* J. Franklin Snook's work on Biblical solutions to America's economic and social problems; *Know Your Enemies* by Colonel Gordon "Jack" Mohr, a comparison of Judaism and Anglo-Saxon Identity; and *Prepare War!* by CSA Enterprises, a scriptural background for the army God is raising.

To make his organization complete, Butler designed a uniform for the men to wear to church services and ceremonial functions. It was a light blue shirt with SS-like insignia on the collars, dark blue trousers, black Sam Browne belts with straps crossing over the left shoulder, and black clip-on ties. Most of it was purchased at the local J. C. Penney store.

Services at the Church of Jesus Christ Christian were held each Sunday morning and Wednesday evening. At 11 A.M. sharp, Ione Dunn would sit at the piano and begin "What a Friend We Have in Jesus," followed by such traditional Christian songs as "In the Garden" or "Blessed Assurance, Jesus Is Mine."

Butler, wearing a dark blue suit with an Aryan Nations patch on the left shoulder, then would move behind the pulpit, extending his right arm up and out in a salute. The congregation, mostly couples with children and a few single adults, would rise and salute as well, reciting the Pledge of Allegiance but altering one phrase to say "One *Aryan* nation, under God . . ." The salute, Butler's followers say, is an open-handed salute in praise of God, not Adolf Hitler. In fact, some mainstream Christian congregations pray this way too.

Nearby, a trusted follower would pull on headphones and get ready to record Butler's sermon, which later would be sold as audio cassettes. The congregation would then sit as Butler began his sermon.

"You don't have anybody today who is a man, who has stood up for his race," Butler preached. "Name me one politician in the last fifty years that stood up for the white race. To be against the white race, to act for the destruction of the white race, any politician does that. Wake up. You haven't been conquered by the sword of the Jew. Of the black. By the Mexican. By the Asians. They didn't come in and storm your ramparts and beat you down and those they left alive are now to be slaves. No. You were deceived by your own weakness and allowed 19 million of your babies to be butchered by abortion.

"You've gone against every constitutional principle. The Constitution was destroyed in 1868 when they adopted the 13th, 14th amendments. Take affirmative action. The Drake Law Review from Drake University says that affirmative action bars any white man from full citizenship in the United States. So it is a violation of the Bill of Rights of the Constitution."

Butler switched gears to a more religious course: "I'm convinced that we have to return to the laws of our father, God, the natural law. If we can't do that, our white race is through. We're declining all over the world at the greatest rate in all history. East Germany now is declining faster than any other species on the face of this earth. There is three deaths in East Germany for each birth. England, the white population is going down. America, the white population is going down. In Canada it's going down. That's why they're talking about bringing in the Asians for population since the whites aren't reproducing.

"The only ones that ever bought the zero population growth has been the white man. It was calculated. In colleges they teach women not to get married. Get a job, get your briefcase and you can have your office on the 57th floor and make a million dollars and be happy ever after.

"But that's contrary to natural law. The women are the bearers of our race, and if they refuse to bear, what's our race's future? And of course they say if you are a white woman, you have a duty to get a black husband because the white race is evil. How we can overcome it is only by the grace of God."

As Butler approaches the end of his forty-five-minute sermon, he often would end with a catch phrase that is his rallying call: "As long as this alien tyranny evil occupies our land, hate is our law and revenge is our duty."

If there were new men joining the church, Butler would hold an initiation after the sermon. The initiate knelt at the altar and took an oath "never to betray my Aryan brothers, never to rest on this earth until there is created a national state for my Aryan brothers, one God, one Nation, one Race." As the assembled brethren face the altar, they would give the stiff-armed salute while Butler placed the sword, with the swastika on the hilt, on the new member's shoulder, saying, "I lay upon you the sharp, two-edged sword of truth."

After services, the men would step outside for a smoke while the women chatted indoors, preparing fresh pastries and pouring hot cups of coffee. The shrill sounds of children playing often floated on the air, but no one objected. Family is the core of the Identity Christians.

Many of the people who worshiped at Butler's church were friendly, outgoing, and down-to-earth folks who had no trouble getting along with people in the panhandle. They didn't think of themselves as threats to anybody. In fact, quite the opposite, they felt they were the ones threatened by an increasingly godless, inhumane culture spreading across the land.

DENVER DAW PARMENTER II was nursing a beer in one of the Eastern Washington University campus hangouts in Cheney in 1977 when he noticed a man about his age, mid-twenties, tossing darts in a corner of the bar. The man's hair was thin on top, but he wore long sideburns and a small, Western-style mustache. In a student body of mostly teenagers, such men were few. Wondering if the man might be a military veteran like himself, Parmenter picked up his beer and sidled through the crowded tables. Extending his hand, he politely introduced himself.

The man responded with a quick smile that his name was Randy Duey, and sure enough he was an Air Force vet who was working as an instructor in the survival school at Fairchild Air Force Base outside Spokane, besides going to college classes.

Parmenter was born in the military hospital at Wiesbaden, West Germany, son of a career Air Force officer. When he was young, the family moved to Florida, where his parents divorced. He lived with his mom until he was twelve, then went to live with his father in Brownwood, Texas, southeast of Abilene. He graduated from high school in 1970 and joined the Army a year later, serving three years as a clerk-typist at a NATO installation in Turkey. After his honorable discharge, Parmenter moved to Bellingham, Washington, to be a clerk and administrative assistant to the vice president of finance at Western Washington University. Three years later he moved across the state to Cheney, 15 miles southwest of Spokane, to attend Eastern Washington. He washed dishes and did janitorial work to make ends meet.

Standing 6-foot-2 and weighing 180 pounds, Parmenter had hazel eyes, thick brown hair, and a bushy mustache that made him a hit with the women. His chief enemy was the bottle, to which he turned whenever the pressure started to build. And after a few belts, he was quick to provoke a fight. Active in EWU fraternities, Parmenter was considered a financial whiz kid. Administrators liked the maturity he had gained from his military service. A conservative by nature, he worked in the Youth for Reagan group in the 1980 election. He was a good student and popular enough to run for student government president in 1981, although he lost.

Randolph George Duey, a much quieter man, was born in New York and had an insatiable interest in history, which he pursued at EWU as a better-than-average student. But he was continuously switching majors so, despite having 244 credits when only 180 were needed to graduate, he never received a degree.

Soon after meeting Parmenter, Duey dropped out to get a full-time job with the U.S. Postal Service, delivering mail at Fairchild. While living in Cheney, Duey attended a Baptist church for three years before determining he wasn't growing spiritually. Once he'd begun that spiritual and intellectual odyssey, however, he became engrossed in the search. He explored political as well as religious ideas. In the course of his reading, he came across John Birch Society literature and became familiar with the conspiracy idea, the notion that power throughout the world is wielded by international bankers who buy politicians, police, and the press.

His odyssey also led him to Christian Identity tracts, which aroused his interest. He started mailing up to $100 a month to various groups for their tapes, books, and pamphlets. Gradually, he accepted racism not as a doctrine of hate for races but as a matter of pride and love for his white race. Blacks, browns, and others celebrated their racial identity, so it couldn't be wrong, he concluded, for whites to feel good about their race as well.

Duey kept up his friendship with Parmenter after leaving EWU, and they often discussed Duey's evolving beliefs over beers and darts. Parmenter at the time was confused about his life's direction. He married his girlfriend, Janice, in May 1981 and got a job as a parts manager at Utility Equipment Company in Spokane for $7.70 an hour. He had graduated with a degree in political science and economics, so it wasn't exactly the life work he wanted. And while he couldn't admit it, Parmenter was drinking too much too regularly.

He was fascinated by Duey's philosophy. Despite all the things he was not, Parmenter would always be white.

*   *   *

AMERICA'S PRISONS SEEMED to demonstrate Butler's point about segregation's being a natural law. Behind bars, where different racial and ethnic groups live at close quarters under the most difficult of circumstances, animosities breed like bacteria in a laboratory. And, as Butler would say, "kind clings unto kind," as gangs form in the prisons along racial lines.

Butler assigned his church secretary, Janet Hounsel, the responsibility of his "prison ministry." Hounsel, a small middle-aged woman, wrote to hundreds of white inmates, spreading the Identity message that Aryan men are God's chosen.

Butler gained some converts from prisons, but it didn't always work. One man who came to Hayden Lake after his release from a federal prison in Colorado took over for Hounsel and soon was corresponding with 1,200 inmates all over the nation. After a while, however, Butler and the man soured on each other. The ex-con didn't think Butler was the genuine article. Butler found the man's life-style—partying and getting high on drugs— distasteful. But the worst part was that the new prison minister turned out to be homosexual. Gay Nazis didn't fit into Butler's new Aryan Nation, where men were obligated to plant their seed where it could bear fruit.

Before long, Butler was doubting that the prison ministry was producing the Aryan warriors needed for the impending race war. One day, two of the recruits pulled onto the compound in a freshly stolen car, hotly pursued by the sheriff. This was the incident that broke Butler's patience. He turned the entire program over to a group in Michigan and booted his prison outreach director off the compound.

But that didn't exemplify the experience of all ex-felons who were contacted by Aryan Nations. In 1980, an inmate doing time for burglary in the Arizona State Prison at Florence was so inspired by the literature he received that he vowed to move his family to Aryan Nations to start a new life as soon as he was released.

After a long and arduous spiritual search, Gary Lee Yarbrough finally found a religious philosophy that corresponded exactly with his beliefs.

There weren't many people around Amado, Arizona,

who hadn't heard of the Yarbrough family. R. B. "Red" Yarbrough, his wife Bertha "Rusty," and their four red-haired boys and red-haired daughter were about the only trouble that part of the mesquite- and cactus-covered country a half-hour south of Tucson ever needed. In the late 1960s, the family staked out a few acres in a make-shift mobile home subdivision at the base of the Santa Rita Mountains. In time, they accumulated three mobile homes for themselves and the kids, clustered among sheds, chicken pens and dog runs for the greyhounds they raced at the local dog tracks. Red made a living in the mines and construction, and Rusty waited tables for twenty years.

It was a rough and sometimes violent home life for the children. Their mom once stabbed their dad during a fight.

The oldest boy became a disc jockey for a Tucson radio station and went on to better things. But his three brothers, including Gary, fell into trouble with the law. Gary was eighteen when he and a younger brother broke into another trailer and stole the owner's rifle, cash, and car, then trashed a school building.

In 1973 Gary was arrested for grand theft in Tucson and, after pleading guilty, was given the option of jail or the Marine Corps. He took the latter and ended up in Hawaii. It didn't take long for him to go AWOL and get arrested for burglary. Gary pleaded guilty to grand theft and was sentenced to five to eight years at Florence, Arizona. The prison time gave him plenty of opportunity to read the literature mailed in by Aryan Nations.

By the time Yarbrough arrived in Idaho, he had a wife and a couple of daughters and no immediate prospect for work. But his limited Marine Corps experience gave him a military bearing Butler admired. Before long, he made Yarbrough a security officer and gave him a job printing the voluminous bundles of literature Butler sent out weekly.

BUTLER SET OUT under the religion of Identity to win the hearts and minds of white Christians. He wouldn't stop until he'd reached the choir of 144,000 foretold in Revelation. If enough came to the Pacific Northwest, they could slowly build their empire from within, taking political control by sheer weight of numbers. They'd continue to expand until they had control of five Western states: Washington, Oregon, Idaho, Montana, and Wyoming. Butler's plan became known as the "10 percent solution," one-tenth of the United States.

Butler first invited a convocation of other Identity ministers to his Aryan Nations headquarters in 1979 for several days of lectures and services. Butler wanted to play a leading role in the movement, and there was no better way to do that than to have the others come to his home turf. The Pacific States National Kingdom Identity Conference was small in scale, but it planted the seed for an annual event that brought Butler national attention.

Dan Gayman, leader of the Church of Israel in Schell City, Missouri, was the featured speaker. Gayman, a former high school principal, considered himself an Identity bishop. He ran a school on his compound near the Ozark Plateau and published *Zion's Watchman*. He organized his church in 1973 as the Church of Our Christian Heritage and operated a cassette tape ministry like Butler. His talks frequently centered on the need for fundamental Christian education. Gayman was a round-faced, balding man who with his wife had three daughters and two sons.

By the next year, Butler had decided to broaden the scope of his conference. He invited not only Christian Identity ministers but leaders from the Posse Comitatus and various neo-Nazi and Klan sects. He scheduled it for a motel in Hays, a small farming community in western Kansas, on April 12, 1980. The location, he figured, was central to all.

At the conference, Butler told the assemblage that granting citizenship to non-Christians and nonwhites was part of a Zionist plot to adulterate Aryan purity. Then he introduced his 10-percent solution, saying Armageddon was at hand.

Butler wanted to unify elements of the right, but in the end his call to arms was somewhat divisive. One who openly opposed his methods was Gayman, who, as soon as he returned to Schell City, took to the pulpit to tell his startled congregation: "There are those who say the time has come when we must go into the streets and bring the government of God with the barrel of a gun. But I am not going on a Kamikaze mission to make National Socialism the next high Christian culture in America. My god is not George Lincoln Rockwell. My god is Jesus Christ. If your god is Adolf Hitler, then let it be so."

But Butler's idea attracted a goodly number of supporters, and he returned to Idaho with plans for an organizing swing through southern Idaho and eastern Oregon. But hotel reservations for meeting rooms were canceled when word leaked out about his intentions, leaving Butler furious and frustrated.

One of the goals of Aryan Nations was to "foster national and international Aryan solidarity." So it was with great honor during the summer of 1980 that Butler received a visit from one of Europe's most famous neo-Nazis, Manfred Kurt Roeder, then fifty-one and recently disbarred from practicing law in West Germany for his involvement in a number of terrorist organizations.

Born in Berlin, Roeder lived in the capital throughout Hitler's reign. He is quite proud that in 1945, at age sixteen, he fought in the battle of Berlin as a Hitler Youth. In 1975, Roeder founded the Liberation Movement of the German Reich and a second group, the German Citizens' Initiative. Through them, he demanded the release of Rudolf Hess and issued pronouncements that disputed the Holocaust.

Two years later, when Roeder visited Butler, the two became fast friends. Roeder traded names of sympathizers with Butler, providing him with contacts in Spain, Switzerland, Scandinavia, and even Hong Kong, Australia, and New Zealand.

Roeder returned to West Germany and in 1981 was arrested for instigating a series of bombing and arson attacks by Deutsche Aktionsgruppen (German Action Groups), a terrorist group that targeted memorials to victims of the Holocaust and a home for Ethiopian refugees in the town of Loerrach. In one of the attacks, a Hamburg shelter for Vietnamese boat people was firebombed and two Vietnamese died. Roeder was convicted and sentenced to thirteen years in prison.

As the meetings with right-wing figures continued at

Hayden Lake and Butler's joint Klan–Nazi meetings went on the road, some people in Kootenai County started to object. Being a good neighbor was one thing, but they didn't want to acquiesce by their silence, like the German populace of the 1930s.

One morning Sidney Rosen, one of the few Jews living in the area, arrived for work at his Hayden Lake steak house and found someone had spray-painted swastikas and the words "Jew swine" on his building. It so horrified Rosen that he immediately put up "for sale" signs. Within a year he was out of the business. Butler adamantly denied he had had a hand in the desecration.

A short time later, blacks living in Coeur d'Alene started receiving letters in the mail stating: "Niggers, don't let the sun set on your head in the Aryan Nations." Then posters began appearing in Coeur d'Alene and nearby Spokane depicting a target with a black man's silhouette. The words "Official Running Nigger Target" were printed at the bottom. It was not long before one of Butler's former followers, Keith Gilbert, admitted he had distributed the posters, although he denied defacing Rosen's restaurant.

Gilbert was a graduate of San Quentin, where he served five years after a 1965 arrest for having 1,500 pounds of dynamite at his home in Glendale, California. He claimed he was planning to use the explosives to kill the Reverend Martin Luther King, Jr. In 1974, Gilbert arrived at Butler's compound, but several years later the two parted company with Butler accusing Gilbert of being a welfare cheat.

In retaliation, Gilbert organized the Socialist Nationalist Aryan People's Party in his home in Post Falls, a lumber town of five thousand sandwiched between Coeur d'Alene and the Washington state border. He boasted of fifty followers, although Butler scoffed and called him a "noisy one-man band."

Butler continued his meetings with leaders of the radical right. In April 1981 he sponsored a series of meetings at Aryan Nations with such people as James Wickstrom of Wisconsin (later of Pennsylvania), one of a few outspoken leaders in the Posse Comitatus. It became common outside the compound to see an orange glow among the dense trees from lighted crosses.

LATE ON A WARM evening in June 1981, Butler locked his church doors and walked the short distance to his home. About half an hour after he and Betty went to bed, the house shook violently from the impact of an explosion. Jumping up, Butler looked out to see smoke billowing from the side of Aryan Hall. He pulled on his clothes and ran to the building while Betty called the sheriff's office.

Kootenai County Undersheriff Larry Broadbent inspected the splintered beams, shredded insulation, and other debris of what had been Aryan Hall's kitchen. The chain-smoking career cop, with his unfashionable 1960s haircut and rumpled suits, had become Butler's chief antagonist in Kootenai County. But he played by the rules. This bomb could have killed Butler, and Broadbent took the case seriously. But he shook his head at the irony. He would have expected the right-wingers to be perpetrators, not victims, of a bomb attack.

Butler and his faithful retreated to the farmhouse to assess the situation, and the two favorite theories focused on conflicting ends of the spectrum. It was either the Jewish Defense League, they agreed, or Keith Gilbert. While they were talking, the farmhouse phone rang. Betty Butler answered it and handed it to her husband. The man on the line claimed he had planted the bomb.

"Is this Levy?" Butler demanded, thinking it was Mordecai Levy of the JDL, since it didn't sound like Gilbert. But the caller hung up. Butler turned to his group, a look of resolution taking over his worried face. There were children on the compound, at the school. They had to protect themselves.

"All right," Butler said. "As of this moment we will have around-the-clock security. I want armed men on the compound at all times. I want a security gate installed and I want a watchtower constructed and manned at all times. We'll show whoever did this that we won't take it."

Although he suspected Levy, Butler a few days later publicly accused Gilbert of bombing the church. Gilbert lashed back: "As surely as Sid Rosen desecrated his own restaurant, Dick Butler blew up his own church. He simply was trying to arouse attention and sympathy for his cause."

Immediately a frenzy began to build at Aryan Nations. Along with repairs to the kitchen, a 29-foot guard tower went up just south of Aryan Hall, like a prison watchtower with a railed catwalk. A pole gate was built at the end of the drive off Rimrock Road, and in time a sentry station was added next to the gate. On the side of the small hut a sign was posted: "Whites Only."

All these precautions soon gave Butler and his church a fearsome reputation as a paramilitary outfit. Stories in newspapers, magazines, and even accounts in books referred to Aryan Nations as a heavily fortified compound where regular shooting sessions were held. They never set it in the context of Butler's need to protect his people. Writers who'd never even seen the compound reported as fact that there was a high chain-link fence topped with barbed wire surrounding the property, that attack dogs roamed freely on the compound, and that land mines had been planted in the forest.

In reality, the fence was the same one that was there when Butler bought the property, a rusted, three-strand barbed-wire cattle fence common in all rural areas. Aryan Nations was on open range. The attack dog was a German shepherd more suited for coercing strangers into playing "fetch" with pine cones. And the land mines were fiction. After all, there were so many children wandering about.

But the armed guards were real. After the bombing, anyone who attended functions on the Aryan Nations compound saw men with rifles on the guard tower and handguns in holsters. No shooting took place there, although the younger men took target practice at a dump an hour's drive north.

Newspaper reports on the bombing eventually drew the attention of the two young men in Cheney, Randy Duey and Denver Parmenter. The former Eastern Washington University students were intrigued by the notion of a church for far-right theology. Until then, they'd never heard of Aryan Nations. Looking at a map, they found the compound was only an hour's drive from Cheney.

Deciding they had nothing to lose by checking it out, they climbed into a car one weekend and headed for Hayden Lake. As they turned off dusty Rimrock Road, Duey and Parmenter were struck by the layout and security of the place. Neither had seen weapons and fatigues displayed so openly since their discharges from the military. They were ushered into the office, where they met Pastor Butler, whose soft-spoken personal approach impressed them. They talked for hours about the Aryan Nations philosophy. Before many Sunday services went by, both newcomers found themselves kneeling before the altar as Butler placed the broad sword on their shoulders and they swore an oath to a white God.

But it was more than philosophy that drew them into Aryan Nations. They had already been getting far-right philosophy through the tapes and periodicals that came with detached regularity to their mailboxes. But at Aryan Nations they found that theory became practice. With a communal feel that was an offbeat blend of Walden Pond and Berchtesgaden, there was insular affection intermingled with the fortress mentality among the people there.

Before long, Parmenter was spending every weekend at Aryan Nations. Janice was not enchanted, and it was causing problems in their marriage. It also caused problems at work, and Parmenter's job was "phased out" some time after he began talking at Utility Equipment about his attendance at Aryan Nations.

That injustice fed his sense of outrage, but he found the commiseration he needed at Aryan Nations. Butler trusted Parmenter and put him on his security staff under Bud Cutler and Howard "Corky" Witherwax. Corky, thirty-four, was a former deputy sheriff from Stockton, California, married to Butler's daughter, Cindy.

For Parmenter and Duey, it was an exciting experience to be on the inside of a group that was so exclusive and unusual. For them, it was living on the edge.

BY THE SUMMER of 1982, Butler was becoming a leading figure in the racist movement. His 1982 Aryan World Congress from July 9 to 11, the annual event that grew out of the 1979 Kingdom Identity Conference, would be his biggest yet. And it would serve well Butler's ambition to unify the fragmented radical right. All of the important figures in the movement would be coming to his turf.

Scheduling accommodations and food for more than two hundred participants, given Hayden Lake's limited capacity during the height of tourist season, was no small task. Many brought campers and tents and were welcomed to make camp under the canopy of Butler's beautiful pine-covered spread. Thirteen different Ku Klux Klan organizations and a number of neo-Nazi groups made reservations.

Butler's array of guests and speakers came from across the country. They included Alexi Erlanger of Buffalo, New York, a Russian immigrant who was Manfred Roeder's point man in the United States; Robert Miles, of the Mountain Kirk of Jesus Christ in Cohoctah, Michigan, one of Butler's closest allies, who served six years in the federal prison at Marion, Illinois, for his role in the bombings of empty school buses in Pontiac; J. B. Stoner, head of the National States Rights Party in Georgia, who had yet to serve prison time for his role in the 1956 bombing of a black church in Birmingham, Alabama; Louis Beam, Jr., a Texas Klan leader who led a paramilitary training camp at Anahuac, Texas; and Traudel Roeder, Manfred's wife.

The day before the congress, cars, campers, and pickups began winding down Rimrock Road, several of them skidding across the gravel as they came over the rise just before Butler's driveway, nearly missing the entrance. Snaking through the short tunnel of trees that led to the sentry station and lift gate, they were met by two men in pale blue uniforms carrying sidearms, motioning them to stop.

"Hail victory!" the red-haired Gary Yarbrough saluted the arrivals as he opened the gate after identifying them.

A road-weary red Pinto kicked up the pebbles as it wound up the drive from Rimrock Road. The driver, a tall, sandy-haired man in his early forties, had taken the lonely drive across the mountains from Golden, Colorado, outside Denver, to be at the congress. David Lane, a longtime KKK activist, was glad to be away from Denver because of a run-in he had had with the cops. He and two friends had been driving to the 1981 NAACP convention in Denver to distribute some of their racist literature, but the police department's intelligence unit got wind of it and pulled Lane over. Lane was sure they intended to take him somewhere and beat the daylights out of him, and only the arrival of two Aurora, Colorado, officers who weren't "in" on the deal had saved him. But the police had confiscated his leaflets.

A large reviewing stand had been constructed just under the trees about twenty steps from the door of Aryan Hall. Three tall flagpoles stood to the side while smaller flags from the twelve Aryan nations were placed around the railing of the reviewing stand. The crowd, more than two hundred, gathered by the stand on opening day, giving the stiff-armed salute to each flag as Butler stopped in front of it.

After the pastor gave the convocational prayer, the congress was under way, its common thread an antigovernment theme. These people even had their own name for the federal system, the Zionist Occupation Government—ZOG—since they felt it was of, by, and for the Jews.

There was no mistaking the desire of these folks, gathered under the tall pines, to work for a drastic change in the system. Butler hoped a number of them would accept his plan to migrate to the Northwest. But most, especially the Southerners, would never entertain the thought of leaving their own soil behind.

It wasn't all work, however. There were excursions on Coeur d'Alene Lake, gift-givings, and the awarding of the "Aryans of Outstanding Valor" honors, which went to Miles, Stoner, Beam, and, in absentia, Manfred Roeder. A special "Mother's Cross of the Reich" was presented to Traudel Roeder. Miles, one of the movement's experts in "Klankraft," the ceremonial customs of the KKK, was the ritual master for the Saturday night cross-lighting. In his elegant Klan robe, he set ablaze a huge cross representing "the light of this world, which is Jesus Christ," while four smaller crosses placed around it to represent the points of the compass were lighted to symbolize the history and heritage of the white race.

In the brilliant orange glow of the fires, men and women in white robes with crosses on their left breasts, and men in uniforms resembling those of Nazi Germany and the modern army, stood ramrod straight and raised their right arms to the sky. The flags of Dixie and the Third Reich waved in the breeze. Duey and Parmenter, standing guard with other young men in their Aryan Nations uniforms, were awed by the pageantry. But they were perched on a "slippery slope." Once they started exploring this extremist fringe, forbidden by the mainstream, their fascination drew them ever deeper. They never regained their footing.

NEARLY FOUR MONTHS later, on November 28, David Lane's sister, Jane Eden, exchanged marriage vows with Carl Franklin, a veterinary supplies dealer from Easton, Pennsylvania, in front of Pastor Butler. Franklin was Butler's representative in Pennsylvania. Lane escorted his sister, who was dressed in a high-neck blouse and a dark skirt and jacket. A large white daisy was fixed in her hair, and an Aryan Nations pin was in her lapel. Franklin was in full uniform.

The altar was a sea of sweetheart roses and white daisies as the couple took their vows. Afterward, with the Aryan Victory Singers providing the music, the couple turned to face two rows of uniformed men in a "Corridor of Honor," forming a canopy of Nazi salutes under which Jane and Carl moved in procession.

Such ceremonies had no meaning to the folks living in Hayden Lake, however, and at times there were so few people at the compound, it was hard to believe anyone would find it a threat. But Butler's regular trips to the post office were a reminder that their community, indeed the Pacific Northwest, was getting a reputation as a right-wing haven.

In September 1982, Undersheriff Broadbent, along with the Reverend Rick Morse, citizen activist Dina Tanners, and a few others from Coeur d'Alene, formed the Kootenai County Task Force on Human Relations. One of the first items on their agenda was to push for legislation making racial and ethnic harassment a crime. They were prompted not so much by Butler as by his former follower, Keith Gilbert.

A woman named Connie Fort had moved to Coeur

d'Alene in 1976 from Los Angeles. She had grown up in Holland during the Nazi occupation and could remember the clacking of the jackboots on cobblestones outside her house. Now Gilbert came into her life, and it was déjà-vu.

Fort married a Native American after emigrating to the United States. The marriage didn't last, but it produced a son named Scott Willey. Next she married a black man and had two more children, Lamar and Neisha Fort. When that marriage failed, Fort decided to look for a less crowded place to live than Los Angeles.

By chance, Gilbert spotted Lamar walking a sidewalk in Coeur d'Alene and became incensed that race-mixing had come to his corner of the world. When he found there were three such mixed-blood children around, he devised a despicable campaign. One day, he walked up to Scott on the sidewalk and spat on him.

"Your life is condemned," Gilbert intoned before the startled boy. "You shall be served in front of the devil." Scott ran home in tears to his mother to tell her about this "man with a mean face." Gilbert knew where Fort lived and started to drive by the house, shouting obscenities, racial slurs, and threats at Lamar and Neisha, then nine and eight. Once, he terrified the youngsters by swerving his camouflage-painted Volkswagen Thing at them as they crossed the street.

"You have betrayed your race to conceive niggers," Gilbert yelled at Fort one day, "and your time shall perish!"

Each night, Fort tried to calm her children's fears and fought to calm the anger in herself as well. But the nightmare continued. After one sleepless night, Lamar said resolutely to his mom: "When I grow up, I'm going to kill that man."

In February 1983 Gilbert was charged with misdemeanor assault on Scott Willey. He was convicted, fined $300, and sentenced to forty-five days in jail. But that wasn't enough for Fort. She sat down with the kids and penned letters to their legislators, urging them to make racial harassment a felony. Broadbent picked up the letters and made the ten-hour drive to Boise to deliver them in person.

Butler spoke out against Gilbert's tactics. He hated

miscegenation, but he felt children should not be blamed for the parents' sins. He also feared Gilbert's behavior would cause a backlash. That's just what happened. Residents of Coeur d'Alene got up a petition with more than eight hundred signatures backing Connie Fort. Trying to soothe the situation, Butler drove down to the Capitol in Boise to testify. Such a law could make his very ministry vulnerable, since verbal attacks on Jews and "mud people" were at the heart of it.

"This bill," Butler maintained, "would take away sovereign, inalienable rights of white Christians." But lawmakers, after reading the letters from Fort's children and seeing the backing from Idaho civil rights groups, passed a bill making it a felony to intimidate anyone because of race. The penalty is five years in prison and a fine up to $5,000.

David Lane, by this time Butler's "information minister" in Colorado, wrote letters of encouragement to members. In March 1983 Lane wrote a short note from his home in Golden to Randy Duey, encouraging his writing:

> Just wanted to tell you I enjoyed your writing. Two years ago, you submitted some things and I didn't know how to tell you that you weren't ready yet. You have learned and developed a lot in two years. Sincerity and commitment must be mixed with polish and experience to be a leader, you have potential.
>
> I hope you have taken the time to study Mein Kampf. It is my belief that no one has a total understanding of Races, Nations, Cultures, History, etc. etc., 'til he studies that book.
>
> Thank you for the many nights you have stood guard over our church.

Yours for the Race, David Lane

THAT SAME SPRING, Butler invited Colonel Gordon "Jack" Mohr of the Christian Emergency Defense System in Mississippi to give a lecture on the dangers of communism. Mohr was one of the most popular and charismatic speakers on the extremist circuit. Identity folk would travel hundreds of miles to hear him.

Denver Parmenter arrived early to get a decent seat, but Aryan Hall was already filling up. Parmenter scanned the crowd and noticed a stranger standing in one group. The man looked about thirty, muscular, with dark, intense eyes, which caught Parmenter's as he walked toward the stranger.

The man flashed a toothy smile, and Parmenter, returning the smile, asked, "You ever hear Colonel Mohr speak before?"

"Yeah. He's great," the man answered enthusiastically.

"I haven't seen you around here before," Parmenter continued, extending his hand. "My name's Denver Parmenter, I live over in Cheney." The man looked at Parmenter's outstretched hand and grasped it firmly.

"Glad to know you. My name's Bob Mathews."

Chapter 3

Establishing the White American Bastion

How Robbie Mathews found himself at Aryan Nations after so many years of keeping his word was a matter of great consternation to his parents. He had been a steadfast worker at Bunker Hill Mine. From the electrical department in 1974, he worked his way to hoistman, one of the most trusted positions. His few years' experience in the copper mines of Arizona's desert hills proved of great value.

But he worked even harder on the 60 acres he and his dad bought up on the mountain. It was a herculean effort to carve out a clearing in the dense pine forest off Boundary Dam Road. After his shift at the mine, he crossed the river and took the fork that wound about 4 miles up the mountain to Mathews Acres, and worked until the last ounce of daylight was wrung from the spacious sky.

By the end of 1975, the land had become Robbie's new obsession. There was no Armageddon, no crawling over the hot sands of Cave Creek in the desert north of Phoenix preparing for the communist invasion. Robbie now had his place in the mountains and the hope that his entire family would be living there. It was such a complete turnaround, his family once again began to feel pride in him. It was difficult not to feel that surge of emotion when they visited on summer vacations and saw how much Robbie had accomplished.

His parents could not imagine that Robbie would go back on his promise to stay away from the dark fringe of politics.

He found this land the first weeks after he arrived. He was hiking in the Lead King Hills on the west bank of the Pend Oreille River one weekend when he came across a small meadow filled with wild raspberries. At one corner he heard the sound of fast-moving water. Winding down an overgrown trail threaded around huge cedars and hemlocks, Robbie came across Beaver Creek.

Tiger lilies, wood violets, and wild ginger grew along its banks as it rushed downhill to a 130-foot shale cliff into the Pend Oreille. The land was alive with wildlife. Robbie was captivated by the contrast with the Arizona desert, almost lifeless by comparison. The next day in town, he learned the parcel was for sale.

He had only one constant companion as he worked the land. Four miles away, Hooknose Mountain jabbed its windswept, treeless point almost a mile into the northwest sky. All winter it was buried in white powder. Then the late spring warmth melted the cover to reveal the jagged rock outcroppings of its vaulting, pyramidal summit, which tilted northward toward Canada. Hooknose presided over Robbie's every success and failure on the land, an immutable presence symbolic of his longtime love of nature and his desire to live in harmony with it.

Mathews shed the childhood name of Robbie among the folks in Metaline Falls. He was now known as Robert Jay Mathews, or simply Bob.

Bob staked out a homesite in the middle of the parcel and started to clear timber. He cut a road into the dense woods, twisting it through the pines like an S so that his house would have privacy from the road where the Seattle City Light crews passed on their way to work at Boundary Dam.

Summer is short in the north country, but its days are long. Bob could work on the land until 10 P.M. before returning to the hotel with his two dogs. But during the winter, when daylight was lost by four o'clock, it got very lonely. There wasn't much for a single man to do in Metaline Falls. There was no place to meet eligible women, and for the first time in his life, Bob wanted to meet women. The cycle of life he observed on his land made him yearn for a family.

Bob's approach was unconventional. He used the personals columns of the nationally circulated *Mother Earth News*, to search for a woman to be his bride. "Looking for a mature, intelligent woman, 18–25, to share my life and land in Washington," he wrote.

Debbie McGarrity grew up on the flat, broad plains of Kansas. But every summer her family vacationed in Rocky Mountain National Park in neighboring Colorado. She grew to love the outdoors and the mountains in particular. From hiking in the park's tundra to exploring old mining towns nearby, she fell in love with the Western mystique of adventure and self-reliance.

When she got out of college, she moved to Jackson, Wyoming, at the southern end of the Teton Range, and worked as a clerk in a gift shop in Grand Teton National Park. Her goal was to be either a national park ranger or, she sometimes joked because of her fondness for nature, the world's foremost authority on the moose. Her favorite time was the off-season, when the streets weren't filled with summer campers or winter ski bums. The Tetons arguably were the most magnificent range in America, and some of the best powder skiing in the Rockies could be found at Targhee and Jackson Hole.

Debbie almost never read *Mother Earth News,* but she picked up the issue that carried Bob's ad. After some giggling over it, Debbie's roommate dared her to answer. So she wrote to this man she had yet to meet that she was no women's libber. "I really feel the most important job a woman can have is to raise children. You can't have a good society unless the home is a decent place."

It reminded Bob of his Mormon days. Debbie's was the eighth letter he got. Eventually, 130 women responded to his ad.

He drove to Jackson late in 1975 to meet Debbie. He saw a pretty young woman with dark hair and big, round eyes, eager to hear about the life he dreamed. What Debbie saw was a vibrant young man, a little shorter than she might have wished but without a single extra ounce on him. He had dark hair, with sideburns trimmed to the bottom of his ears. His face still bore babyish traces, not pudgy but soft. It radiated excitement, even in his pensive times. Bob's face was an inviting trap door through which, if opened, one would fall helplessly into his contagious love of life and catch his infectious, unbridled enthusiasm for this dream world he was building.

He was twenty-two, but his voice sounded like he was still thirteen. It wasn't just a natural lilt, it was a childlike voice filled with intensity. But what stood out from everything else was his smile. He had a smile filled with unfeigned affection. And whenever his smile grew, his eyes lit up and sparkled.

Bob normally was shy with women. But he talked unhesitatingly with Debbie about his land and how beautiful it was. He also told her he saw himself eventually as patriarch of a large brood of Mathewses. Debbie knew right away Bob was the man for her. She moved to Metaline Falls and married Bob in February 1976.

Life was difficult at first. They rented a $45-a-month house in town near the river. It was a small, metal-roofed bungalow nestled under a couple of towering pine trees. The floors tilted, but the price was right.

The remainder of Bob's paycheck went into his land, but it was never enough. They both picked up extra jobs. Debbie worked for a time at the small hospital down the street from the house. She also managed Kaniksu Village, a new apartment complex two blocks away. For about a year, Bob did maintenance work there after his shift at the mine. They also ran the NuVu Theater for several months.

Bob got a part-time position as a weight training coach for the Selkirk High School wrestling squad, a few miles upriver. He loved working with the kids and appreciated having free access to the gym equipment, with which he worked out tirelessly.

Mindful of his Scottish heritage, Bob scraped together money for bagpipe lessons. Each Monday evening for about three months, he and Debbie drove 100 miles round trip to Nelson, British Columbia, to study the odd instrument with a teacher from Scotland. Bob's goal was to entertain Metaline Falls at midnight on New Year's Eve, dressed in a kilt and playing his music down Grand View Street.

Unfortunately, his fingers were too short to handle the chanter.

IT WASN'T OFTEN when Bob worked his land that anyone came by. But on a hot afternoon in August 1976, he looked up from digging at tree stumps when he heard a car coming down a nearby gravel drive. Bob hailed the driver, who brought the car to a stop and got out. He was a stocky man, taller than Bob and weighing about 200 pounds. He looked to be in his mid-twenties, just a year or two older than Bob. He had brown hair and hazel eyes, and a scar was visible on his chin.

The car had California plates, common in the Northwest, where Californians make up a good portion of the tourists. Mathews wondered if the guy was lost.

"Hi. I'm Bob Mathews," he said, extending his soiled hand in greeting. "I'm clearing some land here for a house."

"Pleased to meet you, Bob. I guess that makes you a neighbor," the man replied. "My name's Ken Loff. I own the parcel next to you here."

The two men chatted for some time about the land and about living up near Hooknose. Before long it was dinner time, and Bob invited Loff to town to meet Debbie, wash up, and share a meal.

Loff said he had come from Southern California to visit the property, which he had bought in 1973 with an eye toward homesteading someday. Over dinner, Bob told Ken he ought to consider moving up now. The area could use more young people, he told him. Ken replied he might consider it if the right opportunity came up.

"Well, I'll keep my eyes open for you, Ken, and let you know," Mathews said.

Ken Loff was an unlikely recruit for the north woods. A betting man would have given odds early on that he would be a big-city dweller his whole life.

Born in 1951 in Oceanside, Long Island, just east of New York City, Loff grew up in an Irish-Catholic and Jewish neighborhood. He spent more than a year in trade school before finding a job with a refrigeration and air conditioning company. Then for four years he was a meatcutter at an A&P supermarket.

But after an unnerving experience on the business end of a mugger's pistol, city boy Ken Loff yearned for open country. On a trip to the Pacific Northwest in 1973 he came across Metaline Falls and bought an 80-acre parcel on Boundary Dam Road. He and his girlfriend, Marlene Tait, shared a dream of farming there.

Ken and a partner ran a minimarket on Long Island

for two years until, in 1975, Marlene had a job offer in California. When that company offered Ken a position as well, he pulled up stakes and followed her to Long Beach, in crowded Los Angeles County. He and Marlene were married there that year.

Ken didn't realize until he left New York just how rooted he had been. He never felt comfortable in California. On Long Island he had several friends who were so close, it was like tearing his flesh away to leave them. It left him feeling unfulfilled in Long Beach. Then, only a month after meeting Bob Mathews on his visit to Metaline Falls in 1976, he answered his phone in Long Beach to hear that same high-pitched voice, surprising in its sincerity.

"Ken? Hi. This is Bob Mathews. Remember me?" the voice asked.

"Sure, Bob. What's up?" Ken replied.

"I told you I'd let you know when opportunity knocked. Well, buddy, here it is. The gas station's for sale. It's the only one in town, and it comes with two rental houses to boot. I think you can get a good price on it," Bob said.

There was no mistaking the encouraging tone in his voice. Loff was surprised Mathews would even keep his number, let alone scout business deals for him.

Ken brought Marlene to Metaline Falls in September and looked at the service station, which had a good location just up from the bridge. They agreed to buy it, and by November they were running it and living in one of the rental houses.

Una Mathews retired from First National in Phoenix in April 1977, and the next month Johnny left the Graham Paper Company. As they prepared to move, their son Lee stopped by the Meadows with an announcement. He had talked with his wife, Marcia, and they wanted to move with them. Lee and his wife had two small children. He was teaching in a suburban Phoenix school district and had just bought a new house. But, he told his parents, "I want to be part of your dream."

Elated, Una got doctors to approve taking Grant out of the mental hospital and bringing him with them. She thought the small-town atmosphere would help her oldest son. It would be the whole Mathews family, up in the mountains, the way Robbie had planned when they went camping in the White Mountains of Arizona.

They moved on June 1, 1977. But while they packed, Metaline Falls suffered a terrible blow. Bunker Hill Mine closed on May 28, and Bob was among the many men thrown out of work. The mine was crucial to Metaline Falls's economy, and with its closing many families eventually were forced to leave. But Bob had come too far to turn back. Within six weeks he got hired on at Boundary Dam, where Marlene Loff also worked. Three weeks later, on August 5, Bob got a better job at Portland Lehigh.

It was during this time that Bob Mathews grew very close to Ken Loff, who by then had also obtained work at the cement plant. They became like brothers.

Ken had logged his land and made $15,000. The service station got to be a time-consuming effort, so he let Marlene's brother take it over a while before selling it to the owner of the Rexall pharmacy in town. He put his money into a down payment on a 194-acre farm in Ione, a small, upriver town 11 miles south of Metaline Falls. Ken was hired at Portland Lehigh and supplemented his paycheck by raising some cattle and cutting hay. Bob often helped him with the ranch work.

Johnny and Una moved into a second-floor apartment in Kaniksu Village, with Grant taking the unit below them. Una thought she could take care of Grant, but he started to run away. Each time Johnny went out to bring him back.

Lee was fortunate to land a job at the elementary school in town. Sometimes he came up to the land to work with his dad and Bob. The hardest work was preparing to build the houses. Bob dug trenches for electrical lines and water pipes, installed the well pump, and got the foundations ready. They were spending far more money than they made, so they decided instead of the log cabins Bob once wanted, they would purchase prefabricated houses, called "double-wides" because they consist of two sections shipped separately on flatbed trucks. At the rate they were going, they couldn't wait for custom-built homes.

In August 1978, Bob and Debbie moved up onto the

land. Johnny and Una followed a few days later. But Lee and Marcia chose to remain in town near the school.

In the meantime, Grant's mental health continued to deteriorate. He took his parents' old apartment at Kaniksu Village, but soon there was trouble. Grant left the water running in the tub while he dashed down to the hospital wearing nothing but a towel wrapped around his head. The water leaked through to the apartment below, causing major damage. He also threw a radio into the river after hearing strange voices. Next he claimed someone was beaming signals to his apartment from the vacant building across the street. At last, Bob got County Sheriff Tony Bamonte to help place Grant in an institution in San Diego. Bamonte and his wife, who also lived in Metaline Falls, were among the friends Mathews had made.

Several years later, Una was finally able to unburden much of her guilt about Grant's condition. After two decades of wondering what she and Johnny had done wrong, she read about a medical study linking severe cases of influenza in pregnant women to schizophrenia in their children. She remembered that terrible flu she had at Fort Russell while she was pregnant in 1945, and it helped her to think she had at least part of the answer.

After settling on the land, Mathews brought the first Scottish Galloway cattle into Pend Oreille County. Black Angus are bred by Galloways, and Bob erected a sign at his fence, complete with a painting of a hefty bull, saying, "Selkirk Mountain Galloways, Hardy & Thrifty Scottish Cattle." He figured with their thick coats, the Galloways consumed 25 percent less feed in the winter, making them better suited for the climate than the herefords almost everyone else raised there. His bull was named MacGregor. The bull and a cow, Bonnie Lass, sired a calf, Rob Roy.

Mathews tended bees for a few years, but there weren't enough meadows around to make it profitable. He also kept the usual farm assortment of chickens and dogs. He adopted a dog he found abandoned in a snow bank and named Nathan. It angered Mathews that someone would leave a dog to die like that. He loved nature and wouldn't allow hunting on his land. Once, when a pack rat took up residence under his parents' house, 150 feet from his, Mathews set a live trap for the vermin and instead of killing it took it far into the woods to set it free.

Bob had become the incarnation of the all-American man. His favorite snack actually was apple pie, and usually with a glass of milk to wash it down. Sometimes he let his Van Dyke or mustache grow in, but he normally was clean shaven with a short, simple haircut. He didn't smoke, drink, or cuss. He was muscular and fit, and he worked from dawn to dusk on this project or that, frequently leaving it unfinished in favor of the next task down the line.

And he drove a Chevrolet.

IT NEVER OCCURRED to Ken Loff that his friend Bob could be a racist. They grew as close as brothers, closer than Bob was to Lee or Ken was to his brother back on Long Island. Yet Ken didn't see it coming, not even at that Christmas party he hosted. Bob stepped outside into the frigid air when Ken put a Christmas album by the black crooner Nat "King" Cole on the stereo. Ken thought that was odd.

Johnny and Una thought the same after one occasion at the Pend Oreille County Fair in Cusick. While wandering through the exhibits with Bob and Debbie, they came across a white woman arm in arm with a black man. It wasn't unusual for the times, but it wasn't a common sight in Cusick. Bob stopped dead in his tracks and gave the couple a disgusted stare that was almost hypnotic in its intensity. Una was embarrassed. Why was Bob acting this way? In his John Birch days, or during his tax protesting, her son had never expressed any racist sentiments.

Bob Mathews had never had a significant relationship with a black person. Once in the early 1960s, his grandmother took him back to visit Marfa, and he became friends with a black man named Chaney who ran a rib joint. Not long afterward, at a YMCA summer camp in Phoenix, a black boy was his closest buddy. But that was it.

Una didn't associate the troubling new signs with Bob's radical days until one day in 1980 when she drove down to the Metaline Falls post office to pick up the family's mail. Flipping through the letters and magazines as she stepped out of the storefront post office building, Una stopped short when her eyes landed on one of *those* strange newspapers she remembered her son reading in Arizona. A chill went through her when it occurred to her what might be happening.

"I think Robbie's going back on his promise," she fearfully told Johnny when she got back to the house.

She worried that her son's extremism had been like alcoholism, and that he never got over the intoxicating adrenalin rush that came with his involvement in it. Could it be, she wondered, that like an alcoholic Bob never minded the intoxication itself, only the disillusioning hangover?

It turned out that when Bob fled to the peace of Metaline Falls, he wasn't running from the ideas or the philosophy of the radical right as his parents had assumed. He merely was getting away from the hypocrites who espoused it, then wouldn't help him when he got in trouble for acting on it.

During those years on his land, Bob proved to himself that his beliefs in survivalism and individual accomplishment were well-founded. Everyone who called him "friend" knew him as a caring, hard-working man. He'd made it, practically all on his own, and was justly proud of his accomplishments. And by proving to himself the righteousness of his ways, he reinforced his belief in the sinfulness of the federal government, which had come after him with guns for trying to evade his taxes by claiming he had ten children.

During the long winters in the Pend Oreille Valley, when his outside work was severely curtailed, Bob read scores of books. His childhood passion was history, but now his library took on a more political coloration. Bookshelves lined his bedroom and the dining room wall. When the quiet of the mountain forest closed down on his clearing for the night, Mathews's house became a reading room.

He didn't own a television, a choice he made to avoid polluting his mind with the trivial pap that commonly came over that medium. In the spring of 1978, the top-rated network television series—the shows most of America took time out from its busy week to watch—were, in order of their season ratings, *Laverne and Shirley, Happy Days,* and *Three's Company.*

But the spring of 1978 also produced a work that profoundly affected Bob Mathews. It was published by a group called the National Alliance. Based at the time in Arlington, Virginia, the group was headed by William Pierce, a former physics professor and aide to the American Nazi Party leader, George Lincoln Rockwell.

The book's 758 pages of anti-Semitic arguments grabbed Mathews like a boa constrictor. Most of Bob's friends would have shuddered just reading the table of contents. Chapter after chapter offered heavily footnoted and exhaustively documented justification for eugenics, segregation, and Jewish deportation.

The book was *Which Way Western Man?* by William Gayley Simpson. It chronicled what Simpson, by 1978 an elder statesman of the racist right, believed was the decline of white civilization even at the peak of its accomplishments. Simpson, a laborite, an integrationist, and probably a socialist in the 1920s, was involved in the forerunner of the American Civil Liberties Union. He became disillusioned with institutional Christianity in the late 1920s and began an intense process of reformation. He was deeply influenced by the philosopher Friedrich Nietzsche's conception of the overman and his disdain for egalitarian states.

Simpson adapted Nietzsche to his own views of eugenics, natural selection, and racial superiority. In *Which Way Western Man?* Simpson laid out in laborious and monotonous detail his reasons for believing that white Christian people were in mortal danger of losing their race by being persuaded or forced into integration with other races, the result of an organized plot by Jews, who, he declared, most jealously guarded their own racial purity.

Mathews read about the National Alliance in 1980 in a short blurb in *Instauration,* a right-wing publication based in Florida. The group struck him as a more intellectual outlet than the right wing typically offered. He joined it later that year and got hold of Simpson's thick soft-cover book. He read it each night, a red pen in his hand to highlight passages that seemed to explain the uneasiness he felt in his own life.

Abortion, birth control, and zero population growth, readily embraced by many whites, were the knives with which the race was slitting its own throat, Simpson said. The tax burdens placed on society's gifted to support the less capable were stifling the growth of the "best and the brightest."

Special interest groups have seized America's throttle. "Minorities write the law of the land," Simpson wrote. "Minorities of aliens, multitudes of them, grow fat and rule, while the bulk of the people, many of them descendants of those who founded and built the country, who love it and would die for it, are turned into patient, befuddled suckers, who foot the bills to finance their own destruction." Mathews underlined the passage, one of many, in red.

Finally, Simpson proudly called himself a "racist," saying whites were the only race made to feel ashamed and guilty if they took pride in their identity. The campaign to make whites ignore their racial heritage, Simpson charged, was led by the Jews, a divide-and-conquer technique of a wandering people bent on subjugating the Gentiles. Yet Jews jealously segregated their own communities and guarded their genes, "more fiercely determined to keep themselves a people apart from all others," he wrote.

"Race consciousness, and discrimination on the basis of race, are absolutely essential to any race's survival, and to any nation's survival. . . . Unless we recover our race consciousness, and maintain it, and heighten it, and live by it, we shall die."

Red ink flowed freely from Mathews's pen.

THE NIGHT AIR nipped at Bob Mathews's face when he threw open his back door and bounded excitedly into his yard. Grabbing a ladder from the covered back porch, he placed it against the house and scrambled to the roof. The clear, dark sky was full of stars, and the moonlight reflected off the snowy top of Hooknose. Fighting for balance as he made it to the peak of the roof, Bob faced the mountain and cupped his hands around his mouth like a megaphone.

"I have a son!" he yelled, straining his neck muscles. "I've got a son!"

No one but Debbie, down in the house, and Johnny and Una in their home 150 feet away could hear Bob's screams of joy. It didn't matter. He was venting his pride to the stars and to Hooknose. Debbie and Bob suffered together through several miscarriages in the first four years of their marriage. It was devastating for a couple to whom children meant everything. Bob wanted as large a family as he could support.

But when it became apparent Debbie couldn't carry a pregnancy to term, they signed up with an adoption agency. They had waited less than a year when, on November 12, 1981, the agency called. A young unwed mother selected them because she wanted her son reared in the healthy environment of the countryside, around animals.

Mathews was the main influence in the Loffs' decision to have children as well. In August 1980, Marlene gave birth to a boy they named Joseph Robert. Ken, knowing how much children meant to Mathews, asked his friend to be the godfather.

By April 1981, Marlene was pregnant again. Before she delivered her second son, Mathews got the call from the adoption agency. The Loffs were joyous. It meant both couples would have sons. Bob and Debbie named their child Clinton. Loff's second son, born a month later, was named Robert, after his best friend.

Ken Loff started to take Bob Mathews's counsel on many other things. It started slowly and grew steadily, from the day Bob called him in California about purchasing the gasoline station. Loff trusted Mathews implicitly, so in casual conversation, when Bob started to talk more and more about race, Ken didn't question it. Everything Bob said just seemed to be right.

The talk mostly centered on their children's future, even when it was about taxes, economics, school busing, affirmative action, or some other government policy Bob was condemning. Times were difficult in Pend Oreille County. Timber prices were down and sawmills were closing. Some families still hadn't recovered from the mine shutdown, and there was a labor dispute going on at the cement plant. Still, Mathews always couched his discussions in terms of the children.

"We have to secure a better future for our children," Mathews told Loff one day. "It's up to us. The government works against us, the way it taxes middle-class whites into submission. We've got to stand up for our children's rights. Look at all the outsiders Seattle City Light has brought in to work at the dam. Why, there are families just getting by here who could use that work.

"What's left for our children? What will we be able to leave them?"

Bob Mathews was such an upstanding, righteous individual, Loff didn't seriously question what he said. The trust was complete. Then, two months later, in February 1982, Mathews came to Loff with an incredible suggestion.

"I've found a church about three hours away that preaches good news about the white race," Bob said with that excited look in his eyes. "It's a great place for white Christian families. I'd like you, Marlene and the babies to come.

"We're having Clint baptized there."

Loff agreed to go to the Church of Jesus Christ Christian-Aryan Nations. Mathews introduced him to Pastor Butler, who with an officious smile told him to make himself at home. As Ken mingled and made conversation, Bob watched approvingly. Ken wasn't yet involved in the racial aspect of the right wing. But when Ken's love for his children entered the picture, when he thought about affirmative action making his boys second-class, it outraged him. Anyone who opposed his enemy was someone he wanted to know.

So by the end of that visit to Hayden Lake, Ken Loff was watching Pastor Butler baptize his seventeen-month-old and two-month-old boys, alongside three-month-old Clinton Mathews. Loff was born and reared Catholic but fell away over a dispute with the church. The best man at his wedding was a Jew. But now his children, called offspring of an "Aryan warrior," were being baptized by a man who detested Jews and thought Catholics were sheep manipulated by the Zionist conspiracy.

Mathews returned only a few times to Aryan Nations, more for the fellowship than for the religious doctrine. Mathews believed in God, but he assembled his own teleology by borrowing selected tenets from a menu of faiths and from Odinism. He wasn't very impressed with Butler, but those 20 acres under the pines made a good place to meet young men who believed as he did. The annual Thanksgiving dinners were especially intimate events at Aryan Nations.

When Bob told his parents he and Debbie had been to Aryan Nations, Una was disappointed and Johnny immediately became angry. Their son was slipping back on his promise, and once again, as in Phoenix, there was no way to dissuade him.

"Yes, I'm prejudiced!" Bob yelled at his dad during one argument. "I'm prejudiced for my race, just like other races can be proud of their color. And if more white people soon don't realize we have to protect our race, we're doomed!"

During 1982, Bob conceived the "White American Bastion." His intent was to sell the Northwest as a natural territory for white families. He didn't want a separate government but believed by attracting enough like-minded people, sheer weight of numbers would be enough for whites to exert the social, political, and economic influences that would make them the dominant force in the Pacific Northwest. Not that whites didn't already have such force there, but it wasn't a racially based force. Bob wasn't just looking for whites; he wanted kinsmen.

Bob kept file folders on the White American Bastion organized in boxes in his bedroom. He devoured newspapers and clipped stories on what he perceived as injustices to the white race. He placed a small, three-line ad in *The Spotlight* touting the Northwest and his White American Bastion.

The Spotlight was published by Liberty Lobby in Washington, D.C. The weekly paper was one of the right wing's most widely read publications, with a circulation of a quarter million. It regularly featured articles on such topics as Bible analysis, taxes and fighting the IRS, bankers and how they bleed the middle class, and how the nation is manipulated by the dreaded Trilateral Commission and the Council on Foreign Relations. The paper attracted a huge diversity of readers, from survivalists and enthusiasts of unorthodox medical treatments to fundamentalist Christians and anti-Zionists.

Its classified ad section was a potpourri of pitches, a broad spectrum of goods and services. Mail drops, gun silencer parts, Nazi paraphernalia, and false identification instructions were sold along with poetry, laetrile prescriptions, dating services for patriotic Christians, and automotive devices to dramatically increase gasoline mileage—suppressed in the free market, of course.

Mathews received a decent response from his ad. To each person who wrote, he sent a brochure and an invitation to visit. To some who had particularly touching stories of white hardship, he sent money, though he had little to spare.

"Onward, the course of progress takes our people, onward to the stars!" said his brochure, printed by Pastor Butler on the Aryan Nations press. Under a "White American Bastion" banner were drawn two brave-looking white men, one a Viking warrior, the other a caped pioneer, facing each other in a pine forest.

> Look into the window of your mind and picture a vast expanse of mist-shrouded, heavily forested valleys and mountains. It is early morning, and you stand at the edge of a large meadow. Suddenly, the powerful double notes of an ancient horn shatter the quiet, and before your eyes many people start to assemble in the meadow. Your heart leaps with joy because every face in the meadow is kindred to yours. You see an elderly white woman holding the hand of an inquisitive little boy, his dark brown hair the color of the rich earth and his green eyes the color of the grass.

That vision exists in the Northwest, the brochure promised, for all who are up to the challenge of hard work.

Mathews didn't force his beliefs on anyone. That was part of his attraction. He was no longer the teenager barging into his parents' bedroom ready to preach from the Book of Mormon. Unless one were really interested, he wouldn't launch into a sermon. Bob learned to pick his targets carefully. He had grown increasingly frustrated with most whites, whom he called "sheeple" because of their willingness to be shepherded in return for comfort. All they cared about, he said, was sex, drinking, hunting, and their pickup trucks—and not necessarily in that order.

He would come home and release his frustration to Debbie, ranting and raving about the guys down at the plant. Once, his co-workers taped to his locker a picture of a nude black woman, which he promptly ripped down in a rage.

"These people have never been to the big city! They don't know what it's like!" he complained to Debbie. "All they know is what they see on TV. They ought to go into the city and see what it's really like!"

Several people accepted the invitation to visit the Northwest with Bob as host. One was Charles Ostrout, money room supervisor at the Brink's armored car depot in downtown San Francisco. He answered an ad Mathews placed in a right-wing paper, stating simply, "Are you a white man being displaced by minorities?"

Ostrout told Mathews he had been passed over for promotions in favor of blacks because of the Brink's affirmative action program. Bob commiserated and sent him $50. "Hope this helps you out," he wrote. Bob also hosted a few National Alliance members. Two of them were men just turned twenty, high school classmates from Salinas, California, who had gotten involved in right-wing causes as teens.

William Soderquist was highly intelligent and, among the older National Alliance members, was being nursed as a *wunderkind*. Somewhat chubby with curly hair, he joined the John Birch Society at eleven, just like Mathews, and graduated to the National Alliance as a high school junior at sixteen. He met Mathews at the group's 1981 convention in Arlington with his friend, Richard Kemp.

Kemp was tall, lanky, and handsome, with dark hair. A former high school basketball star, he was very industrious. Soon after his arrival in Washington State, he was helping Loff brand cattle in Ione and finding work at Boundary Dam.

But despite all the time and money Mathews invested in the White American Bastion, only one couple moved to the Northwest because of him. Mathews was very frustrated. The country was falling apart, and he couldn't take it any more.

And what happened to Gordon Kahl only made Mathews's frustration worse.

GORDON KAHL WAS a hard-working, God-fearing farmer in Heaton, North Dakota. He had done his patriotic duty as a turret gunner in a B–25 during the big war, then returned to the expansive plains of the upper Midwest to rear his family. But something wouldn't let him rest, some uneasy sense, aquired during the war, that there were sinister forces pulling America's strings. Traveling the same paths Robbie Mathews would take a decade later, Kahl flirted with the Mormon church and later the John Birch Society. He eventually joined the ultra-conservative Constitutional Party of North Dakota.

Through all this, Kahl met people whose beliefs in Jewish conspiracies and Christian Identity crystallized the unfocused frustration that tugged at him since the war. It didn't take long for them to convince him that paying taxes was not only illegal but sinful as well, financing the destruction of Christian America. So in 1967, he wrote the IRS that he would no longer pay taxes.

After fall harvest, Kahl and his family spent winters working in the west Texas oil fields. There he joined the fledgling Posse Comitatus in 1973, soon becoming Texas coordinator. Despite not paying taxes since 1967, Kahl found the IRS didn't come after him in earnest until after he appeared with other tax protesters advocating their beliefs on a Texas television show in 1976. Kahl ended up serving under a year in Leavenworth, but when he got out, he was more strident than ever.

Kahl looked around at his fellow farmers and counted them an endangered species. Encouraged by government farm policies, they brought in a good crop each year by keeping abreast of the latest in technology. But when the economy tightened after the Arab oil crisis in the early 1970s, they found no matter how good they were or how many newfangled pieces of equipment they bought, their harvests wouldn't pay for what they had put into the ground. At an alarming and accelerating rate, family farmers were financially going under while city folk went about their business well-fed and apparently unconcerned.

"Economic conditions" is an abstract term, hard to hate because it's faceless. One sees only its effects. Since the banks had all the farmers' money, bankers became the face on their plight. Kahl found a compassionate ear for his Posse message at farm auctions and rallies across the heartland. As his anger built, Kahl honed the commando skills he learned in the war by attending Christian survivalist camps. He warned he wouldn't be arrested again, and he never went anywhere without firearms.

In February 1983, as a Posse meeting was breaking up in Medina, North Dakota, Kahl got word that federal marshals were planning to arrest him on the road home for violating probation. Riding with a friend and followed by his son, Yorie Von Kahl, and several other Posse members, Kahl came over a hill on the highway north of town and saw two cars on the next rise blocking the way, red lights flashing. From behind, another police vehicle closed on them. The Kahl entourage stopped in a driveway, and Kahl, his son and another man jumped out with their weapons and took positions near their cars. Six officers—four U.S. marshals and two local cops—surrounded them at close range. A lot of screaming and hollering began, then a shot rang out. A marshal yelled he was hit. Another shot came, and Yorie yelled to his dad, "I'm hit! I'm hit!"

"Yorie!" Kahl shouted, and brought his Ruger Mini-14 automatic rifle to bear on the marshals. As he fired, blood splattered from two of the lawmen who fell mortally wounded. Three others were injured but lived, and Kahl's son was seriously wounded. But Kahl managed to escape.

For four months, Kahl squirreled away with movement sympathizers until one tipped off the FBI that he was hiding in a bunker-like hideout on the edge of the Ozark Plateau near Smithville, Arkansas. Kahl's hosts, Leonard and Norma Ginter, were fellow survivalists and had the earth-and-concrete house stocked with goods and weapons. Federal agents surrounded the farmhouse on June 3 and nabbed Leonard Ginter outside. His wife quickly came out, leaving Kahl inside with his Mini-14. Lawrence County Sheriff Gene Matthews entered the house with a federal agent to arrest him. As Matthews stepped into the kitchen, Kahl emerged from behind the refrigerator and sprayed the lawman with bullets. Matthews fired simultaneously, and another agent sent a shotgun blast through a window, again striking the sheriff. Matthews was dragged from the house, and he later died.

Not realizing Matthews's shot had hit Kahl in the head, killing him, the federal agents spent hours peppering the house with tear gas and weapon fire. One agent placed a container of fuel over a rooftop vent and drained it into the house, touching off some kindling inside. The house went up quickly and Kahl's body was nearly incinerated.

The use of such force against the 63-year-old farmer earned Kahl the rank of martyr among his right-wing allies, who considered him a patriot rather than the killer he was. His death weighed heavily on the minds of dedicated "superpatriots," who wanted to avenge the deed.

THE FIRST TIME Bob Mathews took a leader's role, it was an impromptu act that grabbed the other men's attention. Butler scheduled an Aryan Nations rally in Spokane's Riverfront Park, site of the 1974 world's fair, for June 26, 1983. It was three weeks after Kahl's death. The rally attracted massive publicity as community leaders urged citizens to stay away. But a leftist group, the International Committee Against Racism from Seattle, planned to counter-demonstrate.

Butler asked Mathews to join his security detail in case there was trouble. He wasn't disappointed. In addition to the leftists surrounding the perimeter of the park's grove on Spokane Falls Boulevard, a group of punk rockers showed up who didn't like either the racists or the anti-racists. Police screened everyone entering the park for weapons while police snipers kept watch from rooftops across the street. Still, about three hundred Butler supporters showed up.

At the base of the stand where Butler spoke, Randy Duey, Denver Parmenter, and Gary Yarbrough stood guard in their blue Aryan Nations uniforms. The protesters out on the edge of the crowd, one manning a bullhorn, shouted "Racists!" and "Nazis!" A few began to push and shove. A woman in the group kicked Bud Cutler, Butler's security chief, in the groin.

That's when Mathews emerged. Dressed simply in jeans and a worker's t-shirt, the muscular sentry spread his arms as he moved toward the rowdy protesters, whose signs read, "Smash Racism. Build Multiracial Unity." There was a fearless and determined look in his eyes, as though he were driven by a great inner resolve. Among those who noticed it was one of Butler's newest converts, a Kentucky native named Bruce Carroll Pierce. They all watched as Mathews moved.

When Mathews reached the protesters, he exchanged angry words with those who were shoving. They stopped. Pierce and some of the others then felt themselves pulled to Mathews's side, linking arms to form a moving wall and pushing back the protesters. There was a strength in that chain, and every man felt it.

After police came to separate the antagonists, the guards felt they had achieved a small victory. They admired Bob's courage. Something about him had made a lasting impression. It was that look in his eyes. It was fearless. Clearly, they said later, this is a guy who puts action behind his words.

The following month, there were plenty of words.

The second weekend in July was the date for the annual Aryan World Congress at Butler's church. Many of the same folks from the previous year returned, but the talk was much more militant than in 1982. Louis Beam, a fiery young ex-Klansman from Texas who had taken up residence in Hayden Lake as Butler's "ambassador at large," gave a moving talk about white men securing the future for their children. "We are at war!" he yelled at one point. "We must pledge our blood for the new nation! There's nothing we won't do to bring about the new kingdom, the new nation!"

Ken Loff was seated next to Bob Mathews during Beam's talk, and when he turned toward his friend he could see tears welling in his dark brown eyes.

With a flourish, Beam tossed a chunk of raw meat onto

the pine needles and dirt in front of the bandstand and warned against infiltrators: "I know some of you federal dogs are among us today! I dare you to come forth and take this!" In fact, there were in the crowd at least half a dozen such informants who were gathering information for the FBI.

The sounds of children at play rose from the swing set and jungle gym at the base of the guard tower, while the adults listened to calls for war against the Jews. Many of the women felt comforted by talk of the men laying down their lives to protect their families and values. Some of the women cut locks of their hair, tied them with ribbons, and presented them to their men, so that they could carry them into battle. But most of the people took such talk figuratively.

Butler's camp took on a jamboree flavor during his congresses. The grounds were covered with tents, trailers, and pickups with camper shells, and people walked among them to socialize. One group had gathered near some lilac bushes in the clearing south of the church. Bob saw a pretty woman in jeans standing among them. The woman's brunette hair was straight and long, a simple fashion Bob liked. She was slender and somewhat short, with a fresh look about her. Her mouth was small and pert, and she was wearing attractive wire-frame glasses.

He hadn't seen her here before, but she apparently was with David Lane's group from the Denver area. Mathews knew Lane from Aryan Nations. He wondered who the woman was, and whether he could get David to introduce him.

During the congress, Butler hosted private leadership meetings to push his theme of unity. At one session in Aryan Hall, thirteen men representing Texas, Montana, Michigan, Arkansas, California, Pennsylvania, and North Dakota discussed the prospects for a white homeland. Afterward, a sheet of paper circulated through the group so they could list their mailing addresses. Jim Ellison, the erratic leader of the Covenant, the Sword, and the Arm of the Lord, a Christian Identity survivalist commune in Arkansas, then stood and held the list aloft.

"I want you all to realize that each of us in this room has just committed treason!" he bellowed, astonishing those who thought it was only a mailing list. They were aware of Ellison's eccentricities, having anointed himself King James of the Ozarks. However, his gunsmiths were among the best in the movement and his survival training course was top-shelf. So Ellison was humored.

At another meeting, in Butler's house, a group talked obliquely about how it was "time for action" to establish an Aryan homeland. But no one seemed ready to act. That was one of Mathews's greatest frustrations.

Bob Miles, the former national Klan leader who ran a racist church in Cohoctah, Michigan, told the group the right wing needed money, a lot of it. "If we were half the men the leftists were," said Miles, recalling the 1981 attack on a Brink's armored truck in Nyack, New York, by the Black Liberation Army and Weather Underground, "we'd be hitting armored cars too." The attack had left three dead.

Later on during the congress, Miles, considered the movement's chaplain, staged a peculiar ceremony for the men. It was a blessing of the guns.

JOHNNY MATHEWS HAD a sense that something was going terribly wrong with his youngest boy. But Johnny had more serious problems. His lymphoma was flaring, the third time the cancer threatened his life. He discovered a sore spot in 1976 while playing golf in Tempe. After a lengthy stay in the VA Hospital in El Paso, lymphoma was diagnosed. Still he went ahead with his move to Metaline Falls, thinking the change might do him good. For seven years he'd already beaten the odds given most people with lymphoma.

He was irritated with his son and his friends, with their talk about guns and action. They reminded him of Bob's friends in Phoenix. One day during late summer, Johnny walked into his house, where Una was reading.

"We're moving," he announced in a determined, exasperated tone. "I don't want to live here any more. I'm worried about what Robbie's getting into. Things aren't right and I'm not sure I want to be here when it falls apart."

Una weighed the options for a while. Moving closer to Spokane would put Johnny nearer his doctor, whom he had to visit once a month. But Johnny was losing ground to the disease, and the last thing Una wanted was to move somewhere away from family. "Honey, I don't want to move," Una finally said to Johnny. "I don't want to leave the grandchildren."

Johnny perceived Una's real fear. She soon would be alone, without him for the first time since she had gone back to Detroit in 1945 to give birth to Grant. On her account, he dropped the notion of leaving Mathews Acres.

By August it was apparent Bob was making moves of his own. To accommodate the visitors he anticipated he hired Daniel Bauer, an Aryan Nations member and contractor, to erect a building next to his double-wide that he could use as a guest house. Bauer, a father of four, was a former Minuteman who had joined Butler's church in 1975. He was a church board member and managing editor for Butler's newsletter in the late 1970s and had met Mathews and Loff when they brought their wives to Aryan Nations for Thanksgiving dinner in 1982.

Kemp and Soderquist, Mathews's National Alliance friends from California, helped build the guest house. It would be the Ellis Island of the White American Bastion, where his immigrants could stay until they were settled. With a gambrel roof over its second floor, the "barracks," as it came to be known, was primitive when it came to comfort but provided privacy for Mathews and his friends.

The 20-by-35-foot building was sheathed with corrugated metal siding, aquamarine in color, and had a silver sheet metal roof. On the first floor, a wood stove was placed along the west wall. The floor was bare concrete. A fine wooden door, dark stained with a small window, was hung in the main entrance in the southeast corner. A smaller white door with a large window went into the north wall, leading outside to a small woodpile. The back door was only a few feet from a set of steps leading down a long, steep wooded slope to Beaver Creek.

The second floor of the barracks was gained by a precipitous staircase on the south side of the room. Its floor was particle board, its walls unfinished. After people moved in, carpeting strips were tossed down, old furniture placed here and there, and bunks stretched end to end. Soderquist toted his books from California on Nazis and the German view of World War II, and they were arranged upstairs on a six-shelf bookcase. There was an open balcony at the north end.

Mathews, Bauer, Kemp, and Soderquist put the finishing touch on the barracks by pouring two small concrete steps outside the back door. On the top step, they scratched inscriptions: "8–16–83, D.B., B.M., R.K., B.S." Then a swastika was scrawled on the lower left corner. On the bottom step, they wrote three lines: "WHITE PRIDE, WHITE UNITY, WHITE AMERICA."

Marlene Loff gave birth to her third child, Jamie Anne, on August 23. Ken had grown very close to Richie Kemp and asked the young man to be the godfather. In September the baptism was held at Aryan Nations. But the Loffs stopped going to Hayden Lake after that. Ken watched as his friend Mathews became more obsessed with getting money to aid the right-wing cause. It intensified in the late summer as more young men, all eager for action, came to visit Mathews Acres.

Bauer spread word that there was work at Mathews's farm. Denver Parmenter and Bruce Pierce, hungry for the opportunity, brought chainsaws. Mathews told them they could cut trees to expand his clearing, then sell the timber themselves and keep the money. Pierce, a recent Aryan Nations convert, was grateful for the chance. He and his wife, Julie, were in a financial bind, struggling to rear three children.

Pierce, a proud man, was embarrassed one time when he was down on his luck and Mathews offered him money as a gift. When Pierce politely declined, Mathews insisted and said something Pierce never could forget. "Bruce," Bob said, extending the money, "please do me a favor. Be a gracious receiver."

Bob got pleasure from giving. He was known among his friends as an extremely generous man, and the trait startled some who weren't used to seeing such compassion. In fact, Debbie sometimes complained, Bob let himself be taken by people looking for handouts. But these new men were eager to work. They cut trees, hauled gravel, and did other ranch chores. Randy Duey also visited, along with the older David Lane, who had taken a liking to Mathews at the congress.

They called Bob a "spark plug," some of them remembering the day in Riverfront Park when Bob had taken charge and others fell in beside him. Now, as they discussed race and the right wing during more peaceful times at Mathews Acres, they sensed Bob wanted to take the next step. Pastor Butler was lavish with words, but the younger men were restless. When would it be time to make a stand, they wondered? Now came Bob Mathews. They had no doubt, when Bob said they could raise money for the right wing, that they could do it.

Bob reminded them of Miles's speech about the right wing's need for money. Then Bob gave them National Alliance literature and led discussions about such books as *The Road Back, Essays of a Klansman,* and *The Turner Diaries.*

The Road Back, published in California by the Noontide Press, was an instruction manual on assembling a terrorist group, including sections on living underground, secret communications, and intelligence gathering. *Essays of a Klansman* was Louis Beam's recent work, which included a point system for Aryan warriorhood, assigning values to certain killings and criminal acts.

The Turner Diaries is fiction, written by William Pierce, the National Alliance head—no relation to Bruce. It depicts an underground army that foments race war in the 1990s against a Jewish-controlled American government, told in diary fashion by one of the guerrillas, Earl Turner. In the book, the "Cohen Act" has made gun ownership illegal, and human relations councils are invested with police powers to force integration, even miscegenation, on the public. In response, a white underground called the Organization has been formed. Its secret leadership clique is named The Order, an elite sect of commanders who oversee a truck-bombing of FBI headquarters and a mortar attack on the Capitol.

The group makes up for its lack of numbers by staging small-scale strikes, counterfeiting, armored-car robberies, and assassinations. It is organized in small cells, similar to Bob's Sons of Liberty. In the end, the whites win after gaining territory in Southern California, massacring

Jews and minorities, and commandeering the nuclear missiles at Vandenberg Air Force Base to annihilate Israel. The year is 1999, just before the millennium.

The fictional Earl Turner's first diary entry sums up Bob Mathews's desire: *"September 16, 1991.* Today it finally began! After all these years of talking—and nothing but talking—we have finally taken our first action. We are at war with the System, and it is no longer a war of words."

IN SEPTEMBER, BOB left for Arlington, Virginia, to attend the National Alliance convention. He took a speech he had drafted at his dining room table, a report on efforts to recruit farmers and ranchers into the "white racialist movement."

People who hadn't seen Bob since the 1981 convention were surprised at the change. His hair was cropped short in a military style, and he was in incredible physical shape. He was a celebrity among the hundred or so attendees, because the current National Alliance bulletin featured his picture.

"My brothers, my sisters," Mathews spoke into the microphone with a stilted delivery that gradually smoothed out. "From the mist-shrouded forested valleys and mountains of the Pacific Northwest I bring you a message of solidarity, a call to action and a demand for adherence to duty as members of the vanguard of an Aryan resurgence and ultimately, total Aryan victory. The signs of awakening are sprouting up across the Northwest, and no more so than amongst the two-fisted farmers and ranchers, a class of our people who have been hit especially hard by the filthy, lying Jews and their parasitical usury system."

Mathews gave accounts of "yeoman" farmers who had been radicalized after the economics of the times dashed their dreams for the land. They must be brought into the struggle, Mathews declared in that still boyish voice of his. "The task is not going to be easy," he warned in grandiose terms. "TV satellite dishes are springing up like poisonous mushrooms across the domain of the tillers of the soil. The electronic Jew is slithering into the living rooms of even the most remote farms and ranches. The race-destroying dogs are everywhere."

Then he spoke of his plans for his friends at Mathews Acres.

"Let us not only preach, let us live racial economics," he said. "In Metaline Falls, we are not only eating, breathing and sleeping, we are growing together as one mind and one body. We have broken the chains of Jewish thought. In Metaline Falls, we know not the meaning of the word *'mine,'* it is *'ours,'* our race, the totality of our people!

"Ten hearts, one beat! One hundred hearts, one beat! Ten thousand hearts, one beat! We are born to fight and to die and to continue the flow, the flow of our people," Mathews rolled toward his crescendo. "Onward we will go, onward to the stars, high above the mud, the mud of yellow, black and brown! Kinsmen, duty calls! The future is now!

"So stand up like men, and drive the enemy into the sea! Stand up like men, and swear a sacred oath upon the green graves of our sires that you will reclaim what *our* forefathers discovered, explored, conquered, settled, built and died for! Stand up like men and reclaim our soil! Kinsmen, arise! Look towards the stars and proclaim our destiny!

"In Metaline Falls we have a saying: Defeat, never! Victory forever!"

The audience erupted in applause, giving Bob the only standing ovation of the convention.

At the conference, Bob renewed acquaintance with a Philadelphia man he'd met in 1981, Thomas Allen Martinez. Despite his surname he was an avowed white racist and angrily responded to those who insinuated he was Hispanic. He claimed Aryan blood from his Swedish-Castillian father, and his Welsh-Greek mother. Instead of mar-TEEN-ez, he pronounced his name mar-tin-EZ.

After a small group socialized in Martinez's hotel room, Mathews and Martinez were left alone. Bob confided that he couldn't wait any longer.

"Clint will have no future unless I stand up and provide it for him," Mathews said. "I'm going to give my land to Dr. Pierce to bring the National Alliance out west. That's where the white territorial imperative exists, Tom."

"Wait a minute, Bob, you're not serious?" Martinez responded. "That's very foolish. What would happen to your family then?"

"But Tom, I've got to do something. The country's falling apart and I just can't take it any more," Mathews answered.

There was something in his tone that frightened Martinez.

By LATE SEPTEMBER, the first cool breezes signaling the coming winter were blowing into the Pend Oreille Valley from Canada, rushing through the pine branches and down the mountainsides with a rumble like a faraway stampede. The earth was browning below the evergreens, and the shortening days were cloudier. One brisk evening, several cars wound through the gravel drive from Boundary Dam Road into secluded Mathews Acres, parking just within the four-rail wooden fence setting off the residences from the rest of the clearing.

Debbie frequently cooked for Bob's guests, and this night there was a grand banquet for eighteen people, including wives and children. The occasion was a formal meeting to address the issues the host and his guests had discussed informally in recent months.

After dinner the men excused themselves, leaving the women to clean up. Women were excluded from the decision-making process by biblical proscription.

In the darkness, nine men led by Mathews clambered down the wooden steps from his back porch and walked across the 25-foot path to the barracks. With the moonlight, they could see Hooknose still had a naked summit, but the crisp air indicated that it wouldn't be long before snow fell in the north country.

To Mathews, who studied Odinism, it was significant that they numbered nine, the most mystical number in Norse mythology. He was mindful that Odin learned nine magic songs and hung for nine nights on Yggdrasill, the world tree, to acquire the wisdom of the dead; Heimdall, watchman of the gods, had nine mothers; and, more appropriately, Thor stumbled nine steps before falling dead in the Great Battle.

Bob had set up a blackboard on the first floor of the

barracks. The wood stove was fully stoked. After they settled, Bob surveyed each man, satisfied he had gathered kinsmen who would understand implicitly everything he had to say.

Seated near him were the youngest faces, Richie Kemp and Bill Soderquist. There was his trusted friend, Ken Loff, and David Lane. Then there was the group from Aryan Nations: Dan Bauer, Denver Parmenter, Randy Duey, and Bruce Pierce.

"I've asked all of you to come here because I think we share a common goal," Mathews said, picking up a piece of chalk. "I intend to form a group of kinsmen who will let their deeds do their talking for them. And I'm telling you now, if any of you don't want to get involved in this, you're free to leave."

All looked around, but no one left.

"I've given a lot of thought to our philosophical discussions these last months and I've organized some ideas into a plan with six basic steps. The first is to form the group, which is what we're doing tonight. The second is to set goals—what exactly do we want and how far are we willing to go for it.

"Step three is to procure funds. I've got some ideas about that, which we'll discuss in more detail later. The fourth step is recruitment, and using these funds for financing right-wing causes."

No one disagreed so far, but several were uneasy about that third step. What did Bob mean, "procuring" funds? Bauer and Loff shifted uneasily.

"Before we go on, if all of you are willing to join with me, we first must bond to one another as blood brothers."

This isolated hideaway, tucked deep into the woods, was an ideal place to hatch a conspiracy. Here they heard only Mathews, who had befriended them, who had given them whatever was his without asking anything in return. He had challenged their beliefs and, satisfied they were true, urged them to live by them.

"I'm going to ask each of you to take an oath that you will remain true to this cause," Mathews said. "I would like to remind all of you what is at stake here. It is our children, kinsmen, and their very economic and racial survival. Because of that, I would like to place a white child before us as we take this oath. Denver, can we use Kristin?"

"Sure, Bob!" Parmenter replied, honored that Mathews would select his five-month-old daughter. Parmenter darted back to the house, where the women were entertaining each other. But Janice Parmenter refused to allow her daughter to be used that way. She did not approve of a group of men chanting mumbo-jumbo over her little girl.

Denver went back to the barracks, where the men had moved upstairs. Going up the steps, he saw candles had been lighted in a circle. A blanket was in the center, presumably for Kristin. But Denver told Bob his wife wouldn't cooperate.

"That's all right, kinsman," Bob said, putting his hand on the taller man. Then Bob asked Loff to get six-week-old Jamie Anne.

When Ken returned, the girl was placed on the blanket, where she stared up into a circle of men looming over her in the eerie glow of the candles on the floor. The men clasped hands, repeating an oath Mathews recited:

"I, as a free Aryan man, hereby swear an unrelenting oath upon the green graves of our sires, upon the children in the wombs of our wives, upon the throne of God almighty, sacred is His name, to join together in holy union with those brothers in this circle and to declare forthright that from this moment on I have no fear of death, no fear of foe; that I have a sacred duty to do whatever is necessary to deliver our people from the Jew and bring total victory to the Aryan race.

"I, as an Aryan warrior, swear myself to complete secrecy to the Order and total loyalty to my comrades.

"Let me bear witness to you, my brothers, that should one of you fall in battle, I will see to the welfare and well-being of your family.

"Let me bear witness to you, my brothers, that should one of you be taken prisoner, I will do whatever is necessary to regain your freedom.

"Let me bear witness to you, my brothers, that should an enemy agent hurt you, I will chase him to the ends of the earth and remove his head from his body.

"And furthermore, let me bear witness to you, my

brothers, that if I break this oath, let me be forever cursed upon the lips of our people as a coward and an oath breaker.

"My brothers, let us be his battle ax and weapons of war. Let us go forth by ones and by twos, by scores and by legions, and as true Aryan men with pure hearts and strong minds face the enemies of our faith and our race with courage and determination.

"We hereby invoke the blood covenant and declare that we are in a full state of war and will not lay down our weapons until we have driven the enemy into the sea and reclaimed the land which was promised to our fathers of old, and through our blood and His will, becomes the land of our children to be."

It was a highly emotional moment for all the men, especially for Mathews. He now had a new Sons of Liberty and an expanded cause. After they reassembled downstairs, Mathews announced that step five was assassination of racial enemies. On the radical right, everybody had a hit list, and talking about killing an enemy wasn't regarded as unusual. Most often, it was viewed simply as hot air.

Mathews talked about doomsday assassinations. If the group was attacked by the authorities, each man had a target he was supposed to track and kill. They ranged from Henry Kissinger and the banker David Rockefeller to the heads of the three television networks, all of whom were perceived as enemies because they were either Jewish or fronts for the Jews.

Step six, Mathews said, was the formation of a guerrilla army, a strike force with the ability to carry out sabotage in urban areas.

"Now, how do we get money?" he asked them. "Do you remember Bob Miles saying the right wing needed money however it could get it? Kinsmen, how far do we go?"

Robbery immediately became an option. But Bauer, who had an offshoot Identity church in Coeur d'Alene, raised a religious objection. "The Bible tells us it's wrong to commit crimes," he told the group.

Soderquist, noting that the men had made some money by logging Bob's property, said the Forest Service regularly put out contracts for clearing timber and brush and they could bid on one. Lumberjacking appealed to some of the men's visions of themselves as Nordic woodsmen. Mathews told Soderquist to look into it.

Lane brought up counterfeiting, which would serve two purposes. Successfully passed, the counterfeit money would raise clean money for the movement. Also, introducing bogus currency into the system would devalue real money and thereby undermine the government. Mathews liked the idea and commissioned Lane to investigate further.

Duey and Parmenter raised the notion of approaching Arab oil countries for funding. They shared a hatred of Jews and might be willing to see the cause funded in America, Israel's strongest ally. Again Mathews approved.

When the subject of robbery surfaced again, Loff suggested they might erase the religious objection by targeting pimps and dope dealers, who made a fortune trading on people's vices. It would be efficient for the group to rob such trash and accomplish two goals, raising money and ridding society of its undesirable elements.

Eventually, this Robin Hood approach appealed even to Bauer.

Chapter 4

The Turn to Crime

Denver Daw Parmenter was a strapping young man, his head slightly small for his muscular torso. He loved the bitter cold of the Northwest forests. While being jostled around in the cab of Bob Mathews's pickup, going up twisting Sullivan Creek Road above Metaline Falls, Parmenter contrasted the north woods to the hot Texas plains where he grew up.

The truck skidded to a stop in a gravel lot. A car pulled in behind it.

Despite a steady drizzle, Parmenter and the others looked forward to the work ahead. Parmenter climbed into the truck bed and started handing out the equipment. Then, grabbing a chainsaw, he vaulted over the side, his breath billowing in a chilly mist as his feet hit the ground. The group looked at the trail into the forest, then up at the miserably gray skies, then at each other.

"This was your idea, wasn't it, Billy?" Parmenter said lightly.

Since Bill Soderquist had suggested they bid on Forest Service contracts, he and Loff visited the Colville National Forest ranger station at Sullivan Lake, a resort area east of Metaline Falls. They won a contract to clear brush and timber from a trail in the Salmo-Priest Wilderness. It wouldn't bring a lot of money, but it was honest work. They came prepared to camp, since it was more than a one-day job.

Mathews, Parmenter, Lane, and Kemp grabbed a few saws, picks, and poles, leaving the large array of camping equipment for Pierce and Soderquist.

They set up on the trail and began clearing, but it didn't take long for the cold to numb their fingers. As hours dragged by, they kept glancing at each other. Machismo prevented each from being the first to suggest they stop. Through five hours of raised and broken blisters they maintained this front, until finally Mathews stopped to scan the saddle between the peaks ahead. The ridge line was being dusted with snow, though it was still rain at the lower elevation.

"We're not going to make it, guys," Mathews said. "It's snowing up there and we've got to go to that pass. I think we ought to go back."

The others weren't sure the trail ascended to the pass at all, but they happily agreed. Mathews quickly folded his map. On the hike back to the trailhead, David Lane muttered the obvious: "Well, we're going to have to be better thinkers than our fathers were, because we're sure not the men they were."

One by one, they joined in the laughter. "Heck," Bob said—he almost never cursed—"we couldn't fund the right wing for a week off this job anyway." Ken Loff's robbery idea started to look more appealing. Pimps and drug dealers carry a lot of cash, and no one would feel sorry if they were robbed.

Bob worked a full shift at the cement plant and, after a snack, would kiss Debbie goodbye and drive to Spokane, two hours away. It was like having two jobs, blue-collar laborer by day, Robin Hood by night. He'd meet different men each time, and they would cruise Division Street into the heart of Spokane, capital of the Inland Empire region. Spokane is small by big-city standards at 170,000 people. But to Bob and his crew of neophyte Aryan warriors it was like visiting Sodom or Gomorrah. Bob thought cities were places of evil, prisons of the spirit.

In their daydreams, they were a breed of supermen, Nietzsche's overmen. If they grabbed a pimp or pusher, they told each other, they'd make him say where his money was stashed. Then, they agreed, they'd probably snuff him.

In reality, however, they were frightened men, feeding off one another's bravado, playing an adult game of double-dare. None had ever committed a violent crime before, and their cold feet ruled their action for several nights.

All they knew about how a pimp or dope dealer looked

was what they had seen on television. Lost in their stereotypes, they sought black men who they felt resembled Superfly. Bob would target a Cadillac piloted through downtown by a flashily dressed black and follow it. They followed their marks to houses, thinking loads of cash were inside. But they found it wasn't like the movies at all. It's damned hard to follow people without being obvious.

In time they found some bars frequented by blacks. Mathews and Pierce walked into one across the street from Riverfront Park. As they entered a hallway between the lounge and the dining area, they could see several white women in the bar with black men, who they assumed were pimps.

One of the women came out and saw Bob staring at her, his eyes narrow and his mouth tightened into a smirk. "Whatchoo lookin' at?" the woman demanded. He and Pierce wanted to whack her across the face, but they held back.

They ended up at a black bar about 2 A.M., nursing a few drinks. It took Pierce a while to figure out why the black guys kept casting wary glances his way. Then, reaching back on his stool, he felt his knife handle protruding from his belt. Nonchalantly, he draped his shirttail over it.

"Crazy white boy," Pierce whispered to Mathews, explaining the gaffe. "See, they won't mess with someone they think is a crazy white boy."

After following blacks on several occasions, Mathews steeled his nerve. Dan Bauer, Randy Duey, and Parmenter were with him. They had been behind a targeted car for a short time when Mathews roared ahead at an intersection to block the other car. All four men got out and approached the frightened black man. Mathews, brandishing a gun, pulled the protesting man from his car and patted him down. To trick the victim, Duey grabbed the microphone of Bob's CB radio and pretended to be a police officer. At that point the motorist became more cooperative.

But a Spokane police car cruised down the street, forcing Mathews to shove his handgun into his jacket. He issued a stern warning to the black man, called the guys back to his car and left.

Despite all the dress rehearsals, it wasn't until a Friday evening several weeks after the oath-taking that they committed their first crime. Mathews targeted a pornographic bookstore they spotted during one of their rides.

On October 28, 1983, he gathered Pierce, Duey, and Bauer at a shopping center at the Colville-Newport junction north of Spokane. The four men piled into one car and drove into Spokane, then east on Interstate 90. Mathews took the exit where the freeway crosses over Sprague Avenue, drove a short distance, made a U-turn, and parked in a lot 100 yards from the highway's on-ramp.

Before them was World Wide Video, at the time Spokane's only XXX-rated pornography shop. Such establishments were new to the valley, and there had been a mild uproar over them. Bob figured he'd do his part to get rid of them.

World Wide was part of a California conglomerate dealing in adult materials, and its manager was proud of its extremely explicit merchandise. The store was half cinderblock and half frame, a low-lying building in a commercial strip with an electronics store on one side and a warehouse on the other.

But best of all, it was close to that freeway ramp.

The tension was thick in the car, but Mathews figured all they needed was one watershed event to get over it and unleash a flood of confidence. Courage was easier to find in a group. When Mathews opened his car door, he touched off a chain of events that none of them could summon the righteous courage to stop.

Bauer slipped into the driver's seat, keeping the car running. The robbers had darkened their faces, and Mathews glued a phony mustache to his upper lip. One by one they entered the store, the enemy's den, an outpost of the army of moral decay sweeping over their race.

It was 7:30 in the evening, and there were a few people inside. Mathews went to a display case, barely glancing at blond-haired Teresa Sullivan, the clerk behind it. Pierce went to the arcade area, asking the manager, Ken Taylor, to give him a hand. Duey stayed by the front door. When the last customer left, Mathews pulled out his handgun and went behind the counter toward Sullivan.

"We're going to be robbing the store so take it easy," Mathews said.

"Hey, don't hurt her," Taylor said as he started across the store. As he passed the door, Duey stepped out and slugged him on the left cheek. Taylor's head snapped back but he remained standing, looking shocked.

"That was a stupid move," Mathews told Duey. "He wasn't doing anything."

Duey turned the lock on the door, shaking his head in amazement. His punch hardly fazed the shorter man. On TV, guys always dropped to the floor like a sack of flour when hit. They'd have to stop getting their impressions from television.

Bob rifled the till. Pierce kept silent, slowly scanning the scene from side to side, keeping the action in front, ensuring nothing went wrong. Duey was very nervous. He was a mailman, not an armed robber. Yet here he was, taking that first step he now believed had to be taken. They herded Taylor and Sullivan into a rest room, where in a rush Duey used so much tape to secure Sullivan's wrists, there wasn't enough to bind Taylor.

"You just stay here," he told Taylor as he left.

Outside, Bauer was getting nervous. He knew the Bible's admonition against stealing and had tried to rationalize what he was doing. While he waited, firecrackers went off nearby. Thinking his friends were shooting inside the store, Bauer came close to putting the car in gear and leaving. Before he made up his mind, the three men ran outside and scrambled into the car. Bauer headed straight for the freeway ramp. They were halfway to downtown Spokane by the time Taylor got the nerve to leave the bathroom to answer his telephone. It was his business partner.

"Get the cops," he told him. "We've just been robbed."

The car was filled with delirium. It was easier than any of them dreamed possible, almost like an out-of-body experience. But the euphoria fell with a dull thud as they returned to their parked cars and Bob counted the take. It came to only $369.10. Some revolution!

They stopped at a bar to calm down. Bob said he would set aside 10 percent as a tithe to the movement—$37.

It was an inauspicious start as they evenly split the rest of the money among themselves.

But one result was lasting. Taylor told police the man who grabbed the cash looked Mexican. It was Mathews, who had darkened his face to match his hair and brown eyes. When it hit the newspaper that the suspect was Mexican, the men started calling Mathews "Carlos." It became his code name.

They met several days after the robbery in Bauer's camper near Newport, Washington. Bauer expressed serious moral doubts about what they'd done. Meeting later in Pierce's house in Hayden Lake, the men finally agreed that whatever the morality, a $300 robbery wasn't worth the time it took to do it.

ARMORED CARS, THOUGH, were worth every second of their time.

Taking time from work on November 8, Mathews organized a trip to Seattle. In two cars, his and Bauer's, they piled guns in the trunk just in case they scouted a heist they could do immediately. Mathews, Bauer, Pierce, Kemp, and Soderquist left the barracks, stopping at a Cheney restaurant to pick up Duey and Parmenter, then made the five-hour drive to downtown Seattle, across the inland desert and over the Cascades at Snoqualmie Pass, into the green forests of the Puget Sound area.

Seattle is draped over the hills on an isthmus between Lake Washington and Elliott Bay, an arm of Puget Sound. The deep blue water of the natural harbor is framed on the western horizon by the rugged Olympic Mountains. Mount Rainier, a huge volcanic dome covered with snow year-round, dominates the southern view 60 miles away. The downtown is built on hills as steep as San Francisco's, making some of the new skyscrapers appear even taller.

For a city of half a million, Seattle is surprisingly cosmopolitan because of its role as the region's leading city, its access to foreign markets, and its mixed ethnic population. More than 1.8 million people live in the area. Metaline Falls could fit snugly into one of the freeway interchanges near downtown.

Mathews and his confederates checked into the Golden

West Motel on Aurora Avenue North. The porno store
loot didn't go far. They could afford only one room, all
seven cramming into it. They were so jammed, they
arranged the second night for a larger room down the
hall, although they still stayed together.

Their plan was to scout armored cars, which they had
no trouble finding.

Soderquist went to a Giant T store south of town.
Since he had worked in California for Thrifty, owned by
the same company, he thought he might know more
about Giant T's money handling. Parmenter went to
K-mart and Fred Meyer stores on the north side, taking
notes on times armored cars arrived, where the guards
walked, how they brought out the money, and where
they drove. They watched the stores for several days to
determine a pattern.

When Mathews decided to focus on the Fred Meyer
store at Aurora Avenue near North 185th Street, they
swarmed over it, inside and out. They sat in the parking
lot, loitered at the nearby Radio Shack, and wandered
the store's aisles, making notes all the while. Then in the
evening they looked over the results in their motel room.
They decided the best way to rob it was to hit the guard
as he left the office with his cash bags on a cart. The aisle
was partially hidden by high display cases, and they could
run out the northeast entrance into waiting cars.

Then a new plan distracted them. They came across a
newspaper item on Baron Elie de Rothschild, a relative
of the international Jewish banking family hated so much
by the radical right, who was soon to speak to a Jewish
fundraising group in Seattle. Was Yahweh dropping an
opportunity right into their laps?

Bauer had experimented in two-component explosives,
so the men discussed bombing the reception area at the
Olympic Four Seasons Hotel, where Rothschild was to
speak. Bauer and Parmenter drove to the elegant hotel at
Fourth Avenue and University Street in the heart of
downtown. They inspected the marble-paneled lobby area
and discussed placing a bomb in the room above the
baron's podium, or even the possibility of a suicide mission in which one of them would wear the bomb into the
reception before detonating it near Rothschild.

Bauer and Parmenter went to the library at the University of Washington northeast of downtown to research Rothschild and explosives. While there, they passed an office marked "Arab American Student Association." Looking at each other, they thought the same thing: "Arabs! They hate Jews as much as we do!"

Writing an oblique note about "common goals" and looking for financial backing, Bauer and Parmenter attached the note to the group's door along with a way to get in touch with them. The Arab group never responded.

Mathews was troubled by the distraction Rothschild's appearance caused among the men. He wanted to keep the focus on robbery. Assassinations would come later. Going from a porno store robbery to killing a Rothschild baron was too big a leap. They had to build a bigger war chest. Besides, they had no explosives and no time to concoct a plan on such short notice, Bob argued.

Pierce and some of the others held out for trying to kill Rothschild. Then Bauer began to change his mind about the robbery. Mathews was incensed by the split. Unable to reach agreement, the group returned to Metaline Falls on November 12 without having taken any action in Seattle.

Mathews figured it was time to turn to David Lane. The former Denver Klansman had been busy since the oath-taking setting up a counterfeiting operation. Lane quietly went to Aryan Nations to look over the press there. But he was also interested in how to disable telephone lines on a big scale. If the gang ever tried a big robbery, it would help to knock out alarm systems.

During a breakfast meeting at the Owl Café in Hayden Lake, Lane sat at a table in the rear dining room with Pastor Butler; Randy Evans, a Butler follower and Klansman from California; Roy Mansker, whose son Bob worked for the telephone company; and a man introduced to Lane as Peter Lawrence.

Lawrence actually was Peter Lake, a freelance writer from Marina Del Rey, California, who was infiltrating the radical right for a short-lived investigative magazine published by the pornographer Larry Flynt called *The Rebel*. In his hand, under the table while others sipped their coffee, was a pocket tape recorder.

"I need to know something about phone systems," Lane said, asking Mansker to write a short letter to his son in Weiser, Idaho. "You can't talk on the phone, there's no way."

"Well, you tell me what you want to know and I'll find out for you," Mansker replied. "If he knows it, he'll tell you."

"Good," Lane said. "I have to totally disable the phone system in a major metropolitan area for at least an hour."

"Uh huh," Mansker responded nonchalantly. "I think he can tell you how to do that." This conversation went on as a waitress approached to ask Lane if he wanted more coffee. Lane politely declined while Mansker continued: "Everything, one place you can blow it up in?"

"There's places where if you know where to go," Lane explained, spreading his arms, "there's a pit this big around with nothing but those cables." Lane wanted to know the location of one of the underground vaults the Bell companies use as junctions for major cables. Each cable carries 10,000 strands of wires. Knocking out one small pit can disrupt phone service for many days and prevent any phone-based alarm from functioning.

Lane wrote a word on a napkin, the name of a city that Peter Lake couldn't see. "Tell him I need to know for . . ." said Lane, handing the napkin to Mansker.

Experts believe terrorists would have no trouble wreaking havoc in America's major cities. The nation's utility lines are so poorly guarded that a gang with a minimal amount of reconnaissance could cause widespread chaos. Bombs or chemical weapons can be made at home with no greater difficulty than brewing bathtub gin. More than two thousand how-to manuals on weapons, bombs, and terrorist tactics are available in this country. Potent explosives in four or five strategic locations could black out the northeastern United States for weeks, conceivably for months—electricity, natural gas lines, communications.

GARY YARBROUGH'S PINK skin burned easily in the sun. His bushy hair flowed to the back of his head in great waves of red fire. A magnificent Smith Brothers beard bristled out several inches from his chin. Framing his thin-lipped mouth was a riverboat gambler's mustache, long and bushy. Yarbrough unconsciously rolled the ends between his thumb and fingers almost constantly. Built gangly as a walking stick, he looked like a skinny version of the cartoon character Yosemite Sam, which accounted for his nickname of Sam. He held odd jobs, once as a dishwasher at Schooney's truck stop on U.S. 95 in Athol just north of Hayden Lake. He also ran Butler's offset press.

Bob thought of recruiting Gary in his initial group. But Yarbrough had four daughters, his eldest very ill with kidney disease, and he was needed often at home. Besides, he was the best security Pastor Butler had, and Duey and Parmenter were concerned about Butler's safety. Someone might try to kill the pastor, as they had bombed his church in 1981. So Mathews figured Gary was needed in Idaho.

But in the print shop, Yarbrough might find time to slip on a few different plates for Lane's operation.

On November 24, 1983, after Aryan Nations' big Thanksgiving dinner, Mathews, Lane, and Yarbrough played chess in the office with some of the others from the compound. After checkmate, Mathews ordered the others out of the print shop. Yarbrough had agreed to run the press without telling Pastor Butler what was being produced.

The press, a metal crucifix glued to its side and a picture of Adolf Hitler adorning a nearby shelf, demanded Gary's full attention. So he was startled one night when he turned and found David Tate watching him intently. David, twenty-one, was a son of Charles and Betty Tate, faithful members of Butler's congregation. Despite the differences in age and experience, Yarbrough and Tate hit it off. Tate looked up to the older man, with his tatoos and prison record.

Tate moved from California as a boy with his parents to live near Butler in Careywood, north of Hayden Lake. He went to school with his brother and sister in a trailer behind the office on Butler's grounds. Butler's Aryan Academy was where white children learned the "four Rs": reading, 'riting, 'rithmetic, and race.

The boy grew up around weapons, not unusual at all in

that part of the country. David got used to carrying a handgun, the same as Gary who, despite his felony burglary conviction, often wore a gun in a holster.

Tate often carried a Bible as well as a gun. The Second Amendment was a nice backup, but Luke 22:36 provided all the justification a warrior for Christ needed to be armed: "He that hath no sword, let him sell his garment, and buy one."

The same New Testament would have provided wiser advice for Tate, who was headed for disaster when he handled those weapons: "Then said Jesus unto him, 'Put up again thy sword into its place; for all they that take the sword shall perish with the sword' " (Matthew 26:52).

Tate saw Yarbrough printing the phony $50 bills. Thus compromised, there was nothing to do but enlist the young man in the scheme. Tate watched the clean white paper whip through the press, which spat out $50 bills on the other side. It took about a week to make $200,000. But there was a problem.

The bills looked strangely blanched. To fix that, Mathews asked Loff to save his coffee grounds. Loff brought the grounds to the barracks and watched Mathews, Lane, and Kemp dip the sheets of fifties into a basin of green dye. Loff helped pin them up to dry on a rope strung across the upstairs room. They then rubbed the coffee grounds on the dry sheets to make them look more authentic. The bad ones were tossed into the wood stove and burned.

Counterfeiters don't ordinarily make fifties, since most of the popular places to pass bogus money don't take bills that high. The most frequently counterfeited bill is the twenty. It minimizes risk while maximizing profit. With a small purchase of a pack of cigarettes or newspaper, the return in real currency is tremendous.

Bob asked Ken Loff whether he would accept the responsibility of caring for the families of those who got into trouble, as they had stated in their oath.

"You know I won't do anything illegal, Bob," Ken told him.

"I won't ask you to, Ken," Bob replied, cognizant that Ken had already helped with the phony money. Ken also had helped one of the men already. Richie Kemp bought

a new Toyota Celica with $1,500 he earned at the Vaagen
Brothers sawmill in Ione. Loff co-signed the note for the
remainder. He was quite fond of Kemp.

After Mathews bought his new Chevy and financed it
through the dealer, Soderquist suggested he quit his job
at the cement plant to undergo the same hardship as his
unemployed kinsmen. It was a persuasive argument to
Bob. Besides, it would force him to advance on his plan
since he would need the money. Bob quit his job, hoping
the act would inspire the men.

After the dye session in the barracks, Lane hosted a
bill-cutting party. Pierce, Bauer, and Kemp attended.
When they were done, all but Kemp agreed to go on the
upcoming spending spree in the Yakima Valley.

Bob was preoccupied during much of this time because
of his dad's cancer. Johnny was admitted to Sacred Heart
Hospital in Spokane the day after his son returned from
the surreptitious trip to Seattle. Doctors told Una the
end was near. This time it would be impossible for her
spunky husband to fight it.

Bob and Debbie made several trips to visit Johnny, but
the cancer had weakened him and he was unable to carry
on long conversations. Johnny didn't have much to say to
his youngest son anyway. He glared at him with anger
and disappointment. He had learned in twenty years that
he couldn't win an argument with Robbie, but he had
hoped his influence was moderating. Now he was fearful.

Bob loved his dad more than he ever told him. But
even during the years when they had their truce in the
late 1970s, they weren't good at talking. Bob thought he
was providing the best future for his family. That Johnny
didn't see it that way caused friction and drove brother
Lee, once Bob's closest friend, away for good. Bob's
enthusiasm for the White American Bastion, which he
believed would save his family, actually was destroying it.

Johnny Mathews died on December 1, 1983. A hard-
nosed American patriot and onetime pursuer of equal
opportunity for minorities, he died the father of a man
whose ambition was to form a white resistance movement
to fight the government Johnny so staunchly supported.
He was his son's last mooring to normalcy.

The night Johnny died, Una walked over to her son's

house and found Bob crying on his back porch, under a soft light. "At least now," he said quietly, "I can get on with the rest of my life." The remark frightened Una.

In the barracks 20 yards away, Bob's pals were bundling up phony $50 bills.

THE REVOLUTION BEGAN on December 3, 1983. It was a bad day for the white guys.

Lane, Pierce, and Bauer left a day earlier to pass phony money in the Richland-Pasco-Kennewick area southwest of Spokane near the Oregon border. After a successful day, they spent the night near Yakima, where they passed $200 in a K-mart. Each purchase was a small one, breaking fifty after phony fifty.

On Saturday, December 3, the trio went through the Valley Mall in Union Gap, each taking a wing. Pierce considered himself a charmer and distracted clerks by keeping them talking. He was carrying a thick wad of $541 in good money by the time he got back to the center court. Then he saw Bauer nervously approaching.

"I'm being followed," Bauer whispered tersely. Looking past Bauer's right shoulder, Pierce saw a guard observing them. "I tried to pass a bill at Radio Shack, and now he's following me," Bauer said, then suddenly split through a side door. Pierce inherited his tail.

What do I do now, Pierce thought? He couldn't go back to the car because that would bring everything down. So he began walking through the mall, his pursuer following. Passing the Radio Shack, the guard told the clerk to call the police. Pierce ducked into an arcade, losing the guard for a short time. But when he dashed to a side exit, he was spotted again.

In the parking lot, Pierce saw Lane approaching. As they drew near, Pierce mouthed the words, "You don't know me." Lane walked on by like a stranger.

Pierce, still carrying shopping bags, went into a Skippers seafood restaurant nearby. Through the window he saw two police cars approaching. He slipped into the men's room and locked the door. Furiously, he began to empty his pockets of his remaining $50s, dumping them in the toilet and flushing several times. There soon was a knock on the bathroom door.

"Police. Open up, now!"

"Just a minute, I'm using the bathroom!" Pierce yelled. He didn't think he could get all the money to go down. After a final flush, he unlocked the door and was grabbed by an officer. They patted him down and found a boot knife. One cop poked his head into the toilet stall. There were still ripples in the water from the last flush. The money, however, had vanished.

But with Pierce's shopping bags and receipts, the police retraced his steps and gathered enough evidence to book him. Meanwhile, out in the parking lot, a passerby found the bag Bauer had discarded with some of the phony fifties. Not realizing they were counterfeit, he used them to pay off a debt to his mother-in-law.

That same night, in Kagel Canyon in Los Angeles's San Fernando Valley, Pastor Butler and fourteen others were arrested after lighting three crosses at a Klan rally.

Butler was wearing bright red robes and hood, courtesy of Shirley Silva, the wife of the rally host, Frank Silva, Exalted Cyclops of the New Order Knights of the Ku Klux Klan. As a police helicopter whirred overhead, Butler flicked his Bic and was promptly arrested. Also arrested was Tom Metzger, a former Klansman who once ran for Congress in San Diego County. Silva and his friend Randy Evans, both members of Aryan Nations as well as the Klan, were arrested too.

Up in the quiet of Metaline Falls, Mathews was still grieving for his dad when he heard about Pierce's arrest, then the cross-lighting arrests. In just three days his world had crashed around him. Around 11 P.M., Bob called his National Alliance friend Tom Martinez. It was 2 A.M. in Philadelphia.

"Tom! This is Bob Mathews!" he yelled into the phone as Martinez tried to shake himself awake. "Do you know Dale Strange?"

"Yeah, Bob, I know Dale," Tom replied. Strange was a former law officer convicted of marijuana possession in 1980 in Philadelphia. He had established an Identity church near Williamsport, Pennsylvania, in 1979.

"Call Dale and tell him the revolution has begun!" Mathews demanded.

*   *   *

BRUCE PIERCE WAS taken to an interrogation room in Yakima, where he met a Secret Service agent from Spokane. Pierce faced charges of passing counterfeit money and carrying a concealed weapon. He had made no statement so far and was determined to give no leads. But he inadvertently dropped one.

"Mr. Pierce? I'm with the Secret Service, my name's Dennis Rosedahl," the investigator said as he entered the room.

"Rosedahl. Rosedahl," Pierce mused momentarily. "Hmm, sounds Jewish."

The agent sized up Pierce and concluded: "I'll bet you're from Hayden Lake."

Rosedahl couldn't have said that just a year earlier. At that time, Pierce had never heard of Identity, Aryan Nations, or the Jewish conspiracy for world domination. At twenty-eight, he was an underemployed white man eking out a subsistence-level living with his wife, Julie, and three children. They lived in a ramshackle wooden cabin on a mountain lot outside Plains, Montana, population 1,100.

His wife was on welfare. Bruce worked at odd jobs and supplemented that income with food stamps. The trailer had only a 12-volt electrical supply and a gravity water system from an outside reservoir that froze in the deep, cold Montana winter.

Pierce could not have guessed that in just a year he would go from no racial awareness at all to the top lieutenant in Mathews's racist underground. Of course, he had imagined more glamour to it than flushing funny money down the john at a suburban fast-food restaurant.

Bruce Carroll Pierce was the antithesis of Bob Mathews. While Bob grew up steeping himself in the conservative movement, the radical fringe, and finally his paramilitary Sons of Liberty, Pierce grew up in the prosaic rural atmosphere outside Frankfort, Kentucky. His childhood was about as unremarkable as Bob's was frantic.

Pierce was born May 14, 1954, the last child of Eugene and Lucilla Pierce. He had a sister and three brothers, all much older than he. His first memory of meeting his sister, twenty years older, was that he shook her hand.

Pierce's ancestors settled in the Frankfort–Lexington

area around 1800 and owned land west of Frankfort. His grandfather and uncle lived up Pierces Lane from him. The road that led into town reminded Bruce of something out of Edgar Allan Poe, how it wound through dark tunnels of hardwood trees, several miles from Daniel Boone's grave. It was called Devils Hollow Road.

As a youngster, Bruce spent a lot of time alone. With few neighbors out in the country, he amused himself exploring the woods and had several vantage spots from which he could look down on the small capital city and the Kentucky River.

He longed for the day he'd be able to turn some of those magnificent trees into beautiful pieces of furniture, as his dad did in his carpentry shop. Eugene Pierce's cherry, walnut, and maple pieces were so well crafted that his customers included Kentucky governors and politicians. His older brothers learned the trade before him. Bruce awakened mornings to the sounds of his dad's planer rasping across a board in the shop 200 feet down the hill.

But at age thirteen, before Bruce was old enough to apprentice, a fire set by an arsonist destroyed the shop. Eugene Pierce, who had arterial sclerosis, didn't rebuild it. By then, he could afford to take it easy.

Because of marital problems between his parents, Bruce moved to Atlanta and lived with his brother Greg during his freshman year at Eastpoint High School. He moved back the next year when his parents paid extra for him to go to Frankfort High in the city rather than the county school. The basketball coach recruited Bruce, who was topping out at 6-foot-2.

If there were any Jewish students at school, it would have been news to Bruce. He didn't even know what a Jew was. There were blacks on the basketball team, and he never gave them a second thought. Once a pretty black girl asked him for a date, but he declined simply because he was dating someone else. On the playground, Bruce readily joined pickup games of basketball with blacks. Race to Bruce Pierce simply was something incidental.

It took quite a few dates before Bruce and his first serious girlfriend, Elizabeth Scott, made love. But once started, it wasn't long at all before "Scotty" became pregnant. They married on April 1, 1972, and continued going to school since Bruce had only a few months to graduation. Their classmates remained unaware they were husband and wife or that Scotty was having a baby.

At the same time, Bruce's parents were splitting after thirty-seven years of marriage. Amid the tension at home, Bruce and his mom had a blowup over his personal affairs. One thing Bruce never tolerated was someone butting into his business. He dropped out of school right before graduation, packed his new wife and their few belongings into the orange Karmann-Ghia his dad had bought him, and drove to Atlanta for a tearful reunion with brother Greg.

The baby, named Jeremy, was born in October. Bruce supported his small family working for his oldest brother's carpentry shop. He also worked in circulation at the *Atlanta Constitution*. He and Scotty earned their diplomas at night going to Brown High School.

In 1973, they moved back to Frankfort. For a while Bruce commuted to Atlanta to work. It was an eight-hour, 400-mile drive, and racing his Karmann-Ghia over the Appalachians every weekend grew very tiring. He got a job at a convenience store in Frankfort while he looked for better work at home.

He found it as a circulation district manager at the *Lexington Herald Leader,* an ideal job because he could take Jeremy along. Scotty, meanwhile, found work with the state. Pierce worked for the newspaper for five years, winning several commendations on the job. But more and more responsibilities were placed on the district managers, and Bruce didn't like it. In 1979, he left in disgust.

By then a new aspiration was consuming him. It was the West.

Pierce dreamed of living in the wide-open expanses of rugged mountains, canyons, plains, and deserts of the West. He viewed the crowded East as stifling. By contrast, the West is awesome, at times overwhelming, in its openness.

He had seen this during a camping trip to Colorado in 1978. Pierce and a friend went backpacking in Rocky Mountain National Park, west of Estes Park. Pierce was blown away by the big sky, the clean air and the grandeur of the Rockies' jagged gray peaks. Once he returned to Kentucky, he began to read everything he could about the West—demographic studies, travelogues, even Western fiction.

Bruce Pierce was not religious at all at this point in his life. He was, in fact, a philanderer or, as he put it years later, "an asshole." He had several affairs, and Scotty knew it. He disliked preachers. Once when he was a teen, a preacher put him on the spot in public by asking, "Bruce, when are you going to accept Jesus as your personal saviour?" Embarrassed, Bruce turned and left. They wanted commitment from him, and he was of no mind to give it. He was rather aimless until his Western dream began to change that.

He talked his brother Greg, who was married and had six children, into moving with him. Unfortunately, he couldn't talk Scotty into it. She didn't want to leave the civility of the Bluegrass State for the life of a pioneer woman in some remote box canyon in Montana. On a humid day in June 1979, with a U-Haul trailer out front of their house, Bruce and Scotty had a fight that ended with Scotty forswearing any move to Missoula, Montana, the town Bruce had selected.

Greg drove on to Missoula while Bruce remained in Frankfort for six weeks, trying to reconcile with Scotty. But by August divorce papers were filed, and Bruce followed Greg to Montana.

Missoula is a university town of 33,000 snuggled in a brown valley at the edge of the Sapphire Mountains' sparsely vegetated hills, where the Bitterroot River flows into the Clark Fork. Greg found a house at 123 Saranac Street and invited Bruce to live with him. Bruce quickly found work at a Western wear store in Trumpers Plaza. While driving home one evening in his Land Cruiser, a pretty young woman in a red Peugeot sped by and waved at him. He didn't know her, but he sure wanted to meet her. When he arrived home for dinner, he glanced out a picture window and was startled to see the same woman in the yard next door. Pierce scrambled outside to get her attention, and they talked for hours.

She was Julie Wilson, a teen mother going through a

divorce and living with her mother next door. They began to date, and by early 1980 their relationship had grown to the point where they moved in together with Jeremy, who had come to visit his dad and stayed, and Julie's infant daughter, Jasmine. Then in 1981, in the midst of a custody battle with Scotty over Jeremy, Bruce's lawyer told him it would look better to the judge if he were married. So Bruce and Julie visited a justice of the peace in Missoula.

Bruce had always considered himself a good father and, after a tug of war over Jeremy, he ended up with custody. But his son was already back in Kentucky with Scotty. Eventually Bruce returned secretly to Frankfort and, posing as a family friend, spirited his son out of elementary school and whisked him across the border to Cincinnati. Soon they were on a bus bound for Montana.

Bruce had different jobs on and off. Once he laid carpet for a man who had moved from Denver and who told him that the city had become an unpleasant place to live, beset with gangs and racial problems. But talk of race breezed right by Bruce. He had more immediate concerns, like feeding his family.

Bruce wasn't exactly happy with how his life was turning out. It occurred to him that he had left behind a rather easy life in Frankfort. He certainly had more friends and more possessions back in Kentucky. He reveled in materialism, enjoyed soft rock, and occasionally smoked marijuana. He yearned for new cars and nice clothes. It was almost too important to him. But now he was stuck in a small trailer, with little money, a new wife, and another man's daughter.

There was one advantage that offset the hardships. Bruce was now in the West, where he felt more self-reliant and less wrapped up in the rat race. All of his senses were heightened by the experience. Once in a mountain canyon, he stood still because of the unreal quiet and heard something he'd never heard before—a bird in flight, high up in the blue Montana sky. It was as close to a religious experience as he'd ever had.

In the fall of 1981, Bruce and Julie found land and a broken-down cabin in Plains. Bruce was doing odd jobs at the time, and Julie collected $110 a month welfare.

They survived with the help of food stamps. On November 22, 1982, his second child, a daughter, was born. They named her Kristi.

Such was the state of Bruce Pierce's life in the fall of 1982, when a completely fortuitous occurrence changed it forever.

Jeremy was going to school in Thompson Falls, about 25 miles down Clark Fork from Plains. The high school was connected to the elementary, and Bruce talked the principal into letting him work out on the weight machine while he waited to pick up his son. On a chilly November afternoon, while Bruce was changing in the locker room before working out, a group of students were arguing nearby.

The quarrel was about the Nazi Holocaust. Four youths were ganging up on a boy who maintained the Holocaust was a hoax. Pierce became aggravated because the group was teasing the classmate.

"Hey, over there!" Pierce yelled, anxious to restore peace. "Knock it off and let the boy finish talking, willya? Everybody's got a right to talk."

The adult's voice startled the youths, and they quickly turned and walked away. Dropping it from his mind, Bruce walked into the weight room. A few minutes later the boy who had been teased approached to thank him for intervening. He introduced himself as Mike Butler. Then he began to preach again.

"Everybody just accepts what the Jews say about the Holocaust," the boy preached. "There couldn't have been six million Jews killed by the Nazis, it just doesn't add up." As the boy went on, Pierce became embarrassed. He had never given much thought to Jews, Hitler, or the Holocaust. He just wanted the boy to go away. Then a week later, the boy returned to the gym with a stocky fellow wearing a full beard, whom he introduced as his dad, Jefferson Dwayne Butler.

"I wanted to thank you for sticking up for Mike the other day," Dwayne said to Bruce. "It's not often someone defends our right to express our beliefs."

The older Butler then treated Pierce to the Christian Identity philosophy and finished by inviting Bruce and his family to visit his house.

The Butlers—no relation to Pastor Butler, although they subscribed to the Aryan Nations philosophy—lived about 8 miles from Pierce toward Thompson Falls. The family proved to be friendly and pleasant, extremely helpful, offering but never forcing their views on their visitors. Their demeanor was quite at odds with Bruce's notion of typical right-wingers.

"Now don't get mad, Dwayne," Bruce said after a few weeks of socializing, "but y'all have been so nice to us, I kind of think it's all a put-on."

Butler laughed. "No, I just treat people the way I want to be treated."

By early 1983, Bruce decided to take a closer look at the things Dwayne said about the Bible, racial pride, and the lost tribes of Israel. He was impressed when he found some of the details Butler told him were indeed in library books. They started Bible study together with one of Dwayne's neighbors, Jim Tappeny. One day Bruce stopped to make an observation.

"You know, Dwayne, I think I got a problem here. The Bible says the meek shall inherit the earth. Well, I'm not meek at all," Pierce chortled.

"You misunderstand, friend," replied Dwayne. "Yahweh doesn't want you to let others step all over you. That's not what meek is. Meek is when you abandon your own desires and do what Yahweh wants, when you seek His will and obey."

In March 1983, Tappeny invited Pierce to Aryan Nations and introduced him to Pastor Butler. Bruce immediately took a liking to the people at the church, the Tates, Dan Bauer, and Corky Witherwax. Gary Yarbrough was aloof at first but soon became friendly. These people extended more care and concern to Bruce than he'd felt in years. He thought Richard Butler was a wise man, although a little rambling and verbose. "Must be a trait of the Butlers," he joked to himself.

He returned with Julie several times and soon was comfortable enough to wear the blue uniform of an Aryan Nations security guard.

One morning Julie revealed something that reinforced Bruce's beliefs. She had a vivid dream the night before and got a message that everything they were learning was right. The white racism, the anti-Jew preaching of Butler, the Identity message of salvation for the true Israel, the seed of Isaac, the white race—it was all true. Bruce felt a chill when Julie told him of the dream.

Bruce was summoned East in August to help with another brother's contracting business in Toledo while his brother had surgery. Bruce sold his cabin and land in Montana for $5,000 and went to Toledo. While there, he paid four visits to Bob Miles's farm in Cohoctah, Michigan, a two-hour drive north.

Pierce had met Miles at the Aryan World Congress and was heartily welcomed by the racist leader. Miles was a down-to-earth, jovial fellow who believed that if he had it, it was yours as well. Miles's religion, dualism, was different from Butler's. Miles believed Yahweh and Satan are equal forces doing battle for souls on earth. Bruce learned a lot about the racist movement from Miles.

Returning to Idaho in September, Bruce moved into a cabin north of Hayden Lake and enrolled Jeremy in Butler's Aryan Academy. Enthusiastic about everything he'd learned in nine months, he approached Jim Tappeny, fired up for action.

"Let's do something, Jim!" Bruce said. "Let's fund ourselves, get things going, and keep ourselves free!" Tappeny backed away from the idea.

But later Dan Bauer suggested Pierce should visit Bob Mathews if he wanted action.

Mommy, is Bruce dead?" stepdaughter Jasmine asked her mother when Pierce was stuck in the Yakima jail. He wasn't dead, but he felt like it. Kristi was just a year old, it was three weeks to Christmas, and the judge ordered Pierce held on $25,000 bail. They had nowhere near that much money.

Bob Mathews left for Denver with David Lane the day after Pierce's arrest. Lane thought he could get a deal on a printing press so they wouldn't have to sneak into Aryan Nations. Coming through Wyoming, Lane wanted to spend the night at a friend's place in Laramie. On December 5, just as darkness descended over the dusty high plains town, they pulled into a small trailer park.

Zillah Craig, twenty-seven, still dressed in her nurse's

uniform and student smock, was preparing supper at her stove for her two young boys when there was a knock on her trailer door. She answered to see Lane standing on the stoop with another man behind him on the gravel driveway.

"Hi, David, come on in!" she said with delight. She had met Lane at the Church of Christ in Laporte, Colorado, an Identity congregation about an hour's drive from Laramie down U.S. 287 near the mouth of the Cache la Poudre Canyon.

Bob looked closely at Zillah for a moment before it came to him: She was the pretty, long-haired brunette he had seen near the lilacs at the Aryan Congress in July. Bob had never seen anyone as pretty before. Zillah had soft features and blue eyes that, when they glanced at Bob, forced him quickly to turn away.

He didn't make the same impression on Zillah, who found him peculiarly quiet and shy. She didn't find him particularly handsome either.

After Zillah prepared a quick meal for the men, David left to visit another friend, Kathy Kilty, at her apartment about a block away. Kilty had accompanied David, Zillah, and another man to the Aryan Congress. After David left, Zillah turned to Bob. "I've got to study for a nursing test," she said. "Would you mind helping me with the Latin?"

Mathews smiled, glanced around the kitchen, then said, "I'm not much good at Latin, but I'll try." She handed Bob the book and he started off well, but became barely audible when he came to the Latin terms for "testicle" and "vagina." How quaint, Zillah thought. Before long, he put the book aside and talked.

"I saw you at the Aryan Congress in Hayden Lake," he said.

Zillah studied him but couldn't distinguish him from among the throng. As they talked about the congress, Bob became more animated.

"They talked of a war to make a white nation, but that's all it was, talk," Bob said. "I'm through talking. I've formed a group that'll do more than talk."

Zillah remembered David telling her about a meeting with some men who held hands in a circle and took an oath while standing over a baby. He wouldn't tell her any more. Suddenly, it struck her that this shy man who could barely utter normal anatomical words was the man who was supposed to lead them to a new nation. He certainly didn't impress Zillah as a leader. He had the disheartened tone of a man near rock bottom.

He told Zillah of his father's death, of Pierce's arrest and the exorbitant bail, and about Pastor Butler's being apprehended in Los Angeles.

Bob told her he was a believer in Identity and was appalled Butler was treated so rudely in Los Angeles. Actually, Mathews was an Odinist, which he didn't admit to Zillah until much later. Lane had warned him that Zillah was an Identity Christian, so he could speak her language.

"I've got to do something!" he exploded. "I can't just sit by and let them take us down. The revolution has begun!"

It was then, feeling the fervor of his beliefs, that Zillah was swept into the hypnotic fury of his eyes and began to sense the sway he held over the minds of his men. She decided to offer him a lock of her hair to carry into battle—unless, of course, he had a wife. She waited for an opening.

"So, Bob, are you married?" she finally gathered nerve to ask.

Bob stopped short in a thought, and a sudden calm came over him. As the fire diminished, a smile crept into his eyes. "No. No, I'm not married," he replied.

Walking to the kitchen cupboard, Zillah took out a pair of scissors and snipped a lock of her hair. She found a red ribbon and tied it around the lock.

"The red is a symbol of our blood," she said. "Take this lock with you so you'll know there is a white woman praying for your success."

It was a bit melodramatic, but she was still caught up in the intensity of the Aryan Congress. Bob said nothing, but she could tell by his look that he was moved. Before the men left for Denver the next day, Zillah told Bob he was welcome to stop any time. He thanked her, pocketed the lock of hair, and left.

When Bob got back to the Northwest, he called a

meeting at the Bigfoot Tavern in Spokane to try to keep
the men together. Parmenter was gone, trying to patch
up his marriage with Janice. Soderquist went back to
California for Christmas and didn't know when, or
whether, he'd be back. Lane left the area because of the
counterfeiting. Only Loff, Bauer, Duey, and Kemp showed
up at the Bigfoot to meet Bob. They were upset that
Pierce was calling people from jail, thus linking them as
known associates of a counterfeiter. They were becoming
disenchanted with the entire notion of Bob's "action
group."

But Bob's concern was getting Bruce out, and with the
bail so high, he might even try to break into the jail to
free him. But the others were noncommittal. In the end,
Duey went back to Aryan Nations and Bauer dropped
out. Only Mathews, Kemp, and Loff, the trio from the
Pend Oreille Valley, agreed to stick together.

Bob passed through Laramie several times, staying in
Zillah's trailer. The top half of her couch came off to
make a bed on the floor. But the first few times he slept
over, Bob kept to himself. He soon admitted to Zillah he
was married, but said Debbie could not have children
and he no longer loved her as a wife. He was attracted to
Zillah, but he was too shy to suggest sex.

In talking about his plans for a white underground, he
told Zillah he had robbed a shoe store in Spokane, so he
knew he could do it alone. Now, to get the money for
Bruce's bail, he told her, he was going to rob a bank.

On the night of December 14, Bob made his first move
toward Zillah. He was very nervous about the coming
bank robbery, he told her. "I may never see you again,
Zillah," Bob said. "But this is something I have to do. I
hope to come back to you afterward."

"I understand, Bob. I'll be praying for you," she replied.

"Can I ask you for one last favor?" Bob said as they
settled into the makeshift bed on the floor.

"Sure you can," Zillah answered, thinking he wanted
to make love.

"Can I hold you close to me through the night?" he
asked.

Zillah was startled by the meager request. They slept

that way on the floor that night, his arms around her, not making love but just lying still.

On December 17, Ken Loff saw his best friend driving up to his farm in Ione. Bob was extremely nervous and wanted to see Ken in the basement.

"I'm letting Bruce down, I'm letting everyone down," Bob said, his voice quivering. "I can't let all this go down the toilet now." Ken noticed Bob was white as a sheet, as though his blood had drained.

"What are you thinking of doing, Bob?" Ken asked, afraid of the answer.

"I have to help Bruce," Bob replied. "You may never see me again. If you don't, please see after Debbie and Clint for me."

"Bob, I'm afraid you'll be in too much danger," Ken said.

"Fearlessness is better than a faint heart," Bob replied. "The length of my life and the date of my death were fated a long time ago."

With that, Bob left Ione and headed west over the back roads to Seattle. His target was a bank he had spotted during the abortive November trip. On the way, he stopped in Colville to mail a letter he had just written to Zillah.

When we first started in the direction we are now going [he wrote of his group], we had a large number of men. When it became obvious that we were going to do more than just talk, most of the men started backing out and turning their backs to those of us who have retained our manhood and our Aryan pride. So be it!

Monday afternoon will bring either victory or my death. Sometimes, in the dark hours of the night, I wish I was a normal man so I could enjoy life unhindered. But I know what future awaits our children unless I stand up like a man and fight. If enough of us stand up and fight then your two fine sons will have the future they deserve. They will be able to stand up and say, "I am white, I am proud and I am free," and no Jew or mudman will dare stand against them.

*Outside of my heart, only God knows how much I
miss you.*

"HI! MAY I HELP you?" The nameplate at the teller's
cage identified the woman with the chipper voice as
Tammie. She had just opened her station at the Innis
Arden branch of City Bank, north of Seattle near the
Snohomish County line. Mathews smiled and handed
Tammie a plastic bag.

"You're being robbed," he said calmly. "Put the money
in the bag."

Without a word, Tammie complied. But she wasn't so
nervous that she forgot her training. While stuffing bundles of cash into the bag, she activated the special bundle
with an exploding dye pack that tellers keep handy, and
put it in the bag with the rest of the money. Mathews
stepped back and walked toward the area where the
drive-up teller worked. Three other women were in the
bank.

"Everybody, this bank is being robbed! Nobody move."
He pulled back his sleeveless jacket to expose a gun
tucked into his belt. "I don't want to hurt anyone. I just
want the money."

After taking more cash from the drive-up window cage,
Mathews ordered the women into the vault. "I'm sorry to
be doing this, but I need this money for a sick child,"
Mathews said. "Merry Christmas." He shut the vault
door on them.

Tammie waited a short time before opening the vault.
The last rule when a teller gives out a dye pack is to lock
the front door as soon as the robber leaves. But when she
poked her head out, the man still was there.

"Get back in there!" he ordered. She ducked inside.

Tammie counted another thirty seconds, then ran for
the keys to lock the doors as quickly as she could. She
pressed her face against the glass to see where the man
had fled. It was snowing heavily, unusual for the Puget
Sound area. Suddenly to her left, Tammie saw a puff of
red near the corner of the parking lot.

The blast knocked Mathews on his rear end in a cloud
of dye. Stunned for a moment, he then made a not-so-
clean getaway.

* * *

"WHEN YOUR ASS is on fire, you don't run," Bruce Pierce thought during those long days in his jail cell. He still was angry at Bauer for sticking him with the tail at the mall. "You roll to put out the fire. You stay calm and don't panic."

While he languished, Loff and Kemp tried to help Julie with food and firewood when both ran low at the cabin. Kemp donated his $500 paycheck for Julie to hire a lawyer. But it was Julie's persistence that eventually freed her husband on bond. She set up a conference call with the judge and the prosecutor during Christmas week, and negotiated the bail down from $25,000 to $2,500.

Bruce's brother Greg scraped together the $250 surety in Missoula and posted it at the federal courthouse there. On December 23, Bruce stepped out into the bitter deep-freeze of winter's first cold snap. The open landscape around Yakima was hard as permafrost. The Northwest's interior was locked in an Arctic layer of air. Pierce was 250 miles from home and penniless.

Out at a freeway rest stop, Pierce saw truckers stoking small fires underneath their tractors to keep the engine oil circulating. He found a driver headed for Spokane who agreed to give him a ride. The driver bent Pierce's ear clear from Ellensburg to Spokane about the state of the trucking industry.

"We can't make a living no more in this business, because of them damn Jew middlemen," the driver said. "They're taking over the whole industry."

Pierce kept fairly quiet during the long ride, so the driver never knew how receptive his hitchhiker was to the remarks. Hearing such unsolicited commentary from the "sheeple" always helped to strengthen Pierce's commitment.

Julie drove into Spokane to fetch her husband. They spent that night in the city and did some shopping the next day, Christmas Eve. On the way home, they stopped at the Yarbroughs' house, where Gary and Betty were watching their three children. Then came the surprise. When Bruce walked into his house for the first time in almost a month, he laid eyes on the largest Christmas tree he'd ever seen. Presents were arranged around it. It had been set up by Loff and Kemp. Pierce was so touched, he cried when he saw it.

Mathews showed up on Zillah Craig's trailer stoop in Laramie right before Christmas, holding a Halloween candy bag filled with $25,952 in loot. Much of it was splattered with blood-red dye. Bob wanted her to help clean the bills.

"Yahweh was with me! I could feel Him!" Bob told Zillah excitedly. "It hardly ever snows in Seattle, but while I was in the bank, it started to snow and it covered my tracks! I know now for sure we are doing Yahweh's will!" Zillah didn't doubt for a moment that what had happened truly was a miracle.

They worked with turpentine and paint thinner, but the money still looked red. They bought some Zip Strip paint remover, which seemed to work. Some of the money was ruined, but a substantial portion was passable. Unfortunately, it retained a bluish tint and looked as if it had been laundered a dozen times. They jokingly called the money "bluebacks."

As they worked, Bob talked about the battles ahead. Zillah began to see Bob in a new light. She could still hear echoes of the martial speeches at the Aryan Congress. It had made a deep impression on her. She knew her Bible and normally abhorred stealing and shooting. But then, the Bible also foretold the coming of the millennium and the great struggle prior to Christ's earthly rule. A large number of people believed they were living in such times.

Then into her life comes this intrepid man weaving his tales of revolution. The Bible talks about a war, and maybe this is it, Zillah thought. Maybe now it really was the time. And while so-called Christians hid their lamps under bushel baskets, Identity was holding them up for the Lord to see. Yet she was deeply troubled by the idea of killing and told Bob so. They had their first argument.

"We are commanded by God to struggle to the death with His enemies," Bob explained. "If that means killing, then my sword is in the hands of the Lord."

"In the Bible, God says, 'Thou shalt not kill,'" Zillah argued.

"He also says, 'Bring my enemies before me and slay

them,' " Bob shot back. If need be, he could match her verse for verse. "They are the enemies of our race—Jews, mud people and white traitors."

Zillah didn't win the argument, just as Johnny Mathews never could.

SHORTLY AFTER NEW YEAR'S DAY 1984, Bob flew to Philadelphia to visit Tom Martinez. Tom was thrilled that his friend was coming and planned to show him around the City of Brotherly Love. The Liberty Bell, Independence Hall, and other Revolutionary era sites should be on the itinerary of white Christian patriots who believe the United States was divinely ordained.

But Bob wasn't interested in the sights. He called the city "Filthydelphia." It was a cesspool as far as he was concerned. He wanted Tom to move out to the White American Bastion, away from the bad influences of the city.

Martinez lived in a house on Weikel Street in the city's white working-class neighborhood of Kensington. The Frankford Avenue Elevated ran nearby. About a mile and a half away was a big sewage treatment plant on a bow in the Delaware River called Point No Point, near the mouth of Frankford Creek. It was a teeming enclave of lower-to-middle-class whites in a city that is half black.

Tom had quit high school in the eleventh grade, and he blamed it on blacks. With forced busing for integration, the complexion of Edison High School changed drastically. One day, a boy with whom Tom played hockey was killed by a black youth in his class. Then Tom got threats. He dropped out in fear for his life.

After his introduction to the Ku Klux Klan through a television talk show in 1976, Martinez joined the Knights of the KKK in Philadelphia. He was twenty-one. In 1980, tiring of the Klan, he joined the National Alliance.

Martinez was one of William Pierce's best money-raisers. He sold National Alliance literature on street corners and sent up to $150 a week to Arlington. He lived and breathed racism, an embittered man who thought he got his janitor's job with the Philadelphia Housing Authority only because of his Hispanic name.

His burnout in the movement began in the summer of

1983. He and a friend, Howard Brown, were in a restaurant on the way back to the city from some National Alliance activity. Brown used the term "nigger" in conversation, and a woman in the next booth took offense. A ruckus started and the township police charged Martinez and Brown with creating a disturbance. Each was fined $354.

Tom was hard up for cash. The house, which he recently had bought, had rotting beams that needed to be replaced. So he asked William Pierce to pay the fine, since he had been on "company" business.

The National Alliance leader refused, and Tom was insulted. He had sent the group thousands of dollars, and it wouldn't come through for him when he needed it. Tom went to the convention in September, but within two months he quit.

Bob was disappointed that Tom had quit. Bob's enthusiasm was so high, Tom just never clearly explained to his friend that he was simply burned out. Instead, he listened to Bob's ramblings about a great warrior named Carlos.

"Carlos is going to be a big help to the white movement," Mathews said.

"Is he a Latin?" Martinez asked.

"No, Tom!" Bob laughed with that adolescent voice of his. "Carlos is a great Aryan warrior! He is going to help us by all means necessary." While playing with Tom's son and daughter, Bob was feeling Tom out about bank robberies.

About two weeks after that first short visit, Mathews returned unannounced to Philadelphia with David Lane, this time by car, and knocked on Tom's door. They had sleeping bags and wondered if they could crash on his living room floor.

This time, Tom tried to tell his friend that he was completely disenchanted with the racist movement. He had met a number of Jews and blacks in his trips around town and was discovering that there is good and bad among all races.

Bob didn't want to hear any of it. He just wanted to talk about Carlos the warrior, and getting Tom to help. They sat down on the living room couch for a discussion.

"Tom, you're very good at passing out literature, you're the best there is!" Bob said. "And we can get you all the literature you can handle."

"Well, sure, I'll pass literature, Bob, but I don't want to join no groups," Tom replied. "I'm through with joining groups."

"That's great!" Bob said, filled with that fervor he got when he was at his persuasive best. He was a master at switching channels, tuning out disagreement until he hit the right frequency to reach people. "There's something else I want to tell you," he went on, having hooked his friend. "Remember Carlos, the warrior I told you about? Do you know who he is?"

"No, Bob, how would I know?" said Tom, becoming nervous.

Bob sat back so his friend could take this in. Then he pointed at himself with both thumbs and said with pride: "Me Carlos!"

Tom was dumbfounded. His friend, a bank robber! Bob told him about Innis Arden, the dye bomb, and the Zip Strip. Then Bob opened a bag, showed him the "bluebacks," and asked him to help pass them. Tom, thinking of his rotted beams, the cast on his leg from an on-the-job injury, the late disability checks, and, frankly, the entire deadend course of his life, gave in to greed.

Martinez, hobbling on crutches, went with Mathews and Lane around the stores in Philadelphia, exchanging the hot money for cooler cash. Because of the amount, Martinez got one of his friends, George Zaengle, to help.

Mathews watched intently. Perhaps his group had a chance at resurrection.

WITH MATHEWS GONE so much, the rumor mill at Aryan Nations worked overtime. Dan Bauer told the folk about the surreptitious use of their press, and the men who had joined Mathews's faltering group were being ostracized after Pierce's arrest.

But Pierce and Yarbrough felt they had to continue preparing for revolution. Electronics, Pierce thought— ZOG's got it and we don't. Making a list of gear they needed, such as police scanners, bug detectors, and portable computers, they robbed Radio Shacks around the

Spokane area for about $10,000 worth of equipment. Soon their car trunks were filled with scanners, telephone equipment, and lap-top computers. Then they targeted cash.

Yarbrough knew that each Monday, someone from Schooney's truck stop took the weekend's cash deposit, up to $8,000 in a zipper bag, through the parking lot on the way to the bank. Gary used to wash dishes at Schooney's in Athol, about 10 miles north of Aryan Nations on the Kootenai–Bonner county line.

It was an extremely cold Monday morning, continuing the same cold snap that had covered the area since Bruce left the jail. Bruce loitered by Schooney's dumpster. When passersby asked what he was doing, he said he was looking for lettuce for his rabbits. Gary, whose build would be recognizable even through his layers of clothing, stayed in the woods behind the restaurant, holding a rifle.

Finally, a man with the money pouch emerged and walked across the parking lot. Bruce, coming at an angle, intercepted him from behind, cuffed him across the head, grabbed the pouch, then made a beeline for the woods. Gary's job was to fire warning shots at anyone who might try to give chase. Since Bruce heard no shots as he huffed and puffed down a wooded trail with the money, he assumed he was in the clear. Suddenly he heard a man's voice behind him.

"You ain't gonna make it, dude!" a man who was chasing Bruce said.

Bruce was chilled with dread. The man's steady voice indicated he wasn't even winded, while Bruce was ready to drop. Where the hell was Yarbrough?

During the long wait, Gary had gone over the ridge to check his car. When he returned, he saw Bruce running down the trail with the man in pursuit. Bruce, his voice quivering, yelled: "Be-hi-i-nd me-e-e-e!" Gary squeezed off several shots high over their heads, bringing the man to a sudden halt, and they got away.

Yarbrough quickly fell under suspicion. Undersheriff Larry Broadbent's deputies headed straight for Aryan Nations to investigate. They were met at the entry gate by Corky Witherwax, the security chief, who had strolled down the hill from the compound when he saw the police car. Pierce and Yarbrough followed, trudging through the knee-deep snow down to the gatehouse.

"Hello, Corky," one deputy said, extending his hand to the ex-cop. "Schooney's was robbed the other day. We're looking for two men. Don't know about the one that hid in the woods, but the one who grabbed the cash was kind of a tall guy, stocky build. Had a down jacket on. Any idea who it might be?"

Corky sensed a bad situation. Slowly he turned to glance squarely at Pierce, and the deputies' eyes followed. Bruce nervously unzipped his down jacket and dropped his hands at his side, then realized the deputies might think he was going for a gun. The deputies stepped back, and there was a tense silence.

Then Corky turned and grinned, telling the deputies he was sorry, but he couldn't think of anything that would help them. As the patrol car backed down the long drive, Bruce and Gary figured the cops knew but just couldn't prove it.

Still, the folks at Aryan Nations were getting nervous about the pair. Corky suspended Yarbrough for misusing the compound's press, and that led Tom Bentley, principal of the Aryan Academy, to write to Yarbrough. "Due to your suspension, according to the rules and regulations outlined by Aryan Nations Academy," Bentley wrote in a letter dated January 27, 1984, "we must ask that you keep Annette and Spring Yarbrough home."

There was also talk of expelling Jeremy, but Pierce, extremely angry, took his son out instead. When Pastor Butler returned from a trip East and learned about all this, Pierce and Yarbrough went to see him.

They met in a cabin near the gatehouse at Aryan Nations. Bentley, a middle-aged racist who had come a year earlier from the Corning, New York area, was living there at Butler's hospitality. Butler excoriated Pierce and Yarbrough for using his press to counterfeit money. "Why are you doing this?" he demanded of them.

"Hold it there, pastor!" Pierce commanded, causing Butler to step back in bewilderment. "We're all building the same house. It's just that you have one function and we have another." Dick Butler was not used to being confronted by his people. Pierce's behavior surprised him.

Butler sensed that his hold was not powerful enough, not measured against what Bob Mathews offered.

Pierce and Yarbrough next graduated to banks. After casing the Washington Mutual Savings Bank at East 11205 Sprague in Spokane, a few miles from World Wide Video, they figured it would be as easy as their other crimes had been.

Shortly before 4 P.M. on January 30, they dropped a brown package at the door of Two Swabbies, a clothing outlet near World Wide. Then they went to a Mr. Steak restaurant next to the bank. From there they phoned Two Swabbies and told them a bomb was about to go off. The call drew the available police units in the east valley area to Two Swabbies. Police found a brown package with a battery, timer, and wires and did not spot it as a fake. As planned, it kept police from swiftly answering the next call, a report of "a man with a gun at Mr. Steak" phoned by a diner who saw Pierce fingering a handgun.

Gail Bailey had just popped a piece of candy into her mouth at her teller's station in Washington Mutual when she saw a tall customer waiting. She smiled and apologized, then Pierce handed her a piece of paper. It read: "Put the money in the bag and we won't hurt you." Stunned, Bailey looked up to see who "we" was.

"I mean it," Pierce said. "Give me all your money."

Bailey stepped on the silent alarm button and looked down the counter. Her colleague, Gail Fox, appeared to be engaged in a similar transaction with a shorter bearded robber. Fox cried out as she read her note: "No, this can't be true! Do you really mean this?"

"Just do what the note says," Yarbrough said, "and we won't hurt you."

After they stuffed money into the men's bags, Bailey boldly challenged them.

"Why don't you leave?" she demanded. "You've gotten my money."

"Look at the ground," Pierce ordered. Then he and Yarbrough fled.

Their take was only $3,600. Pierce sent $200 of it in a money order to Bob Miles, the racist leader in Michigan, without telling him it was stolen. The robbers dropped $100 more in the collection plate at Aryan Nations.

*   *   *

ZILLAH RAPIDLY CAME to see her lover as a race warrior, exactly the kind of man her leaders had been imploring Yahweh to deliver to them. She was taken by his boyishness and timidity when they were alone, by his power and command when he was dealing with his group. By Christmastide, after several times of only sleeping together with their arms around each other, they were making love.

Once unleashed, their physical relationship was vigorous. Bob was a tender and imaginative lover who got better than half of his pleasure from making Zillah feel good. He was inventive in bed, sometimes docile and other times wild. He was the best lover Zillah ever had, and unlike Bob, she had plenty of basis for comparison.

Zillah's love for Bob was based on the physical relationship. For the men he attracted to his group, it was psychological. He would find the one part of a person that was aching for affirmation and mine it as efficiently as he had mined copper and zinc in the 1970s. Then he would haul that ore to the surface of the person's psyche and process it into a shiny bar of pure metal. It was how he had brought them from purely innocent tree-cutting to robbery and counterfeiting.

Bob also was attentive to Zillah's two boys, Dustin, then ten, and Caleb, three. Once during a visit, Caleb climbed up on Bob's lap and felt the pistol in his jacket pocket. "What's in there?" the boy asked innocently.

"Oh, don't put your hand in there, son," Bob said, wanting to shield the boy from the harsh reality of the weapon. "Why, I got a critter in there, a chipmunk. He might bite you." Caleb laughed. Bob's mind was increasingly distracted by the fanaticism engulfing his life, but he remembered the incident. On the next visit, when Caleb climbed up again and felt something hard in Bob's pocket, Bob invited him to see for himself what it was.

Caleb reached into Bob's pocket and pulled out a plastic chipmunk. The boy squealed with delight as Bob broke into a big, hearty laugh.

Zillah was not used to such treatment from anyone. Her life in Wyoming, in many ways, had been more miserable than those of girls who grew up in the squalid cities she feared so much, and she was cynical about relationships.

On January 20, 1984, not seven weeks after she first laid eyes on him in her darkened driveway, Bob seduced her once more. This time, when she started toward the bathroom to get her diaphragm, he pulled gently on her arm.

"Forget about birth control tonight," Bob told her. "We don't need it." Bob told Zillah he loved her. He said he would divorce Debbie to reproduce his "seed" with Zillah. They made love that night with the intention of having a child.

Bob was just as manipulative with the men. Pierce had been trying to reach him since he had made bail, but Bob was off washing his stolen money and visiting his various contacts. Finally, Pierce drove up to Bob's in February, and as he stopped on the gravel drive Bob came stomping out of his double-wide house, a gun strapped to his waist. Pierce marched up to him with equal fury.

They had an angry confrontation over Pierce's calls from jail and the group's failure to rally to his aid. When they had calmed down, they went through the back door into Bob's kitchen. Bob handed Bruce some of the bluebacks, telling Bruce he had done it for him and he was sorry it wasn't sooner.

Bob disbursed the money with ease. After paying the bills that had mounted since he quit Portland Lehigh three months earlier, he gave money that he risked his life to steal to some of the men who didn't have jobs.

RANDY DUEY HAD been a postal clerk at Fairchild Air Force Base for seven years. It was a fairly good-paying job for the area. Yet he quit abruptly on March 3, 1984, the way Bob had quit the cement plant. Neither man had other visible means of support, but they were making plans.

The core of Bob's group was down to only a few. But in the space of five months he had taken these disaffected men and convinced them that now, after all the talk at congresses and rallies, now was the time to act. What kind of men would they be, he exhorted them, if they spent their lives praying for the millennium while never lifting a finger to change things? If not now, when?

His small circle of would-be Aryan warriors were convinced. If they didn't act now they would suffer the consequences the fictional Earl Turner had written in his diary: "No excuse for our failure will have any meaning, for there will be only a swarming horde of indifferent, mulatto zombies to hear it. There will be no White men to remember us—either to blame us for our weakness or forgive us for our folly."

Thus it was possible for Duey, a single man with nothing else to hold him, to be challenged by Mathews to the point where he felt the only way to live consistently with his beliefs was to go along to the next level of conflict.

Low on money, Mathews returned to the Innis Arden area of Seattle in mid-March with Pierce, Duey, and Yarbrough. Bob hocked his ring to contribute to a small fund to buy a getaway car. They were going to carry out the Fred Meyer robbery they had planned during their aborted trip in November. They spent several more days casing the job while staying at a motel south of the city.

The quartet looked over an old blue Dodge Dart Yarbrough bought. It was all they could afford. The owner wanted only $500. The trunk lid had a tendency to pop open, but it would have to do.

"There's just one problem with it," Yarbrough hesitated. "It's got no reverse gear." Duey and Pierce were dumbfounded, but Mathews was pragmatic.

"Just be careful where you park, Reds," he warned Gary with a smile. "We don't want to come out and have to push this thing out of a parking spot."

About 2 P.M. on March 16, a Continental Armored Transport truck pulled up to Fred Meyer's main entrance, and the pickup man, George King, alighted from the rear to go to the office. An old Dodge Dart with a recalcitrant trunk lid idled in the fire lane, a young man with a red beard behind the wheel.

Inside the store, dawdling around the office, three men in jeans, jackets and white t-shirts were idly browsing. King had a habit of taking in details like this. He wheeled a hand cart into the office and soon emerged with six large cash bags and six coin boxes. He turned left to go toward the store exit, passing a tall fellow whose head

was buried in a display case. It was Pierce, who had
darkened his hair and pasted on a beard to fill out his
goatee. Mathews had darkened his face, just as in the
porno store robbery.

Suddenly Mathews blocked King's path.

"Excuse me, sir," King said as he edged his cart forward. Mathews turned, opened his jacket and slipped a
gun out of his belt. Pierce came from behind, grabbed
King's arm and twisted it behind him, removing King's
gun.

"Get face down on the floor and you won't get hurt,"
Mathews told King. "There's another man in the store
with a gun." King complied.

Duey was supposed to be blocking the aisle in case a
customer wandered near, but at one point he came over
to watch the robbery. "What are you doing?" Pierce said
in a hoarse whisper. "Get back to your post!"

They grabbed the money bags, leaving the coins behind, and darted toward the exit. Pierce, Duey, and
Mathews zig-zagged swiftly through the checkout lines,
saying nothing and looking straight ahead.

Yarbrough was waiting. Fortunately no car had pulled
in front of him. Mathews and Pierce yanked the trunk
open and tossed the bags inside. They slammed the lid
several times, but it wouldn't snap shut. After they jumped
into the car, Yarbrough accelerated south to the corner
of the building. There he turned right and the Dodge
Dart, trunk lid flapping, disappeared toward the rear of
the store.

A puzzled customer came upon George King, still pros-
trate in the aisle.

"Are you okay?" the customer asked.

King, a dazed look on his face, glanced up at the
Samaritan.

"I've been robbed!"

Mathews's car was so near, the robbers dumped the
Dart and were headed toward Interstate 5 before police
knew a robbery had occurred. When they got back to
Metaline Falls, the four hustled into the barracks to
count the loot. It totaled $43,345, and no red dye this
time. Ten percent was set aside as a tithe to racist groups.
Each of the robbers kept $7,000, which Mathews called

"salary." The rest was earmarked to finance the group's activities.

Shortly after the robbery, police found the blue Dart in a dentist's office parking lot, just 250 yards north of Fred Meyer, parked nose-in facing Aurora Avenue. Its trunk lid was gaping open. Their case dead-ended there.

Chapter 5

Enter the Zionist Occupation Government

The pitted green doors of the Otis elevator squeaked open on the third floor of the Coeur d'Alene post office building, and Wayne Manis stood facing a hallway lined with frosted-glass doors. Along one wall, to the left of the men's room, was a newly varnished solid wood door with a gleaming deadbolt lock.

Fumbling with his keys, Manis unlocked it and entered a pigeonhole room, filled by an old wooden desk, a couple of chairs, and a bank of file cabinets. Surveying the small room for a moment, he pulled off his coat and hung it on a rack by the door. Then sitting down in the chair behind the desk to get a feel for it, he smiled slightly as he ran his hands through his salt-and-pepper hair.

"My God. What have I gotten myself into?" he mused.

Marine Corps-tough and bureau-trained, FBI Special Agent Manis was a true Hoover man. During his eighteen years with the bureau, he'd taken on some of the most perilous assignments the FBI offered.

An Arkansas native, he was a no-nonsense, action-oriented lifer, specializing in undercover work. He'd infiltrated the Cosa Nostra, posed as a hit man, and been part of one of the biggest sweeps ever of Klansmen in the South.

Among his most prized possessions was the first thing he hung on the shabby walls of his new office, a photograph of himself standing with J. Edgar Hoover.

But Manis wasn't a stereotypical FBI agent. He was more like a streetwise hustler from Jersey City than a hick from Little Rock. He favored a wardrobe that was a little flashier than a conventional G-man's. His wavy hair continued down the sides of his stony face to form a neatly trimmed beard. He walked with a cowboy swagger and had a passion for gold jewelry.

Still, there was something of the farm boy in Manis. His favorite ring was the one with the gold horseshoe studded with diamonds, with a ruby in the middle. He ran an Appaloosa horse ranch 60 miles east of Birmingham, Alabama, calling his Appaloosas "usin' horses" as opposed to the racing-type thoroughbreds they raised in Kentucky.

But in 1983, after closing a long-term narcotics case in Birmingham, he surrendered to restlessness. After sixteen years in the Birmingham office, Manis was starting to think about a quieter clime to cap his career. That was when he heard about an opening at the FBI resident agency in Coeur d'Alene, a one-man operation that had been gathering dust since the previous agent's transfer. Manis was an avid hunter and sportsman, and through his frequent hunting trips, he knew the area as one of the West's most beautiful settings. It took him four months to nail the job.

When Manis arrived in Coeur d'Alene in February 1984, he thought he'd found a quiet corner of God's country, a place where he could live in the serenity of the mountains nestled up against a jewel of an ice-blue lake and maybe do a little big-game hunting after he retired.

Instead, he found himself squirming with uneasiness about the group up the road with its swastika flags. He had a hunch something sinister was hidden behind the rallies, the rhetoric, and the national organizing the leader of the group was conducting. For days he closeted himself in the small office, reading and rereading notes left by the previous agent. Then he called on Kootenai County Undersheriff Larry Broadbent, who was about the only authority on the right wing in the area.

Broadbent, a stocky, old-school cop, told Manis that an informant of his at the 1983 Aryan Congress reported that the talk was a lot more militant than before. Broadbent told Manis about the counterfeiting arrest of Bruce Pierce and the Schooney's robbery he was sure they had committed.

What troubled Manis most was what he didn't see. Some of the young bucks were no longer around, as if they'd gone underground. The older guys and the families were still there, praying every Sunday with their right arms stretched stiffly skyward. The printing press continued to churn out extremist literature, and "running nigger" target posters still showed up on trees. And a few of the young ones still showed up at times to visit and provide security for the elders at special gatherings. At least those were things he could see, out in the open.

But it was obvious some of the younger ones had drifted off. Were they simply tired of the rhetoric? Or had they found a new guru, Manis wondered, one who wasn't as public as the old guy up the road with the swastika flags?

After he read the Aryan Nations file, Manis was intrigued. Attorney General's guidelines no longer permitted agents to jump at will into domestic spying cases, because of scandals in years past. There had to be official approval. Manis felt that if he dug hard enough, fast enough and deep enough, he might be able to get Washington's approval for a six-month look-see.

In March, Manis decided if there was going to be a war, he wanted to meet the opposing general. He invited Pastor Butler down to the Coeur d'Alene post office building for a chat. Butler arrived with Tom Bentley, the Aryan Academy principal, who sat in the chair farthest from Manis's desk and kept to himself. Manis looked Bentley over. The middle-aged retired machinist looked more like a quiet accountant. If this was the best they have to offer, Manis thought, they probably aren't too much of a threat. But the pastor was something else.

With his drooping, basset-hound face, Butler was bold and matter-of-fact about his activities at Aryan Nations, his connections in the movement, and how he saw himself as a unifying force. But Manis sensed deception from him.

Manis remembered the advice an old 'Bama agent once gave him: "What you want to do is make them think you're barely smart enough to find your way back to the car." So Manis played possum, nodding as the pastor pontificated. Had Butler not known better, he might even have pegged Manis as a potential convert.

After they left, Manis was convinced he'd soon be full

time on Aryan Nations' case. Was it simply a right-wing organization with a perfect right to go about its business, or was it involved in criminal activity?

THE FRED MEYER robbery was a turning point for Bob Mathews. In three months he had gone from deepest depression to reinvigoration. After his dad's death, Pierce's arrest, and the abandonment by most of his friends—just as in Arizona—there had been a good chance that Mathews's "action group" would fade from the scene as a penny-ante gang of thugs.

But Bob saw much more peril in the world now than what the Birchers had told him about communism. He saw a world filled with people and systems scheming against his race, all interrelated conspiracies by the international Jews and their political allies. It was not the way most people saw the world.

Bob had revulsion for workaday whites, happy with their paychecks and content in their indebtedness to the banks as long as they had a new car, food for their bellies, and a yearly vacation. Bob couldn't believe the world was that simple. He had delved into the labyrinthine logic of the radical right and no longer could be satisfied with life, and a relatively good life, the way it could have been if he had remained the honest, hardworking man from Metaline Falls.

His sacrifices were always "for the children." Mathews truly loved children—white children. Nothing that a man can do in his life, he said, will outlast his children. They are the future. And right before the robbery, he learned he was going to get the one thing life seemed cruelly to deny him, a child of his own blood, flower of his seed. Zillah was pregnant.

Bob treated her like a queen with the stolen money. Eleven days after the robbery, he moved her to a house at 1620 Kearney Street in Laramie and arranged for her living expenses. He handed her $300 in cash and told her to buy new maternity clothes. Bob paid for all the doctor visits, as with everything, in cash.

New life was conceived within the gang as well. The robbery seemed to work CPR on it, stimulating it to breathe, to grow again.

The first step was returning Denver Parmenter to the fold. One of the initial nine gang members, Parmenter was now working as a mold machine operator at Keytronics in Spokane, making $3.89 an hour separating keys once they came out of the molds. He was driving down a dead end, and he knew it. He kept going to Aryan Nations and stayed in touch with his friend Randy Duey, until they got into a barroom brawl in Cheney in January 1984 and split.

Then, two days after the Fred Meyer robbery, Parmenter went to Duey's house to smooth things over. Duey welcomed him inside and handed him a Spokane newspaper. He pointed to a story about the Fred Meyer robbery two days earlier, the one they had planned together in November.

Denver looked up, his mouth agape. "You guys actually did it?" he asked.

Randy smiled and pulled out a stack of money, fanning it for Denver. It was Duey's $7,000 share. "And we're going to do it again," Duey said. "This is just the start. It's really happening now, Denver. Remember we used to say it was time for action, not talk? Well, the action's happening. Why don't you come back in?"

The next day Denver wrote a note to his supervisor at Keytronics: "Joe, I quit. You may send my final pay to my P.O. address in Four Lakes, Wash."

On March 20, Duey and Parmenter drove to Missoula and met Bruce Pierce as he was coming out of the county courthouse. Pierce, angry at first that Parmenter had returned, later relented and showed them some papers he'd just acquired.

They were voter registrations and other identification in the names of Bruce William Fry and Swift Dana Nelson. Parmenter became Fry and Duey became Nelson. Pierce had a listing of other names, culled from trips through graveyards in the area. Following the advice in such underground publications as *False ID in America*, Pierce searched for names of dead infants from tombstones, particularly those who would have been about the same age as the imposter, had they lived.

It was amazingly easy to obtain duplicate birth certificates and use them to obtain phony Social Security cards, rent receipts, and driver's licenses. With their new identities, Duey and Parmenter set up spurious addresses at mail drop centers across Idaho and Montana, legitimate businesses that provide private postal boxes to conceal where people really live.

Pierce also was doing his best to cloak where he was living. After the Fred Meyer robbery he bought a converted 1951 GMC school bus in Coeur d'Alene and made it his home on wheels—under the name Roger J. Morton. Arriving in Montana, he did some recruiting of his own. He visited the automotive department at the Sears store in Missoula to see a clerk there named Andrew Virgil Barnhill.

Barnhill, twenty-seven, was an extremely bright young man and former seminarian from Plantation, Florida. A whiz at mathematics, he had a high-paying job supervising loan accounts in Florida for General Electric Credit Corporation. His dad, Virgil, and he subscribed to many conservative causes, such as fighting gun control. They were members of the American Pistol and Rifle Association, and Andy happened to meet a group from the Identity camp of the Covenant, the Sword, and the Arm of the Lord while they were attending an APRA survivalist workshop in Tennessee.

Barnhill was so impressed with the patriotism and spartan life-style of the CSA folk, he went to its commune in Arkansas in 1982 to live for a year and train in military survival tactics. But Jim Ellison, CSA's leader, drove a large number of followers away that year with his increasingly controversial style.

Barnhill moved to Joplin, Missouri, for several months, along with two fellow members of his heavy-fire "B" squad infantry at CSA, Rodney Carrington and Pete Travis. Barnhill's parents thought he should find a job tutoring math, one of his best subjects, at the local college. But about April 1983, they all moved to Missoula looking for the "Western spaces." Barnhill and Travis shared an apartment on Third Street until Pete moved in with a girlfriend in December 1983.

Barnhill contacted Aryan Nations, which is how Pierce found out about the ex-CSA folk in Missoula. Pierce subtly approached Barnhill and Travis to "feel them out."

Later, Mathews paid a visit and assured the potential recruits that his "action group" was patterned more after the fictional Order in *The Turner Diaries* than after the CSA. Mathews's men weren't going to shiver in the cold of an Ozark Mountains winter, cutting wood for a pittance. His warriors would get paid regular salaries, which he was going to fund through robberies of the enemies of the white race, namely the Jew-controlled banks. The next robbery, he told them, was planned within the month.

Mathews said his group had no name for the moment. "If we have a name it's too easy for members to talk about us. For now, it's 'the company,' or 'the organization,' or sometimes, like in that book we all like to read, it's 'the Order.' We just want to be a nameless, white underground." Mathews left Missoula for Colorado feeling that both Barnhill and Travis would join. In Denver, Mathews and David Lane tended to the group's other major activity, counterfeiting.

Lane met a man at the Laporte Church of Christ who he later learned had a background—albeit unsuccessful—in counterfeiting. The man was Robert Merki, who traveled under the pseudonym Parry Stewart. In three short, chaotic years, this forty-nine-year-old former industrial engineer had watched his promising life fall apart under the strain of going broke. After getting his entire family involved in a phony money scheme that ended with several arrests, he and his wife jumped bail and were living as fugitives.

AS A BOY IN CHICAGO, Robert Emil Merki showed interest in his dad's printing trade. During summers off from William Howard Taft High School, he studied hot lead typesetting. But it wasn't until many years later that, after a career in industrial and aviation engineering, he fell back on his printing talents.

By rights, Robert Merki should have enjoyed a quiet, middle-class life. A Navy veteran, he owned a company in Chicago before he sold it and moved with his wife and two children to California. Then he got the job of his dreams with the Boeing Airplane Company in Seattle, working on development of the 737 jet and the supersonic transport. After Congress voted down funds for the SST, he was laid off.

He divorced in 1974 and remarried Sharon Stewart, at the time a thirty-seven-year-old divorcee with five children. Together they moved to a beautiful piece of land the Okanogan Valley north of Washington's inland desert. It was in the mountains on the east ˙ of U.S. 97 halfway between Tonasket and Oroville, within hiking distance of the Canadian border. It looked down on the valley floor and across to the magnificent Cascade Range clawing at the western horizon. Into this rustic setting Robert and Sharon moved in the spring of 1974 and built a house resembling an upside-down ark. The shape led to Merki's CB radio nickname, "Noah."

In 1975 Merki went into business again, borrowing $15,000 to invest in what he called the Mountain Life Institute, growing hydroponic tomatoes in a 6,000-square-foot greenhouse. Merki subsidized his labor costs under the federal CETA jobs program, hiring some of the local unemployed to work the nutrient tanks.

Merki was at a point in his life, as were many others who later met Mathews, where he was searching for a deeper spiritual dimension. There were Christian Identity followers in Oroville who told him about their religion. In 1978 Merki decided to investigate. He built a camper and headed east with Sharon and two of her children to Flora, Illinois, for the annual Freedom Festival held by the Christian Patriots Defense League. The festival was a flea market of conservative to far-right philosophy, with emphasis on natural life-styles, bartering goods instead of using cash and other practices prevalent among ultra-conservatives.

At the festival, the Merkis heard lectures by Sheldon Emry, an Identity sage from Prescott, Arizona, and by Colonel Gordon "Jack" Mohr, head of the Christian Emergency Defense System in Mississippi. They signed up to receive taped lectures by mail and ended up on several mailing lists, including Pastor Butler's.

But Merki met another man at the festival who had a much more profound impact on him. He was a man selling silver bars at a festival booth. Merki struck up a conversation and learned the man had served time for

counterfeiting. He had done it, he told Merki, because
he was at the end of his financial rope.

Merki's own rope started to fray by the end of 1980.
Just as the arch-conservative hero Ronald Reagan prepared to take office, the CETA program died, and with it
the source of Merki's cheap labor. He and Sharon were
stuck with all the work in the hydroponic greenhouse. To
make ends meet, Merki opened Oroville Mining and
Supply to process ore after he struck a deal with a young
man with a silver mining claim in the Cascade foothills.
But after opening the store, the young man was in a
motorcycle accident, and the deal dried up.

In the early spring of 1981, Merki told his brother-in-
law Robert Donahue that he was at the end of his rope.
Then he recounted the story of the man with the silver
bars at the Freedom Festival. On a whim, they went to
Seattle to price printing presses. Merki ended up a week
later buying a Multilith 1250 offset press for $1,500. Set-
ting up the operation in his basement, Merki's long-
suppressed printer's instincts quickly emerged.

It seemed, though, that when a private citizen purchases a press such as the Multilith 1250, word filters
back to the Treasury Department. Those units are favor-
ites of counterfeiters. Not long after the purchase, a
Secret Service raiding party went to Merki's house with a
warrant and ripped it apart. But they were premature,
since he hadn't started making plates. Merki convinced
the agents that he was setting up a legitimate print shop,
and the agents left peacefully.

Convinced that the feds had bought his story, Merki
set about in earnest. After considering all denominations,
he decided to counterfeit hundred-dollar bills. The risk
and penalty were the same, and the profit greater, so
why chance passing five twenties?

With a bellows camera, he made sharp negatives of
both sides of a real hundred-dollar bill. From them he
made the plates and ran ten reams—5,000 sheets—of
8½-by-11-inch cotton-bond paper through the press, getting four bills on each sheet. The paper was colored with
RIT dye from the market, sprayed, and ironed with
waxed paper compresses. They lost one or two bills per
sheet to the watermark, and Sharon's eagle eyes disquali-

fied another huge batch, which were burned. By September 1981, out of 20,000 bills—$2 million—they had kept only 150, just $15,000, as good enough to pass.

The Merkis embarked on a spending spree that stretched from Helena, Montana, to San Francisco. They were careful to make small purchases and to pick on store clerks who were young and inexperienced. The Merkis' age and looks—the epitome of middle-class America—helped carry it off. Eric Tornatzky, the boyfriend of Sharon's oldest daughter, Suzanne Stewart, came along but tended to panic when passing the funny money.

The trip was a huge success. Merki's party passed all the bills without a hitch. They cleared $13,000 and paid a year's mortgage on the Mountain Life Institute. The income plan for the Merki household for 1982 obviously was set.

A second set of hundreds was printed. This time $77,000 was kept. Merki called Donahue, a teacher in Eugene, Oregon, who had helped pass some phony money there on the first trip, and he agreed to go along on the second foray. But Donahue told a former student about the plan, and the student notified the Secret Service. When 1982 spring break arrived, Donahue brought his daughter and the student to meet the Merkis in Burns, a tiny settlement in the Oregon desert. As they gassed up at a filling station to head to Salt Lake City, the agents swooped down on Merki.

Several weeks later, the people of Oroville turned out to help the Merkis raise legal defense funds. Merki held a yard sale to gather cash, and even the town policeman helped out by buying some items. After the sale, Merki had $6,000. But he never intended to hire a lawyer. He faced up to 105 years in prison, and he couldn't live with that. With an eraser and pen, he converted the birth certificate of Sharon's ex-husband, Harry Stewart, to read "Parry Stewart," and with equal dexterity changed his wife's from Sharon Donahue to "Charah Donchada."

They took the money, drove to Seattle, and caught a flight to Guatemala City, spending the next six months in Guatemala, Belize, and Costa Rica, while the heat died down in Oroville. They returned to the United States secretly in December 1982 and settled in Fort Collins,

Colorado, where Suzanne and Eric Tornatzky were living under the surname Hamilton.

While working at odd jobs around Fort Collins, the Merkis learned of the Identity congregation at the nearby Laporte Church of Christ, headed by Pastor Pete Peters. Among the people they met there were David Lane; Zillah Craig and her mother, Jean; and Dennis and Mary Schlueter. They grew close enough to make social calls on some of them. After nine months, they all moved to Boise.

Merki took a job with C&J Advertising there, traveling from town to town throughout the mountain states selling advertising space around bowling score sheets. Sharon's youngest son, sixteen-year-old Kurt Stewart, stayed in Boise with his sister Suzanne to attend high school while the Merkis traveled.

When they were near Fort Collins in December 1983, the Merkis resumed going to the Laporte Church of Christ. At the time, Mathews and Lane were in Laramie cleaning the dye off the stolen money. Lane brought Mathews to the church, and several times a group split from the church and met at the Schlueters' home in Fort Collins for a Sunday potluck supper and an evening of religious discussion. There the Merkis met Mathews, a man they both instantly liked. Mathews's intensity set him apart from the others they met in the movement.

In January 1984, Pastor Peters arranged for Colonel Mohr to give a talk at the Laporte church. When word spread that the nationally known anti-Semite was coming to the area, Peters received anonymous threats. So on the night of the talk, Merki and Schlueter, who worked as a security guard, took up positions in the cold parking lot to watch for unwelcome visitors.

The publicity surrounding Mohr's appearance didn't go unnoticed in Denver, 60 miles down Interstate 25 from Fort Collins.

Alan Berg wasn't a religious Jew, but he was nevertheless a vocal one when it came to anti-Semites and others across the spectrum of the radical right. Five days a week, he had the needle to goad them right in front of him. It was the microphone of KOA radio, a 50,000-watt superstation that on clear nights could be heard as far away as Hayden Lake and the bowels of Texas.

Berg loved to get people like Colonel Mohr on his radio talk show. He used them as pincushions, whipped up his listeners with his indignation, and then abruptly hung up on his guests. When Berg read about Mohr's visit in the Denver papers, he arranged for Mohr and Pastor Peters to be call-in guests on his February 13 show—Mohr on a long distance line from Mississippi, Peters from Laporte.

It was a typical Berg show, with the antagonistic host verbally ripping his guests to shreds. It climaxed, as his shows frequently did, with Berg pulling the plug on both Mohr and Peters. It made Mohr's supporters seethe. What they failed to realize was that it was all show business to Berg. He'd forget about it as soon as he left the studio and started working on the next day's show.

But the insult to Mohr wasn't lost on Mathews.

David Lane was living for a brief time in Fort Lupton, Colorado, northeast of Denver, in an apartment with Colonel Francis Farrell. Farrell was an Air Force veteran who flew in three wars—World War II, Korea, and Vietnam. In the 1970s he operated a gasoline station in Pennsylvania's Pocono Mountains. When the Arab oil embargo hit the industry hard in 1973, Farrell's business went under. It set him to reading about world politics, and eventually he obtained literature that laid blame for his problems at the feet of the Jews.

In 1983, Farrell moved to Colorado and met Lane through common friends.

A friend of Lane persuaded him to call Berg's show after the host had hung up on Mohr. Lane sparred verbally with Berg over the "Jewishness" of communism and, satisfied he had won his point, hung up. His friend taped the exchange, and Lane delighted in replaying it for several people at Farrell's apartment. He thought Berg, because of his obnoxious radio manner, was good public relations for the right-wing movement.

In March, when the Merkis were staying at a motel in the Denver suburb of Arvada trying to sell their score sheets at local bowling alleys, Lane called and asked if he could visit. When he arrived at the motel room, Mathews was with him.

Lane handed Merki an inch-thick stack of fifty-dollar bills. "What do you think of these, Parry?" he asked, using the phony name under which Merki traveled.

"A good friend of ours," Mathews added, "was arrested passing these phonies. We thought they were pretty good."

Merki, honored that his counterfeiting prowess was being recognized, gave the fifties a thorough examination before he pronounced judgment.

"A sharp clerk could spot these a mile away," Merki said. "They're no good. The paper feels all wrong."

"Would you help us set up a quality operation, Parry?" Mathews asked him. "Ideally we'd like to use an intaglio method, just like the Bureau of Engraving."

"Much too difficult," Merki answered. "Litho is the way to go. Look, I'll help you out on this by picking a press for you."

"What do you think we should do with these?" asked Lane, holding the remaining phony fifties printed at Aryan Nations.

"Burn 'em," Merki answered.

The last evidence of that earlier scheme was destroyed that evening, as they held the bills one by one over the toilet bowl in Merki's motel room and burned them. It set off the room's smoke detector several times before they were done.

WINDING UP BOUNDARY DAM Road from the main highway, Dan Stadtmueller had to slow to a crawl before he spotted the gravel drive amid the pine trees. Although Mathews had given him directions, it was still difficult to find the little sliver that wended its way back into Mathews Acres. Stadtmueller was rehearsing the sales pitch he'd used dozens of times selling life insurance. Yet this was an unusual case. As a broker for Bankers Life of Nebraska, he usually made cold calls on prospects. But Mathews had called *him* in Spokane, inviting him down to Metaline Falls this Sunday evening because five men wanted insurance.

Most people don't go out and buy life insurance,

Stadtmueller knew through experience. It's sold to them. This, he thought, was pretty flaky.

Then again, it was April Fool's Day.

Mathews wanted to run his underground in as businesslike a way as possible. It was logical that he and his Inner Circle of aides should have "key man" policies before risking their lives. Mathews escorted the agent to Una's house, where the agent described the basic whole-life policy to Mathews, Pierce, Duey, Yarbrough, and Parmenter. All decided on $50,000 policies except Mathews, who wanted two.

Stadtmueller took the necessary information on each man. Mathews said he worked at Theta Demographics. Bob loved telling people he worked in demographics. In a twisted sort of logic, he was. On his first policy, Mathews named Zillah Craig as beneficiary. Despite all the talk in the right wing of morality, Bob had no qualms about keeping a mistress. On his second policy, Mathews named William Pierce and John Ireland, leaders of the National Alliance.

Bruce Pierce said he was a carpenter at $8,200 a year and named Julie as beneficiary. Duey, who was unmarried, said he also worked for Theta Demographics at $16,000 a year. His beneficiaries were Debbie Mathews and Betty Yarbrough. Gary Yarbrough said he was a carpenter at $10,000 a year, and listed his wife, Betty, and four daughters. Parmenter listed his occupation as "construction" at $15,000 a year. Janice and their daughter Kristin were his beneficiaries.

Stadtmueller was jotting all this down when Mathews pulled a roll of money from his pocket. Stadtmueller's eyes widened as Mathews counted off enough cash to pay for all six policies, then handed it to the agent. Warning bells clanged in Stadtmueller's mind as he returned to Spokane. After processing the policies, he reported the situation to the police. His home office eventually rejected Mathews's policies because of the beneficiaries, although the other four were issued.

The following day, Duey rented an isolated house on Scotia Road outside Newport, Washington, midway between Metaline Falls and Spokane, to use for the new counterfeiting operation. It was hidden from the main road by a stand of trees, and the owners were on a year's holiday in Mexico.

A neighbor named Larry Cada, representing the owners, walked Duey through the house and showed him how to run the appliances, but the new renter didn't seem interested.

Over the next few weeks, Cada could see through the trees from his house 600 feet away that the tenants indeed were peculiar. They seemed to be living out of suitcases and sleeping without sheets, which they hung instead over the windows.

On April 3, 1984, two days after applying for his life insurance, Bruce Pierce went to federal court in Spokane to settle the counterfeiting charge. After talking with his lawyer, Pierce had decided to plead guilty. It was his first offense, and chances were good he'd be considered for probation.

But Judge Robert McNichols took note of Pierce's silence since his arrest about how he got the phony money, and Pierce's ties to Aryan Nations. McNichols sentenced Pierce to two years in prison. Pierce was stunned.

Quickly the lawyer asked the judge to give Pierce time to settle his affairs before reporting to prison. McNichols gave Pierce three weeks on bond and ordered him to report to the U.S. Marshal in Spokane no later than noon, April 24. Pierce told the court he would be living with Robert Mathews in Metaline Falls.

But Pierce left the courthouse that day with no intention of coming back.

A TROUPE OF WOULD-BE robbers left Mathews Acres on April 19 for Seattle, planning a long weekend to complete an armored car robbery Mathews had scouted earlier. Richie Kemp had gravitated back to the group after the Fred Meyer heist, quitting his $12-an-hour job at Vaagen Brothers sawmill despite Ken Loff's pleas that he keep it. Mathews asked Kemp to wait at the bastion for Pete Travis, the former CSA member living in Missoula, who was supposed to come along.

Andy Barnhill, who had quit his job at Sears and moved into the barracks, rode with Mathews and Pierce. Parmenter drove his pickup with Duey and Yarbrough as passengers. On the outskirts of Seattle, the men checked in two to a room at the Motel 6 in Issaquah. Mathews and Pierce went out to a pay phone to check on why Pete Travis hadn't shown up.

The men had gotten into the habit of carrying large amounts of change to make long distance calls from phone booths. They made it a rule not to use motel room phones. Pierce dialed Travis's number in Missoula and pumped in quarters.

"Hello?" Travis answered.

"Pete? This is Bruce. Got any news?" Pierce said, his standard opening.

"No, nothing."

"We're waiting on you. There's a guy waiting in Metaline Falls. Are you in?"

"I'm sorry, but I can't go fishing with you," Travis said cryptically, then hung up. Pierce stared at the droning receiver a second, then turned to Mathews.

"He said he can't go fishing!" Pierce exclaimed.

"Forget him. Let me call Rich and tell him to get over here now," Mathews answered. Kemp gunned his Celica across the inland desert and over the Cascades in less than five hours, meeting the men at the motel.

The next morning, a Friday, they began preparations for the robbery. Four of the men led by Mathews went up to Northgate Mall, on the east side of Interstate 5 at 105th Street. From a rise on the south side of the parking lot, they watched an armored truck make a swing around the perimeter of the large shopping center.

The Continental Armored Transport truck looked identical to the one they had hit at Fred Meyer. It stopped first at Nordstrom, a fashionable department store on the west side of the mall, then picked up at J. C. Penney and Seafirst Bank before pulling into a tight corner next to the Bon Marché department store.

"That's the spot," Mathews said, approving of the geography. "It's closed in to minimize witnesses. And he's made all of his pickups so we'll get more money."

That same morning, Pierce, Kemp, and Barnhill scanned the classified ads of the *Seattle Times* for secondhand vehicles they could use in the robbery. Finding a van and a big car in the right price range, they called the two sellers, both of whom lived in Everett, north of Seattle.

On the way to Everett, Pierce and Barnhill stopped at a Seafirst branch and changed some of the Fred Meyer loot into larger bills. They asked the tellers to put the cash into two bank envelopes, $900 in one and $1,000 in the other. After returning to the car, they wrote meaningless phone numbers on each envelope.

Kemp dropped off Pierce down the street from Mike Mathis's house. The first Mathis knew his buyer had arrived was when he saw a tall man with a goatee walking down his long driveway. Pierce gave Mathis's white van a cursory look. It had no back windows, which was good, and a sunroof, which was better. "I want a truck that performs quickly," Pierce said. "It's got to have fast acceleration."

"This one sure does," Mathis replied. "You'll like it."

They went into the house to do the deal. As Mathis began writing a bill of sale, he asked Pierce, "What's your name?"

"Just leave it blank, I'll fill it in," Pierce replied.

Mathis shrugged and finished. When he did, Pierce handed him the Seafirst envelope with the $900 cash, as agreed. While Mathis counted the money, Pierce acted as though he suddenly realized something.

"Oh, Mike, can I have that envelope back? I've got somebody's phone number on there I need." Mathis looked at the brown envelope and saw a number on it.

"Sure. Here," he said, handing back the only piece of paper that contained Pierce's fingerprints. The men devised the ruse so when authorities traced their getaway vehicles, there'd be no latent fingerprints left behind. Pierce had never touched the cash.

Barnhill did the same at the home of Cliff and Phyllis Mitchell, who were selling a 1973 Chrysler Newport. But another problem cropped up there. After they sealed the $1,000 deal inside the Mitchells' house, and Barnhill pulled the same envelope routine, they returned outside to the car. Suddenly Phyllis Mitchell showed up with a camera. A sentimental sort, she wanted to get a snapshot of her old car with its new owner. She turned to aim the camera and Barnhill panicked.

"No!" he yelled out, putting his hands over his face

and ducking. "I'm never in pictures!" The Mitchells looked blankly at one another, then with a shrug, Phyllis returned to the house.

On Saturday night, Gary Yarbrough assembled a small bomb in his motel room and put it in a paper bag. He used a high explosive main charge, an Eveready lantern battery, and a Westclox pocket watch timer. Then on Sunday, he and some others drove into downtown Seattle with the firebomb.

Their target was the Embassy Theater, a pornographic movie house at Third Avenue and Union Street, a commercial area near the Pike Place Market. About 5 o'clock, Yarbrough went in and saw about twenty people crouched down in their seats intent on the panting action on the screen. Reaching into the bag, he switched on the timer, pushed it under a seat in a vacant section, and left immediately. One of the gang then placed a call to the Embassy.

The female cashier answered the phone. "The place is going to go sky high," said a husky, whispered voice. Before she could do anything, a loud boom and blast of hot air rippled through the lobby, followed by billows of smoke. Patrons spilled through the exits. The damage was minimal, a few seats and no injuries to customers. But Mathews's crew made its point. Pornography was not to be tolerated.

However, the bombing also was part of Mathews's strategy to create a diversion for the next day's events.

Around noon on Monday, April 23, the crew headed north on the freeway to Northgate. As they passed through downtown Seattle, Kemp tossed boxes of roofing nails onto the highway where it passes through the Freeway Park underpass, hoping to create a massive traffic jam caused by flat tires to add to the confusion.

About a mile and a half from the mall, they parked their own vehicles at a Royal Fork restaurant and climbed into their switch vehicles. A phone call was made to the Embassy Theater, warning that another bomb soon would explode. They figured that police were sure to take the threat seriously because of the earlier bomb, tying up patrol units in another part of town.

Parmenter drove the Chrysler to Northgate, carrying Barnhill, Pierce, and Duey. The latter two were dressed

in tan work clothes and had buckets and sponges.
Yarbrough drove the van with Mathews and Kemp.
Parmenter parked on the rise south of the parking lot to
watch for the armored truck. Yarbrough pulled his van
into the area Mathews selected for the ambush, finding a
spot right next to the Bon Marché side entrance. They
waited several hours.

The Continental Armored Transport truck arrived about
3 P.M., stopping first at Nordstrom. As it continued its
rounds, Parmenter drove slowly into the lot, stopping
some distance from the ambush site to let Pierce and
Duey out of the car. Parmenter's job was to use the
Chrysler to pin the truck into the corner.

Pierce and Duey moved to the J. K. Gill office supply
store just outside the covered side entrance to Bon Marché,
in an L formed by two wings of the mall. With the
buckets and sponges, they posed as window washers,
concealing their handguns under their work clothes.

When the armored truck approached Bon Marché, it
parked nosefirst, instead of backing into the fire lane,
and stopped in the corner. The pickup man got out. As he
rounded the truck toward the door, Pierce glanced over.

"Holy shit!" Pierce snickered. "It's the same guy we
hit at Fred Meyer!" Pierce remembered from newspaper
stories that the guard's name was George King.

Parmenter drove the Chrysler to the fire lane and pulled
to the curb. There were several cars between him and the
armored truck. As each car left, Parmenter backed up
the Chrysler, edging closer to the truck each time.

King returned with several money bags from Bon
Marché, wheeling his cart wide of a car in which he
noticed a man reading a newspaper. He'd become more
cautious in the five weeks since he was robbed at Fred
Meyer. He never imagined that he was about to be
blindsided. King went to the passenger side of the truck
and began to open the money compartment.

"Shouldn't we go now?" Duey said to Pierce, dropping
his sponge and reaching for his gun. Pierce then moved,
pulling his 9mm semiautomatic and passing Duey around
the back of the truck. He got to King at exactly the right
moment, as the side door was unlocked, and pressed the
muzzle behind King's ear.

King's eyes widened with alarm. He tripped on his handcart and fell face down onto the floor of the compartment, cutting his finger. "You know the routine, George," Pierce said, calling him by name. "Give me your gun."

Robert White, the armored-car driver, heard a commotion in back and looked through the gunport from the cab.

"What's going on back there?" White yelled. He pulled out his gun and pointed the barrel through the gunport at Pierce. Duey, who was behind Pierce, saw the barrel sticking out. He climbed into the truck and shoved his own pistol the other way through the gunport toward White, creating an unusual standoff.

"Bobby," King yelled to White, "don't do nothing!"

By this time, Yarbrough had pulled the van to the side of the truck, blocking the narrow drive. Mathews jumped out and was pounding on the side window of the truck. White looked over and saw a tall young man—Richie Kemp—holding a shotgun in one hand and a hand-lettered sign in the other that read: "Get Out or You Die."

"Get out! We're not playing!" Mathews yelled.

Barnhill got out of the Chrysler, brandishing a .308-caliber Heckler & Koch 91 rifle. He jumped on the car's trunk and scanned the parking lot. On the driver's side of the truck, Parmenter stood watch with a .223-caliber Ruger Mini-14 he had borrowed from Duey. He yanked back the bolt, not thinking there was a round in the chamber. But a live round ejected, clinking onto the sidewalk and rolling off the curb into the gutter of the fire lane.

There was a mall entrance about 100 feet south of the robbery, past Shoreline Savings. As Parmenter watched, an elderly woman came out and walked toward the armored truck. "Stop there, lady!" Parmenter yelled at her.

The woman seemed oblivious to his voice as she kept walking toward the Bon Marché entrance, her eyes fixed on the strange events before her.

"Lady, turn back! Go away!" Parmenter yelled. Finally she realized what was happening and quickly turned back toward the mall in fright.

Robert White left the cab and was forced into the back

of the truck with King. Pierce began tossing money bags
into the white van, taking only a few minutes to finish.
"Stay in the truck until the police come," Pierce told the
guards. "There's a man in the parking lot with a machine
gun."

Pierce, Duey, Kemp, and Mathews jumped into the
van, and Yarbrough peeled out. Parmenter and Barnhill
got into the Chrysler and followed east out of the parking
lot, then south to where the switch cars were stashed.
Pierce was ready to pop the sunroof and fire at anybody
who might try to pursue them.

When it seemed obvious the robbers were gone, King
and White started to the cab to radio for help. They saw
a witness standing nearby.

"Call the police!" White called to him.

"I already did!" the man yelled back.

The switch to their own vehicles went smoothly. Pierce
tossed King's .357 magnum revolver onto the van's floor
as they left, so he wouldn't be caught with any evidence.
By the time a television news helicopter found the getaway vehicles at the Royal Fork about 4:40, the robbers
were well up Stevens Pass. They crossed the Columbia
River above Wenatchee and started out across the dry
interior.

A mile west of Waterville, Douglas County Deputy
Gary McLeod had his radar gun set up. Inland Washington is so boringly flat that cops can catch speeders there
all day. About 6:30 P.M., McLeod clocked three vehicles.
The first was Mathews's Chevy Cavalier doing 64. Next
came a white Ford pickup at 61. Playing catchup in the
rear was a Toyota Celica going 74 mph. McLeod pulled
out after it.

Kemp saw the patrol car coming up behind him and
pulled over. At least he didn't have the money. That was
in the bed of Parmenter's pickup, covered with a load of
firewood. But he and his passenger Pierce were carrying
weapons.

The deputy radioed the license plate number to dispatch and walked up to the driver's side, checking the
back seat before he confronted the driver.

Both Kemp and Pierce could feel sweat breaking out
on the backs of their necks. Pierce kept a hand near the

butt of his pistol in case the computer check came back against them. Kemp handled McLeod's questions coolly and waited for his speeding ticket, wanting to give the deputy no reason to search the car.

After the deputy left, Pierce got angry at Mathews. They had agreed to obey all speed limits so they wouldn't be stopped, but Mathews would drive the lead car like a maniac one minute, stringing out the caravan, then drop below the speed limit the next, causing them all to bunch up like an accordion. It was when Kemp was trying to catch up that McLeod caught him.

When the robbers stopped at a restaurant outside Spokane, Pierce was steaming mad. He got out of Kemp's car and stomped toward Mathews. Barnhill saw Pierce coming like a raging bull and stepped between, holding up his hands to try to head off the confrontation.

"Outta my way, Andy!" Pierce bellowed as he brushed by Barnhill to get to Mathews. The two strong-willed men stood toe to toe yelling for several minutes about how to drive properly before the kinsmen could calm them both down. But the men noticed a simmering struggle between Mathews and Pierce.

The seven robbers ended the day at Duey's house in Newport. Parmenter now was living there as well. Dumping their haul on a table, they separated the checks from the cash, then began to count. It came to $230,379, plus $4,432 in Canadian currency that could be exchanged easily.

Newspaper stories later put the robbery at a half-million dollars. Counting the $301,334 in checks, that would have been true. But what good are checks to thieves? They were quickly burned. Bob set aside $85,000 for the group's activities, then they voted to send a $40,000 donation to Aryan Nations, via Tom Bentley. The rest was split among themselves.

A BENCH WARRANT was issued for Pierce on April 26, three days after the robbery and two days after he failed to show up for prison. The next day, armed with the arrest warrant, Deputy Marshal William Miller and a few of Sheriff Bamonte's deputies went out to Mathews Acres, Pierce's last known address. Debbie Mathews met them at the end of the gravel drive between her house and Una's.

"Mrs. Mathews, we're looking for Bruce Carroll Pierce, we have a warrant for his arrest," Miller said. "Is he here?"

"No, he isn't," Debbie answered, holding her ground. "I haven't seen him in about a month."

"He told the court three weeks ago he was living here," Miller prodded.

"He was, but he's not here now," Debbie replied calmly.

"Do you know it's against the law to harbor a fugitive, Mrs. Mathews?"

"There's no one here except me and my son," she replied.

"Do you mind if we look around?" asked Miller.

"Yes, I do," Debbie said. "You can't look in my house without a search warrant." Miller glanced at the parking area and saw a Jeep wagon with Montana plates. He knew it belonged to Pierce. But, he thought, Debbie's probably right, Pierce wasn't there at the moment. Miller returned to Spokane to draw up a search warrant to take back to Mathews Acres. It was worth nosing around there to see what might turn up. But a judge ruled there wasn't enough probable cause.

Sheriff Bamonte, who liked Mathews despite Bob's unorthodox racial feelings, issued a press release asking the public to watch for Pierce, calling him an "Aryan counterfeiter." It was published in the weekly *Newport Miner*, to which Bob sometimes wrote letters to the editor. Bob responded angrily after the piece on Pierce was published. In a letter headed "For the Resurgence," Mathews lashed out at Bamonte and the system:

> *To the Editor:*
> *In regards to your article on the "Aryan counter-feiter," I wish to know how the story would have been written if Mr. Pierce was a Baptist or a Catholic in-stead of a member of the Church of Jesus Christ Chris-tian, Aryan Nations. Would you have reported that a "Baptist counterfeiter" had been spotted or referred to him as a "confirmed member of the Catholic Church"?*

I would also like to see your written description of the various pro-black or pro-Mexican organizations in this country which are treated as gently by the press as the pro-white organizations are treated harshly. Would you refer to the Mexican organization, La Raza, as a "neo-Communist racist group"?

Yes, Mr. _____ was scheduled to go to prison for daring to compete with the Federal Reserve, a non-government entity owned and controlled by international financiers. He was also, because of his religious and political opinions and activities, given a prison sentence far more harsh than given those whose motivation was personal and not based on political ideals.

I have a high opinion of Mr. Pierce. He is not, as the federals claim, "paranoid." He is a strong Aryan man with a pure heart and a keen mind who is concerned about the future of his three children in a nation controlled by a coalition of white racial masochists, Zionists and non-white racists.

As for Mr. Bamonte and his thinly veiled threats, if he thinks Mr. Pierce is hiding in my home then all I can say is I thought Mr. Bamonte was a more honorable and intelligent man than he apparently is.

I, along with Mr. Pierce, have no fear of the federals who came to my home while I was gone and who, after trying to intimidate my wife, threatened my two-year-old son. If Mr. Bamonte wishes to throw in his lot with such cowardly men, then that says a lot about Mr. Bamonte's nature.

I know not what the future will bring for men like Mr. Pierce and myself. What I do know is that while our fellow whites sheepishly continue down the path of racial and national suicide, tolerating homosexuality, abortion and miscegenation, we will stand strong for our race and our heritage even if it costs us our lives.

For the resurgence of my people.

Robert Mathews
Metaline Falls

". . . even if it costs us our lives." People were not used to reading such things in their local weekly. But the authorities took notice.

After leaving Newport, Mathews and Barnhill went to Missoula, flush with loot for a buying spree. Topping their list was weapons. At Brady's Sportsmen Supply in Trumpers Plaza, where Pierce used to work, Barnhill selected several items, including a new Smith & Wesson 9mm semi-automatic pistol, model 469. When the clerk handed Barnhill a standard federal firearms form, he filled it out "Andrew V. Barnhill, P.O. Box 20109, Missoula," and plunked down his cash.

Barnhill hadn't been in the group long enough to have amassed a large amount of bogus IDs. That seemingly innocuous slip, using his real name while buying that pistol, eventually would have dire consequences. No other single lapse by any kinsman had the impact of this slip of paper left at a gun shop in Missoula.

The men bought numerous weapons, including such exotic items as crossbows and throwing stars. Several also shopped around for computers that would allow them to link by modem with the computer network that the former Texas Klan leader Louis Beam was establishing at Aryan Nations.

The Aryan Nations Liberty Net operated like a typical computer bulletin board, with a full menu of essays, notices, and listings of race enemies. It included, for example, a list of the locations of all regional offices of the Anti-Defamation League of B'nai B'rith, which racists believe wields great power and influence over American institutions. The Liberty Net's message of greeting:

> The Aryan Nations Liberty Net welcomes you. This on-line computer bulletin board is for Aryan patriots only. This is a pro-American, pro-white, anti-communist network of true believers, who serve the one and only God—Jesus the Christ. Hail His Victory!

"Hey, Richie, I just armed this thing," Bruce Pierce casually mentioned as Kemp drove his Celica down Bannock Street in Boise.

"You did what?" Kemp yelled, imagining them both going up in a fireball with the car.

"I don't think it'll go off here," Pierce tried to reassure Kemp as he cradled the box containing his homemade bomb. He was very nervous. It was his first bomb. He'd followed all the instructions in his manual, part of his growing terrorist library. He had gotten the dynamite in Missoula from Pete Travis, who said he had found twenty sticks in a mine shaft while cross-country skiing. It was on the spur of the moment that Pierce sat in his converted school-bus home on wheels and patiently wired up three sticks to an electric blasting cap, battery, and timer.

On April 29, it was ready. He decided to test it on a synagogue west of downtown Boise, and got Kemp to drive him. Taking the bomb and a container of gasoline, they waited until several hours after the people left the building.

Kemp dropped Pierce near the corner of North 27th and West Bannock streets, where Congregation Ahavath Israel sat on the edge of a quiet grid of residential streets containing small single-family homes. Although 27th is a four-lane arterial, it was about 4 P.M. Sunday and there was little traffic.

Bruce walked to a parking lot in back of the unassuming building, which was completely visible from 27th. The synagogue was a modest, faded stucco building more resembling a residential duplex than a house of worship. It was one story with a flat roof. Two entry doors gave out on a small front porch three steps up. The only thing marking the synagogue was a gold Star of David mounted above the porch roof.

Bruce pried open the covering to a crawl space below the rear of the synagogue and wiggled his way under the building. He set his timer for less than thirty minutes and crawled back out to rejoin Kemp at a prearranged spot.

The resulting blast did little damage. The dynamite's percussion dissipated through the crawl space and only buckled the synagogue's kitchen floor. Actually, it did more harm to Mathews's group. Bob was irate that Pierce carried out an "unauthorized" action, and others in the group also made their displeasure known.

Besides, Mathews later stewed about the minimal damage; Pierce should have used a much bigger charge.

THE RADIO CRACKLED in Pend Oreille County Deputy Dave Jackson's car as he patrolled near Scotia Road

south of Newport: "We have a complainant who says the
subject we are looking for was sighted in your area driving a late-model white Ford pickup, partial Washington
plate 5591."

Jackson, one of Sheriff Bamonte's patrol deputies, had
been keeping his eyes open for Pierce. Now, on May 14,
he was getting a solid tip. He drove to the access road
leading to Duey's rented house and waited for backup
from Deputy Major Bambino. It was a rainy day, typical
for the Northwest in spring, and both lawmen were wearing yellow slickers.

The tip came from Larry Cada, the landlord, who had
gone to Duey's house earlier in the day. He saw a printing press in the living room just before Duey hustled to
the door holding up an open suitcase to block his view.

As the deputies approached the house, they noted the
windows covered with sheets and blankets. The pickup
with license plates HN-5591 was parked nearby.

Inside the house, Robert Merki was teaching printing
to David Lane. Lane had bandages on his left hand and a
bruise on his face, the result of some racist epithets that
got out of hand at a bar near Newport and ended in a
donnybrook.

Merki now was working for Mathews's "company."
After agreeing to help Lane select a press sold by a
cryptic gentleman over a lunch meeting near Denver's
Stapleton International Airport, he was drawn in deeper
when the men needed help learning to operate it. Mathews,
in his inimitable style of pushing his recruits ever farther,
charmed Merki into taking charge of the counterfeiting.
Merki agreed and took the Aryan oath in the Newport
house while setting up the print shop.

Merki bought paper, both linen and cotton bond, and
other supplies in Spokane while the others built a light
table. After lengthy discussion, they decided to do ten-
dollar bills, which were common and would be easier to
pass.

But then, after all this preparation, Larry Cada came
over demanding a landlord inspection the next day. It
wasn't just the printing press that made Cada nervous.
His phone bill included toll calls from the rental house,
and since Duey moved in there were calls to Robert

Mathews's house in Metaline Falls—the "Aryan counterfeiter's" friend—and to Aryan Nations in Idaho.

Just after lunch, the men in the house spotted the sheriff's vehicles coming down the drive. Duey went outside to greet the two deputies.

"Hi, I'm Randy Duey," he said. "Something I can do for you?"

"Yes sir," Jackson replied. "We have a report of a wanted party seen driving this white pickup here." He never mentioned Pierce by name.

"That truck belongs to my roommate, Denver Parmenter. He's out of town and I've been driving it. We're not wanted for anything, are we?" Duey asked.

"No sir, not that I'm aware," Jackson said. "Is there anyone else inside?"

Duey admitted there was, and Jackson asked Duey to have him step outside. When Lane came out, the deputies noticed his bruised face and bandaged hand, but they concluded he wasn't Pierce, either. Although Duey and Lane seemed nervous, the deputies had no further reason to stay. But Duey was curious.

"Wait a minute," he called after Jackson as the deputies walked toward their cars. "Could I ask you a few questions?" Duey paused, wondering how he could pick Jackson's brain without making him suspicious. He concluded it wasn't possible.

"Well, I guess under the circumstances I don't need to know any more," Duey stammered. That afternoon, Lane and Merki loaded the press into Mathews's pickup and abandoned the Newport house for safer haven in Boise. Merki rented a rundown bungalow on North 10th Street in Boise, with a view of the Idaho Capitol's dome down the street. He set up the press in the adjoining garage, safe from the tightening noose in Pend Oreille County.

A METAL PLATE in Jim Dye's head covered an injury he had suffered in Vietnam. An exploding mortar round caught him in the head, leg, and arm, resulting in slight brain and nerve damage, including memory lapses. Still, he had been proud of his "red badge of courage" and felt he had done right by his country, until he returned stateside to Pittsburgh. Here, he was treated with scorn for having served bravely and with honor in the Marine Corps. He came to believe that it was a useless war and the men who fought it had been pawns in a rich man's game. The experience embittered him, weakened his self-esteem, and drove him to drink.

At age thirty-six, Dye was underemployed and, influenced by his friends, blamed minorities for it. He joined the Ku Klux Klan in Philadelphia, then the National Alliance, and became friends with Tom Martinez. He was a heavy drinker who saw minorities as inferiors. None of them worked, he thought, they just sat back and collected welfare.

Dye met Mathews through Martinez and accepted an invitation to visit the White American Bastion. Mathews offered him a role in something Dye thought was important to his nation and his race. Dye clearly understood it would involve violence. Dye had earlier helped to pass some of Mathews's stolen loot in Philadelphia, and it appealed to Dye, who had left the Klan because there wasn't enough action.

Mathews wired $500 via Western Union to Martinez, who bought a one-way plane ticket to Spokane for Dye and gave his friend the change.

On May 3, Jim Dye landed in Spokane, where Mathews and Barnhill met him at the airport. His code name became "Mr. May" because of his arrival. After dinner in Spokane, they drove to Metaline Falls for a night's sleep in the fresh mountain air. It was quite a thrill for the hard-as-nails city boy. He spent a week at Mathews Acres, doing chores and meeting some of the other men.

During the first week, Dye sat in on an unusual meeting. Some of the people from Aryan Nations were upset about a member there, Walter West. They said West was getting drunk in the bars around Hayden Lake and repeating things he'd heard on Butler's compound about Yarbrough and his friends committing robberies.

This could become a huge problem, according to Tom Bentley, the mild-mannered principal of the Aryan Nations Academy. Most people at Aryan Nations knew about Yarbrough's suspension and the counterfeiting, and they suspected robberies too. But they didn't talk to outsiders about it.

West once asked Duey if he could join the new group, but they were convinced West had no idea what the group was really doing. Duey and Parmenter told Mathews the diminutive forty-two-year-old West wouldn't be a good recruit. They knew of at least one occasion when, after drinking, he'd beaten his wife, Bonnie Sue.

"How about if we pick him up one day," suggested Mathews, "take him to another state, way out of the Northwest, and just drop him off?"

That might make him talk louder, the others responded.

"Let's look for a better solution, then," Mathews said. "Think about it, and we'll decide later."

I HAVE JUST a few words to say to you," Andy Barnhill said over the long distance line to Randall Rader, his old field commander from the CSA.

Rader, living in his native West Plains, Missouri, was startled by Barnhill's tone. He'd known him three years and guessed that Andy was mad about something. He hadn't seen him since spring 1983 on a visit to Joplin, where Barnhill, Pete Travis, and Rodney Carrington lived after leaving CSA. All he knew was they'd moved to Montana. Now, Barnhill said he was coming to Missouri.

"Well, stop in and see me, Andy," Rader said. "I'd be happy to have you."

"I'll be there in about a week," Barnhill replied.

Barnhill and Parmenter were being sent by Mathews on a diplomatic mission across the country. It included a stop in Philadelphia, so they asked Jim Dye if he'd like to share driving chores in Parmenter's new pride, an Oldsmobile Cutlass.

Their first stop was Missoula, where Barnhill went to see Pete Travis at the convenience store where he worked. Mathews wanted to know why Travis didn't show for the robbery. Later at Travis's home, he explained he was too involved with his pregnant girlfriend to join them. Parmenter scratched Travis from his list. But Mathews wouldn't give up. He continued to count Travis as a potential recruit and even assigned him an appropriate code name: "No Show."

On May 12, Barnhill, Parmenter, and Dye arrived in West Plains, a town of 7,500 located 50 miles from the

198 The Silent Brotherhood

CSA camp. They stopped at a roadside motel called the Capri. Parmenter found the Capri a touch seedier than he liked, and went on alone to the Holiday Inn, leaving Barnhill and Dye to share a room at the Capri.

Around the survivalist movement, Randall Rader was considered one of the foremost civilian authorities on paramilitary training. Under his tutelage, the CSA's Survival Training School had become the Fort Dix of the radical right. Now that Rader abandoned CSA, due mostly to a falling out with the leader, "King James" Ellison, Barnhill believed that getting Rader into the "company" would make Mathews's planned step six—racist guerrilla training—first rate.

Before heading to the Capri, Rader drove down to Mountain Home, Arkansas, where Jackie Lee Norton, a former classmate and CSA member, now lived, to bring his friend along—a 100-mile round trip that made him feel more secure since he didn't know if Barnhill was angry with him. But when they arrived at Barnhill's room at the Capri, Andy greeted both of them with a broad smile and introduced Jim Dye.

Barnhill sat down and grabbed a tennis racquet case off the floor. Opening it, he handed the contents to Rader. His game clearly wasn't tennis. Inside was a German-made Heckler & Koch Model 94 assault rifle, a 9mm semi-automatic carbine that had its 16-inch barrel sawed off to just under a foot. It was impressive, even to a man like Rader used to handling sophisticated weapons.

"How do you like it, Randall?" Andy asked. "Cost me $500 out West."

"It's a beauty, Andy," he replied, looking it over thoroughly before handing it to Jackie Lee. "And lookee here, it's got a collapsible stock!"

Barnhill next opened a briefcase, and Rader could see a 2-inch stack of money in its corner. Barnhill reached for a handgun inside and gave it to Rader.

"Try this one out," Andy said.

"Whew-ee, they don't come like this from the factory, that's for sure, said Rader, admiring the pistol. It was a Walther PPK, .380 caliber, and it was top of the line—two-toned, with a blue steel slide and a silver-finished frame.

After more talk, Parmenter arrived and was introduced as "Sandals," his code name. Before they broke up, Barnhill told Rader he had something important to ask him the next day. Rader drew him a map to his parents' farm, where there would be a family gathering the next day for Mother's Day. When Rader got home that evening, he rushed for the telephone and called Rodney Carrington in Missoula.

"I just met with Andy Barnhill," Rader told Carrington after exchanging initial pleasantries. "You should see the firearms he's got."

"Yeah, I know," said Carrington, who ran the machine shop for Rader when CSA was converting assault rifles into full machine guns.

"Just what is Andy getting into up there?" Rader asked.

"I don't think I should say over the phone," replied Carrington, who knew pieces of the puzzle from talking with Pete Travis about Mathews. "I'll send you a letter on it." That evening Carrington wrote to Rader as much as he knew about Barnhill's new friends.

On Sunday morning, Barnhill drove alone to visit Rader and asked him to go for a ride through the rolling Ozark countryside around West Plains.

"Randall," Barnhill began as they started down the highway, "there's a true white man up in the Northwest, his name is Carlos, and he's forming a real white underground. I know because I'm in it.

"He's got a plan for making that area a homeland for the folk. Part of that plan includes a guerrilla force to strike at the enemy. That's when I told Carlos about you. You're the best there is, and Carlos would like to hire you for a month to do some initial training of the men we've got together.

"He'll pay you $1,000 for the month."

Rader's mouth fell open. He hadn't had regular work in some time, and he could use that money for his wife and three kids. And Barnhill was offering work he loved. He relished the idea of commanding another regiment.

"You can make more money than that, too," Barnhill continued. "Carlos is going to want a lot of guns, and you know how to get them. We've got the money."

"Where's Carlos getting all this money?" Rader asked. Barnhill savored the moment before turning to his friend.

"We robbed an armored car," he said with a smile.

"You did what?" Rader responded with shock.

"You heard me right," Barnhill replied. "Look, if you come up to Metaline Falls for a month, you'll need expense money." Keeping one hand on the wheel of the Olds, Barnhill reached into his briefcase and extracted a pile of money, placing it on the car seat between them. "There's $500 there for your expenses."

Rader looked at the money for a moment, then reached over and picked it up. "When do you want me to come?" Barnhill was elated. He also was in the market for weapons. Knowing Rader kept some from the CSA, he asked if any were for sale.

Rader thought for a minute, then directed Andy to a wooded area about 20 miles outside West Plains. There, Rader spent a short time digging a small hole before he hit a plastic pickle barrel. He pulled the soiled container up to the surface and opened the lid. Inside was one of the most gruesome weapons made, the Ingram MAC-10 machine pistol. With limited accuracy over distance, it was a meat grinder at close range. Formerly manufactured by Military Armament Corporation—hence MAC—Rader's .45-caliber version was assembled by RPB Industries. It could fire more than nine hundred rounds per minute, fifteen bullets a second.

It resembled a small metal box mounted lengthwise on its side, a trigger on the underside, with the slot for the ammo clip serving as the grip. The short barrel was threaded for a silencer. The sight groove was enlarged, and Rader had put sling swivels on the side. A new takedown pin was installed, and the bolt handle was made bigger than normal. The grip was wrapped with camouflage tape.

Also in the pickle barrel were several accessories: a silencer made from a grease gun by Carrington, several flash suppressors that would swallow the flames spit out by the immense firepower, nine thirty-round ammo magazines, pouches, and ammo.

Rader had bought the MAC as a legal semi-automatic

at a Mountain Home gun shop in 1979 and had converted it to full automatic. Numerous students at CSA's survival school had fired it. Barnhill offered $500 for it. Rader agreed, and threw in a hand grenade as a freebie, making his morning worth $2,000, thanks to Carlos.

Leaving on Monday, Barnhill, Parmenter, and Dye backtracked to Mountain Home, a small, pleasant town set on the hills separating Bull Shoals and Norfolk lakes. Barnhill met another CSA friend, Henry Hubbard, who sold him a German Schmiesser MP40 machine gun, made in World War II. It had a specially made silencer, a spare barrel, two original German magazines, and its original sling. Barnhill bought it along with 3 pounds of C4 plastic explosive.

Barnhill placed it all in the trunk of Parmenter's Olds, along with the MAC, and started toward Philadelphia, where Dye would try to persuade some of his friends to join Mathews's army.

When they arrived in the City of Brotherly Love, Dye directed them to the home of George Zaengle, another right-wing friend of his and Tom Martinez's. There, they met Zaengle and another potential recruit, Bill Nash, both of whom agreed after hearing about Mathews's "company" that it sounded like something they'd want to join. Martinez, who came along for the visit, was still hesitant.

Dye brought money to pay moving expenses for Zaengle and Nash to the White American Bastion, but Martinez wasn't so sure they should go. Instead, Martinez told them he'd go to meet with his buddy Mathews to check out the bastion. Then he'd let Zaengle and Nash make up their minds. Martinez had a growing uneasiness over Mathews's activities, even though he was profiting nicely from them.

Martinez and his wife, Susan, hosted a cookout in their small backyard. Inside the house, Barnhill continued to tinker with his PPK, and Martinez's daughter saw it. Martinez became upset and asked Barnhill to put it away. "No way," Barnhill replied. "I have to carry this at all times. It's for gunning down the feds." Parmenter was less boisterous as a guest. He gazed for hours at Martinez's television, playing and replaying a tape of D. W. Griffith's *Birth of a Nation*, the 1915 movie classic depicting the Ku Klux Klan as the avenging angels of the white race, on Martinez's VCR.

They left in a few days with instructions from Martinez on meeting Frazier Glenn Miller, leader of the Confederate Knights of the Ku Klux Klan in Angier, North Carolina, a crossroads town between Raleigh and Fayetteville. It is near Fort Bragg, which provided a source of sympathetic recruits and pilfered military hardware.

A week before Barnhill and Parmenter arrived, Mathews had asked Martinez to secure an introduction to Miller for the two emissaries from Bob Miles. Martinez knew Miles well and once spent time on his Michigan farm with his family. He called Miles on May 10, and Miles was happy to pave the way by phoning Miller to tell him some friends were headed his way. An introduction from Miles was a prudent and sufficient entrée for someone making the rounds of strangers.

Miller, forty-three, was a wiry man with dark, deep-set eyes, sideburns, and a thick mustache on his thin, rugged face. He ran for governor of North Carolina in the May 8 Democratic primary, two weeks before Barnhill and Parmenter visited. He came in eighth of ten candidates.

He spent twenty years in the Army, leaving as a master sergeant in the Special Forces. He was in Greensboro in 1979 during a Death to the Klan rally and said he was proud at the outcome, when an amalgamation of Klansmen and neo-Nazis drove up to the rally and opened fire, slaying five communists. "I was more proud to have been in Greensboro for eighty-eight seconds in 1979 than twenty years in the U.S. Army," he told people. "It was the only armed victory over communism in this country."

He claimed to have one thousand followers, although precise numbers at any given time couldn't be known even by Miller. But he regularly drew up to four hundred people to rallies, where his cadres marched in battle fatigues instead of sheets.

Miller received Barnhill and Parmenter at his farmhouse on May 22. They told him they represented a group in the Northwest that wanted to fund white organizations. They were checking out Miller's operation as a potential grantee.

Miller showed them his newsletter, *The Confederate*

Leader, and the home base of his telephone message service for people with questions about the white power movement. He also had a small firing range in his backyard. The guests were impressed, and gave Miller a $1,000 donation, adding that there'd be more coming.

After the brief visit, Barnhill and Parmenter left that afternoon for Florida. Barnhill had a friend in Stuart, Florida, he wanted to recruit, Richard Scutari, a martial arts expert and master of the voice stress analyzer. Barnhill told Mathews that the device could weed out potential informants.

While in Florida, both Barnhill and Parmenter took time to visit some family members. They took their time on the return trip to the bastion, stopping at survivalist stores along the way to buy more supplies. It was June 2 when they pulled into Metaline Falls. As they began to unload, Mathews called Parmenter aside with some shocking news that changed the complexion of the group forever. They had blood on their hands now, all of them.

As HIS FLIGHT approached the runway in Spokane, Tom Martinez could see out the window why Bob Mathews liked the Northwest. It was much different from the East, where children grow up on concrete instead of grassy meadows. Jim Dye felt the same. Seated next to Martinez on the jetliner, Dye was glad Martinez had come to see for himself what the White American Bastion was like.

It was May 23, the Wednesday before Memorial Day weekend. Mathews stood in a phone booth to watch Martinez and Dye arrive, to make sure the Philadelphians weren't followed by the FBI. He knew by this time he was a matter of interest again to the feds. Lane and Kemp were there as well. All of the men jammed into Mathews's truck and drove to a body shop, where Lane retrieved his yellow VW bug. He was headed to Boise to check the progress of Merki's counterfeiting.

Then Mathews, Kemp, Dye, and Martinez made the two-hour drive to Metaline Falls, where Tom spent the next four days socializing, doing some farm work, and running errands with Bob, who bent his ear about moving out there with his family. Tom had to admit, it sure had appeal.

Martinez slept in Mathews's guest room, on the opposite end of the house from Mathews's bedroom. The
other men slept in the barracks. Tom liked the ambience,
but he felt something was different from a typical house-
hold. Then it hit him. There was no television or radio.
Bob wouldn't have such mass-culture purveyors in his
house. In their stead was a police scanner, set to local
agencies' frequencies.

Martinez had to be home by Memorial Day. On Saturday evening, the day before he was to leave, he sat on
the second floor of the barracks, in the corner by the
bookshelf with Bill Soderquist's collection of World War
II books. He flipped through back issues of a racist
magazine while Mathews, Dye, and Kemp held a quiet
conversation on the other side of the room as they cleaned
some weapons.

"Tom Bentley says they're still having that problem
with West at Aryan Nations," Kemp said. That caught
Martinez's attention. When Bentley lived outside Corning,
New York, Martinez had met him. "He says something
has to be done about him."

"What exactly is he doing?" Mathews asked.

"He's running his mouth about 'Gary's army,' " Kemp
reported. West evidently thought Yarbrough was a ringleader. "And he offered his first wife's new husband
some of our counterfeit money."

Mathews became alarmed. "Then it leaves us no room,"
he concluded. "We have to do it. But I can't tomorrow. I
have to take Tom to the airport and then go to Boise."

"I can handle it, Bob," Kemp volunteered. "I want to
do it."

"Get Jimmy to go along," Mathews said to Kemp, out
of Dye's earshot.

"I'll ask him. But how do we get West to go with us?"
Kemp asked. Mathews thought for a minute, then remembered Bentley said that West's wife had left him to
live at Aryan Nations after West beat her in a drunken
stupor.

"Let's get Duey to tell him his wife wants to see him,"
Mathews suggested. "He'll trust Duey. And don't use a
gun. Too noisy. Use a sledgehammer."

Martinez wandered over to the table, and they abruptly stopped talking about Walter West.

On Sunday morning, Mathews and Martinez ate breakfast, then threw their things into the trunk of Mathews's car. Bob was sorry he didn't get a commitment from Tom to move to the bastion. But he'd keep working on him. He even gave him a preliminary code name, "Spider," because of a black widow tattoo Tom had.

Before leaving, Martinez saw Dye. Quietly, he said to him: "Be sure you know what you're getting into, Jimmy."

When they reached Newport an hour later, Bob told Tom he had a stop to make. South of town on Scotia Road, Bob turned at the driveway that led to Duey's house. Randy came jogging out when he saw the car.

Bob got out and walked to the front of the car. He and Randy talked, but Tom couldn't hear much of what was said. When Bob got back into the car, he seemed upset. Tom didn't ask him why. Later, when they were near the Spokane airport, Bob asked Tom whether he owned a gun. Tom said he didn't. Immediately, Bob pulled into a sporting goods store and told Tom to look over the selection.

"Every white man should own guns, Tom," Mathews said as he bought a .45-caliber Smith & Wesson for Martinez. "They're gonna need them."

On the drive to the airport, they talked about Jews and blacks, the way Bob always did. Then in a serious tone, Bob turned to Tom. "I want you to keep your eyes and ears open," he said. "A guy in Colorado is going to be taken care of."

"Who?" Tom asked.

"You don't need to know that, buddy," Bob answered. "Just keep your eyes and ears open. This guy's just got to go."

That same day, Kemp asked Dye to accompany him in his car. As they drove down the mountain from Mathews Acres, Kemp asked Dye if he would come along while they took care of Walter West. They needed another man, and Dye wouldn't have to do the actual killing.

"How would you feel about that, Jimmy?" Kemp asked.

Dye's loyalty was vested entirely in Bob Mathews. This man who had been a stranger just two months ago had already given the embittered Vietnam veteran a new sense of worth. Mathews had given him everything without strings attached. As a result, Dye had told Mathews freely that he would do almost anything for him and the group. Dye felt obligated to go with Kemp.

The two men took some shovels and a 3-pound sledge and drove to the Garwood Tavern, a roadside bar at the corner of U.S. 95 and the turnoff to Aryan Nations. Around noon, they met Duey and David Tate, the young man from Aryan Nations. Tate knew the woods around the region better than the others. They headed north, Tate leading the way in his car. Driving about two hours, they ended up on a logging road in the Kaniksu National Forest, about a mile from the highway. The four walked into the forest about 30 yards from the road. There, between two tall pines, they selected a gravesite.

Dye and Tate dug a hole 5 feet deep, 5 feet long and 3 feet wide while Duey and Kemp left to find West. It took three hours to dig the grave. Then Dye and Tate waited in the brush for their accomplices to return.

West lived near Athol rent-free in a house on Homestead Road owned by Aryan Nations security chief Bud Cutler. He was divorced once, and had a nine-year-old son in Spokane. He and Bonnie Sue had a six-year-old daughter. Bonnie Sue called Aryan Nations after West beat her sometime in the spring. Several of the men went up to the house and saw she was pretty well bruised. They helped her move to Aryan Nations. West later complained to a friend that Tom Bentley had threatened to kill him. Bentley had a romantic interest in Bonnie Sue, and he was angry that Walter could have beaten her that way.

When Duey spotted West, he noticed West was carrying his Mini-14 rifle.

"Your wife's lookin' for you," Duey said. "Wants us to bring you along."

West complied, pushing the rifle onto the seat of Kemp's car. They headed back to where Dye and Tate were waiting.

West was supposed to meet a friend named Don from Colville, Washington, that afternoon. When Don came by the house, West was already gone, although his car was there. He never heard from his friend again. Four days later, it was he who filed a missing person report on West.

Dye and Tate crouched behind some bushes when they heard Kemp's Toyota Celica rumbling up the dirt road just after 6 P.M. The sunlight cut through the pines at a sharp angle, lighting the scene in a golden glow. If West wondered why Bonnie Sue might be waiting in such a forsaken place, he didn't ask.

After West got out of the car, Kemp grabbed the sledgehammer from under his seat. Walking up behind West as Duey was talking to him, Kemp swung the hammer in a mighty arc and brought it crashing into the side of West's head, then quickly hit him again. West crumpled to the ground, dropping his rifle, and slouched against a tree. Blood oozed from the wound.

Kemp and Duey turned to look for their companions when they heard a cry that curdled their blood.

"What's going on here, Randy?" West yelled in bewilderment to his friend.

Both men had thought West was dead from the hammer blows. Duey, tensing from the shrill sound that broke the quiet of the woods, instinctively reached down and grabbed West's Mini-14. Spinning with the rifle at his hip, he squeezed the trigger without taking time to aim. The slug smacked into West's forehead and blew out the back of his broken skull.

Dye rose from his hiding place 20 feet away. Vietnam had inured him to such gore. The others were momentarily stunned. After composing themselves, Kemp and Duey each grabbed a leg and dragged West's body 25 yards to the grave. When they looked back, they saw the dead man's brain trailing on the ground behind them. Dye scooped the brain matter off the forest floor with a shovel and tossed it into the grave with the body.

The men then filled in the hole and, as they scattered brush and moss over it, heard several loud retching noises. It was Tate, the boy with the gun and a Bible. He'd fired plenty of guns before but had never seen a man shot to death. He was down by the cars, heaving his guts out.

On the way back, the four stopped at a stream to wash their shovels. Their nerves were so edgy, they stopped at a bar to down a few beers. There had been nothing noble about what they'd just done. All those years of talk about being brave Aryan warriors, and this was how it finally came down, killing a friend.

The killing of West was a giant leap beyond their other crimes. They had carefully planned them so that no one would get hurt.

But in the very heart of the idyllic White American Bastion, where white families were supposed to find a future free from the madness of the violent, polluted society, a white man had been killed by his white brothers.

Leaving the tavern, Duey and Tate went off into the night. Kemp and Dye went to Metaline Falls, back to their bunks in the barracks. In the dark, walking from the driveway, Dye stopped on the long back porch behind Bob's house. He propped his shovel against the house. No one ever touched that shovel again.

Chapter 6

Alan Berg: The Man You Love to Hate

Bob Mathews rose from the floor, out of breath, after roughhousing on the floor with Zillah's two boys, Dustin and Caleb. All three were laughing while Zillah, prominently pregnant, smiled from a chair to the side of the living room. This was how she had pictured "family."

"Okay, you guys go on and play outside now," Bob panted, a wide grin on his tired face. "You wore me out!"

Zillah loved Bob's visits. Although he was married to another woman, Zillah considered herself his wife. Zillah was the one bearing his child, and Bob said she was the one he wanted. But Bob's work usually kept him away. So his visit the week after Memorial Day pleased her immensely, even if her mother would ruin it.

Zillah's mother had phoned with news of a successful mission. She would be right over with her "intelligence folder" on Alan Berg. For some reason it didn't seem incongruous to Zillah that this gentle man who was so good with her children would send them out of the house so he could talk of murder. But Mathews, just in from Metaline Falls, was progressing immediately from approving Walter West's killing to planning another. This time he wanted to make a statement to the world. It would be an assassination.

There was a deep animosity between Zillah and Jean Craig, and Bob was caught in the middle. As handsome as he was, he wasn't a ladies' man. Debbie and Zillah were the important women in his love life, and both drove him to distraction. The men used to joke that one reason Bob got involved in the movement as heavily as he did was to get away from Debbie's nagging. And where did he run? To Zillah, who dumped on Bob to fight her insecurity. Bob's friends gave her the nickname "Godzillah."

And then there was Jean, Zillah's mother, whom they called Rainy because she cried on cue. Bob frequently tried to bridge the chasm between the two. That was how Jean ended up with the task of following Berg.

Mathews and David Lane were visiting Laramie the week of May 11 when Jean drove up to Zillah's house, walked in unannounced, and started toward the bathroom where Bob was taking a shower. Zillah screamed at her mother and pushed her toward the door. Hearing the scuffle, Mathews jumped out of the shower and pulled a towel around himself, then took Jean gently by the arm and steered her to the front porch, dripping wet while he talked to her.

"I have a job for you and I'm really counting on your being able to do it," Mathews said solemnly.

Jean Craig worshiped Bob. Zillah suspected that her mother, in fact, loved him and was jealous of her daughter. Jean saw in Bob a poise, confidence, and sense of purpose she'd never seen in any man, least of all her two ex-husbands. The gods, she believed, watched over him. To assist, she had been reading the runes, an ancient Norse art of fortune-telling, before each robbery to see what the fates portended. Now Bob had a more active role for her.

"You know we've been knocking around the idea of having a talk with that radio guy in Denver, Alan Berg," Mathews said. "Talking with" was a right-wing euphemism for killing. Jean nodded. She had heard about the February 13 show in which Berg denounced Colonel Jack Mohr, who enjoyed demigod status in the right wing. It had made some of Mathews's friends angry.

"I'd like you to spend some time in Denver gathering information on Berg, where he lives, where he works, what kind of car he drives, everything he does," Mathews said. "Then bring it back here for me."

Jean agreed. She was in Denver frequently anyway, seeing a chiropractor and attending seminars on nutrition, acupressure, and holistic health.

Bob walked her to her car as he explained the assignment, and Jean started crying. He put his wet arm around her shoulder, comforting the overweight woman, who was twenty years his senior. He helped her into her car, then leaned through the window and patted her arm lovingly. Jean's eyes met and held his for a moment.

"Oh, Bob, you're all I have," she said as she turned on the ignition.

Jean Craig was a lonely soul. She was born in Kansas on January 20, 1933. Four of her seven brothers died in infancy. The family moved to Rawlins, Wyoming, where her father was in the restaurant business.

After a stint in the Air Force, Jean returned to Rawlins and got pregnant out of wedlock at age twenty-three. The father refused to acknowledge the child, and Jean went to a friend in Minneapolis to have her baby. When Zillah was nine months old, Jean moved to Worland, Wyoming, and worked as a telephone operator. If Zillah ever wanted to reach her mother, all she had to do was dial 0.

Jean got married when Zillah was three, and it lasted exactly a year. The husband beat Jean so badly one night, she screamed for Zillah to run outside and get help. At four, Zillah was terrified of the dark and didn't know where to go, so she just stood outside on the sidewalk crying in confusion.

Jean took out some of her frustrations on her daughter, most often snapping at Zillah with a wet dish towel. When Zillah became pregnant at seventeen, Jean wanted her to give the baby up for adoption. That demand sent a devastating message to Zillah: "Don't make the mistake I made in keeping you."

In her loneliness, Jean turned to religion. Through her Aunt Helen, she became familiar with the Christian Identity message of the Reverend Sheldon Emry of Arizona, a noted anti-Semite preacher. Soon she was buying his tapes and accepting his racial theology.

Jean's second marriage, also brief, was to a man she met over the phone while working as a night operator. On a cold, icy Sunday morning, her husband was towing Jean's disabled car with his pickup truck while Jean steered the car. He rounded a corner too fast, whipping Jean's car with such force into a pole that she had to be cut out of the wreckage. She came close to dying while spending two months in the Veterans Administration hospitals in Cheyenne and Denver. During that time, her husband never once came to visit.

But the accident opened doors for Jean. Qualifying for vocational rehabilitation, she moved to Laramie to attend the University of Wyoming and found it to be a most positive experience. She studied anything she wanted. But through it all, she never mended her relationship with her daughter.

Jean arrived at Zillah's house the day after Memorial Day 1984 and strode straight to Mathews with a manila folder. "I visited the radio station in Denver," she told him. "I told them I was a journalism student gathering information on Mr. Berg, and they gave me some promotional material."

Jean and Zillah watched while Mathews took the folder to read its contents. On top was a photocopy of a full-page article from the *Rocky Mountain News*, with an artist's drawing of Berg, headlined, "A Man You Love to Hate."

Berg's cars were easily spotted. Most often he drove his black Volkswagen bug convertible. But in the garage of his townhouse he also kept a Bricklin and a DeLorean. He liked to eat at Gyro's Place, a small Greek restaurant on East Colfax Avenue near East High School, or at the White Spot diner on East Colfax near Colorado Boulevard. But both places were often crowded.

Jean had taken photos of the parking area on the alley side of the building that housed KOA studios. It was near Larimer Square, a pioneer-era historic district that is one of Denver's big tourist draws. The University of Colorado's Denver campus was also nearby. The area was usually mobbed with people.

But Berg's house was another matter. His address, 1445 Adams Street, was listed in the Denver telephone book and was only half a block off East Colfax, Denver's major east–west street. Yet Adams was little-traveled, and Berg usually came home after dark. After Mathews digested this information, he closed the folder and looked at Jean, his intense brown eyes alive with admiration, making her blush.

"Jean, this is excellent, just excellent," he bubbled.

"This is fantastic work!" He heaped praise on Jean for several minutes. Then he walked to the fireplace and put a match to the lower corners of the folder. He let the flames get a good start, then tossed the burning papers into the hearth.

Turning to Zillah, he said, "Let's get those kids back in here!"

"IF YOU WANT SOME facts instead of whistling Dixie here . . . ," Alan Berg roared at his guest, but the agitated man on the phone cut him off abruptly. He didn't like the Dixie reference. Berg had already accused him of anti-Semitism, and he didn't want to add racism to the list.

"Hey, I am not whistling Dixie!" protested Roderick Elliott of nearby Fort Lupton, Colorado, publisher of the *Primrose and Cattlemen's Gazette* and head of the National Agricultural Press Association. The group catered to farmers in the Midwest and Plains, where the American Agriculture Movement, tractorcades, and a more militant breed of farmer all had their start.

Elliott had become a telephone guest on Berg's KOA radio show through a complicated set of circumstances. His paper ran a six-part, anti-Jewish series by Francis Farrell on the *Protocols of the Learned Elders of Zion* called "Open Letter to the Goyim." Farrell was the former Air Force colonel who had lost his filling station in the Pennsylvania Poconos during the Arab oil embargo and had moved to Fort Lupton, sharing his apartment for a short time with David Lane.

In those same issues, Marine Corps recruiters ran their "Looking for a Few Good Men" ads. Denver's liberal Democratic Representative Patricia Schroeder, an influential member of the House Armed Services Committee, got the Marines to pull the advertising because of the publication's blatant anti-Semitism.

Berg got Elliott on his show on June 15, 1983, by claiming Schroeder violated Elliott's First Amendment rights by instigating an advertising boycott. Besides, Berg observed on his show, rednecks and Jew-haters might make good Marines.

"As a matter of fact," he joked with one caller, "if she

ran this in the B'nai B'rith paper she'd be wasting her money, ha ha!"

But while he appeared to defend Elliott's First Amendment rights, Berg was merely baiting him to get his phones buzzing. Berg was not about to share his microphone with Elliott when things really started to cook. His loyal listeners knew it was only a matter of a few more barbs at the beleaguered Elliott before the phone would be slammed in his ear.

"You're whistling," Berg shot back in his nasal, staccato voice, "because everything that you have said is a lie, okay? But I think you have a right to advance your lies. See, I'm still protecting your right to lie, okay?" Elliott kept trying to interrupt, but Berg wasn't about to give him a chance to speak.

"Tell you what," Berg shouted. "As long as you lie, I like it open like this because you have no facts. You have made them up and you have inferred a thought like all fanatics, like John Birchers, like Klansmen, like all of these folks!"

"You're crazy!" Elliott interjected when Berg was forced to come up for air.

"I'm crazy, sir? You're a healthy person? Thanks so much for calling! And I stood up for you, believe it or not!" Slam! Berg pulled Elliott's plug. "All lines are open, 861-TALK, 861-8255. What do you think about this thing here? It's kind of sickening. It really is." He cut to a commercial.

Alan Berg was a controversial personality wherever KOA's 50,000 watts could take him from his downtown Denver studio. At night with KOA's clear channel, that meant parts of thirty-eight states, and into Canada and Mexico. He resembled an oversized gnome, his fiery eyes and large nose emerging under a massive haystack of salt-and-paprika hair and beard. His friends knew him as a fun-loving but insecure hermit whose iconoclasm extended even to his favorite drink in his post-alcoholic days, tomato juice laced with Tabasco sauce.

His careers—he had had several by age fifty—always involved his mouth. All required a fast lip and smooth delivery. Promoting jazz concerts, steering johns to a cathouse while driving cabs, badgering Chicago criminal court juries, selling shirts and shoes and, finally, provoking audiences over his radio talk show all called upon his polished gift of gab. Dusty Saunders, the broadcasting critic for the *Rocky Mountain News,* described Berg as "alternately arrogant, witty, rude, erudite, opinionated, intelligent and, at times, just plain nasty."

A moderately successful criminal lawyer in Chicago in the late 1950s and early 1960s, he started having petit mal seizures, which destroyed his confidence and slid the cocky young man into the bottle. Because of Alan's drinking and infidelity, his wife, Judith, left him to come home to her parents, a socially prominent Denver couple. Alan followed, vowing to dry out, which he did. The couple got back together and went into the shirt and shoe business before Alan began a lengthy affair with a black woman and left Judith again.

His introduction to talk radio came in the autumn of 1975 when a friend on KMGC, a small station in suburban Englewood, invited Berg to share his microphone to help liven up a limp Sunday afternoon broadcast. The show started with chitchat, the phones as lifeless as a mountain ghost town. But Berg, a natural provocateur, gradually warmed up and the phones started jingling. Abortion, religion, birth control, one sacred cow after another was led into Berg's slaughterhouse to be ground into hamburger. Berg later was offered his own show on KMGC.

After moving in March 1978 to the area's top station, KHOW, Berg honed his caustic style fending off calls from teens who wanted their rock 'n' roll back. Seventeen months later, KHOW fired Berg when the station was sold and changed to "family-oriented" fare. He returned to the Englewood station and brought his heightened "insult" style, imitative of the late Joe Pyne, with him.

Of his style, Berg once said: "I stick it to the audience and they love it. They can't stand me, man, but they sneak back and listen because they don't know what I'm gonna do next and they want to be there. They don't know when I'm gonna be funny or serious or blow my career or go off the deep end, because I don't know that either. That uncertainty drives them up the wall. It excites them. They don't have much excitement in their lives. Compared to what goes on in Denver, I'm damned exciting."

One afternoon, Berg was baiting the Ku Klux Klan and its local leader, Fred Wilkins, who had sued Denver District Attorney Dale Tooley. Wilkins had charged that the DA glossed over allegations that blacks and Jews had attacked Denver Klansmen at Jewish community meetings in the city. When Berg saw that in the papers, he challenged Wilkins on the air to confront him, calling the Klan "slime."

On Tuesday, November 6, 1979, a week after he dared Wilkins to "take me on," Berg was broadcasting when Wilkins burst into the studio. Startled listeners heard: "I'm Fred Wilkins. You're gonna die!" Then Wilkins left.

Berg told police Wilkins had a gun. But Wilkins, a fireman in suburban Lakewood who was suspended after the incident, said he only pointed his finger at Berg. He claimed Berg blew it out of proportion to milk the ratings. Wilkins was charged in Arapahoe County with felony menacing, but he and Berg later reached a confidential settlement, each claiming vindication. Shortly thereafter, Wilkins quit the Klan. Berg later went to KOA when the Englewood station changed to all-oldies.

Wilkins had struggled in the small Denver Klan faction with David Lane, who distributed neo-Nazi literature along with KKK brochures. Wilkins wanted no part of that. "I ran him out of the Klan," Wilkins later said of Lane, "because I didn't like his way of doing things."

In February 1984, Morley Safer of CBS's *60 Minutes* came to Denver and interviewed Berg for a piece on nasty radio talk show hosts. KOA's brass wasn't thrilled with the outcome, but Berg loved it. Then the March 1984 Arbitron ratings for Denver radio came out, showing Berg with an astounding 10.9 audience share. Eleven out of every 100 people with their radios on at the noon hour had their dials set on 85 AM. Berg was at his best.

"We are with Greeley," Berg said after a commercial, the Roderick Elliott fracas lighting his entire board. "You are on KOA. Hello, caller, are you there?"

"Yes," answered the woman from Greeley, in the agricultural belt northeast of Denver. "I don't want to make an argument or anything, but several comments were made by Alan, and what I was concerned about, one where he was talking so much about Israel. The American people are not concerned about the economics in Israel as opposed to the ones here. We have over 10 million unemployed, we have people on welfare, the senior citizens' Social Security is being cut. What are we doing for the American public, that's what we're concerned about. Isn't that . . ."

Berg jumped in, sensing the woman wasn't going to agree with him. He would play out a little line, let her struggle, then quickly reel her in like a plump Rocky Mountain rainbow trout.

"Are you trying to say we should totally abandon foreign aid altogether?"

"What I'm saying," she replied, "is in your discussion with Mr. Elliott and a Colonel Farrell, the subject of Israel was brought up and their economy and how they live. What we want to know . . ."

Berg stopped her in midsentence. "Well, the reason I brought that up . . ."

"Wait a minute, wait . . ." the woman implored.

"Excuse me, excuse me, caller!"

"No, you excuse me . . ."

"If you want to know why I brought it up," Berg stormed on, "they contended every Israeli is receiving $10,000 a head from the U.S. government. That's a lie." Then the Greeley woman voiced the frustration numerous callers and listeners felt, the very emotions Berg purposely stimulated for his ratings.

"Why don't you listen to me?" she cried. "Why don't you give me a chance? You wanted to roast everybody else. As an interviewer, you are to hear both sides, not to take one side and roast them, but give them an opportunity."

Berg explained he was simply supporting Elliott's right to speak any lies he wanted, but the woman reprimanded him. It was the signal the end was coming.

"Now you're calling me a liar," Berg broke in. "And you don't know me very well to know that I wouldn't take a stand that I didn't believe in."

"As an American citizen, you're telling me that I

should . . . ," the woman began another statement. But Berg was finished.

"You're a jerk, honey, take a walk!" he said as he punched the cutoff button. "Okay, the line's open, enough is enough here!" The show aroused so much rancor that Elliott's wife, Karla, received some telephone threats while Berg was still on the air. Elliott called KOA, and Berg asked listeners to cool it. At the same time, he turned up the heat.

"Brighton, you're on KOA," said Berg.

"Yes, sir, I happen to be Jewish and I have to agree totally with Rick Elliott," the caller from Brighton said.

"Well, what do you agree with?"

"Everything he said."

"Well, what did he say?" Berg prodded. "What do you agree with, sir, as a Jew? I'm curious now. As a Jew, you agree with what?"

"I agree that they are trying to take over the nation."

"How exactly are *they* doing that?" Berg asked.

"Going through the farms," the caller answered.

"Through the farms?" Berg was incredulous. "How many Jewish farmers do you know? Do these Jews go in for plastic surgery and are now looking very goy down on the farm?"

"That's not what I'm saying," the caller insisted. "I'm saying that the Jews are going around buying up the land from the farmers and letting them set."

"Can you give me some documentation?" Berg asked. "Tell me the names of the Jews who have bought farmland and abandoned it. See, I think a Jew's a better businessman than to buy more farms today because it's probably one of the worst businesses you could ever go into today."

"I agree with that," said the caller. "But I believe that they are going to the government in order to come over here and buy up our land and let it set."

"You don't have one shred of evidence to back up what you said," Berg stated flatly, tiring of the call. "You are the most tragic human being. There's nothing more sickening than a Jew who isn't proud to be a Jew, sir, and you are the most sickening being I know on the face of the Earth. Get out of here."

Bang! He slammed down the phone and continued without skipping a beat.

"I tell you, that's the person I could throw up on. I'll tell you, I will respect Farrell and Elliott all day long more than that particular Jew who came on with that fallacious story. Oh God, that Jew! He ought to be over in Israel about a week and a half. Oh my God, would they make mincemeat out of that cat! Okay! One-thirty-seven in the afternoon, the lines are full!"

The show was vintage Berg and he reveled in it. "Whoa!" he cried at one point, "we have got a lot of anti-Semitism cookin' here! You can smell it in each one of these callers."

After the show, other advertisers in Elliott's paper pulled out with the Marines. A few weeks later, Elliott filed an $8 million defamation suit against Berg, KOA, and Peter Boyles, another talk show host who had Elliott on his program. He acted as his own attorney, a piece of advice he often gave farmers. But the suit went nowhere and was dismissed more than a year later.

Elliott was forced to close his paper and lay off his employees. One was a security guard at the *Primrose and Cattlemen's Gazette* office. He was David Lane. Because of Berg, Lane lost his job just weeks before driving to the 1983 Aryan World Congress with Farrell, Zillah Craig, and Kathy Kilty, and hearing all those speeches calling for war against the Jews.

Bob Mathews knew what Alan Berg had done to the *Primrose and Cattlemen's Gazette*. He brought copies of the issues with Farrell's articles when he gave his September 1983 speech to the National Alliance convention in Arlington, Virginia.

"This is an excellent little rural newspaper with a considerable circulation which is geared towards the needs and interests of farmers and ranchers," he told his audience. "What's interesting about this newspaper, in this issue is an excellent little article on the Protocols of Zion. In this issue here is a full-page advertisement for a very anti-Jewish, pro-white racialist organization.

"The Jews are coming down hard on this brave little newspaper like chickens on a June bug, and it appears that it might eventually fold up, but the seeds have been sown," Mathews asserted.

BRUCE PIERCE DROVE his bus-camper north through Salmon, Idaho, into Montana scouting for a secluded house for rent. The fugitive tried to skip through Missoula, where too many people knew him, but during a quick stop at a campground there, a woman he and Julie knew spotted them. Pierce went to his brother Greg's house in Arlee, reading real estate ads and supermarket bulletin boards along the way.

Bruce and Julie spotted an ad for a house for rent in Seeley Lake and drove up to look at it. What happened illustrated the problem of carrying too many false identities.

When the woman showing the house asked Julie her name, she answered "Mary" at the same time Bruce chimed in with "Beth." They looked at each other for a second, then began laughing. The confused woman joined them.

"She goes by Beth," Pierce excused lamely. "But her given name is Mary."

Pierce and his family meandered north to Kalispell, where he put the bus in a storage yard. Then, taking a beat-up Chevrolet Vega, he drove west to Libby and Troy, two small towns surrounded by national forest on the Kootenai River. While sitting in a diner in Libby, he scanned the weekly *Western News* and found an ad for a house far off the main road in Troy. The landlady, Ella Ackley, worked in a nearby restaurant. She drew him a map to the location.

The next morning, Ackley's son met Pierce at the house, a contemporary, wood-sided mountain home built on the crown of a forested knoll by Lake Creek. It was very private, just what he wanted. He returned that evening and told Ella Ackley he'd take the house if he could move in quickly. She agreed to vacate the house within a week.

Pierce moved in on May 17, as Ackley was moving out. He told Ackley his name was Roger Wilkins and gave her $350 for the first month's rent, but he wouldn't sign the rental papers. Ackley turned to Julie to ask what name she should write on the rent receipt.

"Sandra," Julie replied.

"Sandra what?" Ackley prompted, pen in hand.

"Sandra, uh, Sandra something . . . ," Julie trailed off in embarrassment.

"Gleed," Bruce jumped in. "Sandra Gleed is her name."

Ackley thought it odd that "Sandra" couldn't recall her own name. Then she watched Pierce carry green metal ammo boxes into the house. Later, as her son and a friend installed some siding, they looked inside a glass door and saw an odd-looking weapon propped up against a wall. It wasn't a handgun, it wasn't a rifle; it was a sinister hybrid.

Ackley's suspicions gave her no rest. That same evening, Sherry Flatten, the nearest neighbor to the house, called Ackley. "Who in the hell is up at your house?" Flatten asked. "Someone up there is shooting a machine gun."

"That's my new renter," Ackley answered. "He does seem sort of strange."

The next morning Mathews showed up on his way from Laramie, where he had given Jean Craig the Denver mission. He and Bruce took turns emptying ammo clips through the machine pistol down by Lake Creek. Later, Pierce made man-sized silhouettes from plywood, then chopped them in half with .45-caliber slugs.

Flatten and her young daughter were outside their house in a clearing about 300 yards from the knoll when Pierce and Mathews started firing. Flatten dove for the ground, grabbing her daughter, when she thought she heard bullets whizzing by. There was no way the slugs could round the knoll and reach Flatten, but Pierce had underestimated the echo effect down the creek valley.

Flatten reported the gunfire to the Lincoln County sheriff, then called Ackley again. "Ella," she said firmly, "you've just got to do something about your renters."

Later in the afternoon, Pierce and Mathews were in the living room, on the second level, when someone knocked on the downstairs door. Pierce slid open the door to the deck on the opposite side of the house and peeked out. Below, he saw a sheriff's car in his driveway and two deputies standing by the door.

"It's the cops!" Pierce whispered frantically to Mathews.

After a moment of panic, Julie walked toward the stairs. "I'll go down and talk to them," she said calmly. Julie spent several minutes telling the deputies in her sweetest voice that she hadn't heard any machine gun fire. They soon left. But Ackley had reached her limit. Several days later, she left a note on Pierce's door saying he'd have to leave. That night, Pierce called Ackley in such a huff, he again stumbled over his identity.

"Hello, Ella?" he said. "This is Bruce."

"Bruce?" Ackley asked. "Bruce who?"

Pierce slapped himself on the forehead at his stupid mistake, and quickly tried to talk around it.

"Roger, I mean. Roger Bruce. Bruce is my middle name," he fumbled, hoping she'd buy the explanation. "Hey, what's this about leaving the house?"

Ackley explained her misgivings about the machine guns and told him he'd have to leave. But after some discussion, they agreed he could stay through June.

"Your ancestors must have come from Salem," Pierce upbraided Ackley when she visited later with a friend. She looked confused until Pierce added, with all the smugness he could muster: "They burned witches there too."

About two weeks later, on June 6, Pierce was riding dirt bikes through the woods with Jeremy when he spotted a vacant house on North Keeler Creek Road, with a majestic view of 4,943-foot Keeler Mountain in the distance. Although it was less than 4 miles from Ackley's, it was the ultimate in seclusion. The last house on the road, the nearest neighbor to it was a mile downhill.

Pierce stopped to talk with the neighbor, Stacia Fifield, who said the owner lived in Walla Walla and would rent it, but it needed work. "That's no trouble," Pierce replied. "Tell him I'll pay for it." Pierce hired carpenters to do $1,500 worth of improvements on the house and arranged to stay at Ackley's another month before moving.

Pierce was able to strike up one real relationship, as real as it could be using a phony name, while living in Troy. On a Tuesday afternoon, while taking some refuse to the sanitary landfill, he introduced himself as "Roger Morton" to the man working there, Jim Montgomery. Pierce noticed Montgomery's belt buckle had a carving of a fish with "Jesus" spelled in Greek, a common Christian symbol.

"Are you a Christian?" Pierce asked.

Montgomery replied that he was. And he was a devout one at that. During the hour they discussed Jesus and the Bible at the dump, Pierce took an instant liking to Montgomery. He sized him up as the epitome of honesty, sincerity, and integrity, and decided to test him. Asking Montgomery whether he could get him some firewood, Montgomery said he could for $45 a cord. Pierce then handed him $50.

"That's too much, and you don't have to pay me now," Montgomery protested.

"No, it's okay," Pierce replied to the puzzled man. "Fifty dollars is worth the price to find out if you're the man you appear to be. If you don't bring my wood, then I'll know my estimation of you was wrong." He didn't wait long.

The next Saturday, Montgomery trucked a cord of firewood to Pierce's house, bringing two of his six sons. As they unloaded the wood, one of Jim's boys spotted a shell casing on the ground and retrieved it.

"Hey, neat," the boy said, then looked at Pierce. "Can I keep it?"

"Sure, son," Pierce replied. "It's yours." Montgomery paused. Another man was calling his boy "son," yet it sounded so loving to him, he wasn't offended a bit.

During the time Pierce lived in Troy, he and Montgomery enjoyed what Christians call "fellowship." They talked about salvation and things of the Lord, and Pierce hazarded a few advances about Identity. There was absolutely nothing Montgomery sensed in his friend's demeanor that hinted he could kill another man.

THE JETLINER'S WHEELS touched down on the runway at Spokane International Airport shortly before noon on June 4. As the passengers filed off, David Lane studied each until he spotted a slender man of medium height with short dark hair and a matching, neatly trimmed beard. The man carried a large briefcase.

"Richard?" Lane ventured. The man stopped, then nodded. "Andy Barnhill gave us your flight number,"

Lane said as they shook hands. "You got any luggage?" The man nodded again. As they started down the concourse, a second man stepped out of a phone booth, looked around, then approached with an infectious smile.

"Hi. I'm Bob Mathews," he said.

"Richard Scutari," the new arrival said.

They got into Mathews's car in the airport lot and drove north toward Metaline Falls. Mathews delighted in pointing out landmarks during the two-and-a-half-hour trip. The scenery impressed Scutari, who was from the flatland of Florida. The highest hill there was where they buried the garbage.

Once they got to Metaline Falls, Mathews offered each a cold drink. "So Andy Barnhill tells me you might be thinking of joining us."

Ignoring the overture, Scutari put his briefcase on the dining room table. "Before we go any further, I want you both to go across this machine," he said solemnly, opening the briefcase to reveal an instrument panel containing dials and lights.

"What exactly is that machine?" Bob asked, although fully aware what it was since he had used a primitive version in the Sons of Liberty.

"It's a voice-stress analyzer," Scutari answered while searching for an electrical outlet.

"What does it do?" Lane asked as Scutari plugged in the cord.

Scutari looked Lane straight in the eye. "It lets me know if you tell the truth. I'm sorry, but I'm wary. I've trusted people before and been burned. Now either both of you go across this machine, or I pack up and head back to Florida." Scutari had to be careful. It was a covert FBI operative who had goaded the neo-Nazis and Klansmen into attacking the communists at Greensboro in 1979, killing five people.

"Okay, okay," Mathews laughed, sitting down next to the box. Scutari was soon satisfied that Mathews was exactly what he claimed to be. And, as Mathews introduced Scutari to his "action group" and his plans for the White American Bastion, Scutari felt the authenticity of Mathews's approach.

"The idea is to get enough kinfolk who believe as we

do to move up here and take over towns, then counties, and finally states," Bob said excitedly. "We either fight now to save the race, or we're doomed.

"We start with Metaline Falls. Can you believe it, up here in white country, we got a goddamn chink for a mayor!" Mathews said. The Chinese man who owned the town hardware store was the mayor of Metaline Falls.

"Once we have a majority here, we create laws banning Jews, mud people, and other minorities from living here," he said. "Once we've secured Metaline Falls, we keep expanding until we are strong enough to create a white nation, separate from the Jew-nited States."

"Be a little tough to start a Civil War against the U.S. military, wouldn't it?" Scutari asked. Mathews gave his most honest response.

"With what we're planning," he confided, "the chances of any of us coming out of this alive or free from prison for the rest of our lives are pretty slim. But somebody has to start it. Once others see us, more kinsmen will be inspired to follow. You and I will probably never see it come to be, but by our dedication and vision, I assure you someday it will be accomplished.

"Cattle die, kinsmen die, and I too shall die. The only thing I know that does not die is the fame of dead men's deeds."

Scutari had heard enough. At that moment he realized he had finally found a group willing to take action, to organize for the battle Scutari believed had to be fought to save America.

The journey through the right wing that led Scutari to Metaline Falls began in 1973 when he was working the cold North Sea oilfields as a diver. War was raging between Israel and the Arab countries, and Scutari was glued to his radio. British sources reported the United States was on stage-three nuclear alert, meaning Nixon had his finger on the nuclear button. There was talk among the allies of not letting American forces mobilize from England, West Germany, or Spain, or allowing U.S. planes to fly over those countries because of neutrality pacts. Scutari listened apprehensively, because his company had divers in the Persian Gulf.

When he came back to the States, however, Scutari

discovered that nobody knew how close the country had come to nuclear war. It troubled him deeply. An American history buff, Scutari was greatly disturbed that the press hushed up what was happening. Eventually, in trading books with his fellow divers during the long spells on the offshore platforms, Scutari came across some literature from the John Birch Society. One item was titled "Gun Control Means People Control." It fed his distrust of the government.

Although he didn't see action in Southeast Asia, Scutari couldn't look at the Vietnam Memorial without tears coming to his eyes. He felt 58,000 Americans died so fat cats back home could line their pockets with money. His country's course confused him. Here, American soldiers had been told they were going to protect the country from communism, yet the United States continued to trade with communist countries, keeping them afloat.

All his life, Scutari held that if you believe something, you live it.

Scutari had enjoyed the outdoors from the time he was a child. Born on April 30, 1947, in Port Jefferson, New York, he inherited his swarthy complexion from his Italian-German father, a native of Brooklyn's Bedford-Stuyvesant, and his Italian-Irish mother from Corona in Queens. He lived in East Patchogue, Long Island, where his dad shot squirrel in the still-rural surroundings. His father was a foreman for Republic Aviation, and his mother worked in a laundry.

His dad visited Florida when Richard was nine and liked it so much he moved the family to West Hollywood, on the edge of the Everglades. That was where Richard and his brother, Frank, three years his senior, grew up. While Frank was on the honor roll, Richard maintained a C average. It seemed Richard discovered that the girls at Driftwood Junior High were more fun than studying.

Richard was an industrious teen who worked after school. He loved to camp in the nearby swamps. Reared Catholic, he lost interest in the faith after his dad had a dispute with a parish priest.

After his junior year, Richard dropped out to join the Navy in Fort Lauderdale. He shipped overseas to Rota, Spain, and drove occasionally to Torremolinas in Málaga for bullfights. And he fell in love—incessantly. American women on holiday or the women of Cadiz—it didn't matter to him.

Scutari took a nine-week course at diving school in Washington, D.C., and diving quickly became his passion. He loved the work, going underwater to remove valves, work on sonar, and change 11-ton propellers. Then, as he was about to reenlist after four years, he got a notice from his father about a company looking for experienced divers for $40,000 a year, kingly wages in 1968. He took the job, with Taylor Diving & Salvage in New Orleans, and soon was working with the company's best divers on underwater oilfield pipelines.

Scutari loved the heady rush of danger that came with the undersea work. Normally he worked the Gulf of Mexico, but often he went overseas. He made exceptionally good money, earning $68,500 in five months during his best year. But he watched in sadness as his friends became statistics in a frighteningly hazardous business. In five seasons in the North Sea, eighty divers lost their lives.

Scutari met his first wife, Linda, in New Orleans while he was dating her mother. Linda was twenty-one and Richard twenty-three, and they courted for nine months before she became pregnant. Richard married her in 1970 in the local Lutheran church.

Soon after Tina was born, Linda was pregnant again. Rachelle was born in 1971. But Richard's extended absences hurt the marriage. Arguing became their pastime when they were together. They were divorced in 1976.

During the marriage, however, Richard acquired a love for martial arts. Linda was 4-foot-11 and weighed 95 pounds, so he encouraged her to learn self-defense. She started with a tae kwon do class, but soon dropped out. Richard, however, was hooked. Eventually, he became a black belt in tae kwon do and hapkido, and a brown belt in combined shorin-ryu goju-ryu karate styles.

In 1976 Scutari remarried. His wife, Michele, soon became a young stepmother when Richard gained custody of his daughters. Michele moved to downtown New Orleans with the young children and watched her new husband sail out into the gulf for four months.

But 1979 became his last season with Taylor Diving. He was among the top twenty divers in a company of 350, but he knew he was defying the law of averages. When he reported for his physical for the 1980 season, he abruptly quit. Richard and Michele then bought some land in Port Salerno, Florida, and built their own house. In 1982, Richard and Michele had a child of their own, Danielle.

Richard formed a construction company named Chel-Ric Enterprises and started doing business with his brother Frank, who was a school counselor in nearby Stuart but also had a construction company. They had a deal to build some homes and condominiums in 1982, but it soured when interest rates skyrocketed.

To his neighbors, Scutari was a friendly, honorable man who gave free karate lessons in his garage to the neighborhood children. He asked only that they bring their own boards to break. By this time he had gone beyond the Birch Society literature and was deeply immersed in right-wing politics.

In 1979, he attended a seminar held in Fort Lauderdale by the Minutemen leader, Robert DePugh, who told him that God was a figment of man's imagination. DePugh encouraged Scutari to seek the truth for himself. While at the seminar, Scutari met a man who belonged to the American Pistol and Rifle Association. Scutari, who first fired a shotgun at age five on Long Island, was a member of the National Rifle Association and the American Legion, but he had never heard of APRA.

The man told him APRA was like the NRA, only more grassroots, more locally centered, and more into survivalism. They taught not only how to handle guns but how to freeze-dry foods and manage finances in times of civil distress. Scutari was intrigued. He believed the country was headed for disaster, whether through economic collapse, civil strife, or nuclear warfare. Curious, he visited APRA's range in Naples, Florida, and liked the people, so he joined.

In Port Salerno, he organized his own APRA unit and

over time built it up to forty members. He set up a shooting range on a tropical fish farm, where shooters as young as eight practiced on combat courses. Members of his unit included Martin County sheriff's deputies and city police, who said Scutari's course gave them better training than the police academy.

Scutari knew Andy Barnhill's dad, Virgil, who was a member of the Fort Lauderdale APRA chapter and lived in nearby Plantation. Virgil was also a member of the ultra-conservative Florida Patriots, an enemy of gun-control laws. Scutari agreed to take Andy with him to the national APRA rendezvous in 1981, which brought together diverse elements of the survivalist movement. Andy met Randall Rader and eventually decided to move to the CSA camp in Arkansas.

It also was through APRA that Scutari renewed his search for religion. In 1980, while attending APRA's national rendezvous in Benton, Tennessee, to teach a course in unarmed self-defense, a friendly looking gentleman who identified himself as Ardie McBrearty approached him with a religious pamphlet.

"Keep that pacifist crap away from me," Scutari said. "Not interested."

"No, my friend, this is Christian Identity," McBrearty told him. "If you've been away from Yahweh all these years, you should read this. It'll open up a whole new way of looking at the Bible."

Scutari took the pamphlet and, as soon as he was back in Florida, grabbed his Bible and set out to disprove what he read about Identity. Michele, also a fallen Catholic, was curious and asked Richard about it.

"I've been going back through the original Greek and Hebrew," Richard told her after a period of studying, "and I've found that 'Adam' actually means 'capable of showing blood in the face.' That's something you never hear. The Bible doesn't say there wasn't anybody here before Adam. Just says Adam was the first man capable of showing blood in his face."

"What does that mean?" Michele asked.

"It's talking about the white race," Richard answered patiently. "Adam was the father of the white race."

Scutari also concluded that the Bible didn't contradict science.

"You see, there are people who say man never set foot on earth until 6,000 years ago and here scientists find man 10,000, 15,000 years ago," Richard explained. "But when you look at the Bible, in fact, there were two creations, Genesis 1:26, and Genesis 2:7. Two creations. That explains it!"

While Michele remained skeptical, she knew these findings were having a profound effect on her husband. Her interest was in the political aspects of the movement. But Identity strengthened Richard's already conservative political posture.

"We send Israel grants—not repayable loans, but grants—over $9 billion at a whack, yet our farmers are losing their farms and others are homeless," Scutari observed. "And you tell me the leaders of this country are for our people? No way. Capitalism and communism are the biggest crimes that ever happened to our people.

"We give grain to Russia to keep them from starving. The Republicans are the ones, when the Polish people were ready to kick communism out, who said, 'No, we can't have you do that. Here's so many billions of dollars to keep the government going.' Yet we'll send some more American boys to die fighting communism.

"We have more political prisoners than any other country in the world, be they white, black, Indian, or Hispanic. This great human rights country lets old people eat dog food, then puts in 25 percent of the money for the World Bank.

"I just know there's only one solution to the problem, and that's getting back to the white Christian nation it was supposed to be," he concluded. "Our Constitution and the laws this country was founded on come straight from the Bible. Only when we get back under God's laws will we have peace and harmony."

Then, in May 1984, Andy Barnhill came calling. For a month's pay and expenses, Andy asked him, would Richard be willing to come up to the Northwest and check out a group that was going to quit talking and start doing?

Hell, yes, Richard replied. He bought a round-trip ticket to Spokane and left the return date open.

*   *   *

THERE WERE FEW customers in the early morning at Vick's Café in downtown Boise. Seated alone at the front was a measly looking middle-aged man sipping his third cup of coffee and staring out the window down 10th Street.

At the corner of 10th and Idaho streets, a bright red-and-black Wells Fargo armored truck squealed to a halt in front of the Idaho First National Bank.

The man gulped his dregs, threw $2 on the table, and strode to the door. He got into an old brown Chrysler station wagon and, putting it into gear, grabbed a CB microphone and thumbed the button.

"I'm off again, honey," Robert Merki broadcast.

In her kitchen on North 10th Street, Sharon Merki went to the base unit and set the mike. "Okay, dear, let me know how it goes."

The Wells Fargo truck lumbered away from the curb. Merki slowly steered out into traffic and dropped in behind the truck while penciling his starting time, 7:30 A.M., in a notebook. In her kitchen, Sharon kept her own notebook and cocked her ear for transmissions over the twenty-channel scanner on the table. Each time a Boise police officer radioed his location to dispatch, she noted the time and place. She was hoping that over time, she'd be able to establish the patrol patterns and staffing levels on the day shift.

It was Bob Mathews's suggestion. At his farm, he kept some of the Northgate loot hidden under a false bottom in a grain barrel. When the barrel came to have more grain than money, Bob held a meeting at the Newport house with some of his people. They had only a few thousand dollars left. It was time to replenish it.

So in addition to pushing Merki to finish the phony tens, Mathews decided another armored car robbery was imperative. He put the Boise crew to work on Wells Fargo, while he set out to prime Charles Ostrout, his Brink's contact from California. Ostrout had visited Mathews Acres and had complained about all the blacks getting the jobs and promotions at Brink's.

Merki learned a lot about armored cars in the few weeks he followed them. The first thing he learned was they didn't look so formidable up close. After locating the Wells Fargo depot, he was amazed. It was off the main thoroughfares, sitting in the middle of a rundown neighborhood at the junction of three narrow side streets, Miller, Ash, and Grand.

It was an unmarked, white cinderblock cubicle, with two garage bays on the right side and a heavy door with a small glass window on the left. A red gasoline pump sat between the garages, and a newer pump was around on the left side. A surveillance camera was mounted on the upper right corner, aimed downward toward the door, and a radio antenna was mounted on the side.

A community center was directly across Ash Street, with a playground and basketball court facing Wells Fargo. South of the depot was an apartment complex, and more apartments lined Grand. The neighborhood looked practically deserted. Merki couldn't believe Wells Fargo stored millions of dollars in such an area.

Then, when Merki started to follow the trucks, he noticed the drivers were adept at running traffic signals about to turn red, speeding up to scoot through and cut off anybody following them. He also learned their weekly routes, and saw that they never stopped at the same places two days in a row.

When he needed hard data on departures and arrivals, Merki enlisted his youngest stepchild, Kurt, by now seventeen. "I want you to take your basketball, maybe a book, and ride your bike down to that playground," Merki told him. "Keep track of when the trucks come and go." Practicing layups, playing around-the-world, and sharpening his hook shot, Kurt dribbled and rebounded for hours, always keeping an eye on the Wells Fargo garage across Ash Street. A jungle gym made of wood poles obscured the view somewhat, but the angle was such that when he concentrated on the basket, the depot was directly ahead in the background.

Pierce and Jimmy Dye arrived a few weeks later to help. They waited outside the depot in the morning for a truck to leave, then stayed with it all day. They used two cars to remain inconspicuous, coordinating their movements over the CB. When they got back to the depot, they watched from their parked cars as the guards got out in the parking area in front. One guard drew his handgun. Big deal, Pierce thought. Then the guards wheeled out a cart and loaded it with money bags from the truck before pushing it inside through the door.

"This is a piece of cake," Pierce leaned toward Dye. "Three girls armed with water pistols could pull this job."

Jean Craig and Sharon Merki, now forty-six, were among the few women that Mathews's gang trusted. Sharon, a committed Identity follower, was forthright rather than deferential in her dealings with the men. While surveilling Wells Fargo, Pierce found chatting with her an interesting intellectual exercise. He regarded her as a female version of Randy Duey, the contemplative member of the Inner Circle.

The men called Sharon "Mother of God" because she had a theory that God was female, or at least sexless, and exhibited female characteristics. This didn't go over at all with the men. The right wing is very patriarchal, and generally the women take positions in only three places: the kitchen, bedroom, or nursery. Women are the bearers of the race, not of the weapons of war. And God was a man of war.

As a result of his work on Wells Fargo, Robert Merki was able to construct a chart with schedules, routes, estimated values of shipments, plus escape routes and police patrol patterns. A command decision from Mathews was now in order.

But Mathews was busy with a more significant decision, moving on Step 5. He had set the wheels in motion with Jean Craig despite a split among his Inner Circle and despite assuring some friends that assassinations had been shelved.

Pierce and Yarbrough favored a hit, an assassination that would show that the right wing was not toothless. But at one meeting in Boise to which Mathews brought his manila folder stuffed with papers and clippings labeled "Step 5 Intelligence," Duey and Parmenter were opposed.

Bob pulled out the folder's contents. The name on top was Morris Dees, leader of the Southern Poverty Law Center and the Klanwatch Project in Montgomery, Alabama. An arch-nemesis of the Ku Klux Klan, Dees pioneered the use of civil suits to combat right-wing organizing. He was the personal foil of Louis Beam, the Texas Klansman, who once challenged Dees to a duel in the woods.

The second name was television producer Norman Lear, who kicked off the popular trend of ridiculing white values twelve years earlier when he depicted Archie Bunker of *All in the Family* as a witless buffoon. He followed with shows like *Sanford and Son, The Jeffersons,* and *Good Times,* which portrayed blacks in a positive light, then the trashy *Hot L Baltimore.* Mathews held Lear responsible for reshaping television into pandering, race-mixing, free-sex garbage.

The third name was Alan Berg, about whom the group already knew much.

Duey rose in protest. While he agreed with the need for killing at some point, the embryonic army they were forming was likely to collapse under the heat an assassination would focus on them, he said. Parmenter agreed, saying the proposed Aryan Academy training camp should be in operation at least a year before such a great leap was taken. But Mathews knew Pierce and Yarbrough agreed with him. The propaganda of the deed was a powerful force.

"Leave us out of it then," Parmenter said on behalf of himself and Duey.

"Well," Mathews sighed as he lifted himself out of his chair, "this is a situation then that'll be taken care of by those who want to do it."

He folded the file shut, and a tattered newspaper clipping fluttered to the floor. Parmenter picked it up, glancing at it before handing it back to Mathews. It was about William Wayne Justice, a federal judge in Clarksville, Texas, who had ordered elderly whites evicted from a public housing project to make room for poor blacks. Mathews refiled it with several dozen other notations in the folder.

RANDALL RADER FLEW into Spokane four days after Scutari, and Andy Barnhill and Scutari picked him up in Mathews's Chevy. He was excited about the prospect of training men again, which he missed since leaving CSA.

When Rader arrived at the barracks, Mathews welcomed him and said he hoped Rader would join. Rader recognized Dye and Parmenter, and also Yarbrough, who had visited CSA in 1982. During the next week, Rader met others whom he was to train, including Loff, Lane, Kemp, Duey, and Soderquist.

Another new recruit was there as well, a Klansman from Rosamond, California, named Randy Evans. Evans, twenty-nine, was a follower of Butler and among those arrested at the San Fernando Valley cross lighting. Upon hearing of this new "action group" through his Aryan Nations contacts, Evans had decided to investigate. He'd been to Aryan Nations before, but Mathews's group gave him the impetus to move his family—two wives—to the Northwest.

Shortly after Rader's arrival, Mathews called a meeting in the barracks. For the newcomers, he went over the "six steps" and introduced the staff, including Rader as prospective director of training. He went over the "doomsday plan," under which each man was to track and kill a prominent target—a Rothschild, a Rockefeller, Henry Kissinger—if the gang were cracked by the FBI.

Mathews discussed the plot of *The Turner Diaries* and handed out copies to anyone who hadn't yet read it. Then Mathews held another swearing-in ceremony, much like the first, except that instead of holding hands, the men in the circle saluted over one of Loff's children. Scutari and Evans were the initiates.

After the meeting, Rader told Mathews he liked the thought of training guerrillas, but when he realized how that training ultimately could be applied, assassinations, he was hesitant. Men still at Rader's level of commitment bothered Mathews. Yet, to keep Rader on track, Mathews mollified him.

"Don't worry about it, buddy," Mathews said. "Step 5 will be discontinued. We got too much going on trying to raise cash."

With that, Rader jumped into rifle and pistol training for a half-dozen men. They set up a shooting range in the woods behind Mathews's house. Rader lectured on weapons and ammo, and how different ones are used for different purposes. After a week, he began lessons on squad tactics, map reading, and such techniques as hiking in silence through the woods. Scutari gave some martial arts lessons.

But all the shooting attracted the attention of neighbors, one of whom complained to Una Mathews. That put a stop to the shooting on Mathews Acres.

Rader liked what he saw in the Northwest. He believed racial chaos was coming, and when he saw his friends Barnhill and Scutari committing to this new group, it made him give serious thought to it. Everybody moving up to the Northwest seemed to have one theme in common: Enough talk, it's time for action.

When Rader heard Mathews talk, he understood why the men followed him. It was Mathews's knack for building people's sense of outrage at the way things were until they felt they had no choice but to act. Mathews never gave up on anyone. In fact, he was still counting on recruiting Pete Travis, who had abstained from the Northgate robbery. Rader had worked with Travis at CSA and advised Mathews to drop the idea. Since Travis had told Rodney Carrington all about Andy Barnhill's new friends, Rader warned, he was apt to talk.

Mathews nodded in agreement, then promptly disregarded the advice.

On the morning of June 14, Scutari told Rader he was leaving with Mathews but that Rader should continue the training. "We got a big mission down in Denver," Scutari said. "Couple of military-type guys down there are thinking of joining so I'm gonna run 'em across the lie box."

"Seems like Bob's really got a viable movement going here," Rader observed.

"Yeah," Scutari answered. "We're taking along that MAC you sold Andy last month, by the way." An alarm was triggered in Rader's mind. He had bought that weapon in his own name in 1979 and converted it into an illegal machine pistol.

"You use that gun somewhere and it can come back to me!"

"Naw," Scutari replied. "We took care of it. We drilled out the serial number." Then Scutari turned to leave with Mathews.

"Richard," Rader called out, "be careful. Don't get

sucked into anything bad." Scutari waved goodbye as he walked.

That evening in the barracks, Rader settled into a bunk as David Lane came upstairs. Lane was going to ferry Merki's phony tens to the East Coast for some operatives to pass. Rader had seen some of the phony money and thought it looked good. As they talked, Lane mentioned that he too would be leaving the next day.

"Where you off to?" Rader asked.

"Denver," Lane responded. "You know why Bob's heading there? They're going to kill this big-mouth Jew down there, a talk show host named Berg. He's been giving our people nothing but trouble. We're gonna make an example of that kike."

Rader said nothing. It didn't seem like his business.

RANDY EVANS LOOKED down the bar of the Rialto Tavern at the thin woman with long, blond hair, seated on a barstool. She had large-framed glasses and was sucking on the filter of a long cigarette. He sidled down the bar next to her.

"Hi, my name's Bob Brenner," Evans introduced himself.

"Stacy," she offered. She was wearing a light sleeveless top and cutoff jeans. They stayed a few hours until closing time, talking and drinking.

The Rialto was in Madras, Oregon, a small town on the desert side of the Cascades. Evans had borrowed Denver Parmenter's pickup truck and was headed for California to pick up his other wife, his first having already relocated to Sandpoint. Andy Barnhill had come along for company.

It was June 17, and they had logged more than 500 miles by the time they hit Madras, so they decided to stop for the night. Barnhill got a room in the Madras Hotel-Motel and collapsed in exhaustion, but Evans wanted to check what little night life he saw, which brought him into the Rialto.

When the bartender called last round at 2 A.M., Evans said to Stacy, "How about we get some beer and go someplace else?" She agreed.

They drove in Parmenter's pickup to the City Center

Motel and checked into Room 35. Evans signed the register "Bob Brenner, Yakima, Wash." Stacy said she was from Toppenish, Washington, on the Indian reservation south of Yakima.

In the room, they cracked open a sixpack of Schlitz and shortly before 4 A.M., when both were feeling a buzz from the alcohol, Evans made his move.

"C'mon, Stacy, it'll be good," he said as he moved close to her.

"No, Bob, I can't!" she protested, backing up toward the bed.

He reached out and grabbed her, pulling her close. As he did, he worked one hand inside her pants where he anticipated the soft feel of a woman. Evans's eyes widened in shock when it dawned on him that his fingers had just touched a penis.

She was a he!

Incensed and disgusted, Evans threw a fist that caught Stacy in the stomach and propelled him onto the bed, gasping for breath. Then Evans crawled on top of the frightened transvestite and pulled a knife with a 2-inch blade.

"I'm gonna cut your phony nipples off!" he growled. Stacy yelled, shoving Evans off of him. Evans punched Stacy in the mouth. In a trembling voice, Stacy pleaded with Evans not to hurt him any more. Evans, who had retreated to sit in a chair and sort out this turn of events, began to laugh and reached for his handgun.

"You don't deserve to live," he said, pointing the gun at Stacy. He got up and locked the door, but Stacy, taking advantage of Evans's indecision, edged toward it, twisted the lock, and rushed out. Evans drove the truck back to the Madras Hotel-Motel and slipped into bed without waking Barnhill.

Stacy made a report to a Madras police officer, Bob Dispennett, and Jefferson County Deputy Sheriff Rick Doan, giving them "Brenner's" license plate number and description. Doan spotted the white pickup parked at the Madras Hotel-Motel, but a more urgent call prevented him from checking it.

About 6:45 A.M., Barnhill and Evans left the motel. Doan saw them and called Dispennett from a nearby pay phone. Dispennett caught up with the pickup by the Madras Auction Yards and pulled it over. Doan covered him. As Dispennett was radioing the license number to dispatch, Evans walked toward the police car.

"Who's this truck belong to?" Dispennett asked.

"A friend," Evans replied. "What's all this about?"

"It's about an assault at the City Center Motel this morning," the officer replied. Checking the truck, the officers saw a handgun on the seat. As one of the officers reached for it, a scuffle broke out. Evans and Barnhill were quickly handcuffed and under arrest, Barnhill charged with unlawful possession of a weapon, Evans with second-degree assault and menacing. A search of the truck turned up three loaded handguns inside.

"If you're talking about that thing at the motel," Evans told the officer on the ride back to town, "it's not a girl."

"The subject," Dispennett replied, "is assault, not whether the victim is female or not."

Back at the station, the police were curious after they found that Barnhill had two identifications, one a birth certificate for Keith Merwin. Barnhill told them Merwin was a friend who had given him the ID to hold. Harder to explain was why he also had receipts for various purchases with Merwin's name on them.

Searching Evans's wallet, police found a card from ex-Imperial Wizard David Duke's new group, the National Association for the Advancement of White People. Also, there were two business cards of George Pepper, California Grand Dragon for the Invisible Empire faction, and a handwritten phone number for Tom Metzger, an ex-Klansman in San Diego who headed the White Aryan Resistance and hosted the public access cable television show, *Race and Reason*. Metzger also was among those arrested at the San Fernando cross lighting with Evans and Pastor Butler.

When the Madras police teletyped the Washington State Patrol on a routine check of the truck's plate, the simple assault began to look much more significant.

The patrol wired back that the truck was leased by Denver Parmenter and was connected to a federal counterfeiting investigation. "Please be advised," the patrol said, "you have individuals involved with the Aryan Nations neo-Nazi group." The teletype and phones worked overtime through the morning as Dispennett tried to verify just what he had on his hands.

Then, at 11:10, four hours after the bust, this message hit the teletype:

MKE/WANTED PERSON—CAUTION
ORI/VAUSM0021 NAM/PIERCE, BRUCE
CARROLL SEX/M RAC/W POB/KY DOB/051454
HGT/602 WGT/200 EYE/GRN HAI/BRO FBI/
423334CA3
OFF/FAILURE TO APPEAR—SEE MIS
MIS/EXTRM PARANOID, AFFIL W/ARYAN
NATION-NEO-NAZI GROUP/CCW KNIFE
HIDDEN IN BOOT ORIG-COUNTERFEITING
PH 703-2851100 ORI IS US MARSHALS SERVICE
HEADQUARTERS MCLEAN VA

Then the calls started to come, from the FBI, the Secret Service, marshals, and Alcohol, Tobacco and Firearms agents, all hoping Madras had just landed Pierce. Dispennett quickly flew to Portland with photos of the suspects, and an FBI agent from Portland accompanied him back to Madras. In the meantime, Barnhill was allowed his one phone call. He dialed Mathews's house, the same number he gave on his arrest slip.

At Mathews Acres, Soderquist was walking through the kitchen when the phone rang on the counter near the backdoor. He answered and heard Barnhill's voice: "We're in jail in Madras, Oregon. Start things on your end." Then he hung up, in accordance with one of Scutari's security rules: If arrested, call in with a brief message, then wait.

Soderquist walked out to the barracks and told the few men there what little he knew, which was only the name of the town where the two were in jail. Parmenter volunteered to investigate further, driving clear to Ione to use a pay phone to call the Madras police. All he could get from them was that his friends were arrested because of some kind of brawl, some weapons were confiscated, and there was a question about one man's identity.

By the time Parmenter returned to Mathews Acres, a mad scramble was on. Rader believed Mathews's house had been compromised by Barnhill's call. They had to hide the illegal weapons. Dye, Kemp, and Soderquist helped bury the ammo boxes and assault rifles deep into the woods behind Mathews's house. While running relays from the house to the woods with their weapons, Rader saw Kemp approaching with an M-60 machine gun, a 50-caliber, belt-fed weapon of incredible firepower.

"A gun dealer in Spokane sold it to Duey for $3,000," Kemp told Rader, anticipating his question. "But we can't find an ammo belt for it."

"Don't worry. I know where to get one," said Rader.

After the barracks was cleared of weapons, Rader had Dye, Kemp, and Soderquist pack their gear, some tents, and food. He led them on a camping excursion to Silo Mountain so no one would be at Mathews Acres if the FBI raided.

BOB MATHEWS DIDN'T really have a sixth sense about judging people. Sure, he could get them to follow, but he already trusted some people a more prudent man would have scratched. Richard Scutari was new to the group, yet Mathews had no problem trusting him. Scutari knew his own level of commitment was deep, but he couldn't help wondering what made Mathews so sure of him so soon.

Mathews gave Scutari a code name, Mr. Black, due partly to his Mediterranean complexion. Mathews outlined his plans, and Scutari would shake his head at the potential for disaster. "You know, Bob, it might not be such a good idea to tell everything," Scutari reproached him. "We should start working on a 'need-to-know' basis, the way the military does. Just tell people what they need to know for a specific job, and not stuff that could ruin us if they got caught."

Mathews smiled at Scutari. "You know, I've said that many times myself," he said. "Maybe when we get better organized, you can take over internal security."

In the next breath, Mathews continued on the same course.

"Now, we've got this next procurement coming up in

California that, if it comes off right, should get us more than a million dollars."

Scutari looked at him in amazement. How committed was Mathews to security, he wondered, if he was telling this much to someone he'd known less than two weeks?

Mathews and Scutari left Metaline Falls to meet Bruce Pierce at a truck stop just outside Missoula. When Pierce arrived, Mathews was inside the restaurant and Scutari was in the parking lot, leaning against a car. Pierce parked and looked around slowly, settling on the dark-looking man leaning against the car as the most likely one to be Scutari. The man had a stern look and kept sweeping the lot with his eyes, as though looking for someone. Then Pierce saw Mathews exit the restaurant and walk directly to the stranger, so Pierce went over too.

After exchanging greetings, they stood near Bob's car and talked. As they did, it became clear to Pierce that once again Bob had taken a new man and told him things that could send them all to prison for a long time. Pierce contained himself then. But later, out of Scutari's earshot, he let Mathews have it.

"What the hell are you doing, telling people all this stuff?" Pierce said.

"Richard's a good man and I trust him," Mathews replied. "I felt he needed to know about the next armored car job and about why we're going to Denver."

"Well, anybody could be a good man, but you gotta be cautious as if they're no good," Pierce admonished him. The competition between Mathews and Pierce had been heating up ever since Pierce's counterfeiting arrest, when he and Bob were about the only ones still devoted to the concept of an "action group." They took turns with the derring-do, Mathews pulling the gun to initiate the Fred Meyer robbery, Pierce accosting the courier at the Northgate heist.

But Pierce was firm about the Berg job. He wanted to be the triggerman. Pierce wanted credit for the points that came with killing a Jew. To be an Aryan warrior, racist literature contended, one had to amass fractions of points amounting to one, and a Jew was a sixth of a point. Only one hit automatically accorded a full point—assassinating the President of the United States.

The trio arrived in Laramie on Friday, June 15. Pierce and Scutari got a room at the Motel 6 under the name Joseph Shelby. At the same time, Pierce prepaid reservations for two at the Motel 6 in Denver, at Interstate 70 and Peoria Street near Stapleton International Airport, for Saturday and Sunday nights.

Mathews took Scutari to Zillah's old trailer, which had stood empty since Bob had moved her and the children into town. As they entered the trailer park, Bob saw Zillah and a friend picking up some empty flower boxes.

"Darn!" Mathews said. "I didn't want them to know you were here yet." Seeing there was no way out of it, he parked the car and introduced Zillah to Richard.

"Richard's going to be working with us," Mathews explained. "I was going to call you to let you know I was in town."

Zillah said hello to Scutari, then switched subjects. "You remember we're going to the Denver Zoo with the day care families tomorrow?" she asked Bob.

Bob's eyes softened as he flicked aside a loose strand of her hair, and said, "Of course, I remember. It'll be a great day for the kids."

A BRILLIANT MORNING SUN forced Zillah to squint as she loaded Bob's car with a picnic cooler and snacks early on Saturday. Bob corralled Dustin and Caleb, then drove to the Sunshine School, where Caleb attended day care, to pick up the school's owner, Barb Spaulding, and her husband, Ron, operator of a Laramie radio station.

In short time they headed down U.S. 287 toward Denver, 135 miles south, in a caravan of seven couples and their children from the Sunshine School to a free-admission day at the Denver Zoo. It was called Carousel Days, in conjunction with fundraising by the Juvenile Diabetes Foundation at Denver. One sponsor of the event was KOA radio, which set up a booth featuring its celebrities.

As they drove, Mathews and Spaulding had a lively discussion of politics. Bob complained with resentment that his antitax activities had caused "the sudden withdrawal of my appointment to West Point." It was an example of Bob's selective memory at work. It was he who had soured on West Point because of the court-martial of Lieutenant William Calley. And he didn't pass the math test.

At the zoo, Bob appeared cautious as ever, his eyes darting instinctively, taking in everything. When they approached the Carousel Days booth with KOA's blue-and-white logo, Mathews scanned the crowd for any sign of a tall, thin man with a haystack of hair and a beard. But Alan Berg wasn't scheduled to appear there until the next day.

Ron and Barb Spaulding brought a bag lunch and met Zillah at the refreshment stand. Several picnic tables were arranged on the shaded grass, where peacocks freely roamed through the crowd. "Where's Bob?" Spaulding asked Zillah.

Sipping a soft drink, Zillah nodded and pointed to the left. Ron Spaulding looked over and saw Mathews talking animatedly in a telephone booth.

That evening on the drive back to Laramie, Bob was very quiet. Zillah sensed something was on his mind. Settled into their bed on Kearney Street, she waited patiently for several minutes until Bob was ready to talk.

"You remember all that information your mother brought me on Alan Berg?" Bob said, an uncharacteristic coldness in his gaze. "We're going to do it Monday."

Zillah knew exactly what he meant. "I'm afraid," she snuggled closer to Bob. "Why is it so important?"

"He's a filthy Levite," Bob snarled back. "We are at war, and we have to stand up like men and fight." Zillah was compliant. She had no feeling for this Berg, but she loved Bob beyond measure. If he said it was necessary, it was so.

That same Saturday, Pierce and Scutari drove down to Denver in a four-door Plymouth and checked into the Motel 6 on Peoria. Once settled, Pierce went out to a pay phone nearby and called Julie to let her know he was safe. She had recently learned she was pregnant. Bruce was going to be a daddy again.

ON MONDAY MORNING, David Lane parked his yellow Volkswagen on Kearney Street and beeped the horn. Mathews checked the clip in his semi-automatic pistol, shoved it into his waistband, pulled his jacket around to conceal it, and kissed Zillah goodbye. He told her he didn't know how long he'd be gone.

On their way down U.S. 287, Lane told Mathews he'd like to stop in Fort Collins to visit Dennis Schlueter, whom they met at the Laporte church, and see if he'd received a $2,000 money order the "company" sent him to rescue his house from foreclosure.

"I've liked Dennis," Mathews said, "ever since he had us over to his house for those Sunday potluck suppers. We could use a man like him in the company."

Lane steered into the lot at Foothills Fashion Mall in Fort Collins. He and Bob went inside and had Schlueter paged to meet them at the Orange Julius stand. When Schlueter saw them, he thanked them for the $2,000. He was probably going to lose his house anyway, he said, as he was facing some jail time because he was caught cheating on welfare.

"You come up and join us, pal," Mathews encouraged him. "We know how to take care of our kinsmen." Schlueter asked what they were doing in Fort Collins.

"We're on our way to Denver for a business meeting," Lane answered.

Lane and Mathews drove south on Intersate 25 for an hour before Denver appeared over a ridge. Nestled against the Front Range of the Rockies, the city was a splash of green sprawled across the brown prairie like a rain puddle on a vacant dirt lot. They went east at Interstate 70 toward the airport-area motels.

Alan Berg's day began early, as usual. He got out of bed in his unkempt townhouse rehearsing that day's program in his head. There were stories in both Denver dailies that weekend about Pope John Paul II's stand on the role that love and commitment play in the Catholic view of sex. "Pope Says Sex for Pleasure Is Sinful," one headline read. Good topic, Berg thought.

He called his producer and asked her to locate a guest he could use as a counterpoint for his tirades against sexual conservatism. He dressed in a V-neck sweater with a beige plaid sports jacket over it. From his limitless collection of footwear, he selected a pair of saddle oxfords. Bouncing down the outside stairs to the driveway, he hopped into the black VW with the stark white cloth top and headed for Gyro's Place for a quick breakfast and a skimming of the morning papers before he headed downtown to KOA. When he arrived, his producer said she wasn't able to get anybody on such short notice to stand in for the Pope.

Berg said he'd wing it. He sat in front of the microphone at 9 A.M. and began to rip into the Catholic position on multiplying and replenishing the earth. As expected, the switchboard lighted up.

"Can you figure any way as a man that you could have sex without pleasure?" Berg asked. "I'm just curious now, because I can't come up with the idea.

"Don't you wonder," he baited his audience, "if you hold on to this dogma, how long can people cling to a religious following that advances this kind of dogma? . . . Does it say anywhere in the Bible that you couldn't have pleasure while you're having sex?" It was a standard ploy, to take a piece of information and push it to a distorted conclusion. The Pope had simply said that pleasure for pleasure's sake was not the purpose of sex.

After whipping Catholics the first hour, Berg spent an hour interviewing Colorado's Governor Richard Lamm about an article the Governor had authored for *Playboy*. He then coasted to his 1 P.M. signoff with open lines on any subject. Following the show, Berg taped a public service spot for the American Cancer Society. Sometime before 2 P.M., he hit the streets to sell his ad-lib commercials, which made him extra money. Some of his regular clients were merchants in the fashionable Cherry Creek area near the Denver Country Club.

Cherry Creek is a ten-minute drive down Speer Boulevard from downtown. Berg planned to spend several hours with clients before meeting his ex-wife, Judith, for dinner. She had flown in from Chicago to help celebrate her parents' golden wedding anniversary. As Berg wandered from client to client, the skies darkened, typical of a Denver summer afternoon. Clusters of thunderheads roiled from the west over the mountains. It was raining torrents in some parts of the city.

The downpour washed away Berg's last slim chance of surviving the day.

As the hit squad went over the plan at the Motel 6, the rain kept them inside. Checking into the same motel during the cloudburst was a vacationing couple from Metaline Falls. The man was a teacher at Selkirk High School, right outside Metaline Falls, where Mathews had worked as a weight trainer for the kids on the wrestling squad. The man and his wife ran swiftly to their room after parking their car, trying to dodge the heavy rain.

Had Mathews left the room for a stretch and run into the teacher, exchanging glances of recognition, discretion might have dictated that the attempt on Berg be scrubbed until later, when no witness could place him in Denver. But the couple never looked around as they ran to their room. They had plans for a late dinner with, as it later turned out, the perfect alibi—an old school chum who was a Denver County Court judge.

About 5:30, Judith Berg pulled up next to Alan's car in the Cherry Creek lot and greeted him with a quick kiss. Though divorced, Alan and Judith had remained close friends. Alan suggested that they dine at the Jefferson 440 restaurant in Lakewood. Berg chose the restaurant because its owner was a new advertiser, and Berg hoped to meet with him at the same time.

The Jefferson 440 was one of those dark lounges where it was difficult to read the menu without holding the table candle in front of it. The owner wasn't present, so the couple got right to the meal. Berg ate little of his sandwich. His daily consumption of three packs of Pall Malls and a continuous flow of coffee blunted his appetite, which probably accounted for his slim build. Judith ordered the filet of sole entrée.

By 7 P.M., long shadows were falling across Adams Street. The storm had left in its wake a perfect night—72 degrees and 32 percent humidity.

David Lane wheeled the Plymouth off East Colfax Avenue onto Adams Street, slowing momentarily as he passed 1445 Adams on the right so the others could take a good look at Berg's townhouse. He then accelerated, turning left on East 14th Avenue then left again on Cook Street. He pulled into the rear of the parking lot at Taco John's at Colfax and Cook. They got soft drinks and began their wait.

Lane stayed in the car, listening to a police scanner. Pierce slipped the MAC-10 into a tennis racquet case, then walked from the rear of the Taco John's lot to Colfax. There was a bus bench on the curb in front of Paradise Cleaners, close to the corner of Colfax and Adams. Pierce walked to the bench and sat down, the racquet case tightly in hand, watching the traffic zip by.

Across Colfax was a cascade of lights outlining the marquee of the Bluebird adult theater, advertising *When She Was Bad* and *Virginia*. As Pierce waited, a young boy strutted down the sidewalk near the curb, waving at cars with lone male drivers. East Colfax Avenue, despite massive efforts at prevention, had become notorious in the last decade for its porno houses, blue theaters, and constant parade of female and male prostitutes.

Mathews left the car and walked alone to the corner and down Adams Street, where he studied the layout of Berg's place. Jean Craig had been right on the money. The short driveway ended abruptly at large garage doors, with apartment units on two levels above the garages. It was about the only new structure on the block, the others being older brick singles. He looked up at the rooftop of 1445 Adams as it pierced the deep blue twilight sky. There was no thought of backing out. From the moment he learned of the communist menace at age eleven, Mathews was destined for this night. Somehow, this was part of his war.

"THERE'S AN OPEN space just before the driveway. Pull around there and park," Mathews told Lane after everybody got back into the car at Taco John's.

Lane pulled left onto Colfax, then left again onto Adams, sliding to the curb near a blond-brick one-story several doors north of Berg's driveway. Pierce pulled the MAC-10 from the case and slipped a silencer onto the barrel. He jammed a thirty-round magazine into the weapon and jacked a shell into the chamber.

"When he pulls up, get out and do it quick," Mathews said.

"I know, I know," Pierce replied edgily. "Just stay out of my way. I'll handle it." Mathews was in the shotgun position, with Pierce directly behind him in the rear seat.

Robert Jay "Robbie" Mathews, 3 (center), with brothers Grant, 11, and Lee, 7, on the porch of his home in Marfa, Texas. His parents had planned to raise the boys in the small town but the failure of the family's appliance business forced a move to Phoenix. There, Robbie, at age 11, joined the John Birch Society and began his life-long involvement with the radical right. (Photo courtesy of Una Mathews)

After receiving a misdemeanor conviction for a tax protest, Mathews moved to Washington state and bought some wooded property outside Metaline Falls where he lived in a double-wide trailer home and gained a reputation as a hard-working man. (Photo by Gary Gerhardt)

It was during visits to Richard Butler's Church of Jesus Christ Christian-Aryan Nations outside Hayden Lake, Idaho, that Mathews met some of the men who later formed the core of the Silent Brotherhood. (Photo by Kevin Flynn)

Three of Richard Butler's followers (left, Denver Parmenter, center, Gary Yarbrough, right, Randy Duey) who later joined with Mathews are pictured here, surrounding the podium, as Butler speaks to a crowd gathered at an Aryan Nations rally in Spokane, Washington in June, 1983. (Photo by Vince Musi)

Robert Mathews, pointing angrily at a demonstrator, agreed to help Pastor Butler with security at his Spokane rally. By boldly confronting an anti-racist group, Mathews attracted the attention and respect of right-wing sympathizers. (Photo by John Kaplan)

Bruce Carroll Pierce, left, here with his brother Greg, was introduced to the racist theology of Christian Identity soon after moving to Montana. He met Robert Mathews at Butler's Church and engaged in discussions about how to advance the right-wing cause. (Photo courtesy of Pierce family)

Gary Yarbrough learned of the Aryan Nations compound while serving time in prison. Upon his release, he moved to Idaho with his wife and children and soon joined Richard Butler's security force. Here, in military fatigues, he joins Denver Ku Klux Klansman David Lane in a search for a suspected intruder. (AP/Wide World Photos)

It was at "the barracks," the name Mathews and his friends gave to a two-story metal shed on his property, that he and eight other men took an oath in 1983, in a candlelight ceremony, to work silently, underground, to fund the radical right-wing movement. (Photo by Kevin Flynn)

In accord with his oath, Mathews robbed a bank in Seattle and showed up at Zillah Craig's home carrying a trick-or-treat bag filled with $25,952. (Photo courtesy of Zillah Craig)

Mathews and Craig soon became lovers, and in January, 1984, she was pregnant with his first natural child. Meanwhile, Mathews' gang successfully robbed armored trucks in March and April and grew with new members. (Photo courtesy of Zillah Craig)

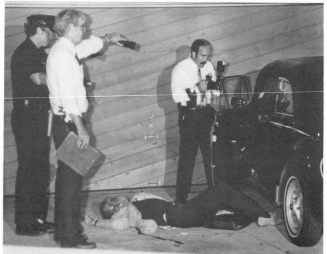

In order to energize their racist underground, the Silent Brotherhood targeted Alan Berg, a Jewish radio talk show host who routinely denounced right-wing groups on his program, as its first assassination victim. He was killed in his driveway in June, 1984. (Photo by Lyn Alweis, *The Denver Post*)

The Silent Brotherhood used a dozen men to stage a $3.8 million robbery of a Brink's Company armored truck in July, 1984. Leaving behind a handgun at the scene of the crime, Mathews inadvertently set the FBI hot on the trail of the gang. (Photo by the *Ukiah Daily Journal*)

Mathews recruited Robert Marki, a federal fugitive from a counterfeiting case, to be the Silent Brotherhood's printing expert. It was in his bungalow in Boise, Idaho, that he produced counterfeit ten-dollar bills and that the Brink's loot was counted and split. (Photo by Kevin Flynn)

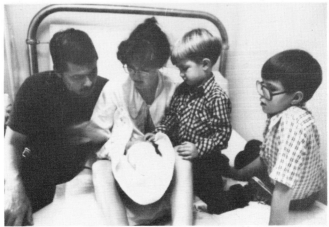

The morning after the birth of a daughter, Emerant, to Robert Mathews and Zillah Craig at her home in Laramie, Wyoming, Mathews spotted the FBI surveillance of him and narrowly escaped. This set off a two-month federal manhunt centered on the Pacific Northwest. (Photo courtesy of Zillah Craig)

Surrounded by FBI SWAT teams for 36 hours at a remote island hideout in Washington's Puget Sound, Mathews engaged in a fierce machine-gun battle before the authorities burned the house to the ground with Mathews in it. (FBI photo)

There was no Aryan World Congress held at Pastor Butler's compound in 1985 due to the federal investigation of the Silent Brotherhood following a massive racketeering indictment. But, in July, 1986, the annual event resumed, drawing right-wing activists from across the nation, including Mathews' widow and son. Here, the next generation salutes a burning cross during the Congress. (AP/Wide World Photos)

They waited at the curb for what seemed a long time.

Shortly before 9 P.M., Alan and Judith left the Jefferson 440 and got onto the nearby Sixth Avenue Freeway back to the city. On the fifteen-minute drive, he told Judith about Tuesday's show. The subject was gun control.

Berg stopped at a convenience store to pick up a can of dog food for his beloved Airedale, Fred, plus some shaving cream. Their plans were to go to Berg's place and phone his seventy-five-year-old mother in Chicago, then cap the evening at the home of a mutual friend, Bobbe Cook. But Berg was getting tired. As he turned from Colfax onto Adams, passing right by Mathews and his crew, he stopped at his driveway without pulling in. "How about if 1 just take you to your car?" he asked Judith. "We can call Mom tomorrow. I'm pretty tired." Judith agreed.

Alan put the car in gear and started back toward the shopping center.

The men in the car couldn't believe what they had just seen. Berg was within inches of stopping and then took off. Did he make them? What scared him off?

Alan dropped Judith at her car in Cherry Creek, and with a goodbye kiss she assured him she'd be fine. Judith got into her car and drove to visit Bobbe Cook. Alan turned back toward his house, just a few minutes away.

At 9:21, Mathews heard the rattle of the beetle's engine before it turned the corner. "Okay," Mathews said. "Let him pull in, then David, pull up to the driveway and Bruce, you take him."

Lane fired the engine as Berg nosed his car up to the closed garage door and shut it off. Lane pulled the Plymouth sideways across Berg's driveway apron and stopped. Mathews quickly got out and yanked the rear door open for Pierce.

Berg, a freshly lighted cigarette dangling from his lips, reached for the small grocery bag, then opened his door.

Pierce was out of the car and starting up the short driveway when Berg thrust his long left leg out and bent slightly to exit the VW. For an instant, Berg's eyes swung around to catch the movement behind him.

As he did, Pierce cut loose point-blank. The fiery lead slugs hit like a jackhammer into Berg's head and body, twisting him violently and sending him swiftly to the concrete. He landed on his back in a hail of .45-caliber cartridges, a can of dog food rolling toward the curb.

Pierce sprinted to the car, and Lane slammed the accelerator to the floor, speeding past East Fourteenth Avenue, where he had planned to turn, and going down a few more blocks before he gained his composure and headed for Colorado Boulevard. Pierce looked at the MAC-10 and saw a spent cartridge stuck in the ejection slide.

"Did you see that?" he asked his companions as the car sped away. "It was like we pulled a goddam rug out from under him the way he went down!"

On Adams Street, a few window curtains were drawn back as neighbors casually glanced out into the pitch-black streetscape, curious about the noise. They had heard a metallic sound, like a log chain being dragged over a car fender. Seeing nothing unusual, they went back to their televisions and card games.

In the apartment immediately above Berg's garage and one floor below Berg's unit, Susan Allen was toweling off after her shower and was walking toward the laundry room when she heard the loud rattle and felt the house vibrate, as if someone had thrown a handful of rocks against the garage.

Frightened, she went back to her bedroom and waited silently a few minutes, not knowing what to expect. Then she reached for her phone and dialed a house about a dozen blocks away, where her boyfriend was visiting friends.

"Are you coming over soon, Charlie?" she asked nervously. "I heard a terrible noise. I think something's wrong."

Chapter 7

Brink's and the $3,800,000 War Chest

Alarmed by the fear in his girlfriend's voice, Charles McDowell drove quickly to Adams Street, parking in the alley behind Susan Allen's condominium. He ran along the south side and rounded the staircase to the second floor, his momentum carrying him two steps up. As he did, he came upon a black Volkswagen, its door open, and a man sprawled face-up on the concrete next to it.

McDowell backed down slowly, focusing hard on the body, the huge pool of blood, and the stream oozing down the driveway. He recognized it as Berg. McDowell ran up to Susan's door and knocked loudly.

"Susan! Open up!" he yelled. "It looks like somebody's mugged Alan Berg!"

At 9:38 P.M., a Denver police dispatcher came on the air. "Three fourteen."

Officer Diane Brookshire, riding with Officer Nina Orton, reached for the radio mike. "Three fourteen," She answered.

"Three fourteen. Fourteen forty-five Adams. In the driveway. Report of a man down, possible mugging. Ambulance is responding."

"Fourteen forty-five Adams," Brookshire repeated in the mike.

"21:38," the dispatcher said, punching the pink card and placing it in car 314's slot. At 9:40 P.M., the policewomen came up Adams Street from East Eighth Avenue and stopped in front of the driveway at 1445. A rescue team from a nearby firehouse and paramedic ambulance had just arrived. Turning on the left-side spotlight, Brookshire sprayed the light over the man's body and saw the large amount of blood. The light reflected off several small objects—shell casings.

Mike Simon, a Denver General Hospital paramedic, walked up to Brookshire. He looked back at Berg's body, then told her, "Looks like he didn't make it."

Orton pulled the two-way from her belt and called: "Three fourteen. Better start homicide and the ME to 1445 Adams," she said.

Detectives Erv Haynes and Ray Estrada arrived shortly before the medical examiner. They instructed uniformed officers to block the street and put up the yellow "crime scene" tape across Adams Street to keep the growing crowd back.

One of the detectives bent down to look at the victim. "You know who this is?" he said to his colleagues. "It's Alan Berg!" Realizing the death would stir media attention, he asked the dispatcher to go "two-way," meaning only the dispatcher could hear the transmission.

Investigative Division Chief Don Mulnix was home when the dispatcher called, informing him who had been killed and how violent it had been. He ordered the dispatcher to notify the skeleton night crew that he wanted every working detective at the crime scene immediately. He also said to call Captain Doug White, Lieutenant David Michaud, and Sergeant Tom Haney of the crimes against persons bureau.

"Oh, yeah. And get the PIOs out there. I don't want to answer reporters' questions all night," Mulnix said before placing the receiver back in the cradle.

When the detective went "two-way" to the dispatcher, it was like sending up a red flare to Denver's news media, which closely monitor police calls. If police didn't want everyone to hear, it meant something big was up. Immediately a horde of reporters from the city's two daily newspapers, AP and UPI, four television stations, and several radio stations converged on the scene. Other than KOA's news staff, not many knew the significance of the address.

Mulnix ordered all detectives except homicide, the crime lab, and uniformed officers not busy with crowd control to fan out door-to-door for witnesses.

A fifteen-year-old girl who lived next door to the Berg townhouse said she heard three shots and ran out the door. "I knew what it was right away," she said, but she hadn't seen anyone leave the scene.

"I thought it sounded like a machine gun, but it was quieter," said Kelly Wiggins, who was watching TV with her roommate across Adams Street. "We decided it was probably a pack of firecrackers."

"I was playing cribbage with my roommate when I heard it," Larry Fowler said. "It sounded like a rattling chain." One woman told police she was crossing East Fourteenth Avenue and a car sped across Adams Street, nearly hitting her.

Mulnix stood with detectives Estrada and Haynes as the crime lab took samples and pictures. "Jesus," Estrada said, "those are .45-caliber casings. I've counted nine so far. How long would it take to pump nine shots into a guy?"

"And what about the noise?" Haynes asked. "You know, .45s are loud as hell. It would have sounded like sticks of dynamite going off."

Mulnix had spent virtually all but his rookie year in the detective bureau. He'd seen everything from muggings to gangland slayings, but he'd never seen anyone butchered by a gun the way Berg was. "It's pretty obvious," he said slowly, "this was no mugging. Somebody wanted to send a message with this one."

When Berg's body was placed in a rubber bag and hoisted onto a stretcher, three more casings were found under him. He'd been shot at least twelve times.

Just twenty minutes after his body was discovered, viewers all over Colorado heard of Alan Berg's death as the lead item on the 10 P.M. television news. In the Motel 6 on Peoria Street, Mathews continually switched channels, trying to determine how much was known and whether their car had been spotted.

Pierce inspected the magazine from the MAC-10. "Jeez. It jammed on the thirteenth round," he mused. "I wonder if that has any special meaning?"

Lily Halpern sat up straight in her chair when she heard the lead news item. As Judith Berg's mother, she cared about Alan and knew they had gone to dinner. A chill descended through her body, numbing her with fright. She knew they were supposed to go to Cook's, so she ran for the phone to call her. Bobbe answered.

"This is Lily, Bobbe. Is Judith there?" Halpern asked frantically.

"Yes, she is, Lily," she replied.

"What's she doing?"

"She's just been trying to get a hold of Alan."

"Is your TV on?" she asked Bobbe.

"No. Why? Is something wrong?"

"Oh, Bobbe! Thank God she's there! It's terrible!"

Ken Hamblin, a black talk-show host at KOA, was on the air with a caller when the reporter Rick Barber sat down at the other mike. Sensing something urgent, Hamblin cut off the call and asked what was up.

"Denver police have just confirmed that Alan Berg has been shot," Barber broadcast over KOA. "They also confirm that Alan Berg is dead."

Hamblin stared at Barber in disbelief, then he started to cry. Sobbing into the microphone, he said, "I guess I'm just not network material." After long, agonizing minutes, he regained his composure and spoke to the audience at large.

"I only wish this were a damn hoax," Hamblin spoke into the mike. "I wish it was a damn publicity stunt. But it's not." Then, realizing the killer would still be within listening range, he spoke directly to him.

"I can feel your presence out there. You're a loser, man! If Alan Berg was anything before you blew him away, you have made him immortal."

Berg's longtime friend, the attorney Al Zinn, called Berg's sister, Norma Sacks, in Chicago and told her what had happened. Stunned, Norma and her husband, Martin, debated whether to tell Alan's mother, Ruth, immediately or to wait until morning. It was already after 11 P.M. in Chicago, but they decided they had to tell Ruth now. They prepared to drive to her apartment, but it was too late. Ruth Berg called in tears. She had flipped on the radio to WGN, where the talkshow host Eddie Schwartz was reading the news of her son's death.

The Denver TV news ended at 10:35. Mathews shut off the set and told the others to pack. Then he walked to a nearby pay phone. At 10:45, he dialed his mom's number in Metaline Falls. He talked less than three minutes, just long enough to make sure everything was all right in his White American Bastion.

Shortly after 11 P.M., the hit team silently slipped out of

the Motel 6. Lane started his yellow VW and went off alone, east on I-70 into the dark and empty prairie toward Kansas. He had a load of counterfeit money for Tom Martinez.

About 1 A.M., Pierce pulled up to Zillah's house and dropped off Mathews. He rapped on her door, and Zillah answered. Bob rushed inside, wide-eyed and excited. Zillah was apprehensive. Unable to sleep, Bob sat her down and told Zillah every last detail of the evening.

"Don't ever tell anyone what I've just told you," he said. "Even Bruce, Richard, and David. I don't want them to know I told you."

EARLY THE FOLLOWING morning, Mathews rushed out to buy copies of the *Denver Post* and the *Rocky Mountain News*. The stories dominated the front pages. When Zillah awoke and walked into her living room, she saw Mathews, Pierce, and Scutari sitting quietly with the papers, exchanging them as they read.

Division chief Mulnix formed a "major case squad" Tuesday morning, with detectives from all bureaus, including the crime lab and the intelligence unit. He called for assistance from the Colorado Bureau of Investigation, the FBI, and the federal Bureau of Alcohol, Tobacco, and Firearms. In all, Mulnix assigned more than sixty detectives to the homicide, the largest major case squad in Denver's history. Meeting in the first-floor conference room at Denver police headquarters, Mulnix told the officers he believed this was the work of a right-wing fanatic or terrorist group.

"There's no way someone could fire twelve times with a .45-caliber semi-auto," Mulnix told them. "The gun we're after was fully automatic, the kind that leaves a message as well as a body."

Firearms experts decided that the MAC-10, because of its compact size, was the logical choice. Police technicians began examining the recovered slugs under a microscope to see if they could detect a silencer from the markings.

Mulnix also warned the officers to keep all information to themselves to cut down on cranks. He or Captain White would issue findings to the media. By Tuesday afternoon, calls from around the nation and as far away as West Germany and Tel Aviv had come from people wanting to know what had happened.

Wednesday morning, Mulnix received the preliminary autopsy report. According to Dr. George Ogura, the city's forensic pathologist, Berg suffered thirty-four wounds, all caused by entry and exit of up to thirteen slugs. There were six head wounds, any one of which would have been fatal; two in the neck, both exits of bullets that hit him above and below his left eye; six wounds in the left arm; seven wounds in the chest, one of which penetrated his heart; two in the lower chest; two in the right shoulder; seven in the right arm; one in the abdomen that traversed through his liver and stomach; and one in the back.

"Our one hope," Mulnix told his squad at a meeting in the conference room, "is that they don't dump the gun somewhere. The bullets are in good shape, and we have a chance of identifying the weapon if we find it."

Then Detective Dan Molloy, who had spent seventeen of his twenty-five years on the force in the intelligence bureau, walked to the front of the room. Molloy, a soft-spoken, good-humored Irishman, had been searching through the multitude of contact cards and files in his bureau, looking for one in particular. Now he had it.

"I have a possible suspect," Molloy said to the assembly. "Actually, a prime suspect. His name is David Eden Lane."

Lane's name surfaced for Molloy when he went back through his "right-wing radicals" cards, remembering the incident three years earlier when the Klansman and two friends were intercepted by police while heading for the NAACP convention in Denver with a trunkload of white supremacist literature. The contact card indicated Lane and his companions voluntarily surrendered the literature, and no legal action followed. In fact, they'd broken no law, but police like to let radicals know they are being watched.

Molloy got busy on the phone, calling known friends and associates of Lane, and quickly learned that Lane hated Alan Berg with a passion.

Although Mulnix warned investigators against talking to the press, there were a few old-time police reporters with cultivated sources in the department and in the federal branches as well. One reporter stopped by the homicide unit and asked veteran homicide Detective Peter Diaz if they had any suspects.

"Yeah," Diaz said with a slight smile. He picked up the Denver telephone book and tossed it onto the center of his desk. "All of them."

Still, police close to the case soon realized this wasn't the work of a disgruntled listener. Weirdos and psychotics rarely had access to automatic weapons. And despite Berg's self-proclaimed ties to the underworld as a Chicago lawyer and his associations with gamblers, a scenario involving those elements was discounted. Mafia hit men didn't pulverize their victims. They shot them in the head, mouth, or other symbolic location with a single bullet and threw down the cold piece, its serial numbers punched out so it couldn't be linked to them.

"I can almost profile the man who killed Alan," the noted Chicago lawyer Frank Oliver, a friend of Berg's who also defended underworld clients, said. "He's a guy between thirty-five and forty-two, far right, a gunhead, a good Christian of the evangelical variety, a chauvinistic kind of guy." Oliver wasn't far off.

Berg's killing obviously was intended to serve as a statement. And the killer had to be someone with access to sophisticated weaponry, long a hallmark of the radical right. The investigation quickly narrowed. Within days, detectives learned that Lane had last been in Denver sometime in April, staying with a friend, Warren McKinzie, in Lakewood. Lane had left in a huff after a squabble with McKinzie.

McKinzie scoffed at the notion that Lane was involved in the assassination, saying Lane had once gone into hiding when he was certain the Anti-Defamation League was shadowing him. In fact, in April Lane had told McKinzie the ADL was bugging him again. But McKinzie also said Lane was no longer bothered by Berg.

"We used to listen to Berg because he was funny and insulting," McKinzie told a newspaper reporter. "Dave is not fond of any Jews and I think he has good reason not to be. But as for Alan Berg, he didn't care that much. I'm sure he's owned a handgun or two, but he's not violent. He keeps it in the glove compartment. I'm telling you, I know Dave and he isn't nuts. He's a man with strong beliefs, a strong personality, but not nuts. If he shot Alan Berg, what would that have gained him?

"I can see it now. They'll put him in front of a Jew judge and a Jew jury. I'm not a radical, but I can see his point."

But McKinzie's opinion of Lane was in the minority.

John J. Clancy, a former Klansman who met Lane in the United Klans faction, told Diaz that when he saw the TV news about Berg's killing, his first thought was: "Where were you at 10 o'clock, David Lane?"

Clancy was expecting the police visit. In fact, he argued with his wife for two days over whether to call police anonymously to tip them that Lane might be their man. Clancy knew Lane as a loner, filled with rage over a "Jew-dominated, infested" world. Almost never was Clancy with him that Lane didn't mention Berg. Lane hated Berg and would ask out loud about Berg's personal habits—where did he live, where did he eat, when did he get off work?

Lane listened to Berg on the air and sometimes called to argue, once about integrated housing. Lane had given up his broker's license because he wouldn't sell houses to interracial couples. But invariably Berg would hang up on him.

"There's plenty of David Lanes out there," Clancy told a *Rocky Mountain News* reporter, John Accola, shortly after the murder. "A lot of fanatics, and they could just as easily be on the left as the right. You get around these people and I guess you never get rid of the paranoia. I know I've never gotten over it."

Denver police also located Lane's adoptive parents in a small Douglas County town southeast of Denver. The father, a slight, gray-haired man, was a Lutheran minister and a successful Colorado businessman. In his mid-seventies, with hearing aids in both ears, he was a very private but amiable fellow, living with his wife in a modern ranch home set on several acres.

"We have different philosophies," the father told Accola. "David, he is easily led, misguided. Somebody is using him. He's not a leader. He's being tossed around like a wet rag."

Asked what he knew about the Aryan Nations church, the father responded, "I know this church teaches hate. A real church can't do that, not hate."

As a teenager, Lane had attended Hinckley High School in sububan Aurora and had showed a burning passion to become a professional golfer. He was good enough on the links that he could always hustle a few bucks betting suckers on the golf course. As an adult, David reclaimed his biological father's Danish surname, thinking a golf pro named Lane would be more easily remembered.

He worked as a title searcher for a company in southeast Denver and married a woman named Sue Carol. The marriage ended in divorce just as Lane was getting involved in Aryan Nations as Butler's "information minister." Friends said personal problems, not his racist philosophies, split them up.

In the late 1970s Lane was contacted by his natural sister, Jane Eden, who lived in Boise. She was engaged to Carl Franklin of Easton, the Pennsylvania state leader of Aryan Nations. Lane's association with Franklin and his sister deepened his commitment to the white supremacist philosophy.

Detective Molloy put out word on the national Law Enforcement Intelligence Unit wire that Denver police were looking for Lane for questioning in the Berg homicide. Unfortunately, one man who knew that Lane had recently been at Aryan Nations, Kootenai County Undersheriff Larry Broadbent, didn't subscribe to LEIU. He had no way of knowing Berg's death in Denver had ties in his own backyard.

On Thursday in Forest Park, Illinois, Berg's body was laid to rest in a grave next to his father's in the Free Sons of Israel section of the huge Waldheim Cemetery. Only five mourners were there: Ruth Berg, Norma and Martin Sacks, their son, and Judith Berg. They wanted it kept private. As a result, despite the intense interest, only one reporter managed to find the service. The funeral director, Jules Furth, restrained a policeman after the Denver reporter said he would remain a respectful 25 feet from the service.

MATHEWS AND SCUTARI drove overnight to get back to Metaline Falls from Laramie on June 22, bringing along newspaper clippings about the killing. When they parked at Mathews Acres, Bob called the men still there, Kemp, Dye, and Soderquist, into his living room. "Did you hear about that guy in Denver?" he asked as he spread out the clippings on his coffee table. Bob looked proud as he held court.

"Man, with all this publicity, this guy Berg must have been a member of the Kehilla," Mathews told them. Many on the extreme right believe in the existence of a super-secret Jewish cabal called the Kehilla, which charts the course of the world by controlling money and nations. Somehow, the public's reaction to Berg's murder reinforced the belief. "No matter," Mathews said. "The guy got what he deserved."

Outside in the gravel parking area, Scutari leaned wearily against Mathews's car, propped on his elbows. Rader came out of the woods from the shooting range, and when Scutari saw him, he complained: "Your gun jammed on us, Rader."

"It's never jammed on me!" Rader said, defensive about the MAC's performance even before he wondered how it had been used. "Sometimes it's those factory loads in the cartridges. You get a light one every so often and it won't push the ejector piston." Rader then went inside the house, where Mathews told him to come over and look at the news stories. The men were calling the victim "Iceberg," and the act later became code-named "the genocide in the mountains."

Rader was horrified. He had always had it both ways at CSA, training for guerrilla warfare but not actually doing it. Now he rationalized that he shared no responsibility for Berg's death, despite his implicit approval by remaining with the gang and his explicit act of selling the MAC in the first place.

Ken Loff stopped after his shift at the cement plant and came upon the same scene—men laughing over the brutal killing. "Well, buddy, we shot him!" Mathews told Loff, tossing a newspaper to him. "Read this."

It was the *Rocky Mountain News*, its tabloid front blazing the story. Mathews hunched over the *Spokane Chronicle*, while others shared the *Wyoming Eagle*. Loff, who had never heard of Alan Berg, was upset because

Mathews had told him long ago, after the oath in the barracks, that there would be no killing.

Rader also reminded Mathews that he had said assassinations wouldn't be done yet. True to form, Mathews told each man what he wanted to hear. To Loff, Mathews said there would be no more. But to Rader, who would be training his soldiers, Mathews said that from time to time an assassination might be necessary.

Later, Mathews told Rader to prepare an encampment in the woods for a group meeting in a week, a planning session for the next robbery. Mathews was going to call on his friend from Brink's, Charles Ostrout.

A fifty-year-old money room supervisor at the San Francisco Brink's depot, Ostrout was an extreme example of a disaffected white man. At one time unemployed, he blamed his inability to hold a job in the Bay Area on the large influx of minorities, particularly Asians, and affirmative action programs. He answered Mathews's ad in a conservative newspaper and soon began a regular correspondence. Ostrout felt a close kinship with Mathews, considering him a loyal friend. He complained that Jews were behind the promotions blacks were getting at Brink's, which prevented white men from getting ahead. His feelings seethed while Mathews kept stoking them.

So it was with only slight trepidation in March 1984 that Ostrout complied with an unusual request. Mathews asked him to scout the names and addresses of drug dealers in the Bay Area that Mathews's gang could rob.

Mathews and Parmenter drove to the Bay Area from Metaline Falls on June 24 and checked into a motel in San Pablo. Mathews called Ostrout, who lived with another Brink's employee during the week and drove home on weekends to remote Lookout, California, 330 miles northeast of San Francisco in the Mount Shasta region.

When Ostrout arrived at the motel, Mathews handed him a ream of uncut counterfeit money, saying he could keep a percentage of what he passed and mail the rest back. Then the trio went out for a beer. Mathews sipped on his—his friends couldn't recall ever seeing Bob finish a beer. Ostrout told him he had some friends who were looking for dope dealers who kept money at home.

"That's good, Chuck," Mathews replied. "Let me tell

you what else our group is interested in. Our revolution is in great need of large funds. We've hit porno shops, banks, and armored cars, but we need big money. And fast. If you're really as angry with your company as you say, there's a way to get back at them."

"Yeah? How's that?" Ostrout bit.

"Well, we have enough men now to be a small army," Mathews bragged. "If you could furnish us with any good sites to hit one of your armored cars, we'd get what we need and you'd be paying the company back for what it did to you."

Ostrout had been afraid it would come to this, ever since Mathews started dropping hints a few months back. He started to feel like a man on a speeding locomotive, heading for a trestle that had collapsed. He could either jump from the train, which could kill him, or take his chances when it crashed, which also could kill him. He assumed if he bucked Mathews, he and his family would be marked for death. So Ostrout decided to hang onto the runaway locomotive's throttle, keep his head as low as he could, and ride to the end of the line.

As he was leaving the motel after returning from the bar, Ostrout started for his car, then turned and said, "I'll get back to you."

Returning to Boise, Mathews looked over the potential Wells Fargo job and scratched it in favor of pursuing the Brink's opportunity. Robbing something in Boise would be like fouling their own nests. The Vikings didn't plunder Norway.

RADER DID A YEOMAN job of preparing the campsite. He knew some of the men could be under surveillance, so he took extra precautions. He found a dense stand of trees in the woods about a half-mile from Mathews Acres and got Kemp, Dye, and Soderquist to clear a narrow path to the area. They spent almost three days cutting, clearing, and building. They erected a wooden table for a stove, places for lanterns, and a site for several tents.

On June 29, a Friday night, the company's largest meeting to date began deep in the woods of the Lead King Hills. Sixteen Aryan warriors attended. Three new faces were there: Tom Bentley, who was living with

Bonnie Sue West since Walter West's disappearance; Jim Wallington, whom Pierce had invited during a visit to Aryan Nations; and David Tate, the impressionable youngster who grew up at Aryan Nations. Evans and Barnhill were back from Madras, Evans acting sheepish because of the nature of his arrest. The weapons charge against Barnhill was dropped after Evans claimed the guns were his and pleaded guilty to the assault charge.

Mathews surveyed his "army": Pierce, Loff, Dye, Kemp, Duey, Evans, Barnhill, Rader, Scutari, Yarbrough, Parmenter, and Soderquist. The first order of business was another reading of the oath for Tate, Bentley, and Wallington.

Then Mathews introduced Scutari, who handed out copies of a two-page document and went over it with them. It was titled "Rules for Security."

"Drugs of any type are strictly forbidden," Scutari started. "A few joints may be harmless, but you have to buy from a dealer and that is a security risk.

"Alcohol—never while on a mission, at the bastion, or in training. And a two-drink limit otherwise. Drunkards are security risks, too," Scutari added.

"There is no excuse for fighting in public unless bodily harm is imminent. This means if a nigger spits in your face, you will walk away. When you're around mud people or race traitors, act like they're normal people. Their time will come. It is important the enemy never find out we exist. If he does, he must think we are toothless!

"Never use a motel switchboard. Use pay phones, and make the calls short. When you call someone at his house, use his real name. If you call him somewhere else, use his code name.

"We will operate on a need-to-know basis," Scutari continued, glancing at Mathews. "If you are not on a job, you will not know anything about it.

"Driving. Another sore subject. On the open highway, no one will go over 65. No one will drive more than twelve hours straight even with multiple drivers. If you have a thirteen-hour trip, you'll divide it so you're fresh when you get to the destination, like ten hours one day, three the next.

"If you're stopped by a cop, don't argue. Take your ticket and leave."

Scutari was aware that some of the men had terrible driving records. Andy Barnhill's Florida license had been suspended in April 1982, after he left for CSA in Arkansas, for failure to pay a traffic fine. Barnhill also received a speeding ticket near Ione in June; Parmenter got one in Orlando, Fla., on May 31; Kemp got one speeding home from the Northgate robbery. They weren't the only ones. These tickets, Scutari feared, would create a web of documentation that one day could entangle the company, tie down its members to certain times and places.

Scutari's last item was advice about what to do if they were caught.

"If you're arrested, make one call to the relay number for Mr. Black. Give your location and the charge, then hang up and shut up. Wait for us because we'll get you out." He didn't say how.

Everyone acquired a code name. Mathews, of course, was Carlos. Gary Yarbrough was Yosemite Sam, because of the resemblance. Parmenter wore sandals, so Sandals became his name. Jim Dye was Mr. May because he joined in May. Bill Soderquist became Cripple after a knee operation. Andy Barnhill was Closet because of a sexual fantasy he once confessed about tying up women in a closet.

The others' code names included Field Marshal (Randall Rader, who, some of the men joked, thought he was the second coming of Erwin Rommel), Mr. Black (Richard Scutari), Brigham (Bruce Pierce), Luke (Randy Duey), Marbles (Ken Loff, because of the funny way he pronounced the word with his Long Island accent), Calvin (Randy Evans), Jolly (Richie Kemp; he also acquired the nickname "Hammer" following the Walter West killing, and some of the men would sing the refrain from the Beatles' "Maxwell's Silver Hammer" in Kemp's presence), Ace (Tom Bentley), Ezra (Jim Wallington), and Banty (David Tate).

New people recruited into the gang were assigned code names as well. Eventually there would be members whose real names were never known to some.

After Scutari finished, Rader got up and talked about setting up an Aryan Academy, a training camp for white guerrillas. He and Scutari had gone over the pass from

Metaline Falls to Priest Lake, Idaho, and had seen some suitable terrain. The men would be assigned to the camp once Mathews could afford to operate it.

That brought up the next subject. Mathews got up to talk.

"Kinsmen, we are very low on cash. Very low. We need another procurement, and I want to know who would like to be in on it," Mathews said. All but Tate, Bentley, and Wallington raised their hands.

"We've got business at Aryan Nations," Tate explained. "The annual congress is in two weeks and we're on the security detail." Mathews sent Rader and the trio down the path to stand watch since they had no "need to know" about Brink's.

"Comrades," Mathews told the group after the four men left, "Parmenter and I are going to meet a kinsman in San Francisco who is joining us in our battle. He is in a position with Brink's to target a job that will yield more money than you'd believe." Mathews divided the men into three groups, with one from each designated to call Loff each day. Mathews would notify Loff when the men were to proceed in groups down to California for the robbery.

After an hour the meeting adjourned, with almost everybody returning to the barracks. Pierce, clean-shaven and with brown hair bleached blond, couldn't risk being seen because of the arrest warrant on him. Rader said he would keep him company camped in the woods. Pierce and Rader had just met that night. They spent the hours in the tent talking at first about the hardship of life as a fugitive.

But mostly they talked about the Lord, Yah, who Pierce believed was guiding his every move.

A continent away, that same night, Tom Martinez was languishing in a holding cell in downtown Philadelphia.

THE DAY AFTER Alan Berg was killed, Tom Martinez saw the story in the Philadelphia *Daily News*. Mathews's words came back to him in a rush: "Keep your eyes and ears open. A guy in Colorado is going to be taken care of."

A few days later, Mathews called him to say David Lane was coming with the counterfeit money Martinez had agreed to pass. Tom couldn't hold back his question.

"Bob, that thing in Colorado, was that you?"

"Yep," came the simple reply. "That was us."

Martinez's spirits sank to new depths. His friend had actually killed a Jew. Martinez began thinking of ways to get out of the whole deal.

Lane came to Martinez's house on Weikel Street on June 24 carrying two boxes wrapped in paper, like presents, with the name of Martinez's daughter on them. When Lane opened them on the kitchen table, Martinez saw both were filled with uncut counterfeit ten-dollar bills—950 sheets, which Lane said would be $38,000. Lane pulled out sets of surgical gloves, cutting knives, and rectangular plastic templates to be placed over the bills for cutting to exact size.

When the task proved mountainous, Martinez called George Zaengle to help. Zaengle, a National Alliance friend, had been promised a spot in Mathews's group along with Dye and William Nash. The task took three days. While cutting the phony bills, Martinez asked Lane if he knew anything about the Berg killing.

"Know about it!" Lane snorted. "Hell, man, I was the goddam getaway driver!"

"You've got to be kidding me!" Martinez responded in shock.

"Shit, we watched that Jew-kike eating dinner, our surveillance was so good," Lane bragged. "We waited in his fucking neighborhood for six or seven hours." Now Martinez could think of only one thing: Get this man out of my house.

On Monday, after they had finished, Lane gave Martinez written instructions on passing the bills—what stores to avoid, the types of people to approach, and so forth. Lane told him to cross over to New Jersey to pass them and to keep them out of his own neighborhood. When Martinez got good money in change from the counterfeit bills, he was to get a book, hollow out the center, insert the money minus his percentage, then mail it to Ken Loff.

That Wednesday night, while driving around the city, Martinez passed Miller's Pharmacy at Kensington and Allegheny avenues. Lane told him to stop so he could get something. Martinez waited only a minute before Lane, a huge grin on his face, returned with a single candy bar.

"You see how easy it is?" Lane said, unwrapping the candy bar and displaying $9 plus change.

In his mind, though, Martinez devised another plan. He would pass maybe one-fourth of the money, keep the proceeds to fix up his house, which was in disrepair, then call Mathews and say he was nearly caught and was quitting. Maybe that, he thought, would break him clear.

Lane gave him a phone number, which turned out to belong to Lane's brother-in-law Carl Franklin, about 60 miles up the Delaware River in Easton, where Martinez could reach him through Lane's sister, Jane Franklin. Lane took about $8,000 worth of the phonies with him when he left Wednesday.

Once Martinez started passing the bills on Thursday, he found Lane was correct. It was incredibly easy. Trusting clerks simply took his tenspot for a newspaper, a pack of gum, or some other inexpensive item and turned over real U.S. legal tender as change. Martinez was overcome by greed.

Ignoring Lane's advice to go out of state, Martinez passed roughly $1,500 that first day, right along Kensington Avenue and other main streets in his neighborhood. He capped off the day's spree by stopping in the Beerland Package Store, in a strip center on Aramingo Avenue, and buying a 50-cent Pennsylvania Lottery ticket. Who knows? Maybe he'd hit the jackpot.

After 7 P.M., the Beerland owner, Jerry Stern, counted his day's receipts and the phony ten stuck out from the others like a red flag. He remembered that when a man bought a lottery ticket with it, something about the paper didn't feel right. He turned to his clerk, Carol Achuff, and told her to be on guard in the morning.

Sure enough, a creature of habit, Martinez returned to Beerland about 10:15 the next morning, intent on starting his second day's work where he left off. This time Achuff waited on him as he ordered a 50-cent lottery ticket.

When Martinez handed her one of Merki's bills, Achuff rubbed it and turned to Stern, who was at the other end of the counter.

"This feels like that ten we got yesterday, Jerry," she called to him.

Stern looked over and recognized Martinez. "Hey!" he yelled. "You're the guy that gave me counterfeit money yesterday. I'm calling the cops!" In an instant, Martinez's fantasy world crumbled around his feet. Feigning innocence, he denied knowing anything about it. "You're crazy," Martinez yelled, then ran out the door. Unaccustomed to criminal activity, Martinez ran right to his car.

Stern followed him outside and watched as Martinez climbed into a gray 1983 Mitsubishi and drove away. Stern wrote down the license number—DWM-777.

Martinez panicked. He dashed around collecting the remaining counterfeit money in his car and home, the instruction sheet from Lane, and all other remnants of the scheme, and put them in a bag. Then he called Zaengle and arranged for him to pick up the bag and dispose of it. Later, Martinez wondered whether going back to Beerland and offering a real ten-dollar bill might smooth things over.

Martinez returned to Beerland more relaxed, and called to Stern. "Sorry about that incident this morning," Martinez said, waving a real $10. "Here, I want to make it up. I didn't know that was bad money."

"Well, why did you run?" Stern asked.

"I got scared. I thought you were calling the cops."

"It's too late," Stern replied. "I did. If you want to talk, here's the Secret Service agents to contact"—Stern fumbled for a business card—"Alonzo Webb or Sean Gallagher."

Martinez turned, leaving his money on the counter. "Keep it," he told Stern.

Webb and Gallagher were already aware of the scam when Stern called. The First Pennsylvania Bank branch at Kensington and Allegheny avenues notified the Secret Service that morning that ten counterfeit bills had turned up in the overnight deposits of various merchants in the area. With Stern's call, Webb thought they might wrap up the case quickly.

Zaengle later told Martinez he had gotten rid of the evidence. Of course, more would filter in as merchants around Kensington banked their receipts and Merki's handiwork showed up in deposits. Martinez pulled out Lane's number and dialed.

Lane was visiting his sister in Easton. The Franklins lived in a house on a small spread along Cedarville Road, south of town near the sewer plant, on the hardwood-forested slope of Mammy Morgan's Hill. It overlooked the confluence of the Lehigh and Delaware rivers. Carl Franklin, the Aryan Nations leader for the Keystone State, answered Martinez's call and said he'd have Lane call back.

Soon, Lane called Martinez in Philadelphia. "This is Lone Wolf," he said, using his code name derived from his loner's tendency. "What's up, Spider?"

"I got busted," Martinez replied, "passing the money in Kensington."

"You fucking idiot!" Lane yelled. "Why the hell didn't you go to Jersey like you were supposed to?"

"Look, man, I ain't gonna argue with you! I'm getting rid of the rest of it! I'm through!" After dinner that evening, Martinez was lounging in the back yard with his family when police and treasury agents stormed in. While being cuffed, Martinez was read his rights, then driven to the federal building, where agents asked him to reveal where he got the phony money.

"Are you crazy?" Martinez blurted. "Do you think I want to die?"

The agents then realized Martinez might be involved in something larger than a backroom counterfeiting operation. Still, Martinez said nothing about Mathews or the organization, or what he knew about Berg, Northgate, the porno store, the "bluebacks," and Carlos's plans for a White American Bastion. He guarded his information closely, partly in fear of Mathews but also in fear of being caught up in a larger, more serious set of crimes.

A day later, Martinez was released on a personal recognizance bond. He called Ken Loff and begged him to wire $1,600 for an attorney. But Mathews wouldn't allow it. He needed every cent he had to fund the Brink's job.

"I know you're in a bad spot now, buddy, but try to sit tight," Mathews soothed him. "We've got something big coming down soon, and after that we'll have plenty of money to get you an attorney."

PARMENTER PICKED MATHEWS up July 1 in his blue Cutlass, and they started for California. Bill Soderquist wanted to go home to Salinas, south of San Francisco, to meet with a girlfriend, so he hitched a ride with them. The next day they pulled into the Travelodge Motel in Richmond, north of Berkeley. As soon as they got to their room, Mathews called Ostrout.

Ostrout arrived later with a package. He opened it and handed them photos of a place he said was owned by a local dope dealer. The photos included various shots of the home, the man's vehicle, and his garage. Ostrout said the person who gave him the photos indicated the dealer kept as much as $200,000 in his home.

"Kinsman," Mathews said, shaking his head in dismay, "$200,000 isn't nearly enough money. Maybe months ago, yeah, but we're really gearing up. Have you done anything about the armored cars?"

Ostrout told them of a place in Milpitas, north of San Jose, where they could check on armored trucks as they collected from stores and banks.

In addition, Ostrout said his boss and work-week roommate, Ronald Allen King, forty-five, might be a recruit, and Mathews should meet him. King, operations manager for the San Francisco depot, had an apartment in San Lorenzo since separating from his wife, Lisa, also a Brink's guard, who was dating one of the company's black drivers.

On Tuesday, July 3, Mathews, Parmenter, and Soderquist drove to Milpitas while Ostrout worked. They watched two Brink's trucks make pickups at stores and a bank. Because it looked as though they would yield less money than Northgate, Mathews decided against targeting them.

That night Ostrout called with a better suggestion. There was an overnight depot area near San Leandro where trucks made their relays. Each night, three trucks met and transferred money to be taken to the main vault in San Francisco. Ostrout said he would be gone on a two-day run upstate the next day, the Fourth of July, from San Francisco up U.S. 101 to Eureka on the coast, then back through the Sacramento Valley. He was to fill in for a driver taking the holiday off. He asked Mathews to hang around until he returned.

On the holiday, Mathews and Parmenter drove Soderquist to Salinas, then went to San Leandro, south of Oakland, to watch the three-truck relay point Ostrout had mentioned. The potential looked better, but again Mathews discarded it.

Ostrout returned Friday full of excitement. "Bob, I think I have it!" Ostrout almost shouted. "I just got in from the Eureka run and there's a place north of Ukiah that would be perfect to hit an armored truck." He gave Mathews a map of the run he'd just taken and showed the location where the armored truck had to grind down into first gear to make it up a winding hill.

"It practically stops right here," he said, pointing to a grade on California 20.

At last Mathews was satisfied. "Well, sounds like we need to move our operation to Ukiah for a while," he said with obvious pleasure.

He and Parmenter went to Ostrout's home in Lookout to spend the weekend with him, then headed for the small town of Ukiah, in the Russian River valley in the Coast Range. They checked into the Motel 6 in town and began mapping strategy.

Ukiah is a picturesque Northern California town of about 10,000 near Lake Mendocino, close to the Mendocino National Forest in the Mayacmas Mountains. Ukiah's single main street, State Street, runs north and south. Businesses cluster there or near the four main interchanges of the U.S. 101 bypass, the Redwood Highway, which skirts east of town.

About 6 miles north of Ukiah, where U.S. 101 emerges from Redwood Country at a small town called Calpella, California 20 originates and climbs east across the Mayacmas, 75 lonely, twisting miles to Williams on Interstate 5.

Southbound traffic on 101, as the Brink's truck would be headed, exits at Calpella by way of a sharp jughandle on the right, circling back under 101 to form the beginning of California 20. There is a steep uphill grade a mile east, as the highway climbs 350 feet in less than a mile, a 6.5 percent grade. It was along this stretch of three-lane highway—the uphill side included a passing lane—that Ostrout thought was the ideal robbery site.

At the beginning of the week, Mathews contacted Pierce and told him to bring Duey to San Francisco and wait for a call. At midweek, when they hadn't heard anything, Pierce became angry, and he and Duey drove to Ukiah, where they, too, checked into the Motel 6. Pierce called the message center and left his location. A short time later, Mathews was at Pierce's door. Pierce was miffed, but Mathews's broad smile, as always, dispelled the anger.

"You won't believe it!" Mathews said with a schoolboy exuberance that never failed to amuse Pierce. "We haven't actually seen an armored truck on the hill, but we've seen a lot of other trucks, and they really have to gear down to make it." As he listened, Pierce sensed that the plan was sketchy, but Bob was chairman of the board. Pierce reconciled himself to it and decided to take a look.

Later on Wednesday, Pierce and Duey drove to Santa Rosa, a larger city 60 miles south of Ukiah, and scanned the classified ads of the *Santa Rosa Press-Democrat* for the vehicles they would need. They used the same routine that worked in the Northgate robbery, exchanging their stolen cash for bank-fresh money in an envelope, so the buy money was untouched by the conspirators' hands.

They found two Ford pickups for sale that looked like good deals. Duey returned from buying a blue 1965 Fleetside in fairly good shape to see Pierce glancing over a green 1966 model. Pierce's had no tailgate.

"No problem, Randy," Pierce said. "I'll make one out of wood and tie it on with bunji cord. It's only gonna be used once. For $600, what do you want?"

Thursday was the day the armored truck was scheduled to return from Eureka, turning east on California 20 to the Sacramento Valley and back to San Francisco. Pierce, Duey, and Parmenter drove to the incline, parked a distance away, then hiked back through the woods to the highway. They clambered up the steep slope of a road cut on the north side of the highway and leaned back under the bright sun. They watched trucks lugging down as they struggled to pull up the incline.

The Brink's truck was due about noon, and they strained their gaze down the highway until they saw it coming. Mathews, who waited back near the jughandle, was driving right behind, clocking the truck's speed. In seven days they would be back.

On Friday, Mathews notified Loff that the rest of the men should come to California.

For the most part, none of the men minded the prodigious amount of driving that "company business" demanded. Some, like Pierce and Duey, traveled well together. They developed a different sense of humor from the mainstream. As they went through towns, Mathews would spot a passerby he thought looked like a mixture of races, and challenge his passengers to play "Name that Creature." They had to guess how many different races the person carried in his genes. For people who differentiated not only between whites and blacks but between such subgroups as Alpines and Nordics, the game could get quite involved.

The seven new arrivals checked into various rooms in Ukiah during the weekend of July 14. Mathews was registered under one of the more interesting pseudonyms he'd used—Grant Lee, his two brothers' names. On Sunday they gathered in McGarvey Park, five blocks off State Street, to review the data.

Mathews, who had changed motels once already, decided eleven men in a small town were too noticeable. On Monday they began pulling back to Santa Rosa, using the adjacent Motel 6 and Super 8 on Cleveland Street, near the freeway. Soderquist later drove up from Salinas in his Camaro.

Scutari, trained in survivalism, was amazed when he arrived that the escape, the most important aspect of a successful robbery, had not yet been planned. The men bickered over what to do. Pierce wanted just to drive flat out, to put distance between themselves and the cops as quickly as possible. Someone else suggested getting a plane to fly the millions to the bastion. Others talked about backpacking the loot through the Mayacmas to a rendezvous 25 miles away. Scutari laughed. It would take twice as many men to haul as much loot as they expected.

Scutari's philosophy was to split fast, switch quickly, and lie low. That would give the men time to gauge how much heat the cops were putting on. Scutari drove out with some men into the hills west of Ukiah, since police were likely to assume the robbers would go east toward the major highways.

After some effort, they found an area off Orrs Springs Road, only about nine miles from town but 2,400 feet up in the forest. There was a small garbage dump there with a gravel turnoff so it would be easy to spot.

They cleared a space in the trees about 100 feet down the steep hillside from the turnoff. On Wednesday, Scutari returned with Evans, Merki, and Parmenter, bringing a load of snack foods, water, and other gear to set it up for the next day.

To make the plan work, they needed two more switch cars. A mile east of where they planned to hit the armored truck, there was a large parking area at the Pomo Day Use picnic area on the north shore of Lake Mendocino. It was decided they would park the switch cars there so they could quickly dump the two pickups. Since the parking area was relatively isolated yet close, they could switch the loot and escape to the woods. Some of the men then would go to Ukiah to measure the police response and determine when it was safe to leave.

On Tuesday, Duey located a 1973 Buick Riviera for sale in Santa Rosa. He called the number listed and, after saying why he had called, made the mistake of asking the seller how to get to his house from the Motel 6 on Cleveland Street. Later, Pierce and Parmenter went along.

"The car belongs to my girlfriend," said the seller, Frank McFarland. One man lifted the hood of the green sedan and another ran through the gears while Duey dickered with McFarland.

"We'll give you $700 for it," Duey said after getting assurance from the others that the car looked usable.

"I'll take $900," McFarland replied. After some hushed talk among the trio about the gang's depleted finances, they agreed they could scrounge that much and said they'd come back in the morning for the car.

On Wednesday, Barnhill was sent to McFarland's to get the Riviera. But McFarland's girlfriend had showed up in the meantime and was insisting on $1,000 for the car. Barnhill had brought along only $900, so McFarland drove him back to a spot near the Motel 6. In a while, Barnhill returned with the full $1,000.

Later, Duey found a van for sale that fitted the group's

needs. Joan Cookston's son had gone into the Air Force after making the last payment on his 1971 Ford van, which meant the title would be up in the air when the FBI tried to trace it. It had no back window, precisely what was needed. Duey agreed to pay $1,400.

While the switch cars were being bought on Wednesday, Mathews took some of the men back to Ukiah. It was the day the Brink's truck was due on its first leg to Eureka. Several of them lounged under the shade of a large tulip magnolia tree on the Mendocino County Courthouse lawn. They were careful not to show how closely they were watching the gray truck rumbling up State Street right on schedule.

They saw two black guards in the front. "What if Ron King's nigger-lovin' wife is with them?" one of the men asked.

"We've planned it so that no one is to get hurt," Mathews said with finality. "We come for the money. Don't disappoint us. That's our mission. No one is to get hurt. The race-traitors' time will come."

The men then made a last tour of the robbery site and the getaway routes. Mathews returned to Santa Rosa with a 5-foot length of cardboard tubing, apparently the center spool from a carpet roll.

"Fashion a handle for this and paint the whole thing black." Mathews said, handing it to Parmenter.

"What for?" Parmenter asked.

"A dummy bazooka," Mathews replied. "There's going to be so much excitement when we stop the truck, no one's going to be looking closely. They see what they think is a bazooka, and I'll guarantee you'll have their attention."

Mathews had hoped to obtain a military light antitank rocket tube but had been unsuccessful. Obviously it was still on his mind.

Parmenter wore a skeptical grin. He picked up the tube and asked, "Uh, what should we call it?"

"Well," Mathews said, "how about Ballistnikov?"

With a short laugh and a shake of the head, Parmenter walked out.

THE JULY HEAT was stifling in Agent Wayne Manis's upper floor pigeonhole office in Coeur d'Alene. Fans blew constantly, but the room was like a sauna.

The phone call Manis had just received was the capper. Back on June 29—the day of the meeting in the woods at Mathews Acres, the day of Martinez's arrest, neither of which Manis could know yet—he sent a 4-inch-thick packet of papers to Washington documenting his reasons for requesting a full-scale investigation of Aryan Nations.

The latest call was from a confidential informant attending Pastor Butler's third Aryan World Congress up the highway. Colonel Jack Mohr and Louis Beam, the informant said, had conducted a two-day seminar in urban guerilla warfare.

It troubled Manis when his informant told him the folk, especially Beam, were making far too much of the killing of Alan Berg. Manis didn't yet know about the February 13 show in which Berg pulled the long-distance plug on Mohr, but he had received a teletype from the Denver FBI office saying the Denver police were looking for David Lane for questioning in connection with Berg's slaying.

Publicly, Denver police stressed that Lane was not a suspect. They just wanted to ask him some questions. In reality, Lane was very much a suspect, but police didn't want to be put in a position of having to arrest him, then by law have only seventy-two hours in which to file a formal charge or release him.

Lane's name hit the Denver papers on July 11. When Lane heard of it, he wrote an open letter to the Denver media denying he was in Denver the night Berg was killed. He then returned to Ione to hide, living for a time in the hayloft of Loff's barn.

Since Manis had begun poking around the edges of Butler's operation, disturbing signs had surfaced, chief among them Pierce's counterfeiting arrest and his failure to appear to serve his two-year sentence.

Pierce was so hot that police detained Evans and Barnhill in Madras until their photos and fingerprints could be flown to a U.S. marshal's office in Portland to make sure neither was Pierce. Manis believed that the press at Aryan Nations had been used to make the fifties Pierce had passed.

Right after the congress, Manis went to a meeting of

FBI agents from Spokane and Butte, where informants' notes were compared. At that meeting, Manis first heard the names of Robert Jay Mathews and Denver Daw Parmenter. The word was out that young men who wanted action were leaving Hayden Lake for Metaline Falls. It was the word Walter West was spreading around before he disappeared.

Too much smoke was rising from Hayden Lake—and not from burning crosses.

Manis contacted his boss, Bill Fallin, special agent in charge of the Butte, Montana, office, and outlined his suspicions, saying the case might take all of his time. Fallin agreed. It didn't take Washington long to decide. By mid-July, Manis received a teletype authorizing him to conduct a six-month investigation in conjunction with the Butte and Spokane offices.

THE MORNING OF July 19, Robert Merki walked into Mathews's motel room in Santa Rosa and stopped the conversation dead. Some of the men started issuing wolf whistles and others went limp with laughter.

Merki, who ordinarily looked like an accountant, was dressed in a skirt and blouse, sewn from a pattern by his wife, complete with bra and falsies, panty hose, a half-slip, and a short gray wig. He had purchased a pair of women's black shoes earlier from a store near Ukiah. He borrowed jumbo panties from his wife. He'd even gone so far as to shave his legs, arms, and underarms.

Merki definitely did not want anybody to be able to identify him.

"All right!" Mathews said with approval. The men went to get breakfast, and Merki was pleased that the disguise fooled the waitress, who addressed him as "ma'am."

After eating, they reassembled at the motel. Richard Scutari waited for them to fall silent. Then, in preparation for the day's events, Scutari recited the 91st Psalm. He selected it because legend had it the British 91st Infantry recited it before going into the bloody Battle of Bellau Wood in World War I and emerged from the intense fighting without losing a man.

"God is a refuge and a fortress," Scutari began, eyes

closed and head bowed. "He that dwelleth in the secret place of the Most High shall abide under the shadow of the Almighty. I will say of the Lord, He is my refuge and my fortress; in Him I will trust. Surely He shall deliver thee from the snare of the fowler, and from the noisome pestilence. He shall cover thee with His feathers, and under His wings shalt thou trust. Thou shalt not be afraid for the terror by night, nor the arrow that flieth by day."

Parmenter gave Merki a ride to the Lake Mendocino parking area near Ukiah in his Cutlass, while the others followed. They parked the switch vehicles in the lot, then Merki took the Cutlass down to 101 and drove up to Willits, 17 miles north. Merki had his wife's Ruger .357 Magnum along, but it was in the trunk.

The eleven others, dressed plainly in blue jeans and t-shirts, tied bandannas around their necks, applied Krazy Glue to their fingertips, and slipped on surgical gloves. They then climbed into the two pickups.

Their positions had been worked out meticulously. Scutari, armed with a 9mm H&K rifle, drove the green truck with the makeshift tailgate. Scutari's truck was to cut off the armored truck in front. Next to Scutari was Mathews, carrying the model 469 Smith & Wesson 9mm pistol Barnhill had bought in Missoula afrer the Northgate robbery. Mathews had asked Barnhill if he could borrow it.

In the pickup bed, Pierce sat at the tailgate with an H&K .308-caliber semi-automatic rifle, used for heavy firepower. He had jacketed shells guaranteed to penetrate the armored truck's bulletproof glass. After subduing the guards, Pierce would use the rifle to guard the road ahead. Dye sat opposite him with an automatic AR-15, a .223 rifle meant to support the heavier gun. Soderquist, seated closer to the cab, held a sign similar to the one at Northgate: "Get Out or Die." Next to him, Parmenter settled back, holding on with one hand to "Ballistnikov." By the tailgate was a large box of roofing nails.

Yarbrough drove the second pickup, which was to pull alongside the armored truck when Scutari got in front, to sandwich it to a stop. Yarbrough was armed with the MAC-10 used to kill Alan Berg. Next to him was Duey with a fully automatic Israeli 9mm Uzi. In the rear, Kemp and Evans carried shotguns loaded with buckshot. Barnhill was Pierce's heavy-fire counterpart in the second truck, carrying an H&K .308 to guard the rear. There was also a box of roofing nails.

The men pulled out of the Lake Mendocino parking area and drove to Calpella, turning north on 101 for 2 miles until they reached a gravel turnout on the west side of the highway, straddling a small, picturesque vineyard. It was shaded by a few trees on the little island between the turnout and the highway, but the mid-July sun broiled the men as they waited, bathed in sweat.

Had they been students of local history, they would have realized they were about to recreate a scene from Northern California folklore. In October 1877, Black Bart robbed the stage between Covelo and Ukiah on the Willits grade. It was at a dangerous bend where the stage, coincidentally, had to slow considerably. Then up that same road a bit, four years later, Bart robbed the Wells Fargo stage on the run from Fort Ross to Guerneville.

AT THE SOUTH end of Willits, Merki pulled into a McDonald's parking lot on U. S. 101, which he had scouted earlier in the week. There he'd be inconspicuous while still able to see the road clearly.

The armored truck's last stop before Willits was at a bank in Laytonville, 23 miles north. It was due through Willits at 11:15. Merki arrived an hour early, but as luck would have it for the men sweltering in the pickups a dozen miles south, the Brink's truck was an hour behind schedule.

Shortly after noon, as Merki was beginning to wonder if something was wrong, he spotted the large gray truck lumbering down the street toward him. He let it pass, dropped in behind it for a few miles, then passed it on a hill to put some distance between them.

As he approached the turnout where the men waited, Merki keyed the CB mike. "Breaker," Merki broadcast. "Are you there Mr. Black?"

"Affirmative," Scutari replied.

"Well, have a good day," Merki returned. He roared by and went to Calpella, where he waited in a parking area wedged behind the Club Calpella lounge and the Northwestern Pacific Railroad tracks. He monitored channel 9 on his CB.

"Let's go!" Mathews shouted to the robbers. "We got the word!"

They watched the Brink's truck rumble down the highway past the turnout. Neither guard up front paid attention to the two pickups loaded with men.

Scutari pulled out with Yarbrough right on his bumper. They caught up with the armored truck as it hit the jughandle onto California 20 and geared down to second on the sweeping turn under the main highway. It gathered speed on the flat for about a mile, across the Russian River bridge, before heading into a right-hand curve. The hill began after that curve and steepened into a long sweep to the left, gaining 400 feet in elevation in less than a mile. The overladen truck struggled when it started into the second curve.

"Okay, now take him," Mathews said to Scutari, and the green pickup pulled into the center lane.

"Hey, Aaron," Brink's driver Paul Scott said to his partner, Aaron Davis, after looking in his rearview mirror. "Look at these crazy guys passing us in the truck." Scott watched the green pickup edge into the right lane in front of him, then begin to slow. Preoccupied with that, Scott didn't notice Yarbrough's pickup pull into the passing lane and come alongside until Scutari jammed on the brakes and there was nowhere for Scott to pull out.

The heavy truck ground to a halt just past the left curve. The guards sat in stunned silence as the men in both pickups stood up and leveled weapons at them. One held up a sign that read: "Get Out or Die." All had bandannas over their faces except the tall one—Pierce—who brazenly showed his face.

Mathews jumped out of the pickup cab, ran to the front of the Brink's truck, and hopped on the bumper on the passenger's side, shouting at the guards to get out. Both were too shocked to respond. Their eyes widened when they saw Parmenter pointing what appeared to be a rocket tube at them.

After ten seconds without response, Pierce raised the H&K .308 and blew three dime-sized holes through the glass in the upper inside corner of the driver's windshield. As the guards ducked, Pierce fired a fourth shot through the top right of the passenger's windshield. Glass shards sprayed Scott, slightly cutting his forehead. The shots were deliberately high-centered so Pierce wouldn't hit the guards but would still make his point.

The slugs whined past Mathews's head as he stood on the bumper, and he quickly yelled at Pierce, "Hey! Stop firing!"

The guards stumbled out with their hands in the air. "We'll give you anything you want!" one of them stammered.

"Shut up!" Pierce commanded.

Scott failed to set the brake; as they abandoned the truck, it began to roll backward. The robbers watched in horror as their "golden goose" started drifting back down the highway. Randy Evans turned his shotgun on the rear tandems and blew the tires flat, causing the vehicle to lurch to a stop at a cocked angle to the highway. Scott belatedly yanked the brake.

When both guards had left the cab to lie face-down on the shoulder of the road, their doors slammed and locked. The switch to unlock the money compartment was inside the cab. That meant the robbers had to get the third guard in back to come out.

The highway was filling with traffic in both directions as rubbernecking drivers gawked at the spectacle. Some thought, being in California, they were watching a movie being filmed. Others who saw or heard the gunshots realized something was wrong. Several motorists stopped and took cover behind their cars. Richard Rea, owner of Rea's Dairy in Ukiah, was one of the first westbound motorists to stop. "This can't be," he thought as he gazed at the chaos before him. "This is Ukiah and things like this don't happen here."

A female motorist who watched enough to realize what was happening got on her CB radio and tuned to channel 9. "I'm on highway 20 between 101 and Lake Mendocino," she radioed on the distress channel. "There's an armored truck being robbed here by about a dozen masked men with guns!" Merki, sitting quietly behind Club Calpella only a mile from the scene, heard the transmission.

"Whaddaya tryin' to do?" Merki broke in on the woman. "Start a riot? You can't use the radio to spread false information!"

Evans, standing in the back of Yarbrough's pickup, could see through the side window of the Brink's truck that a female guard inside was reaching for something. Thinking she was going for a weapon, Evans fired his shotgun through the window. The pellets ripped apart the seat cushion she had just vacated.

Badly shaken, she surrendered through the side door facing the shoulder of the road. The door also slammed shut as she left.

"Open that door!" Mathews shouted at her. "Get that door open now!" She fumbled with her keys before unlocking the cab, where the switch to open the rear compartment was located. Evans ran around the truck and as he approached the woman—who was Lisa King, the Brink's manager's estranged wife—his bandanna slid down. She looked directly at his round, cherubic face until another of the men ordered her to lie beside the road with the other two guards. They took the guards' weapons, including King's .30-30 rifle.

"I don't know how I missed her!" Evans gasped, relieved he hadn't killed the woman. His hands began shaking as he dabbed at his face with the bandanna.

Mathews jumped inside the money compartment and paused when he saw thirty large money bags neatly stacked in the rear of the vehicle. Parmenter, Dye, Evans, and Soderquist formed a bucket brigade from the side door to the green pickup.

Mathews bent down to scoop a money sack. As he did, he felt Barnhill's 9mm pistol, which was tucked into his waistband, dig into his belly. He didn't notice as he kept working in the sweltering heat when the pistol worked its way out and dropped to the floor of the truck.

The curve in the road where they stopped the truck was working to the robbers' advantage. There was no way a responding police car could come upon them without being taken by surprise. And, but for the call of nature, that surprise might have been sprung on a Mendocino County deputy who was heading home for lunch and would have been driving eastbound on California 20 at that precise time. Instead, he stopped first to relieve himself at the sheriff's office.

Scutari and Yarbrough sat in the cabs of the pickups, monitoring the police channels on their scanners. They got the frequencies from a Radio Shack guide, tuning the sets into multiple channels of state and local police and the sheriff, and even the frequencies used by forest rangers in the area.

Scutari had a stopwatch and was calling out thirty-second intervals while the money bags were tossed from man to man. As time wore on, discipline in the line gave way to expediency, the men rushing to get as much as they could.

The traffic jam was becoming a problem since it could block the getaway. Randy Duey, holding his Uzi across his chest, stepped out and played traffic cop, shouting, "Let's go! Keep it moving!" as he waved traffic through. But the driver of a semitrailer decided he'd had enough and started inching his rig ahead of the pack. Duey shouted for him to stop, and when he didn't, Duey leveled the Uzi at him. The truck crunched to a stop with a loud hiss of its air brakes.

By the time Mathews had dished out about half of the sacks, Scutari called out they had been there seven minutes, two minutes longer than planned.

Fearful it was taking too long, Mathews left about fifteen sacks behind as he vaulted out the door and ran to the pickup, shouting for the others to leave. Yarbrough's truck left first. Scutari's truck, weighted down by the heavy money sacks, faltered a moment. Scutari feathered the accelerator and it finally started moving up the highway. Dye tossed the roofing nails onto the roadway.

When they were about 600 feet away, Lisa King started to get off the ground. Pierce instinctively snapped off a quick round over her head. She hit the deck.

"Why'd you do that?" Parmenter asked.

"I saw her getting up," Pierce answered. "Shit. I hope I didn't hit her."

Richard Rea, the Ukiah milkman, ran to the semi and shouted to the driver to call for help on his CB. The driver answered that his set wasn't working.

About a thousand feet from the robbery site, the highway leveled off and, within a mile, both trucks turned sharply to the right, squealing through the 145-degree turn onto Marina Drive. As he made the turn, Scutari suddenly saw a young woman in a car talking out her window and not watching where she was driving. It looked for sure they were going to sideswipe until Scutari laid on the horn. The woman's head jerked forward and she let out a little yelp as she swerved, barely avoiding being hit by the truck.

"Man, wouldn't that be something?" Mathews said with a quick laugh. "Pull off a perfect operation and get wiped out in a traffic accident." Scutari's heart was pounding too hard for him to respond.

In back, while preparing to abandon the pickup, Pierce noticed Lisa King's .30-30 rifle among the loot. After the truck made the turn, Pierce flung the rifle into the brush.

The green pickup stopped with its tailgate close to the windowless white van in the Pomo parking area. Slowing to a deliberate pace so they wouldn't draw attention from a nearby swimming party, the men loaded the van with the money and the guns. Then each pulled on a different shirt over his t-shirt.

Dye, Kemp, Evans, and Soderquist slid into the green Riviera and casually drove down the back road toward Calpella. The trick, they knew, was to blend in as quickly as possible. Once the money was switched, the others got into the van, leaving the pickups. Yarbrough drove down the back road west of Lake Mendocino, through Calpella, under U.S. 101, and onto a southbound freeway ramp.

The $1,000 Riviera was used only three minutes before being dumped. Dye went to Club Calpella, just a mile down the hill, ferrying Kemp, Evans, and Soderquist. He parked next to Parmenter's Olds, where Robert Merki waited patiently. The men wiped their prints off the handles and steering wheel of the Riviera before tossing the keys inside and jumping into the Olds.

As they went up the southbound freeway ramp of U.S. 101 toward Ukiah, they saw three police cars headed north, lights flashing, toward California 20. Mathews had counted on the police, once they heard reports of a dozen men with automatic rifles, holding back their response until they had reinforcements.

Shortly after the police arrived, however, they made a startling discovery. One of the officers inspecting the money compartment glanced to the left and spotted a handgun on the floor. Picking it up with a pencil through the trigger guard, he saw it was a 9mm Smith & Wesson.

"Hey," he said, approaching the Brink's guards, "this belong to any of you?"

All three guards looked at it. "Say," said Davis, the guard who rode shotgun, "that looks like the one the ringleader was pointing at us."

AFTER DRIVING 3 MILES toward Ukiah, Yarbrough pulled off an interchange onto the old highway and went another mile to Orrs Springs Road. Up into the pine-covered hills he drove, ascending the twisting road until he reached the garbage dump that marked their bivouac. They spent more than an hour pulling the money bags from the van and hauling them down a steep trail into the thick stand of trees where the snack foods and water were stored.

Using battery packs, they set up their scanners so they could relax and listen to the frenzy of police activity. The plan was for Yarbrough to drive back to check out how much heat there was in Ukiah, and to meet Merki at the Standard station on State Street.

In the woods, Mathews, Duey, Pierce, Barnhill, Scutari, and Parmenter opened one money bag on Mathews's orders, and each took $10,000 in case they got separated. They busied themselves stuffing bills in their pockets and socks.

Parmenter went to take up a lookout point near the road while the others dug into Scutari's food cache. As they ate and began to relax, they couldn't contain their delight at the success of the mission. They recounted their differing perspectives of the robbery, and in time Mathews reached instinctively for his waistband as he recalled grabbing his gun and jumping up on the truck's bumper.

"Oh shit! Oh, son of a bitch!" he jumped up shouting. "I lost the gun!"

Looks of alarm crossed the other men's faces as Mathews continued to run his hands over his pants pockets, still hoping to find what he knew was gone.

Barnhill knew it was the gun he had bought in Missoula with the Northgate loot, before he got his "Keith Merwin" identity. Now for certain, the feds had at least one name to go on. "Oh, Andy," Mathews told Barnhill. "I'm really sorry."

"Well," Barnhill said with characteristic calm, "I guess I'm going to have to make some changes." Mathews was beside himself with remorse.

Meanwhile, Parmenter was keeping watch in the bushes beside Orrs Springs Road when a car slowly pulled off by the garbage dump and stopped. The driver hopped out and came to within 10 feet of Parmenter, unzipped his pants and started to urinate into the bushes. Parmenter froze to keep from being seen. When the man finished, he went back to his car and drove off. It took Parmenter a few minutes to catch his breath before scrambling deeper into the woods.

For the gang that went back into Ukiah, it was a three-ring circus of missed meetings, changes in plans, and just plain panic as they watched the small town fill up with FBI agents from the San Francisco division.

Merki dropped Kemp and Soderquist near the Chevy Camaro Soderquist had driven up from Salinas. From there, the two went to Santa Rosa to clean up the motel rooms, making sure nothing had been left behind. Merki dropped Evans and Dye off at a shopping mall, saying he'd be back in an hour. The two did some casual shopping to kill time while Merki drove aimlessly for the same purpose. When Merki returned, he saw they had bought some shirts and a radio. Merki drove Evans north on State Street to the Aladdin Motel and dropped him off to meet Yarbrough. Then Merki continued to drive around to kill time with Dye.

Evans went into the motel room, but Yarbrough wasn't there. He checked around and, under the bed, found the MAC-10 that Yarbrough had used in the robbery. Deciding to wait for Yarbrough to return, Evans started to relax until he heard car doors slamming in the parking lot. Peering through the curtains, he saw men in suits escorting the three Brink's guards into another room at the motel.

His mind raced back to the instant when his bandanna

slipped and the female guard got a good look at his face. Panicked, Evans waited for them to go inside, then slipped out, circled around the back, and headed for the Lou Ann Motel several blocks south, where he had previously registered. He slipped quickly into Room 233 at the Lou Ann, struggling for breath to calm his nerves.

Merki and Dye missed their scheduled rendezvous with Yarbrough at the Standard station. After waiting fifteen minutes, they drove to the Aladdin, where they saw Yarbrough dressed in shorts and a t-shirt standing in the doorway to his room. He said he couldn't find Evans. Merki, still in his female attire, said he and Dye would check into a nearby motel and would call if they found Evans.

Merki waited in the car at the new motel while Dye went in to sign the register as "Mr. and Mrs. John Carlson." They bought some crackers and beer and settled in for a night of listening to a police scanner and watching television.

Around dinner time, Soderquist and Kemp returned from Santa Rosa. Soderquist dropped Kemp at the Aladdin Motel to link up with Yarbrough, then went on to the Lou Ann Motel, parking a few blocks away. As Soderquist approached the Lou Ann, he saw two men dressed in suits talking to the motel manager.

Convinced that they were FBI agents, Soderquist edged his way around to Evans's room. Knocking on the door, he heard someone inside ask who it was. When he had identified himself, the door opened a crack and Evans all but dragged Soderquist inside. Soderquist quickly locked the door, then turned to see Evans had a wet rag and was washing down the walls in the motel room.

"Come on, man!" he commanded, short of breath. "We got to get rid of the fingerprints!" Soderquist glanced through the open bathroom door and noticed Evans was soaking all of his clothes in the tub.

"What you doing that for?" Soderquist asked.

"Man, we got to wipe away all traces," Evans said as he continued furiously wiping the walls. Evans rushed to the soaking clothes and started wringing them out. When that was done, he threw the clothes under the bed, promptly forgetting about them. The clothes, in fact, remained there for a year until the FBI came to search the room.

"Listen," Soderquist said finally. "I think the FBI's at the motel. We have to split." They devised an escape plan that called for Soderquist to get his Camaro and meet Evans about five blocks away. But they never got together on which direction they would take.

Soderquist slipped out the door and made it back to his car. Gunning the engine, he went to where he thought the pickup point was, but Evans wasn't there. He drove around a while, then decided the FBI must have arrested Evans. So he turned south on U.S. 101 and headed for Santa Rosa.

Evans slipped out but headed to a point exactly opposite to where Soderquist had gone to wait. When Soderquist failed to show, Evans decided the FBI had him. Having no car, Evans took off on foot, jogging straight out of town. He got off the main highway and crashed through the brush, scraping his face and hands as he ran. Reaching the Northwestern Pacific tracks, he turned south along the rails until he thought it was safe to return to the highway and hitchhike.

Up in the hills on Orrs Springs Road, the other robbers had been listening to the police scanners and enjoying the show. They knew the FBI was expected shortly by helicopter from Santa Rosa.

A short time later they heard the clatter of a helicopter, and Mathews, despite the dense forest cover, ran to a tree and hugged the trunk so he wouldn't be seen. He yelled for the others to follow suit, but they remained seated on the hillside and laughed. It was obvious that even if the chopper passed overhead, there was no way the pilot could see them through the thick vegetation.

About midnight, Yarbrough went to the motel where Merki and Dye were staying and told them to take Parmenter's Olds to Santa Rosa and wait. He and Kemp would drive the Ford van to the hideout in the hills and pick up the others.

"Be sure to keep an eye out for Evans," Yarbrough reminded them as he left.

A little after I A.M., Mathews heard a vehicle stop up by the garbage dump, followed by the sound of someone walking into the woods. Then they heard a sharp whistle. "It's Gary. It's the guys!" Mathews started moving toward the sound.

"Damn it, Bob," Pierce said in a hoarse whisper. "Let's wait until he identifies himself before we let him know we're here."

"He won't find us," Mathews argued.

"Well, it's bullshit to walk out there if it's an FBI agent," Pierce's voice was getting a little louder. Before it could be debated further, they made out the silhouettes of Kemp and Yarbrough.

"Man, the heat's really on," Yarbrough reported. "Ukiah's filled with feds, and I'm guessin' tomorrow's going to be worse." Mathews started calculating the next step as Yarbrough continued. "I already sent Merki and Dye on to Santa Rosa. But we got a problem. We can't find Evans or Soderquist."

"Do you think ZOG's got them?" Mathews asked.

"No idea," Yarbrough said calmly.

"Screw it, let's get the hell outta here," Pierce said.

"Yeah. Right," Mathews agreed. "Let's get the money up to the van and get out of here." Dragging the money bags up to the van was a lot harder than dragging them down. It was a monstrous job; the men made trip after trip in pitch blackness. Parmenter finally fell forward and collapsed in exhaustion.

On one trip uphill Pierce put down his sack and patted his socks.

"Damn!" he shouted. "That $10,000 that was in my socks fell out on the trail!" Pierce and Yarbrough got down on their knees and started scouring the trail in the dark, feeling around for the bundle of bills.

"Hey!" Mathews called. "There's plenty more where that came from, Bruce. Don't worry about it. We gotta go!"

With one last check of a thicket, Pierce shrugged and hefted the money sack. The men finished loading the van after 2 A.M.

"There's no sense heading back to Ukiah," Mathews said as Yarbrough started the engine. "Go west on this road and it'll take us to the Coast Highway, and we can get back to Santa Rosa that way."

* * *

FIVE MONTHS LATER, two couples from Ukiah were on a drive in the hills when their car began to overheat while climbing the steep grade up Orrs Springs Road. They pulled off at a wide spot on a curve and got out to let the car cool down.

One of the men went down the hillside 5 or 6 feet into some bushes to urinate. After he started, he heard an odd sound as his urine hit the ground. It didn't sound like a stream splashing on leaves and brush. The man looked closer and was flabbergasted to see a wad of money, all musty and moldy.

He shouted for the others, and they gathered up as much as they could find and laid it out on the hood of their car. Undecided what to do with it, they drove back to Ukiah, where a relative called the sheriff to report the find.

The response by the dispatcher was cool, but the couples were invited to bring in the money if they cared to.

The man who had relieved himself on more money than he'd ever seen before wrapped it in newspaper, walked into the sheriff's office, placed it on the counter, and told a deputy to take a look. Within minutes, the FBI in Santa Rosa was notified. The man found himself in the back seat of a sheriff's cruiser headed back up Orrs Springs Road to show where he'd found it.

Chapter 8

Survivalism: The Man Who Ate the Dog

The ringing phone shattered Ken Loff's nerves. He prayed it wouldn't be the operator again. Uneasily, he picked it up. "I have a collect call for anyone from Calvin. Will you pay for the call?" the operator asked.

Damn, Ken thought. This was the fourth time Randy Evans, using his code name, had called Ken's house in one day. Collect calls could come back to haunt him if whatever happened in California the day before was traced to Mathews.

Ken didn't know the full story, just that something had been robbed. While Ken was working at the cement plant the day before, his wife, Marlene, and David Lane took several calls from the men in California, each saying all was well and they were heading home. Soderquist called to say he feared someone was following him, so he was heading home to Salinas. Now on Friday, Evans was frantically trying to find the group.

"Yes, operator, I'll pay," Loff said.

"Marbles," Evans called Loff by his code name, "have you heard from Carlos? How do I hook up?"

"Relax, Calvin. Where are you now?"

"I'm in Coalinga," Evans answered. Loff had lived in California long enough to know that Coalinga was a small town in the hills on the west rim of the San Joaquin Valley, southwest of Fresno. In his anxiety, Evans was headed toward home in Rosamond.

"You gotta get to Reno, Calvin," Loff told him. "I've talked to Carlos and they'll wait for you there. Get to Fresno or somewhere and catch a bus."

"Thanks, Marbles," said Evans. "And remember, buddy. Don't turn out the light bulb." It was a reference to Loff's role as caretaker of families of men who were caught. Evans clearly was nervous about being separated.

The robbers who hid in the woods met later in Santa Rosa with the ones who had stayed in Ukiah. Only Evans and Soderquist failed to show. Pierce and Duey headed straight east from there, while Mathews and the others went toward Salinas to look for the missing men. Failing to find Soderquist but learning of Evans's plight, Mathews worked out the Reno rendezvous with Loff.

The trip was calm, considering the men's status as the most wanted bandits in the West, except for one incident. A car backfired on Interstate 80 and Scutari, driving the getaway van, heard it. His heart leaped into his throat, and he leaned on his horn for the others to pull over while he composed himself.

Jimmy Dye had fought the Viet Cong. Now he could imagine how they felt—attacking from ambush, striking with speed and precision, then melting anonymously into the countryside. The recurring headaches from his shrapnel wound were a painful reminder of his Marine Corps tour in Vietnam and, worse, of the cold scorn heaped on him by his fellow citizens on his return.

Sharing a van with Yarbrough and Merki, Dye smiled when he realized he'd reversed the roles. FBI agents were still sorting through the truck in Ukiah, not knowing who the enemy was. Dye felt an electric thrill from that realization. He would do anything now for Mathews.

When Mathews sensed his men's allegiance, he was exhilarated. He felt they were at a plateau. His money worries were over. In the trunk of his car, he had the glue to unite the right wing. He had the means now to form a guerrilla army the likes of which the right had never seen, not Bob DePugh's Minutemen, not anybody.

The evening sun lighted the western face of the Sierra Nevada, turning the mighty pines a brilliant greenish-gold, as the convoy of robbers ascended Donner Pass toward Lake Tahoe. It was dark by the time they topped the range and dropped down quickly toward Reno, appearing suddenly as a brilliantly illuminated mole on the face of the Great Basin.

The Reno Holiday Inn is a prominent, gaudily lighted monolith off Interstate 80. As the cars pulled into the lot, the men were still high from the robbery. Knowing they had several million dollars stashed in their trunks, Scutari couldn't contain his excitement at seeing the lights of Reno.

"Hey, Denver!" he said, grabbing Parmenter's arm as they walked toward the hotel. "Whaddaya say? Why don't we take it in there and put it all down at the craps table? One roll, Parmenter! Double or nothin'!"

He was kidding, of course. One big gamble in two days was enough. Scutari didn't even drop two bits in the slot machines.

Evans hitchhiked to Sacramento, then got a Greyhound bus to Reno. He hit town about midnight, and one of the men drove out to get him. The nine men, getting the first good sleep in two days, didn't even bother to post an overnight guard on their cars. Fortunately for them, no car thieves were working the parking lot.

In the morning, Dye and Barnhill drove the getaway van to a car wash and vacuumed it, wiping everything to get rid of fingerprints. On the way out of Reno, the convoy stopped at the Sparks exit and waited an hour while Mathews and Scutari delivered the van to Chuck Ostrout's son-in-law, who lived in Sparks. They gave him money to have it repainted and asked him to sell it.

Pierce and Duey were first to reach Boise, having gone ahead of the group. Their car's rear, weighted down with a third of the loot, nearly scraped the pavement as they sped toward Idaho. They carried the money bags into the living room of the Merkis' ramshackle house on North 10th Street.

Pierce also sensed it was a turning point for the group, and he wanted more responsibility in it. The group was growing too large too fast for Pierce's taste. Mathews had skillfully bridged an underlying schism between the religious and political members of the group. But the competition between Mathews and Pierce kept building. Pierce could accept Mathews as overall leader, chairman of the board, but Bob's short suit was his inability to delegate authority. In the beginning, he had made them feel this was a corporation, that there would be group decisions. But then Mathews tried to control everything himself.

It's a 426-mile drive from Reno to Boise, virtually all

of it through desert. By the time Yarbrough, the last one
to arrive, got to Merki's house, it was well after dark. On
the way, he had nearly given Mathews a heart attack,
and the men were still chuckling. Near Winnemucca,
where U.S. 95 cuts north into Oregon, Yarbrough was
trailing Mathews in the desolate valley near McDermitt.
As darkness came, Gary reached for a portable red strobe
light he kept in his van. He flashed it at Bob's car, as a
highway patrol car would do.

Mathews started to panic, then realized it was Yarbrough.
Mathews responded by shaking his fist out the window.
Yarbrough got a good laugh out of it.

Inside Merki's house, groups began counting the loot,
quickly reaching a million dollars from the contents of
the first carload. As each stack was counted it was piled
on the dining room table. Soon the mound nearly reached
the ceiling.

Sharon Merki and her daughter, Suzanne, kept the
plastic wrap and money bands to burn in their wood
stove, rebundling the money with rubber bands. Scutari,
mindful of the noise, stationed a few lookouts in the
small front yard.

Robert Merki, while counting a stack, noticed some of
the top bills had been stamped "Brink's." He destroyed
those and recommended to the others that they do the
same if they found any. The group counted the larger
bills and set aside the ones and fives to count the next
day. They never finished counting all of it that night.

If they had, they would have totaled $3.8 million.

Euphoria dulled Mathews's sense of dread at having
left Barnhill's gun in the truck. About 11 P.M. Mathews
called Pierce, Duey, Yarbrough, and Parmenter, the Inner Circle, into the tiny bedroom off the enclosed back
porch to talk about his salary system and how the money
would be divided. The timing couldn't have been worse
for Pierce to bring up his beef, but being Pierce, he did
anyway.

"You know, Bob, some of us are concerned about the
way you keep running things from the hip," Pierce began.

"Look, I'm sorry about the gun, I've told you . . . ,"
Mathews started.

"It's not the gun, Bob," Pierce jumped in. "Andy'll

make some lifestyle adjustments. It's bigger than that. You need to delegate more to us. We should break up into smaller groups so we can handle some of the decisions too."

Mathews took the criticism as a personal affront. "Look how far we've come in less than a year," he started to argue.

"But this isn't the understanding we had then, Bob," Pierce replied. Their voices started to rise, interrupting each other to make their points. Mathews wanted to split the money with other white groups, which was the reason he had formed the gang. Pierce shouted that that wasn't his concern. What he and the others wanted was more say in the structure of the group.

The argument got louder, and those outside the room could hear it plainly. Glancing at the piles of money on the dining room table and at the weapons, they got nervous. Not only were they upset because they thought Pierce was trying to dethrone Mathews, but a fight could prompt neighbors to call the cops.

As the shouting grew, Scutari began to pace, upset about the argument but more upset that he wasn't allowed in the room. Instead of bickering, he thought, they should be praying to Yahweh in thanksgiving for a successful mission.

Inside the room, Yarbrough and Duey were getting steamed at Bob too. As tempers continued to flare, Mathews began to shake with anger. He was like a cornered animal, turning around and lashing at whoever came within range. His face became so red that Yarbrough believed Mathews was about to punch him, so he lunged first, jumping at Mathews and shoving him across the tiny room.

The Merkis had heard enough, and the words were very compromising indeed. Sharon was first through the door from the rear of the kitchen.

"Hey, you guys!" she shouted above the roar. "There's an alley out back and houses right next to us. You guys are going to have to just calm down!" Total silence suddenly enveloped the room. The men looked at each other, then back at Sharon. Each fought to control his temper, knowing full well Sharon was right.

"Well, you know, Bob," Duey began with renewed calm. "You are taking on too much. We've all talked about it."

"I don't mind you being chairman of the board, Bob, but you're making all of the decisions," Pierce said in firm but quiet tones. "We're capable too."

The argument, now at least civil, lasted ten more minutes. When the Inner Circle emerged from the back room, Bob gathered everybody for the verdict.

There will be delegating, he told them. Pierce would take a group, a "fire team" of sorts, to a different area. Duey would be in charge of indoctrinating recruits. Parmenter would plan the next procurement—a euphemism for robbery—and Yarbrough would plan assassinations. Mathews would remain as coordinator, plotting strategy and recruiting. Mathews then announced they had selected some white groups that would split the loot.

"We must share what Yahweh has given us," he intoned. The groups selected were his first allegiance, the National Alliance, led by his idol William Pierce; the Carolina Knights of the KKK, led by Frazier Glenn Miller; Louis Beam, the former Texas Klan leader; Tom Metzger, leader of the White Aryan Resistance in California; Bob Miles and his Mountain Kirk; and Butler's Aryan Nations.

Mathews also had some smaller personal grants he intended to make. Among them was $10,000 for Dan Gayman and his Church of Israel in Missouri. He wanted Gayman to look after Zillah if anything happened to him.

Then Mathews ordained that each member of the gang be put on a $10,000 salary every six months, and each participant in the Ukiah robbery get a $30,000 bonus. Pierce would take a chunk of loot with him for his group, Mathews told them, and the rest would be kept in the treasury.

Dye received $45,000 to ferry to Philadelphia; $20,000 was for Tom Martinez—$10,000 for six months' salary and $10,000 for his legal fees; $12,500 each was for George Zaengle and Bill Nash. The first $10,000 was their salary, the rest for their moving expenses to the White American Bastion.

Scutari shook his head. During the fight in the back

room, he had pretty much decided to leave, because he felt the group lacked discipline. But when he saw how it ended, he was amazed. He loved to watch Mathews, the undisputed master of manipulation. It dumfounded Scutari. How could the man fly into a rage, his eyes flashing with murderous enmity one minute, and then speak so lovingly the next? It was more than an act, Scutari decided. It had to be real.

As the meeting broke up, Pierce told Parmenter he would whip his team into shape and volunteer for the next "procurement." At that, Pierce grabbed six duffel bags that had been filled with $107,000 each and left with Richie Kemp.

After Pierce was gone, Mathews became miffed that he had taken $642,000. No one had expected him to take quite that much. He fumed about it a while before deciding he'd have to ask for some of it back.

"WE GOT A TON of money in California, Marbles!" Mathews told Loff on the phone about noon Sunday. "I want you to quit that Portland Lehigh job, get down here, and bring Lane with you. I'm going to pay you $20,000 a year. Tax free."

Loff felt a surge of delirium at his friend's news. He too had believed that someday the battle would intensify. Now he had to put up or shut up.

David Lane had been staying in Loff's barn since the Denver police had announced in mid-July they were looking for him in regard to the Berg killing. His sister Jane and her husband, Carl Franklin, came out to see him, bringing along some articles clipped from Denver newspapers. One reported on the open letter he had sent to Denver media and others denying he was in that city the night Berg was killed.

"We shouldn't have killed him," Lane said to Loff after reading the articles. "We made a martyr out of him." Lane asked Franklin to sell the yellow VW, which Lane had left on Franklin's property in Easton.

Lane and Loff threw a few things into Loff's Toyota wagon, and the pair started the long drive to Boise.

By midday Sunday only Mathews, Scutari, Dye, and Barnhill remained at Merki's house. Already planning his

change of life-style, Barnhill went to the home of Sharon
Merki's daughter, Suzanne Stewart, several blocks away,
so she could dye his hair.

Loff and Lane reached the Merkis' house about 10
P.M., and only Kurt Merki, seventeen, was there. While
they waited for Mathews, Ken noticed the array of duffel
bags and laundry sacks on the kitchen floor and imagined
what was in them. Soon Mathews returned with his entourage, and Loff noticed that Andy Barnhill's hair was
lighter. As he was wondering about it, Barnhill started to
tell Loff about the Ukiah robbery, how smoothly it went
and how few shots had been fired.

There was only one glitch, Barnhill told Loff, and
that's why his hair had been lightened. It seemed that
Bob had borrowed his new 9mm Smith & Wesson handgun, Andy explained calmly, the one he had bought in
Missoula with loot fresh from the Northgate heist. Then
Bob left it at the robbery scene. It was just a matter of
time before the gun would be traced back.

Ken felt frightened, not only for Barnhill but for himself, as his mind reeled into the future. Loff's breath was
still running short when Barnhill gave him the key to his
house in Laclede, and asked him to clean it of any
evidence. Loff said he'd do what he could.

"We got almost four million dollars, buddy," Bob broke
in on a more chipper note. He told Ken how they had
divided the money, then he handed him a small bundle.
It was Bob's own $30,000 bonus, which he wanted Ken to
deliver with a note to Debbie telling her what bills to
pay, since he didn't plan to return to Metaline Falls for a
while. Some of it was earmarked for a surrogate mother
program in Portland, which already had identified a surrogate to bear Bob's child.

Then Bob motioned to a pile of cloth sacks in the
kitchen, saying he had another job for Loff.

"I want you to take those and hide them on your
farm," Bob said, adding that Ken should use whatever he
needed for the farm. "There's a million and a half dollars
in them, which will help supply us for the great struggle
ahead. There's gonna be a guy come up from Arkansas
to set up a training camp for our new men, and I'd like

you to work with him, help set it up and equip it with this money."

They opened some of the sacks and Ken looked at the mountains of green cash inside. The sight overwhelmed him, and in that moment he was convinced that he should go the distance with his friend instead of running to the nearest police station, as he might have done just a year before. It was well after midnight when Loff and Lane stuffed the sacks into cardboard boxes and sealed them with masking tape. After only a few hours' sleep, Loff awakened Monday about 5 A.M., loaded the boxes into his Toyota, and headed north alone for the ten-hour drive.

Richie Kemp, still living in Loff's basement, was at the farm when Loff returned to Ione that afternoon. Together they got several five-gallon plastic tubs and placed plastic bags filled with cash inside them. They buried the tubs inside Loff's barn, in front of the rabbit hutches, in 4-foot holes. Ken got some margarine containers from his wife to bury more money elsewhere. He interred $60,000 in his garden. More went under his carport, near the haystack, and into his attic. In mid-July, his farm truly was sprouting green.

On Tuesday, Loff and Kemp drove to Metaline Falls and up into the Lead King Hills to drop Mathews's share with Debbie. She hadn't been seeing much of her husband lately and asked Loff what Bob was doing. Loff answered ambiguously.

Debbie then handed Loff an article from the previous Friday's Spokane *Spokesman-Review,* which reported the Ukiah robbery. A broad smile spread over her face as he read it, but she said nothing. The men left without confirming or denying anything to Debbie, but Loff believed she already knew. This "need-to-know" crap Mathews preached always seemed to travel in a wide circle.

Una Mathews, widowed eight months and still living in the tidy house next to her son's, also wondered about Robbie. She knew he traveled the country talking about his cause. On one occasion she asked him how he could afford to travel so much. He told his mom a rich benefactor was funding his crusade.

He didn't tell her it was Brink's.

*   *   *

THE SAME DAY Loff left Boise, Scutari picked up a used car and headed south with Mathews, Barnhill, and Dye. When they hit Laramie, Bob said goodbye to the others and got out at Zillah's house. Scutari resumed driving southeast with Dye and Barnhill, stopping in Schell City, Missouri, to visit Dan Gayman, the Identity pastor who several years earlier had been wary of Richard Butler's unity program.

Scutari offered Gayman a $10,000 contribution and told him Mathews wanted Gayman to offer refuge to those in the "underground" who got into trouble. Gayman looked at the cash, then at Scutari.

"Is this stuff good?" he asked. "I mean, the word's out you guys in the Northwest are dealing in counterfeit. I don't want any part of that."

Scutari laughed and assured him they were genuine Federal Reserve notes, although that didn't mean he respected them any more than counterfeit. Gayman took the money, then said a prayer over the three travelers before they left.

After two hard days on the road from Boise, Scutari arrived at Gentry, Arkansas, stopping at the home of Ardie McBrearty, the tax protester who had introduced him to Identity. Ardie was a pleasant fellow with a wry smile, thinning hair, and a slender body. At fifty-six he was flying around the country helping people fight the IRS. Like Scutari, he was an expert at running the voice stress analyzer.

Randall Rader over in West Plains, Missouri, was summoned to come the next day. Rader and his friend Jackie Lee Norton arrived in Gentry just after sunup. Only Scutari and McBrearty were awake. Barnhill, Dye, and McBrearty's wife, Marleen, gradually joined them in the kitchen. After an hour of small talk among good friends, Scutari was ready to do business. He knew why Barnhill had recruited Rader and why Mathews wanted him. Step 6, guerrilla warfare, demanded tough training at their planned Aryan boot camp.

"C'mon back here, Randall." Scutari motioned Rader into a back room off the kitchen, making it clear that Norton wasn't included. There was a table in the center of the back room with a green duffel bag at one end.

"I got something for you, Rader, something you never seen before," Scutari said as he pulled open the top of the canvas bag. Rader's eyes widened when he saw the stacks of money Scutari extracted from the opening.

Scutari got a brown paper bag and whipped it open. Counting out stacks of bills, he placed them into the second bag, stopping when he reached $100,000. He folded down the top of the paper bag and pushed it across the table to Rader.

"That's for company expenses," Scutari said. "Weapons, ammo, supplies, stuff like that. You're the expert on what we need to outfit a training base.

"This," he continued as he reached for his briefcase, "is for yourself." Scutari opened the briefcase. Inside were more wrapped bundles of cash. "There's $30,000 here for your cut of the robbery, and another $10,000 for six months' salary. That's our pay system." Scutari then motioned to Barnhill, who stepped up to the table with a thick wad of fifty-dollar bills. Barnhill peeled off one hundred of them.

"There's $5,000 for your moving expenses to the Northwest," Barnhill said.

Rader was almost breathless. On the table was $145,000, tendered because his friends thought his talents were second to none. He didn't even think of backing down. The sight of all that money and the knowledge it was stolen didn't frighten him, it thrilled him. Stuffing the money into a nylon gym bag, Rader willingly became a member of the underground even though he knew nearly everything they had done, including the murder of Alan Berg.

As he gathered up the money, Rader talked with Scutari about McBrearty. There was nobody in the movement who didn't like Ardie. He was caring and generous, and had often helped the folk at CSA when they were at their poorest. Rader wanted to give Ardie some of the money.

"He loaned me $200 once when I was broke and I'd like to pay him back," Rader said. "He doesn't have much here. I'd like to give him $1,000."

"I'll tell you what," Scutari replied. "Let's split it and each give him $500." Rader was pleased that Scutari agreed so readily, but he was not surprised. The people he knew in the movement were truly watchful over their own. Both Scutari and McBrearty had helped Rader find work when he needed it. The right wing in some ways was like an extended family. They each counted out $500 from their shares and went to the kitchen, where Ardie and Marleen waited with the other guests. When they offered him the money, Ardie smiled and waved a hand at it.

"No, give it to my wife," he said bashfully. "She runs the house."

Later, Rader offered Norton a job as his assistant for $1,600 a month plus expenses. Desperately needing work, Norton accepted. Scutari and Barnhill went on toward Florida, first dropping Dye at the Amtrak station in Little Rock so he could return to Philadelphia with the money for his friends.

At home in Port Salerno, Scutari was like a kid in a candy store with his money. He bought two new voice stress analyzers for $6,800 each, but they turned out to be junk. He continued to use his old reliable off to the side while the lights and gizmos on the expensive ones dazzled his subjects.

He also bought items he imagined would be needed if they were soon to be at war with ZOG, the Zionist Occupation Government. His shopping spree included wiretap detectors, scrambled walkie-talkies, vibrating transmitter detectors, and telephone scramblers, which converted the voices over the wires into meaningless electronic sounds and translated them at the other end.

Barnhill had to stay up the coast from his home in Plantation, outside Fort Lauderdale. The FBI was sure to have his parents' house under watch by now.

In the days after Scutari's visit, the cash burned through Rader's pockets. He wanted to do this job right, with top-shelf equipment. Traveling between shops in Marietta, Georgia, and Fort Smith, Arkansas, Rader amassed a ton of supplies ranging from special boots, packs, and uniforms to flares, tents, and camping equipment.

In Fort Smith, Rader ordered pistols and night vision scopes with television-type screens at $900 each from a gun dealer named Robert Smalley. The order came to

$7,000, and when Rader didn't have enough to pay, Smalley went to West Plains with him to get his money. On the ride, Rader told Smalley he'd have more business for him since he was outfitting a new right wing action group out West.

"I'd like to get some arms and ammo without any paperwork, you know what I mean?" Rader asked after assuring him it was "secure" to deal with the group.

"That can easily be arranged," Smalley said. "I know a couple places we can go." One of his sources was a deputy sheriff in Arkansas who owned a gun shop.

In West Plains, they tried the night vision scopes, which worked perfectly. Rader paid Smalley and placed an additional order for pistols before they parted.

It was Rader who was most responsible for the CSA's enjoying the reputation it had throughout the right wing for militant survival training. It was odd, then, that the CSA had become overtly violent only afrer Rader left at the end of 1982. He had been instrumental in transforming the encampment from a peaceful commune of pious fundamentalists into the Fort Dix of the radical right.

Rader was born on June 16, 1951, to Gilbert and Betty Rader in remote West Plains. His dad, a county agricultural agent, taught Randall a lot about the outdoors. But the boy didn't want to be stuck in the backwater Ozarks country his whole life. After he graduated from West Plains High School in 1969, he fled to Los Angeles with his guitar and spent about five years forming acid-rock groups and playing around Southern California.

During that time he took every type of drug he could get except heroin. Mostly he took LSD, then at the height of its popularity. He smoked marijuana and hashish, swallowed speed, and dropped downers. He sold some acid as well to make a few bucks. It was a reckless life headed nowhere until a miraculous event.

In August 1974, on a visit back home, Rader stopped at a fundamentalist religious revival of the sort popular in the summertime in the Bible belt. There in his hometown, surrounded by childhood memories, something spiritual grabbed him. As he listened to the preacher's booming voice, a great wellspring of remorse for his wanton lifestyle rose involuntarily in his soul. He felt himself being drawn forward to the altar, where he loudly proclaimed his sorrow and asked Jesus to forgive him. It could not have been more of a reversal.

He joined a Methodist church in West Plains and got a low-paying job as a steak house cook. For a time he experienced vivid dreams in which he saw himself leading an army through the rubble of civilization. Maybe it was the Russians he was fighting, but maybe he was part of the unfolding of Revelation. He never knew. But the dreams were powerful forces that helped forge his new identity.

At several Methodist church meetings, Rader and a few other young men met Jim Ellison. Ellison had been an ordained minister in the Disciples of Christ movement before becoming disillusioned in 1962. Ellison felt led by God to the Ozarks in 1970, and he bought a farm in Elijah, Missouri, west of West Plains. In 1975 Rader joined a dozen other men and their families living there in a Christian commune headed by Ellison.

During the nation's bicentennial in 1976, Rader worked as a wrangler with a ceremonial wagon train and used the skills to get a job breaking horses at a dude ranch in nearby Caulfield, Missouri. It was there he met a young woman from Chicago named Kathleen Ann Bator, who was a ranch guest. Kathleen became Rader's bride.

When he was laid off in October 1976, he rejoined Ellison's commune, which had relocated to a 224-acre tract Ellison had bought from the Fellowship of Christian Athletes on the shore of Bull Shoals Lake. It was in Arkansas, 50 miles west and slightly south of West Plains. But its north property line was shoved against the Missouri border by the flooded valleys of Gulley Spring and Wolf creeks, part of the lake; 5 miles to the southeast loomed the Promise Land Ridge.

At high water, the commune was very difficult to reach by the dirt roads that forded across several swollen streams. Its post office was in Pontiac, Missouri, 2 miles away. The nearest Arkansas town, Oakland, was only a wide spot in the road with a dozen buildings, 3 miles as the crow flies over the thick hardwood forest.

The center of the commune was 140 feet above the water and a half-mile east of the lake. Bull Shoals is a serpentine body of water, its numerous tentacles snaking up creek valleys as the water rises for miles behind the dam on the White River, just below the small town of Bull Shoals, Arkansas. There are countless coves in the lake, and spindly peninsulas popular with sportsmen.

About the only building on the property when Ellison got it was a ramshackle one-story wood-frame farmhouse with a covered porch and half-attic. Some of the men logged among the numerous cedar trees on the forested property, and Rader spent the winter helping haul the timber to mills to raise money for the commune.

Ellison named the business venture Christian Brothers Cedar, but the commune itself took the name Zarephath-Horeb. Zarephath was the village near Sidon where the prophet Elijah raised the widow's dead son, and Horeb was the mountain, Mount Sinai, where Yahweh appeared in the burning bush to Moses. As spiritual leader of this new Jerusalem, Ellison gathered a number of well-meaning fundamentalist believers onto the property and added primitive dwellings. About sixteen structures went up in three separate compounds. Only one compound had electricity. Running water was provided through 55-gallon drums mounted on rooftops.

During the first few years, the people constructed a dozen substantial buildings. The most impressive was the combination church-school, a magnificent stone structure designed by Ellison. It had a large meeting room on the first level, dominated by a stone hearth in the center, and wooden benches set auditorium-style before a small stage. There was also a kitchen on the first floor.

Upstairs were school rooms where the children of Zarephath-Horeb learned not only the Christian religion but academic subjects from mainstream texts. It was a clean-living, spartan community of believers who didn't smoke, drink, or cuss.

By the late 1970s, Ellison had plugged deeper into the network of right-wing survivalists and had come to believe that the endtime struggle was approaching. The commune aligned with Christian Identity in 1978, as Ellison built a relationship with Dan Gayman's Church of Israel and later with the Reverend Robert Millar, who ran Elohim City, another Identity encampment near Adair,

Oklahoma. Ellison began to have visions he said were from God, which warned him that war was coming on the land. Zarephath-Horeb needed to prepare a defense against teeming refugees from the rotten cities.

In another vision, Ellison traced his personal lineage back to King David.

Gradually the peaceable nature of Zarephath-Horeb gave way to the more militant tone of its political arm, formed in 1978 and named The Covenant, The Sword, and The Arm of The Lord. Ellison adopted a logo for CSA with a rainbow signifying the covenant, pierced by a flaming sword. The host of believers were the arm of the Lord. They bought uniforms and wore the logo on shoulder patches.

Ellison named Rader defense minister, although Rader had no military experience. The hunting and fishing Rader had done with his dad was about his only preparation. But he threw himself into his job, compiling a huge library of military and tactical manuals, particularly Chinese.

On April 18, 1980, Ellison asked Rader to help his sister and brother-in-law, the Troxells, in an insurance scam by burning down their house northeast of Gainesville, Missouri, only about 15 miles from CSA. Jean and Roderick Troxell needed the settlement to pay off the property.

Following his sacred leader that same night, Rader joined another CSA member and two of Ellison's sons. Ellison had the house key, and the Troxells had removed their most valued possessions. After trying to light a fire inside, the men found a can of gasoline in the barn and used it on the exterior of the house. Ellison tossed a match and they threw more gasoline on it to get it going.

The men then drove to the Tecumseh fire tower and watched the flames lick the northern horizon. They could still see the glow when they turned down Highway 5 back to CSA. The Troxells received an $11,000 insurance settlement, but Rader earned nothing from his first illegal activity since leaving the drug scene.

As Rader became filled with the self-importance of leading an army of God, he felt the world outside become increasingly threatening. By 1980, the skilled men at CSA began converting their semi-automatic rifles into machine guns. Within a year there was a complete machine shop on the grounds, with Rader in charge. The men also began to make silencers and grenades, marketing them to outsiders.

Soon, down in a hollow near a spring that fed into Wolf Creek, work began on a facility that became the pride of CSA. It was Silhouette City, a mock-up of an urban intersection, with seven flat-roofed buildings arranged along the four streets. One building was four stories high. The hulk of an old junker was placed at one curb, and electrical lines dangled overhead. It was like a movie set.

It was meant to simulate urban riot conditions. Trainees were taught the proper technique to storm buildings and rappel down the façades while avoiding live electrical lines. The junker was planted with firebombs to add to the realism. Silhouettes of the "enemy"—a mugger, a ZOG agent—popped up in windows as trainees made their way from house to house. It was shoot or be "shot."

With an adjacent obstacle course and underground bunkers, CSA's survival training school became known throughout the movement. By 1982 applications were being accepted from members of right-wing groups throughout the country.

At one time Rader commanded forty men. He took survivalism to its limits. Once, Rader told his men, he killed and skinned a dog and ate its meat raw just to demonstrate he could do it.

At the American Pistol and Rifle Association's rendezvous in Benton, Tennessee, in 1981, Rader met Scutari, Barnhill, and McBrearty. The three were among a crew Rader led into the woods on a three-day survival hike. Ardie suffered kidney stones and was carried out, but they all became close and stayed in touch.

Scutari was invited to be a martial arts instructor at a CSA convocation in October 1982, the same gathering to which Richard Butler brought a contingent from Aryan Nations. McBrearty donated food and clothing to the poverty-line families living there when he visited to give tax-resistance lectures. Barnhill was even more impressed. He went to live at CSA for a year.

But with all his success, Ellison had planted seeds of dissension. Shortly after declaring himself King David's descendant, he decided he too was a king. He proclaimed in 1982 that he was "King James of the Ozarks." The Reverend Millar of Elohim City presided at the coronation by anointing Ellison's head with oil.

Ellison then proclaimed that it was proper to steal from non-Identity people, a concept he termed "plundering the Egyptians." This caused consternation among some of his followers, most of whom were law-abiding folk uneasy about the car thefts and other crimes a few CSA members committed to meet the $608 monthly mortgage on the land.

In truth, there were many reasons for the mass exodus of families from CSA in late 1982 and 1983. Chief among them was the miserable economy that forced many of them onto food stamps to feed their children. Living conditions at CSA deteriorated even from their substandard level, so the family men migrated to Springfield, Joplin, and even faraway Kansas City to find work. Ellison had trouble with the land payments, so a fundamentalist preacher from Branson, Missouri, eventually stepped in to save the commune from foreclosure.

The last straw was the day in 1982 Ellison declared polygamy acceptable. Ellison was attracted to the wife of a CSA member. After spending several days alone in the brush, he declared that in a vision he had seen the man's spirit leave his body. With the man thus spiritually dead, his wife became a "widow" whom Ellison could take as his second wife. The couple accepted this, and the woman went to live with Ellison and his first wife.

Kathy Rader wasn't thrilled by this new twist at all, especially since one young woman at the compound seemed to have caught Randall's eye.

Some believed it was ostracism after the death of Rader's thirteen-month-old daughter, who drowned in a basement on the compound while he was supposed to be watching her, that led the Raders to leave CSA.

Rader drifted, unemployed much of the time, with his family. After a few weeks with his parents, he stayed with Scutari in Port Salerno for six weeks working in construction. CSA friends Jack Norton and Buddy Lange also were there.

When he returned to Missouri, Rader was a minimum-wage fry cook for a time until he got a job milking cows at a dairy farm. He worked eleven-hour days for $138 a week. By January 1984 he was unemployed again and tried to enlist in the Army. But he had three children, so the Army wouldn't take him. He had been on welfare for five months by the time Barnhill called him out of the blue in May 1984.

After Rader left, CSA went over the edge. Invigorated by the call to arms at the 1983 Aryan World Congress, Ellison returned and urged his men to make war. He hung a Nazi flag in the church and ended his services with the rigid salute. A CSA member being discharged from the Marines stole a load of helmets, uniforms, and other supplies on his way out, at Ellison's command.

A month later, on August 9, Ellison drove a CSA elder, William Thomas, to Springfield, Missouri, and waited while Thomas stuffed a carton of gasoline into the mail slot of the Metropolitan Community Church and lighted it. The church ministered to homosexuals in the area. The gasoline spilled out, and the porch went up in flames, so damage was confined to a small area.

Six days later, instructed by Ellison to "rob something," Thomas and three others, including the ex-Marine, drove to Bloomington, Indiana, to case banks. While there, they firebombed the Jewish Community Center, causing moderate damage.

Then on November 2, five days after Mathews's group robbed the porno store in Spokane, Thomas and another CSA member, Richard Snell, set off a bomb on a natural gas pipeline outside Fulton, Arkansas, believing that the pipeline was the major feeder from the gas fields in the Gulf of Mexico to metropolitan Chicago. They picked a spot where the line crossed the Red River, thinking it would be weak there. The explosives dented the pipe but didn't break it. Later that month in Fort Smith, the squad tried to bomb a major electrical transmission line.

When this band of zealots finally pulled a robbery, it had a deadly result. Thomas, Snell, and Steve Scott, another CSA member, traveled to Texarkana, Arkansas, on November 11 and targeted a pawnshop. During the stickup, Snell put a pistol to the head of the proprietor,

William Stumpp, assuming him to be Jewish, and killed him with one shot. Snell later told Ellison that Stumpp "needed to die."

On June 30, 1984, Snell was pulled over on a routine traffic stop outside De Queen, Arkansas, by State Trooper Louis Bryant, a black man. Snell opened his door, emerged with a pistol, and shot twice from the hip, killing Bryant. The police captured Snell later that day in nearby Broken Bow, Oklahoma; they shot and wounded him in the process.

Six weeks later, on August 13, 1984, Rader packed up the supplies he'd bought with Scutari's money and left the madness of the Ozarks behind. Arriving in Ione three days later, he set up camp near the edge of the pines with his family.

WHEN BARNHILL'S PISTOL slipped out of Mathews's waistband at Ukiah, it was like dropping a key. Bob Tucker, a longtime FBI agent in San Rafael, California, had to find the lock that it fitted. At this point there was nothing to tie together the robbery with Wayne Manis's probe into Aryan Nations.

But very quickly the two FBI investigations collided.

The gun opened a floodgate through which nearly every piece of information in the case eventually poured.

Working closely with Bill tenBensel, an FBI agent in Santa Rosa, Tucker sent the 9mm's serial number to the Bureau of Alcohol, Tobacco, and Firearms in Washington. Records there showed the gun had been shipped to Brady's Sportsmen Supply in Missoula. A Montana agent visited Brady's to check the paperwork.

On Friday, the day after the Ukiah robbery, while the robbers still were headed toward Reno, Tucker got a call from an agent at the National Gun Center in Washington. Records showed the 9mm was sold on April 26 to "Andrew V. Barnhill, Box 20109, Missoula, Mont.," and gave Barnhill's physical description. Agents then obtained Barnhill's Montana driver's license.

Checking ownership on the lime-green Buick Riviera, tenBensel learned from the seller that the man who had bought it asked for directions from the Motel 6 on Cleveland Street. At the motel, tenBensel began the tedious job of obtaining toll call records for the motel rooms, then for all nearby phone booths. Had he not known that a man from Montana owned the abandoned gun in the Brink's truck, tenBensel wouldn't have known where to begin among the mountains of toll records. Given that link, however, he scored. Over a month's time, tenBensel compiled a list of ten telephone calls originating from pay phones around Cleveland Street to various locations in the Montana-Idaho-Washington area.

From a booth outside the Motel 6, he found a phone call made on July 16, three days before the robbery, to an Ione, Washington, number registered to Kenneth Loff. The next day the phone was used to call a Cheney, Washington, number registered to Janice Parmenter, Denver's ex-wife. Then tenBensel noticed Loff's number was also called on July 17 from a pay phone in Elmer's Pancake House, near the motel.

And within ten minutes of that call, the same phone was used to call a number in Laramie, Wyoming, belonging to Zillah Craig.

At 11 P.M. on July 18, just hours before the robbers awoke to go to Ukiah, someone used a pay phone at the Super 8 to call a Sandpoint, Idaho, number belonging to a Gerry Olbu. When agents obtained a copy of an Idaho driver's license issued the previous April to Olbu, it contained a picture of a thin-faced man with red hair and a bushy red beard.

TenBensel relayed this information to Wayne Manis on September 5. Manis staked out the address given by the phone company for Olbu, a well-kept one-story house near the Bonner Mall in Sandpoint. As he watched through binoculars shortly after 6 P.M. that day, a man came out of the door where Olbu supposedly lived.

Manis's eyebrows arched in recognition.

"Hey!" Manis said to himself. "That's Gary Lee Yarbrough!"

Manis watched Yarbrough ride a motorcycle a short distance to a pay phone, make a quick call, and return home. Manis traced the call and found it went to the home of Suzanne and Luke Hamilton on North 8th Street in Boise. They actually were Suzanne Stewart and Luke Tornatzky, Sharon Merki's daughter and son-in-law. Luke was still wanted for Robert Merki's 1982 counterfeiting operation. Manis didn't yet know their true identity, but Boise agents were alerted.

The next day, Manis and his crew watched Yarbrough hop on his Harley and, driving evasively, go to the Careywood post office 25 miles south, then to the Athol post office 6 miles farther on, then back to Careywood. Returning to Sandpoint, Yarbrough went to a storage locker at 3Js Mini-Storage.

Meanwhile, Agent John Nelson of the Butte, Montana, FBI office was following up the Barnhill lead in Missoula. With an address from the post office box, Nelson found Barnhill's former landlady, who knew him as Andrew Smith. Her records showed that when Barnhill moved to Missoula, he gave a Missouri license with a Joplin address. This helped Nelson find Barnhill's associates for questioning.

Checking with Barnhill's friends in Missoula, Nelson learned about his survivalist background. Shortly after that, Rodney Carrington and Buddy Lange left Montana to return to the South, not wanting to be in the way when the FBI moved. They knew too much about Andy's new friends to be comfortable.

But Nelson reaped his big harvest when he entered Barnhill's name in the National Crime Information Center computer. Up popped Barnhill's arrest in Madras a month earlier on the weapons charge with Randy Evans.

On August 2, Nelson got the entire report from Madras. The most revealing item was the second birth certificate police found with Barnhill, in the name of Keith Merwin. Manis's colleague, Joe Venkus, searched records and found that the real Keith Merwin, born in 1957, died in infancy. The items photocopied by Madras police with Merwin's name indicated he lived in a house on "Highway 2, next to church," in the tiny panhandle town of Laclede, Idaho.

Tucker and tenBensel wrote a search warrant affidavit for the house but had a hard time getting a magistrate to sign it until the U.S. Attorneys from San Francisco and Boise intervened. Manis's Aryan Nations investigation was still covert, and busting into Barnhill's house on the Ukiah case, now dubbed "Brinkrob," could blow the lid off it.

On August 4, 1984, Manis drove to Laclede with Agents Venkus and Norm Brown, and kicked in Barnhill's door. Inside they found books on making bombs and racist literature tying Barnhill to Aryan Nations. More interesting was a faded newspaper dated April 24, folded to highlight one article. It was about the robbery of the Continental Armored Transport truck at Northgate Mall in Seattle.

But the most significant find was a two-page photocopied document, the one Scutari handed out at the meeting in the woods June 29, titled "Rules for Security." Reading it, Manis not only had concrete proof that there was a right-wing underground forming in his territory but now understood how it was organized and how seriously its members were taking it.

When the agents left, they posted the warrant on the door as required by law. Shortly after the search, Yarbrough drove over to Laclede with Barnhill's house keys, which Loff had given him, to clean the house. He was too late. He ripped the notice from the door and read it, his deep-set eyes widening when he saw how close the FBI had come in exactly two weeks since the robbery.

In fact, between Manis's notes in Coeur d'Alene and those kept by Tucker and tenBensel in California, the FBI had a list of intriguing suspects for the Ukiah robbery, and possibly the Northgate job as well. They had Barnhill right in the middle. Barnhill's arrest in Madras gave them Evans, and the pickup truck Evans was driving gave them Denver Parmenter. That gave them Bruce Pierce, who had been seen in that truck. It also gave them Randy Duey, Parmenter's roommate in Newport, who had been questioned in May by deputies looking for Pierce. The phone calls from Santa Rosa gave them Gary Yarbrough, and tailing him yielded a mysterious young couple in Boise. The calls also gave them Ken Loff, an Ione farmer.

All of this kept coming back to one man in Metaline Falls, Washington, Robert Jay Mathews. Pierce used Mathews's home as his address in federal court. Barnhill got a speeding ticket in Mathews's car and called Mathews's house after his arrest in Madras. It was Mathews who, police knew, peeled off a wad of cash to buy life insurance for himself and his friends, who defended Pierce in a letter that talked of defending his race "even if it costs us our lives."

FBI agents didn't know it then, but they had in hand the names of seven of the twelve Ukiah robbers, plus leads on Loff and Merki. If it weren't for Barnhill's gun, they wouldn't have had any of it. Had Barnhill bought the gun under a phony name, or had Mathews held onto it, Tucker would have struck a dead end fast.

But Manis always considered himself lucky. He knew a break would come one way or another. Only a month after getting the go-ahead to open the Aryan Nations case, the largest open-road armored car robbery in American history came into the picture. By September, six weeks after the robbery, Manis was convinced that Bob Mathews, former cement plant worker and currently with no visible means of support, was the man in control, the man with the power.

Now he had to prove it.

IF MONEY IS POWER, Bob Mathews was truly powerful. And he was ready to flex his newly acquired muscle. On July 31, after a few days in Laramie, he bought a used Pontiac Bonneville, piled Zillah and her boys into it, and headed east. Tens of thousands of stolen dollars were in his briefcase and in an overnight bag in the trunk. And he always kept at least $10,000 stuffed inside his socks. He dropped Dustin and Caleb at the home of Zillah's grandmother, Marie Craig, in the tiny south-central Nebraska farm town of Wilsonville, and headed off with Zillah.

This was the longest period Zillah ever spent alone with Bob at one stretch. Her mother wasn't there to barge in on them. While Bob kept in touch daily with the message center, there was no phone to summon him away.

That was the kind of life Zillah wanted. Often, when she had Bob to herself, there was no hint of the dark passion he carried. Instead he was gentle and compassionate. He once swerved his car into a ditch to avoid hitting an animal. He even accompanied Zillah to the store to select their bedsheets together—a flower-and-butterfly print for the Aryan warrior.

When they were together, Bob and Zillah seemed like any other couple. Once at the movies they saw the Steve Martin–Lily Tomlin comedy *All of Me*. Zillah laughed the entire time. When it was Bob's turn to select a film, it was a different genre: action-adventure. He once rented Charles Bronson's *Death Wish II* to play on Zillah's VCR. As he slid the tape into the machine, he told Zillah he wanted her to see it so she would understand his motivation.

"This is what's wrong with society today," he said as Bronson annihilated a bad guy. "We have to do that because the government won't. Our police state doesn't do that. We have to cleanse the land ourselves."

During the interminable car ride across the flat expanse of Nebraska and Iowa, Bob and Zillah talked endlessly. He was frustrated with whites, both in and outside the racist movement. He was doing so much, like Bronson, and they didn't seem to appreciate it, he told her. They were nothing but "sheeple."

Zillah had spent almost her entire life within Wyoming's borders. Bob opened new doors for her—dangerous doors, but in Zillah's thinking, ones that had to be opened. She rationalized everything Bob did, even Berg's killing. Berg was only a Jew, she thought, and while she wouldn't have thought of killing him, she did believe in some sort of endtime battle. Who was she to reject the idea that it would be something so simple, like what Bob was doing, that would touch it off?

She suspected by now, however, that Bob lied to her to keep her happy. He swore he was getting a divorce, that he had stopped sleeping with Debbie, but more and more he talked about "plural marriage." Zillah wasn't ready for that. When she protested, Bob tactfully backed off.

"I'm just saying the Bible allows it," he explained, again using Zillah's faith to mollify her. "I only want one family, that's you, the boys and our baby. I'm just saying generally, polygamy is all right. It's biblical."

He also lied about his gang, so she never knew what to believe. In fact, Bob might have believed some of it himself. He daydreamed of Bronsonesque violence.

On March 7, 1984, Bob wrote to Zillah about a mission on which he was leaving the next day. It was the Fred Meyer robbery in Seattle, but that's not what he told Zillah. In his letter, it was a mission of international intrigue.

"If God permits, and I can return home to you, I will tell you more about it," he wrote. "But for now I will just tell you that we are going to attempt to free a Mexican (a white Spaniard) who is being held a political prisoner in Mexico City. The man is a powerful enemy of the Jew bankers and if he ever comes to power in Mexico he will curtail the Mexicans (non-white Mexicans) who are pouring into our country, and that is our ultimate goal of this whole trip." Bob later boasted to her that they had killed a guard and freed the man.

He once told her that when he was in the Sons of Liberty in Arizona, he executed a traitor in the desert by forcing him to write a suicide note, shooting him in the head, and leaving the gun with the body.

The wildest story was about a trip to California with Yarbrough in the spring of 1984. Bob said they became suspicious when they returned to their parked car and found a cigarette butt that hadn't been there before. Searching around, they found a bomb under the car. Suddenly, two men jumped them. Bob told Zillah he and Gary cut the head off one of them, leaving the torso in the street. They later learned the men were agents of Mossad, the Israeli secret police.

None of those stories was true.

Zillah figured Bob was impatient with her curiosity about his activities, and it beat telling her the truth. She accepted it. Twenty-eight years of a pretty unhappy life had taught her how to accept a lot worse.

From the time she was born in January 1956, Zillah was an outsider, even to her mother. Jean Craig lived out her bitterness as a single mother in tiny Worland, at the center of north-central Wyoming's isolated Bighorn Basin. Zillah was orginally named Tommie, after her grandfather, and carried that boy's name for twenty-five years before officially changing it to Zillah, a name meaning "shade." In Genesis, Zillah was the second wife of Lamech, a descendant of Adam's son Cain.

The chasm between mother and daughter became permanent when Jean had Zillah, just turned sixteen, committed for six months to the state mental hospital in Evanston because she'd become extremely withdrawn. What Zillah never told her mom was that she had been brutally raped two weeks earlier, on New Year's Eve 1971, by a Hispanic boy she had seen around Worland. It cost her a boyfriend and cemented in her a pattern of terrible behavior. She became pregnant at age seventeen by a worker in a traveling carnival, then rebelled when Jean asked her to give the baby up for adoption. When she refused, Jean kicked her out.

Her son Dustin was born in June 1974, and Zillah spent several years getting by on welfare while sleeping around, drinking, and smoking pot incessantly.

But about 1979, struck by a longing for something more substantial in her life, she recalled a conversation she'd had seven years earlier with her great-aunt Helen while on a shopping trip into Casper, Wyoming. Helen was a follower of the far-right preacher Sheldon Emry of Arizona, and it was from her that Zillah first learned of Identity. Jean Craig also began following the new religion.

Zillah, married by then to a man who turned out to be withdrawn, found the strength to divorce him and live her own life. She entered nursing school after giving birth to her second son, Caleb, in December 1980.

When Zillah went to Sheldon Emry's talk at the Laporte Church of Christ in February 1983, she discovered a new congregation she hadn't known existed. There she met Kathy Kilty, who lived in Medicine Bow, Wyoming, before moving to Laramie, and was a friend of David Lane. Six months later, Lane invited Zillah and Kathy to go with him and Colonel Francis Farrell to the Aryan World Congress. Stopping at the Custer Battlefield in Montana, Lane posed for a picture with the two women, giving a Nazi salute in front of the Little Bighorn memorial.

The congress was just as David had promised, and Zillah was impressed that all those men would vow to shed their blood for the survival of their race. It set Zillah in the perfect frame of mind to meet Bob five months later.

*   *   *

AFTER TWO DAYS of driving, Bob and Zillah arrived at Bob Miles's farm in Cohoctah, Michigan. A bull of a man with pure white hair, Miles enjoyed a fierce reputation but was a friendly, convivial fellow who moved with equal comfort among genteel religious ladies or exconvict bank robbers.

Miles had grown up in New York City's Washington Heights, near the Harlem River at the north end of Manhattan Island. He graduated in 1940 from George Washington High School, where Henry Kissinger also attended. He was set to enter Union Theological Seminary when the call of adventure overtook him.

It was a loosely kept secret that the Free French forces had a recruiter in an upstairs room above Cartier's. Miles joined as a radio operator and later flew with the RAF to drop spies behind Nazi lines. After Pearl Harbor, Miles joined the U.S. Navy in the Pacific. At war's end he was discharged in the Philippines.

He married and moved to Michigan to work in the sedate insurance business. At one time he was head of the Michigan Association of Insurance Executives.

A conservative by nature, his superpatriotism and anticommunism hardened with the years. In 1968 he was drawn to George Wallace's campaign for president, but Wallace had no formal organization in Michigan. Instead, Miles discovered that the United Klans of America, one of the largest KKK factions, had a realm in Michigan supporting Wallace. He joined in the same spirit of adventure that led him to the second floor of Cartier's to join the Free French. With his forceful character, he soon became Grand Dragon of UKA's small Michigan Realm and later rose to Imperial Kludd, or chaplain, of the entire UKA network.

In 1971 Miles founded his Mountain Church of Jesus Christ, based on the theory of dualism. He interpreted Genesis 6 as supporting a super-race of giant spirits who came from the stars to mate with beautiful earth women and fashion the white race. While his theology differs from Christian Identity, Miles is comfortable with people like Richard Butler.

A federal grand jury in Detroit indicted Miles on October 21, 1971, for civil rights conspiracy and explosives violations over the bombing of ten empty school buses used for integration in Pontiac. Convicted, he served nearly six years of a nine-year sentence at Leavenworth and Marion federal prisons.

He sometimes bragged about how easy it was to raise a racist ruckus in the hinterlands west of Detroit. Whenever Miles wanted publicity, he and some friends would drop a burned cross in a field and scatter dozens of cigarette butts around the perimeter. Then they'd call the media, which would inspect and duly report that a Klan rally had been held. It kept his small Klan group in the papers.

Bob and Zillah spent the night at Miles's farm, and in the morning Mathews and Miles walked out together into a field behind the house for a meeting out of her earshot. After they got back, Bob and Zillah left. In the car, Bob told her he was disappointed with Miles. Bob said he gave Miles a large donation out in the field and asked Miles if he could take over directing the gang for a while.

"I feel like a Pony Express rider, tired and winded," Bob told Zillah. "I'd been hoping Miles could take over, and I really thought he'd say, 'Yeah, I'll take it from here.' But he didn't even give me a fresh horse. Just wished me luck and said, 'See ya later!' "

"Did you accomplish anything at all?" Zillah wondered.

"Well, I got this," Bob added, handing Zillah a letter. "It'll get us in to meet Glenn Miller when we get to North Carolina."

Zillah glanced over the paper. In it, Miles asked Miller to welcome Mathews. "I would entrust my life to this man," Miles wrote in glowing terms about Bob. "You have no reason at all to fear or distrust him."

From Cohoctah they went to Columbus, Ohio, where Bob met a college history professor he knew through the National Alliance. Bob, believing the professor had influence with youth, wanted to underwrite a white-power rock band through him. Bob wanted it to have a he-man image to appeal to the emerging skinhead groups of punk-rockers, many of whom share white racist beliefs.

Mathews prided himself on his tastes in music. He didn't like rock, which he felt was a corruptor of youth. It gave white children bad idols, he felt, making them sway to black boogie-woogie while ignoring their own culture. Mathews loved classical music and the Celtic sounds of the *Thistle and Shamrock* program on American Public Radio. He also shared Zillah's bluegrass taste.

The next stop, Philadelphia, was a shock to Zillah. Having grown up in Wyoming, she had a natural aversion to big cities. But nothing had prepared her for the tumult she felt in Philadelphia. It was a typical hot, humid August day, with a sweaty haze hanging in the air. There were black people everywhere, more on one street corner than Zillah had seen in her entire life.

Fed by Mathews's intractable loathing of any town larger than Metaline Falls, Zillah saw cities as dark and dangerous places, where people looked down in gloom at the concrete; where each day they passed thousands of other frightened people, never speaking; where different races at cross purposes were in constant turmoil with each other. Mathews was unreserved in promoting that view. Those who came under his spell believed the world outside the bucolic Northwest was like the futuristic nihilism of a "Mad Max" movie transformed into horrifying reality.

After checking into the George Washington Motor Lodge, Mathews contacted George Zaengle, Martinez's friend, who had agreed to join him. Zaengle's wife, Maggie, was a hairdresser, and Bob wanted her to lighten his hair. Jimmy Dye also dropped by to tell Mathews he'd given Martinez his money.

Martinez knew the money's origin. The day after the robbery he was traveling through Lancaster, Pennsylvania, when he picked up a newspaper and happened to see an article about an armored car robbery in California. A shock wave hit him when he read the part about a gunman holding up a sign that read "Get Out or Die." He remembered Mathews telling him about such a sign at the Northgate robbery.

Martinez drove to Zaengle's home and told Bob he was getting a new lawyer with the stolen money, having dropped his Jewish attorney. Tom had been arraigned in federal court only three days earlier, and trial was set for September 4. The new lawyer, Perry de Marco, would try to get a delay.

The entire group, including Tom's wife, Sue, went out for dinner. Bob ordered Zaengle and Dye to sit at another table while the two couples squeezed into a booth. Zillah didn't care at all for Tom, who she thought was too wrapped up in his material possessions.

Bob turned on his considerable charm for Sue, trying to convince her that he would never let anything happen to Tom. Sue smiled politely but bought none of it. Then, while Zillah and Sue chatted about their children, Bob began trying to convince Tom he had no real choice but to run.

"If ZOG finds out you're a racist, they'll nail you, Tom, don't you know that?" Mathews told his friend. "That's what they did to another friend of mine."

"Maybe, Bob, but I'm stuck with this turkey of a house that I've dropped a lot of money into." Tom began listing the structural problems with the Weikel Street house. "Then there's my car, they still got my car . . ."

"Tom, your lovely wife and children need a better atmosphere than you can give them here," Bob countered. "You have to cut those materialist strings."

What Mathews failed to perceive was that Martinez was fishing for reasons to turn him down. After Jimmy Dye had told him about Walter West's killing and David Lane had bragged about driving the getaway car from Berg's assassination, Martinez was frightened to death. Dye and Zaengle, drinking one night with Martinez, said bluntly that despite their friendship, they could kill him too if that's what Mathews ordered. Martinez was a man drowning in confusion and fear, and Mathews was tossing him not a life preserver but a cinderblock.

On Monday morning, Bob and Zillah left Philadelphia for a 140-mile drive to Arlington, Virginia, where they checked into a hotel and called on Dr. William Pierce, head of the National Alliance.

A tall, quiet man who used to work with the American Nazi chief, George Lincoln Rockwell, Pierce welcomed Mathews into his small apartment. A baby grand piano took up much of one small room. Pierce showed the couple his secret plans for moving his headquarters to a tiny town high in the Allegheny Mountains of West Virginia called Mill Point, near the birthplace of Pearl Buck.

Bob accorded Pierce a reverence approaching outright worship that he deigned to give no other man. When William Pierce spoke, Mathews became reticent, almost as if he was afraid to interrupt with thoughts of his own. It was decidedly unlike Bob Mathews. Soon Pierce and Mathews went into a bedroom, leaving Pierce's wife, also from Laramie, with Zillah. Zillah listened as she explained her eerie interest in parapsychology and the supernatural. It gave Zillah the creeps.

Back at the hotel later, Bob asked Zillah to help count his remaining money before he set aside an amount in a bag for Dr. Pierce. Later Pierce came to the hotel, and Bob escorted him down to a bench in a shaded, grassy area nearby. From a hotel window high above, Zillah watched as Bob handed his mentor a bag.

Dr. Pierce later relocated to Mill Point, operating out of a metal warehouse-type building on a 364-acre property in the woods.

The next day, Bob and Zillah drove south to visit Frazier Glenn Miller, head of the Confederate Knights of the Ku Klux Klan, in Angier, North Carolina. During the trip, Bob was excited. He said Scutari had called with good news. A representative of the Syrian government had agreed to meet with him. Any enemy of the Jews was a potential friend of Mathews. He also told Zillah that he hoped to work with the Black Muslim leader Louis Farrakhan. Zillah didn't know whether to believe any of it.

When they arrived at Miller's home, Bob asked Zillah to wait in the car while he walked up to the farmhouse with Bob Miles's introductory letter. After reading it, Miller invited them in. His wife was making dinner, and his seven boys were running wild. Lost in the crowd was Miller's youngest, a daughter, whom Miller ignored completely. Playing on the blaring television was *The A Team*. The sight of this Klan leader's children watching the heroics of the black celebrity Mr. T, one of the show's stars, was almost too much for Mathews. It was the precise reason Mathews refused to own a television set.

Nevertheless, after chatting a while, Mathews invited Miller for a visit once he was settled in a hotel room in nearby Benson. He would make a contribution to this

Southern racist leader, who, like Mathews, used the white power slogan "Blood, Soil, and Honor," in his writings.

Bob and Zillah spent five days in Benson. During that time, Scutari and Barnhill invited Ardie McBrearty to assist them in running the voice stress tests on recruits. They hired a Florida pilot to ferry them around the country, and on August 7, they flew to Benson to meet Mathews.

McBrearty had run hundreds of voice tests in the years he'd been in the tax protest movement. He knew IRS agents shadowed his movements. He had to fly under assumed names, because the IRS would seize his plane tickets to settle more than $60,000 in tax liens against him. Mathews knew that just as he had to adopt the Identity approach to reach people like Pierce and Duey, he would have to hone his old tax protest vocabulary from his Marvin Cooley days to win McBrearty over.

McBrearty was a simple man with a consuming passion, the tax rebellion. He entered it, as he saw it, a victim. A construction engineer and electrician in California in 1967, he had applied for a contractor's license to open a business. The application contained a number of questions about the tools he owned, which he happily answered. Later, with his license, came a bill for $32.

"What's this for?" he asked some bureaucrat in the licensing department.

"That's a tax on your tools."

"But they're the same tools I always owned," McBrearty protested.

"Well, yesterday you weren't in business, and today you are, so we tax them," the bureaucrat replied. By 1972, fueled with indignation, McBrearty was sponsoring tax protest meetings in Southern California. He went on to be chairman for four years of the U.S. Taxpayers Union.

Mathews told McBrearty he headed a group of a dozen men who were in the tax fight. He wanted McBrearty to help as legal adviser and design an airtight security system to detect infiltrators. McBrearty was offered handsome pay. The sight of large amounts of cash didn't shock him, since cash-only transactions to avoid paper trails are normal in the world of tax protesting.

McBrearty signed on, and that Friday the Florida pilot flew Mathews back to Philadelphia with McBrearty and Scutari to run the city boys across the box.

Tom Martinez answered his phone to hear first George Zaengle's greeting, then Mathews's high-pitched, sing-song voice.

"Hey, buddy, can you come over to George's? I've got somebody here I'd like you to meet, and take a voice stress test," Mathews said. "We're all taking it."

"What's that?" Martinez asked.

"It tells if you're being truthful. It's for weeding out informers," Mathews replied. That sent a chill through Martinez, whose mind was confused already.

"No way, Bob, I ain't takin' no test," Martinez balked.

Martinez said it was too dangerous to come to Zaengle's house, since he might be under surveillance. He suggested meeting at a nearby hoagy shop. Soon the two friends were seated privately in a booth eating a couple of subs and washing them down with thick chocolate milkshakes.

"Bob, I don't want to meet nobody else," Martinez protested. "Look, how do I know they're not informants themselves? I'm in enough trouble." His reasoning made sense to Mathews, who then turned to Martinez's trial. Prosecutors were talking about adding a third count since another counterfeit bill Tom passed had turned up. ZOG was going to nail him to the wall, Mathews said.

"You'd better skip that trail, buddy, and take off," Mathews said. "I can set it all up for you. We've got the accommodations. Zillah's mom got us a lot of names from cemeteries that we've been turning into genuine IDs. We can set it up for you—Sue and the kids, too. Other guys have their families with them."

It was hard-sell, but Martinez resisted. "No, the trial'll be all right. I'm not ready for this underground stuff," Martinez declined.

Mathews looked sadly at him. "Tom, there's no way you're going to win. ZOG doesn't let its enemies walk free. You have no choice, my kinsman. You come to the bastion now and later we'll send for your family. They'll be there with you."

"I need time to think about all this," Martinez said, acting unconvinced.

"Yeah, of course," Mathews replied gently. "It's difficult to pull up stakes. You take time to think it over and get used to it."

When Mathews returned and told Scutari what Martinez had decided, Scutari was firm. "You drop that guy like a hot potato, Bob," Scutari warned him. "If he won't come across this voice box, he's no good."

"Oh, no, Black," said Mathews. "Spider will come around."

Zaengle and Bill Nash passed their tests and within days flew to the bastion to await the opening of the Aryan Academy training camp.

Bob returned to Benson, where Zillah waited. Glenn Miller came to visit their hotel, and during the meeting Mathews handed him $75,000. Miller's eyes bugged out when he saw the cash, but he kept a lid on his excitement.

Mathews told him the money was his to spend however he saw fit. Miller thought a moment, then looked at Mathews. "Would you mind if I use some to put my kids in private school?" Miller asked. "Now they have to go to school with niggers, and I don't want that for 'em. I want 'em in a Christian school with all white kids. Niggers can't afford to go there. Is that okay?"

"Sure," Bob replied immediately. "Whatever you want. The money is yours. In fact, I'm going to send you $125,000 more. I think you can put it to good use."

Miller had heard a rumor from his sources that Mathews was an FBI plant trying to entrap right-wing leaders. Miller confronted Mathews about it before he departed. Mathews laughed it off. "Don't worry about that!" he told Miller.

Bob and Zillah then drove to Mathews's family homestead near Mount Airy, North Carolina, where relatives still lived, and stayed a few days with aunts and uncles. For the first time on the trip, there was no talk of killing, robbery, or counterfeiting. There was a very good reason.

Mathews's distant cousin worked for the FBI in Washington.

"TURN LEFT HERE, Robert Merki told Denver Parmenter, looking up momentarily from his San Francisco street map as they drove off the 9th Street exit of U.S. 101

toward Harrison Street. "Now down about three blocks and go right."

In less than a minute, Parmenter had turned onto 12th Street and gone a block and a half. He slowed his Olds to a stop around the corner of Kissling Street, a narrow, one-block alley that dead-ended off 12th.

"Holy shit, Noah!" Parmenter said with surprise to Merki. *"This* is Brink's? You were right. It don't look secure at all." The two men were on the corner, looking across at a nondescript two-story cinderblock building that by itself would be unidentifiable except for the heavy trucks parked in a fenced lot on the southeast side with the word "Brink's" on their sides.

It was only slightly more imposing than the Wells Fargo operation in Boise.

"This is where they have their vault," Merki said as he pointed his new camera toward the building at 240 12th Street. It was August 14, and Parmenter was trying to line up the next robbery. Brink's was only five blocks south of San Francisco's City Hall, but the neighborhood was quiet and empty.

Just across 12th Street from the depot was an abandoned metal industrial building with a large overhang above the sidewalk. It would be a good place to station snipers. There was a clear field of fire to the metal stairs that went up to a second-floor door on the northwest side of the Brink's building. Merki snapped another photo of the door. It was a potential entry point.

The Brink's compound looked like a hodgepodge of buildings joined into one. A metal shed adjoined the southeast side of the cinderblock main portion. A chain link fence topped with barbed wire surrounded the truck yard.

Merki and Parmenter returned to their car and drove around the area. They couldn't believe what they found. From 12th and Howard, the next corner up from Brink's, it was only one block to the on-ramp for the Bayshore Freeway. They could be across the San Francisco-Oakland Bay Bridge, or down to Candlestick Park, in a matter of minutes.

Afterward, Parmenter contacted Charles Ostrout, who was still boarding in San Lorenzo with Ron King, the operations manager of Brink's San Francisco branch, during the work week. But Ostrout was at home in Lookout, 330 miles away. They arranged to meet in Reno, which would be an equal drive for each.

The three men met in Nendel's Motel in Reno. Parmenter asked Ostrout to describe the interior of the Brink's depot. Ostrout told them the first floor was the main area, with the vault, garage, and office. The second level, where that northwest side door led, was reserve space and storage.

A periodic shipment of cash from Hawaii, ranging between $30 million and $50 million, was routed through the depot. That's what interested Parmenter. Ostrout handed Merki his Brink's ID, which looked like a driver's license. Merki said he could copy it easily. Ostrout also said Ron King was ready to join the "company."

Then, with a tone of disappointment, Ostrout told them something else.

"You know, since you guys hit the Ukiah truck last month, our drivers are too nervous to take that route," Ostrout said. "I had to drive it myself two weeks ago. I get up there in the hills and you'd never guess what happened. The fan belt broke. I got stuck for a couple hours out in the boonies. I just wish I could have called you because that truck was easy pickings."

Parmenter went back to Spokane to prepare a move to a house he rented near Flathead Lake in Bigfork, Montana. Mathews, Scutari, and Barnhill were looking to move near there as well. The day after Parmenter's return, however, Mathews summoned him to Boise for a meeting. Parmenter would have to be stripped of some of his responsibility to help settle the feud between Mathews and Bruce Pierce.

It seemed that after Mathews returned from the East Coast, he had told David Lane to notify Pierce to bring back half the money he took from the Ukiah loot. Lane had remained in Boise in late July to run the message center Merki had set up in a tiny house off an alley at 4121/2 Thatcher Street. Merki had been supplied with $8,000, all in singles, to operate the message center. He bought a phone and answering machine at a yard sale and set up the Thatcher Street house on the edge of town with a desk, chair, lamp, stove, and refrigerator.

Merki then moved from the shabby 10th Street house to a much nicer split-level ranch home on Greenbrier Drive, near the Hillcrest Country Club on Boise's south side. He taped aluminum foil over the two-car garage windows and erected a metal shed inside to hide the printing press and camera. Jean Craig, at Mathews's personal request, then moved from Laramie to the 10th Street house to help run the message center with Lane. Lane passed the message to Pierce at Bob's request.

"Carlos says come down to Boise and bring $300,000 along," Lane told him. "He wants to clear things up."

"Wait!" Pierce said in shock. "Bob said what? You tell him we decided at Boise on a division of money and that any large expenditures, we all had to agree on. What he's asking clearly breaks the line. You inform Bob I'd like to have a group meeting on this request."

But what Lane told Mathews was something else: Pierce wasn't going to hand over the money. Word quickly spread through the group that Pierce was trying to take over. Several days later, Duey and Yarbrough met Pierce late at night at a rest stop on U.S. 2 west of Troy and told him the rumors.

"David Lane is poisoning me with Bob!" Pierce yelled. "You let Bob know we have to meet!" Pierce told Duey and Yarbrough he had the perfect solution.

"I don't want a separate group," Pierce said. "I accept Bob as leader. But we're getting too big. We should break into cells and each have certain responsibilities to be more effective." Duey and Yarbrough agreed.

Scutari was in Florida when the meeting was set for August 19. Concerned lest someone might try to harm Mathews, he called Loff and asked him to round up the National Alliance folk to support Mathews. Loff got Kemp and Dye to go to Boise with him. Zaengle and Nash, also in Mathews's corner, arrived as well.

Yarbrough roared into Boise on his Harley, and Parmenter and Duey showed up too. They all went to the tiny Thatcher Street house and waited with Lane.

Pierce was pacing across the small living room of the 10th Street house waiting for Mathews. He glanced through the window panes that took up three-fourths of the front door and saw a blond man he didn't recognize approaching.

"Hey, somebody's coming!" Pierce yelled to Jean Craig as he began to retreat toward the dining room. "Find out who it is." The man knocked, and Jean instantly recognized Bob. Pierce emerged from the dining room and stared at Mathews. Sure, it was the same build and the same face, but Pierce couldn't believe how much difference it made in Mathews's appearance to go from dark brown hair to blond.

Mathews was surly. He sent Jean to wait with the others at Thatcher Street, then turned to Pierce. "I can't forgive those who stab me in the back," he began, putting Pierce on the defensive. "I won't sacrifice all that we've accomplished for that. You want to take over? You can do a better job?"

"Bob, you've been misled," Pierce said. "I don't want to take over. I don't have your knack for it. Dave Lane got my message to you messed up." It took over an hour for the two men to straighten out the misunderstanding, then turn the talk toward Pierce's suggestion to break into cells.

"We've got just a big pool of guys now," Pierce explained. "A pool is directionless, a guy here, a guy there. It's just a mess. There's so much wasted manpower. There's no function or goals. We need to break into cells. If you divide it up, five guys, five guys, you can get something done."

After a lengthy discussion of the idea, Mathews agreed. Independent cells could insulate better against infiltrators by holding group interaction to a minimum. Pierce said he'd like a more challenging assignment, like planning the next robbery. To do that, Mathews would have to limit Parmenter's role.

Shortly after 5 P.M., Mathews came to Thatcher Street and said there would be a general meeting soon, but first the Inner Circle would meet at the Holiday Inn near the Boise Airport. The Inner Circle was the same five men who'd fought in the back room at 10th Street in July. They met for three hours to hash out their new roles. Mathews asked Parmenter to relinquish Step 3, robberies, to Pierce. Instead, Parmenter would be the Inner Circle liaison with the training camp Rader was setting up. Parmenter agreed. Duey would get money to open an indoctrination school at Bluecreek, Washington, where he had moved to a small trailer house.

Yarbrough's oldest daughter was having a difficult time with kidney disease, requiring almost constant care and dialysis treatments. Besides, Yarbrough was tiring of the group and annoyed at how big it was getting. He told Mathews if it was all the same, he'd rather stick close to home and possibly be in charge of finding recruits from the prison system. What Gary wanted to do was quietly fade from the scene, as he could see better than the others where they were headed.

Mathews was to remain chairman, with Scutari at his side as security chief. Pierce could take the Identity followers he preferred and plan the next heist. But Mathews insisted on getting back at least $300,000 that Pierce had taken.

Mathews went back to Thatcher Street and explained to the troops what was happening. The leadership crisis had been averted. Then Mathews told Lane he was being replaced at the message center. It was difficult, because the two had been so close. Lane was hurt by it, then got miffed and left.

That night, before returning to Ione, Loff walked around the block with his best friend. So much had happened since that hot day in August 1976 when he first met Bob clearing stumps up at Mathews Acres. They chatted a bit about what was going on in Metaline Falls. Loff told Mathews that he had quit his job at Portland Lehigh last week. But Loff wanted assurance from Mathews on just one point.

"There's been talk," Loff began, "about Scutari. Some of the guys have been questioning his race. He's Italian, and there's some who don't think he should be with us. His complexion is dark, and he's got a rather big nose."

Mathews chuckled over that. Of all the people in the group at this point, Scutari was about the only one on whom Mathews felt he could totally depend.

"Well, the reason I brought it up, Bob," Loff went on, "is that I'm Italian. I want to know where we stand on this. Am I the next one they'll talk about?"

"Don't worry about a thing, Ken," Bob replied. "You're

one of my most loyal friends and I have absolute trust in you. And Mr. Black, he's my right arm."

RANDALL RADER WAS used to remote places, and when the real estate agent John Muzidal took him to the tract across the belly of Big Meadows, 30 miles north of the tiny town of Priest River, Idaho, Rader felt it was right.

There were 110 acres for sale, with more to lease, where Consalus Creek joined Goose Creek and later flowed into Priest Lake, one of the panhandle's larger lakes. A half-mile upstream was the Washington border. Rader liked being a short hop away from state lines. A large open meadow straddled the valley floor below the Pelke Divide, while thick trees grew on the two facing mountainsides of the property. The camp could be hidden from sight in a stand of trees, in a flat area nestled in a curve of the mountain.

"I could hold it for you for $500 earnest money," Muzidal said. Rader looked back, said all right, and reached into his pockets for some cash. "And what name is this under?" Muzidal asked for the offer sheet, which he dated August 25.

"Put down 'Timberline Hunting Club,' " Rader replied without hesitation, agreeing to the $88,000 purchase price.

The site for Mathews's planned Aryan Academy wasn't as remote as Rader thought. It was less than 2 miles to a paved road, where a ranch house was located, and a public dirt road in the Kaniksu National Forest cut through the property. When Rader showed the camp separately to Scutari and Mathews, he brought them in the back way, 22 miles over dirt road from Usk, Washington, 34 miles south of Ione. It looked a lot more remote then.

Rader and Loff spent thousands of dollars to outfit the camp. The rabbits in Loff's barn got hardly a moment's peace. Early in August, Mathews called Loff and requested $230,000, which Kemp would pick up. The following week, Mathews needed $310,000, which David Lane would pick up and bring to him in Boise. As Loff was excavating by the rabbit cages, Lane drove up and walked into the barn, seeing where Loff kept the loot.

Late in the month, Lane returned to Ione on Mathews's instructions to get $100,000 for delivery to Louis Beam, the former Texas Klan leader who'd been living with Pastor Butler. When he didn't find Loff, Lane went to the rabbit cages and dug up the money with Zaengle's help.

In fact, Loff's farm had become the focal point for the company in the weeks before the training camp was purchased. Late in August, Soderquist returned from California and camped at Loff's with Rader, Zaengle, and the others. Parmenter drove over from Kalispell and took Soderquist aside, on Mathews's orders, to grill him about his desertion following the Ukiah heist and about his continued drinking. Parmenter placed him on probation after concluding that Soderquist's mind and heart still were in the right place.

On August 29, Rader used the message center to contact McBrearty, whose legal experience he needed for the September 1 closing on the Aryan Academy real estate. Two days later, Rader and Loff drove to the Spokane airport to pick up McBrearty, who had been working with Pierce in San Francisco. Riding north in Rader's pickup, they discussed what name they would use to buy the land.

"I like 'Amos Able,' " McBrearty said, causing Rader to snicker. "Well, Randall, it's based on the military alphabet, A-Amos, A-Able. Next time, I'll use Bill Baker." They all laughed again.

Back in Ione, they met in a shed on Loff's property, where Rader had set up a business front, Mountain Man Supply, as a conduit for the material he was going to purchase. Rader gave McBrearty $31,500 of the "company money" Scutari had handed him in July for the rest of the down payment. "Won't using that much cash make the agent suspicious?" Loff asked.

"Naw," McBrearty replied with a smile. "People use cash all the time. You're just used to doing things the way the banks want you to."

On September 1, a Saturday, Rader and McBrearty drove to the realty office in Priest River, 8 miles east of Newport. There they gave Muzidal the rest of the down payment and the first $500 monthly payment on the debt assumption. McBrearty signed "Amos Able" of the Timberline Hunting Club on the documents.

Driving back to Spokane, where McBrearty had to catch a flight to Portland, Rader asked McBrearty what he'd been doing in San Francisco with Pierce.

"Runnin' some fellas from Brink's over the voice box," McBrearty said. "Brigham thinks the next procurement will get the company more than $20 million."

BRUCE PIERCE WAS NOT a man who set his sights low. Taking over robberies from Parmenter, he went right to work on what would be the largest cash robbery in history. What Pierce enjoyed most about this Aryan warrior stuff was the heady rush of danger and death that accompanied the difficult planning and commission of the crimes. He wanted fervently to be in the thick of it. All he had wanted from Bob was a looser rein. He was determined to show Bob his trust wasn't misplaced.

Returning to Montana from the Boise meeting, Pierce assembled a group of men who, like him, believed in Identity. He felt most comfortable with them in his cadre: Randy Evans and his two wives; Tom Bentley and Bonnie Sue West, Walter's widow; Jim Wallington; David Tate; and Dwayne Butler and his seventeen-year-old son, Mike, who had filled out tremendously that summer. It was this teenager who turned Pierce toward Identity only twenty-one months earlier. Now Pierce was a leader.

Counting the women and children, there were sixteen people in his nomadic cell.

He made one rule right from the start. In view of Mathews's mistake at Ukiah, Pierce decided his men would tether their weapons with lanyards. If they were injured, their guns wouldn't fall far away. And if they were stupid enough to lay down their guns in the middle of a crime, they wouldn't forget to pick them up.

Pierce arranged a session for August 29 at the Holiday Inn near San Francisco International Airport. Parmenter, the middleman who had met Ostrout, came to help. Scutari and McBrearty arrived to give voice stress analyzer tests to Ostrout and Ron King, Brink's operations manager at the 12th Street depot.

Using baseline questions such as "Are we in San Francisco?" and "Do you sometimes drink water?" Scutari set both recruits up for the real questions: "Is there someone you suspect is an informer?" and "Are you an informer?"

Then McBrearty took over to ask several leading questions: "Do you realize the dangers involved in associating with this organization?" and "Do you realize the price you could pay by being associated with this organization?"

Both recruits answered correctly. Both men passed.

As proof of his loyalty, Ron King drew a diagram of the Brink's building interior, including the vault and the little-used second level with its isolated outside door. King outlined the alarm systems and security procedures at the depot. He identified the people who worked in and around the vault.

More importantly, he provided details about the Hawaiian cash shipment, which came in by plane and was trucked from the airport to downtown. It was quite possible that the cash could run as high as $50 million. With two inside men and Merki's counterfeit ID cards for the conspirators, Pierce felt confident about the odds when he left to return to Montana the next day.

Pierce had a logistical headache waiting back in tiny Troy. He wanted all his men together, and Troy couldn't accommodate them. Pierce and Evans went to Salmon, Idaho, to rent new houses. Pierce had liked that area when he drove through with his bus in May. It was about halfway between Missoula and Idaho Falls, Idaho, near the Montana border.

Pierce found an ideal place with a trailer next to it, for Mathews or other guests. If he was to plan a heist as big as the vault job, he wanted his people nearby so they could brainstorm. Together they rented more than a half-dozen places in and around Salmon, in the shadow of the Continental Divide.

Salmon met the criteria Pierce outlined for his safe houses. It was a small town, about three thousand people, with a local economy depressed enough so that residents didn't look twice at the color of his money. It was near the state line. At his back was the Salmon River Wilderness, one of the largest wilderness areas in the United States, through which flowed the River of No Return. He figured he could lead a battalion of soldiers back there and the feds would never find them.

Pierce had just moved into the house on North Keeler Creek Road in Troy, owned by Richard Gross, from Ella Ackley's house on August 3, but in that short time he had fashioned it into a fortress. The north fork of Keeler Creek flowed through a steep valley sandwiched by Pony and Grouse mountains. The stream ran 100 feet from the house, down through a large clearing Pierce used for shooting practice. The Fifields, a mile downstream, never complained about the noise.

Pierce chained his driveway and began to rim the perimeter of the clearing with tripwire hooked up to a 12-volt system that would light the house at night if an intruder approached. He positioned loaded weapons in every room of his house and had no trouble with the children touching them.

To protect his family when he was gone, Pierce decided to buy a guard dog. One day shopping in Kalispell, 100 miles east of Troy, he saw an ad for a kennel in nearby Columbia Falls. Visiting with the owner, James Kerney, with German shepherds, rottweilers, and dobermans to choose from, Pierce settled on a four-year-old male rottveiler named Kirk, kenneled at the time in California. He paid a total of $3,300 for the dog, counting air fare and retraining.

"I don't frighten easy, but this dog is awesome," he told Julie after he returned. "A doberman is a cross between a rottweiler and a greyhound, so this here's the daddy. You put him out in the yard and point to the corners, say, 'Watch, watch,' you can go to bed and relax. The dog'll take care of it.

"If a doberman saw this dog, he'd go home and train some more," Pierce raved. "If someone puts his arm out to stop him, fine, he'll just break through the arm to get to the throat. In a space of 10 feet, a cop with an unchambered gun would be dead. This dog would vaporize him. If he buys me just one second, that's all I need. He's worth the price if he buys me my life and freedom."

Perhaps the most foresight went into the escape pack Pierce assembled, a canvas backpack into which he put everything he'd need to survive if he had to make a quick break on foot. It had such standard equipment as his sleeping bag, canvas, tarp, and matches. It also contained a small stove with several means of starting a fire, including tinder. He had plenty of dried food and a water filtration device, along with reference books on wilderness survival, recognizing edible plants, and being on the run. He packed several changes of clothes, spare socks, underwear, and toiletries. Also in the pack was a knife, a pistol rolled up in a bag, and some 223 ammo for the rifle he'd bring along.

The most important thing to Pierce, though, was the final item, a vial of microfilm with an available-light viewer. On the microfilm was the Holy Bible.

Pierce didn't keep the pack in his house. At the crest of a ridge south of the house, across an arm of Pony Mountain, he raised the pack high into a tree by rope. Then he tied the rope to another tree down the path and secreted a knife at the base of a tree farther back. It was all spaced so he could grab the knife on a dead run, slice through the rope, and catch the pack as it fell. For good measure, he strung tripwire across his getaway route.

While in Troy, Pierce took up a hobby that nearly resulted in his capture.

He considered himself a natural flier, having taken lessons with his brother Greg in Georgia. In Troy he bought an ultralight plane and found a farmer on Lake Creek Road who let him use an open field. He flew it as often as he could, in early morning and at sundown when the thermal currents are favorable. As he got more proficient, he started to use the paved landing strip a mile north of Troy.

When Pierce was getting ready to leave Troy in September, he disassembled the plane and packed it into an old pickup truck. But he was waiting for delivery of a ski attachment for the landing gear. He drove the pickup to Stacia Fifield's house, and she agreed to let him store it there until the skis were delivered.

Then Pierce looked for his friend Jim Montgomery to let him know he was leaving. Montgomery was at his brother's house, and came outside to greet Pierce.

"I'm being transferred to Fargo," Pierce lied to him. "I want you to have that firewood you sold me."

"Roger," Montgomery answered with surprise—he knew him only as Roger Morton—"I can't take that."

"Sure you can," Pierce insisted. "Plus I'd appreciate it if you would take my Vega. It runs good and, well, I got too many vehicles now."

Montgomery was taken aback by the offer, but on September 1, the Saturday before Labor Day, he went to Pierce's house to load the wood. When he finished, he went into the house with Pierce. It was empty except for a brown couch and chair, a VCR, and a Bearcat scanner. Montgomery heard two transmissions, one from the Lincoln County Sheriff's office in Libby, the other from the Troy police department.

After he helped Pierce strap some tools to the top of the bus, Pierce invited him inside. "I'd like to show you something," Pierce began hesitantly. "Maybe I shouldn't . . ." With that, Pierce pulled back a blanket from a bed inside the bus. Montgomery's eyes widened when he saw an array of weapons laid out on the sheets. They weren't hunting rifles. They looked like military ordnance, with flash suppressors. There was also a crossbow. Pierce had grown so close to Montgomery, he couldn't resist revealing his secret side.

"Maybe," Pierce added afterward, "it would be better at this point if you don't mention my name to anybody." Montgomery was confused by it all.

Before departing, Pierce left the Vega keys for Montgomery. Inside the glove compartment, he hid an envelope reading: "For Jim and Family." It contained $250.

After leaving Troy with the bus and a U-Haul van, Pierce stopped outside Kalispell to pick up the rottweiler. He talked with Kerney for fifteen minutes about the man's kennel business, and was so impressed with Kerney's sincerity that he decided to play Robin Hood again.

"How much would you need to get the business going?" Pierce asked.

"For all I want to do, probably about $25,000," Kerney answered.

"Would $5,000 help?" Pierce asked.

"Sure!" Kerney replied. Pierce then pulled out some money and counted.

"Here's $6,000," he said as he handed the money to a stunned Kerney. "And I don't charge interest. Just give me your address and I'll be in touch."

*   *   *

JUST FOUR DAYS LATER, the FBI hit Troy. Yet another of Bill tenBensel's tedious checks of toll call records turned up a call from a pay phone in Santa Rosa to a phone registered to "Sandra Gleed," Julie's alias, in Troy.

Wayne Manis was working on the Yarbrough surveillance on September 7 when Agent Ernie Smith, now among more than two dozen FBI agents working the case, called to tell him they may have found the trail of Bruce Carroll Pierce. Manis and John Nelson left the surveillance to meet Smith. Together they interviewed Ella Ackley and felt confident that her "Roger Wilkins" was their man Pierce.

The next day, a steady rain fell as ten agents returned to Troy. One was Don Wofford, a veteran of domestic terrorism cases from the Newark, New Jersey, office who had been transferred to Butte for this case. In Newark, Wofford had worked on Weathermen and Black Liberation Army cases. A bit pudgier than most agents, with thick, dark hair and a full beard, Wofford's nickname was "Wolfman."

The agents fanned out to look for the ultralight plane Ackley told them Pierce had. The roads through the forest south of Troy were a confusing maze of dirt paths. Once, when Wofford was stationed at an intersection deep in the woods, the others had a hard time finding him.

Manis stopped in the woods at one point, thinking the plane could be concealed in the trees. He started down a path through the tall grass when he sensed something was moving toward him. Freezing, he reached for his weapon when a black bear suddenly padded around the corner. Face to face, it was impossible to tell which was more startled. But both retreated, the bear scrambling up a tree and Manis heading for the safety of his car.

Manis was riding with Smith and a Lincoln County deputy, methodically going along each road, keeping alert for the ultralight. They nearly passed Fifield's driveway when, from the corner of his eye, Manis spotted the aircraft in the old pickup.

Fifield directed them to Gross's house. For the first time since Pierce had jumped bond in April, authorities found his lair. The house was empty, but Smith found a trash pile 25 feet down the clearing. Manis searched the grounds and came across a plywood silhouette target of a trooper shot full of holes. There were numerous holes in the trees around it, and agents dug out .45-caliber slugs.

Pierce had fired them from the same MAC-10 he had used to kill berg.

At the trash pile, Smith found a list indicating Pierce was well armed: "Sunday evening: Load ammo boxes, guns, except ones may need."

After interviewing Ackley, Fifield, Montgomery, and others, Manis was certain Pierce would return to Troy for the plane. Sure enough, Pierce called Fifield two days later. Fifield told him his ultralight's skis had arrived the day after he left. Then Pierce asked nonchalantly whether anyone had been asking about him. She told him no, as the FBI requested. Pierce then said he'd come and get the ultralight.

Pierce started back for Troy on Wednesday, September 12, riding with David Tate in Tate's Toyota Land Cruiser. Tate had registered it in Kalispell and needed to pick up the permanent plates. When they went into the Flathead County Courthouse in Kalispell, with the police station a stone's throw away, the FBI spotted them.

A mad scramble started. The FBI radioed for surveillance aircraft to take over as they tailed Tate and Pierce west on U.S. 2. The pair spent the night in a motel in Libby, but the agents were ordered to take no action. Being this close to Pierce without arresting him was frustrating for Manis. They had a legal right to arrest Pierce on the Yakima counterfeiting conviction, but it was deemed more important for the moment to see whether Pierce would lead them to the others.

On Thursday morning, Pierce and Tate drove the 18 remaining miles to Troy. As they approached the Lake Creek Road turnoff that led to Fifield's, Pierce told Tate instead to head into town so he could call first and make sure Fifield was home.

Tate pulled into the IGA supermarket lot, the first large business on the southeast end of Troy. As Pierce headed for a pay phone on the outside wall, he looked to his left and saw Jim Montgomery going into the store.

"Hey! Jim!" Pierce called. "How are you? Is there any news?" It was Pierce's standard rhetorical greeting. Montgomery stopped dead and looked at his friend.

"Hi, Roger," he said. "There's a little news, but it isn't good."

Suddenly Pierce's senses heightened. He paused and slowly looked around.

"Damn!" Manis said, spotting Pierce through binoculars from beyond the lot. "He ran into Montgomery! He's going to know we're on him." Manis radioed Bill Fallin, the Special Agent-in-Charge of the Butte division, who was circling high above Troy in a spotter plane. The FBI had two planes working in tandem on this surveillance.

"We're going to have to take him down, here and now," Manis advised Fallin.

"No," Fallin radioed back. "No contact. We're still in the intelligence mode. We've got to see where they lead."

Manis chafed as he watched Pierce maneuver Montgomery closer to Tate's car. He realized Pierce would find out as much as he could from his friend.

"So tell me what's been going on?" Pierce asked Montgomery as they walked.

"The FBI's been around asking questions about you," Montgomery answered. "An agent named Steve Fiddler came to me and said he heard I sold you some firewood, and did I know where you went. I told him you went to Fargo."

"When was this?" Pierce asked, his eyes darting around the parking lot.

"Couple days after you left."

"Praise Yahweh!" Pierce exclaimed. "We got out of the way just in time!"

"What do you mean?" Montgomery asked his friend.

"Come on along with us," Pierce suggested as he reached Tate's car. Montgomery balked when he saw the driver had a handgun in his belt. "Don't worry," Pierce reassured him. The way Pierce said it, Montgomery knew he would not be harmed. They got into the Land Cruiser and headed west out of town.

The agents in the surveillance plane watched the roof of a brown Land Cruiser as it headed toward the hills.

The pilot kept in contact with the agents on the ground, who were ordered to follow at a safe distance.

"What's your name?" Montgomery asked Tate as they left the lot.

"Call me anything you want," Tate grumbled as he headed toward the U.S. 2 bridge over the Kootenai River, a couple miles northwest of the tiny hamlet. He drove about 4 miles out, then doubled back over a side road on the north bank.

"So, Jim, do they know about my vehicles?" Pierce asked Montgomery.

"Yeah, they do," Montgomery answered. Pierce realized he'd have to get rid of the great old bus. He pumped Montgomery for anything he could remember. As they approached the older bridge that came straight into town, Montgomery said he'd rather not go back through Troy with them, if it was all the same to them. Tate stopped at the bridge, where Pierce told Montgomery he could get out.

"If there's FBI in Troy and they try to stop us," Pierce told him, "there's gonna be a lot of dead cops in the road. I don't want you involved in that."

Montgomery got off on the shoulder and looked back at his friend. He still didn't know Pierce's real name. "Take care, Roger," he said. "Take care of your family and take care of your life."

As Tate pulled out, his rear tires spitting gravel, Pierce checked the back for the two AR-15s they brought. Each had hundred-round ammo drums, instead of the usual thirty-round magazines. They also had survival packs in case they had to break for the woods. But they saw no sign of the FBI in Troy. Tate reached the U.S. 2 weigh station just past Lake Creek Road and turned south onto Montana 56.

The FBI plane kept tabs on the brown roof below as it wound up into the high country. It seemed like the exact sort of spot Pierce would select as a hideout. The Land Cruiser hit a dirt road and kept ascending into the deepest part of the woods, until it reached a point high above Troy. It stopped at the last house on the road, under a canopy of pines.

Thinking they had located Pierce's safehouse, about eight FBI agents rendezvoused at the airstrip in Libby, where Fallin landed in the spotter plane. Out on the tarmac, Manis approached his boss and again advocated a quick strike to take Pierce down. The FBI had enough men on the scene to do it, he argued.

But Fallin overruled him. He didn't want to compromise the covert operation and ruin weeks of investigation by taking Pierce prematurely. The potential gain from following him, gathering more evidence about the larger conspiracy, was greater than from popping Pierce here and now on the two-year counterfeiting sentence. Instead, Fallin ordered his agents to surround the house high on the mountaintop and keep the suspects under close watch.

It was near evening when the agents set up along the roads leading to the hideaway. Manis sat in a car with Joe Venkus, who had recently moved to Coeur d'Alene to join the case after closing the Lewiston, Idaho, FBI office. They and the agents stationed elsewhere around the forest settled in to spend a cold night in their cars.

The wait was in vain. Pierce had already slipped through their grasp. While the agents had their argument at the Libby airstrip, Pierce and Tate were well on their way over the Cabinet Mountains, headed south toward the Clark Fork Valley and eventually to Salmon, Idaho, unfettered by a police tail.

Only a thousand people lived in and around Troy. The odds were astronomical that there would be two brown Land Cruisers in the supermarket parking lot, leaving at the same time. But that was what happened. And when Tate pulled out, the pilot had followed the wrong one.

Tate stopped when he saw a pay phone near Thompson Falls so Pierce could call Julie in Salmon. "Tell everybody to get prepared to leave," he said. "We might have to leave within hours." Julie, pregnant and starting to show it prominently, marshaled the other families. Pierce got back to Salmon very late.

As the sun began to light the mountainsides in Troy the next morning, Manis and Venkus were told to approach the house carefully and see who was there. The two veteran agents crawled quietly through the forest and separated when they neared the house. Reaching a window from which he could peer into the kitchen,

Manis slowly edged his face to the side of the glass.

His eyes nearly bugged out of his head when his gaze landed on a woman in a nurse's uniform, cheerily cooking breakfast at her stove. It wasn't until then that the FBI realized it had followed the wrong car. The woman never found out that Uncle Sam had surrounded her house that night.

That same morning, 320 miles away in Salmon, Pierce gathered his soldiers and told them drastic changes were necessary.

"We have to adjust psychologically," he lectured them. "Our lifestyle has to change. Instead of dragging around our possessions like gypsies, we need to get rid of them. This stuff could end up hanging us. Let's cut it down to nothing.

"Being successful," he said, "is more important than possessions."

ANDY ANDERSON WAS a former California cop who relocated to Idaho so he could slow down and prolong his life. But when Wayne Manis moved his investigation to Sandpoint, he called Police Chief Bill Keise and said he wanted Keise's best man to work with him. Keise assigned Anderson, his top police detective. It wasn't long before Anderson began to worry again about his pace and his safety.

Anderson knew Gary Yarbrough was a suspect in the robbery at Schooney's truck stop. Anderson was also naturally wary of the Aryan Nations people, figuring if they were after Jews and blacks, they'd come after him next.

Anderson called himself a Jack-Mormon. That's a baptized Latter Day Saint who, unlike straight-line Mormons, enjoys his smokes and takes a drink once in a while. If his wife would just say the word, he'd be a polygamist too.

One day shortly after Manis set up the stakeout of Gary Yarbrough's house, Anderson parked at Bonner Mall and walked toward the secret command post when a motorcycle roared up behind him. It was Yarbrough.

Yarbrough skidded to a stop next to Anderson's unmarked police car—which, of course, looked exactly like an unmarked police car—and closely inspected the inside before speeding off. Anderson could only shake his head in dismay.

Yarbrough had been aware of the surveillance for some time and was turning the FBI's work into a cat-and-mouse game. He busily amassed home addresses of local police and agents. On one occasion, as agents followed him at high speed down U.S. 95, Yarbrough suddenly pulled off and maneuvered behind the agents to begin following them. When the car pulled off in a gravel lot, Yarbrough doubled back and began roaring in circles, doing doughnuts in the gravel with his bike.

It was hard to miss the FBI's presence in Sandpoint. Agents turned the resort village into Club Fed. By the end of September, forty agents were working on the case. The third floor of the post office in Coeur d'Alene was turned into a war room. A computer kept track of all leads, and a teletype spewed out reams of dispatches with information from other field offices.

The work consisted mainly of tailing the suspects to see where they would lead. At times it had a circus atmosphere. Surveillance teams from Spokane, in a different FBI district, sometimes entered Idaho while tailing Parmenter, Dye, or one of the others. Those agents bumped into crews out of Butte following Yarbrough, and didn't know whether to say hello or pass like strangers.

In addition, it happened that the area around Sandpoint was a thriving clearinghouse for illegal drugs. So when all the agents descended on the town on Lake Pend Oreille, their presence was quickly noted by the local druggies. Word spread that the Drug Enforcement Administration was setting up a sting operation, which made the druggies paranoid. A lot of illegal drugs were flushed down johns in Sandpoint that fall. But the paranoia also became dangerous.

One night an FBI agent returning to his motel room was jumped in the parking lot by a local drug dealer, who brandished a gun and demanded to know what was going on. Other agents rushed in, dribbling the bewildered assailant around the lot for a few minutes before turning him over to the Sandpoint police. Anderson took the dealer aside and warned him not to say another word about it.

"You think they're here to watch you?" he belittled the dealer. "Boy, this is way above little pukes like you. You're dealing with something you have no business in. You just get out of here and keep your mouth shut."

Anderson was one of several local cops trusted by the FBI, which has a history of milking local cops for information then tossing them aside like peons when it's glory time. This one-way street feeds the disdain and mistrust local cops often feel for the FBI. But Manis was different. He and the other agents who joined the accelerating case were ex-officers and military vets who were streetwise and knew how to get results. Once the FBI assembled a good network of locals, it clamped a lid of secrecy on them. Manis was wary of the local cops, some of whom he feared could by Aryan Nations sympathizers themselves.

But some of what Anderson saw troubled him. Manis called him late at night on September 26 to accompany agents on a search of the locker at 3Js Mini-Storage out on Baldy Road, where they had followed Yarbrough one day. Anderson had executed search warrants before, but not often at 1 A.M. It looked like a black-bag operation to him. The agents picked the lock on number 137 and entered with their flashlights. They went through the items inside, which included weapons and explosives as well as medical items for Yarbrough's gravely ill daughter.

The agents made note of everything inside but, oddly enough, didn't take a single thing, not a rifle, not a grenade, not a bullet. They made sure everything was back where they found it and carefully closed the locker door without posting the customary copy of the warrant on the premises or even notifying the storage yard owner that they had been there.

It turned out that Manis had persuaded a federal magistrate in Coeur d'Alene to sign a search warrant at 6 P.M. that specifically allowed the surreptitious nighttime entry and permitted Manis to depart without leaving a copy.

But Yarbrough already knew about the surveillance and by mid-September had had enough. He rented a secluded mountain home 12 miles north of Sandpoint, in the hamlet of Samuels, Idaho. As he hauled his belongings up into the timber, the FBI could only follow by plane and get a general idea of where the house was.

Anderson was sitting at the FBI command post back in Sandpoint, listening to the pilot describe the site.

"He's turning into a clearing off this side road," the pilot radioed. "It's a modern, natural wood house with a large deck, loft windows facing the front, double sky-lights and a basketball hoop to the side."

"Hey!" Anderson, sitting up straight, said to the agents. He couldn't believe the coincidence. "I know that house! I was in there two months ago on a marijuana bust!" By chance, Yarbrough had rented a house where a Califor-nia fugitive had set up a pot farm. Anderson had helped take out marijuana plants growing there. Driving quickly to his office, Anderson got his file, which included pho-tos and an interior floor plan. When the pilot returned, Anderson showed him his photos of the house. The pilot confirmed that it was the one Yarbrough was occupying.

It couldn't have been more strategically placed. The house was screened from Pack River Road by huge pines. Agents had to hike into the thicket to keep an eye on Yarbrough. It was difficult to be inconspicuous under the circumstances.

Manis tried to get close once. He had an agent drive him down the dirt road called A Street, through a canyon of pines, that went past the rear of the property. Jumping out of the car near Yarbrough's back driveway, he eased on foot past a small sawmill on the rear of the land. Suddenly the fender of Yarbrough's truck came into view ahead on a bend in the trail. Manis dived into the brush and froze while Yarbrough passed within 5 feet of him. There had to be a better way.

"AND THEY HAVE TO look like this, with the battle ax set out above the shield," Jean Craig said to the manager at Gem State Crystals. She had a diagram on paper of a medallion she wanted struck for neck pendants.

Christopher Johnston, standing behind the counter of his shop in a restored old building near South 8th and Myrtle in Boise, thought it was more than slightly odd. The diagram showed a shield with a Roman Cross. The ancient Saxon word "Fyrdung" was to be inscribed on the cross. The battle ax was faced right. The hardest part was a scroll waving in an arc above the shield, from which the chain would be mounted. On the scroll were to be the Gaelic words: "IS TUSA MO THUA CHATHA AGUS MO CHALSCE COGAIDH." It means, "Ye be my battle ax and my weapons of war."

Then, across the shield's crest, were two German words: "BRUDERS SCHWEIGEN."

The pendants, Craig told him, were for a group that recreated medieval pageants, the Society for Creative Anachronism. Johnston shook his head and filled out the order sheet.

"Now I want forty-two of them," Craig reminded him. "Make forty out of silver, and gold-plate the crosses. But the other two make out of sterling silver with 10-karat gold crosses. The gold ones are for our leader," she added proudly. Jean Craig loved Bob Mathews and was enormously proud to be the grandmother-to-be of his first natural child. He embodied everything she envisioned in a Nordic god, and when she read the ancient runes like a soothsayer, it was with every ounce of devotion that she tried to determine whether the magic charms of the Norse gods would keep him safe. And indeed they had in Seattle, in Denver, and in Ukiah.

By mid-September, Bob had formulated the new structure for his group along the lines spelled out in Boise. With the structure came a formal name.

The medallions were symbolic of that and of the name Mathews chose. For a year, the group had had no name. With its fitful start, people dropping in and out, unsure of its purpose or direction, choosing a name seemed the least pressing task. Then when it became flush with success, things were happening too quickly to bother. The members most often called the gang "the company," as in "being on company business." Sometimes they called it "the Organization," the name of the guerrilla army in *The Turner Diaries*. Other times, it was "the Order," the name of the Inner Circle that oversaw the Organization in the book.

But Mathews was inspired to give the group a German name, remembering one of the books Bill Soderquist stored on the shelves in the barracks. It was a history of Hitler's Waffen SS titled *Wenn Alle Bruder Schweigen*, from a German soldier's poem penned 170 years earlier by Max von Schenkendorf, containing the line: *"Wenn alle Bruder schweigen und salchen Gotzen traun, wir woll'n das Wort nicht brechen."* It meant: "When all our brothers are silent and trust in false idols, we will not break our word."

So the name of Mathews's group became "Bruders Schweigen."

He translated it "The Silent Brotherhood." In part, it was wishful thinking.

But mostly, Mathews could take stock on the last weekend of September 1984 and conclude that he was organized enough to begin planning the terrorist strikes he hoped would touch off the beginning of the end for ZOG. Most of his staff members were energetically pursuing their appointed tasks, with Mathews, Carlos the Coordinator, at the center of it all.

Scutari was becoming Mathews's closest confidant. The rugged, worldly Scutari was beginning to feel genuine affection for Mathews. As he worked with him, he saw Mathews as more than a believer in the super-patriotic cause. He saw Mathews as an entirely unselfish, dedicated worker for the racist cause. Bob's mind was always abuzz with plots and subplots, working out minute details. When they traveled together, trying to recruit kinsmen, the routine was to be up by 8 A. M., eat breakfast, and hit the road, day after day. Scutari was surprised at the receptive audiences they often found. While he realized how deeply he'd gotten involved in criminal activity in just four months, he had no regrets.

Duey, the intellectual indoctrinator, was getting his trailer at Bluecreek prepared for his school and looking forward to his first two subjects, Canadians who were members of the Western Guard ultra-right group.

Merki, the consummate counterfeiter, turned from phony money to phony ID. He mocked up a driver's license from Costa Rica and ran off duplicates. He told anybody who wanted one to run down to the K-mart photo booth and bring back a picture. He also began work on a counterfeit ID for the National Security Agency.

David Lane, meanwhile, wanted Merki to print a Bruders Schweigen recruiting poster. It was to have photos of white children and a mixed-race couple, with the caption: "An opportunity to take back your woman."

Responsibility for the message center was put in the hands of a newcomer, a Klan friend of Randy Evans named Frank Lee Silva, twenty-six. It was on Silva's land in the San Fernando Valley that the controversial cross-lighting, leading to Pastor Butler's arrest, had taken place. Silva moved into the Ona Street house in Boise that Evans had abandoned when he joined Pierce's cell. Staffing the message center meant being at the nucleus of the white underground.

Yarbrough was spending most of his time near his ill daughter, but Mathews wanted him on his assassinations squad. Mathews was panning to start tailing Morris Dees, the attorney who headed the Southern Poverty Law Center in Montgomery. Berg had been chosen over Dees as the first victim, but now it was to be Dees's turn. The preliminary plan called for kidnapping Dees, interrogating him, then flaying him—peeling his skin from his body—before killing him.

McBrearty set up a hotline for anyone arrested. On September 17 he rented an office in Tulsa, Oklahoma, and installed an answering machine. It was called the Beartrap system. A member in trouble with the law would call the Beartrap number, leave a message, then wait as long as it took for the group to get help.

Pierce, the nomad of the Northwest, was staying one jump ahead of Manis's men while planning the next Brink's heist. He hurriedly left Salmon with his cadre and inadvertently put the FBI a step behind. They piled all their furniture into two of the rented houses and asked a man from whom Pierce had purchased a $2,000 jet boat to donate all of it to the needy. Then he returned the jet boat to the man without asking for a refund. But the man was startled by all the possessions that had been abandoned and on September 17 notified the police of his suspicions.

Pierce's tribe wandered through the belly of the western plateau, staying only a few days in any place. First it was Pocatello, Idaho, then Ogden, Utah. On September 26, Pierce drove to Grand Junction, Colorado, and used his fake Costa Rican license to take the Colorado driving test. He got a phony license, then scouted the lonely Grand Mesa area for safe houses before returning to the Salt Lake area.

Parmenter, the liaison with the guerrillas-to-be, took a vacation back East with Janice, still hopeful of saving his marriage while saving the white race.

Rader, the dog meat connoisseur, was among the busiest of Mathews's staffers. After buying expensive furniture for his house in Ione, he began to outfit the training camp with similar extravagance. In September alone, United Parcel Service made thirty-one deliveries of paramilitary gear Rader ordered from Mountain Man Supply.

Rader's camp rules were that there would be two-week shifts, three men on and three men off. There would be no drinking at bars within a 50-mile radius, and the men would carry no concealed weapons while they were commuting to and from camp. The trainees kept busy cutting trails and digging foxholes, erecting the big tents, building a storage shed, and arranging a lookout perch in a large tree that had a sweeping view of the main road as it came out of the trees across Big Meadows. While they were off, Dye and Zaengle found rental houses in Spokane. Dye also found a girlfriend, Tiffany, a prostitute he met in a brothel in Wallace, Idaho. She moved into his house in Spokane.

When Rader returned to the training camp from a buying trip to the Soldier of Fortune convention at Las Vegas's Sahara Hotel on September 25, Kemp told him that Soderquist, Dye, and Nash had gone to a nearby bar and gotten drunk. Rader was angered that the men continued to drink heavily in defiance of directives. They also violated rules by drinking in a location close enough to compromise the training camp. Rader resolved to take it up with Mathews.

It was frustrating for Rader to make serious plans for guerrilla training, then be stuck with men who didn't seem to be aware of just how serious the Silent Brotherhood was going to be. He picked up Ardie McBrearty at the Spokane airport a few days later and, using a microcassette recorder Ardie handed him, taped a message for Mathews, seeking his advice on handling the drinking problem.

Rader was most concerned with Soderquist, who had already received a warning to curb his substance abuse habits. "As concerning the other two men," he relayed to Mathews, "I will put them on probation as was Bill before he blew his chance."

Mathews later returned a tape with his response, agreeing with Rader's suggestion that violators be confined to camp.

"The abuse of alcohol is indeed a potential compromise not only to the base but to the entire Order," Mathews said on the tape. "And it's unfortunate that you've been saddled with three or four men who seem to have a weakness for this. I'm trying desperately to get you some new recruits."

ON THE WEEKEND of September 29, several events drew a major portion of the gang to Boise. First, several recruits were to receive their voice tests. McBrearty would also give the tests to some regular members he'd missed. Finally, Pierce had a security matter he wanted to clear up.

Mathews first went to the Holiday Inn near the Boise airport. McBrearty gave the voice tests there to two Alabama Klansmen who came at Mathews's invitation to check out the group, which they were told was part of a right-wing unity drive. One was William Riccio, twenty-eight, an organizer for the Knights of the Ku Klux Klan who had done prison time for a weapons offense in 1979. He had met Mathews at the 1983 Aryan World Congress in Hayden Lake. The other was Michael Stanley Norris, a follower of the Knights leader Don Black of Tuscumbia, Alabama.

Norris and Black were players in one of the more bizarre right-wing affairs of the decade. On the night of April 27, 1981, at a marina along the wooded north shore of Lake Pontchartrain near Slidell, Louisiana, federal agents swooped down on ten men about to board a boat bound for the tiny, impoverished Caribbean island nation of Dominica, 2,000 miles away. On the boat were weapons, including machine guns and explosives. Among the group were two Canadian right-wingers, a former Kansas police chief, and assorted Klansmen, including Black, at the time Imperial Wizard of the large Knights faction.

Dominica, only 29 by 16 miles with seven thousand

inhabitants, had a moderate government opposed by some members of the small army still loyal to the imprisoned former Prime Minister, Patrick John.

The ten mercenaries, some believing they had been hired to fight communism, were to slip ashore at Roseau, the capital, attack the island's police station, and depose Prime Minister Mary Eugenia Charles. Patrick John, a black man who had led Dominica to independence from Great Britain, allegedly offered the mercenaries tax-free concessions to the island's resources in return for their help.

Seven of the ten pleaded guilty. Three went to trial. Norris was acquitted. The other two, including Black, were convicted of violating the Neutrality Act.

The FBI's code name for the investigation was "Bayou of Pigs."

After Norris and Riccio took their tests, Mathews went to Merki's house on Greenbrier Drive, where three others waited. They were Merki, who had missed the earlier tests, Frank Silva, and Dennis Schlueter, Lane's and Merki's friend from Fort Collins, Colorado, who attended the Laporte Identity church. Schlueter had lost his guard's job in August after pleading guilty to welfare fraud. He had to hurry back to serve a twenty-day term in the Larimer County Jail on October 1. After that, he told Mathews, he would join the underground. He had nothing else.

McBrearty administered the voice tests in the toy room in Merki's basement. He later ran the test on Pierce's new people, Dwayne Butler, his son Mike, and Jim Wallington. Everybody passed. They always did, it seemed.

The members gathered at Jean Craig's 10th Street house, where the Ukiah loot had been counted, for a formal swearing-in ceremony. Mathews extended invitations to Norris, Riccio, and Schlueter, as well as Pierce's people. All accepted but Riccio, who still harbored doubts that the entire setup wasn't a sting operation. He had heard the same rumors about Mathews working with the FBI that had made Glenn Miller antsy. Miller had been salved with money. Riccio got a similar offer of $30,000 to set up a print shop in Birmingham.

But Riccio was still on probation from his weapons

conviction. He told Mathews he didn't think he could go underground just yet. Norris, however, accepted with one condition. He had a store in Alabama he had to sell first. He expected that would take several weeks, then he'd enroll in the Aryan Academy.

Schlueter was earmarked to replace Silva at the message center, something the unemployed man said he'd accept right after his three weeks in jail was up.

The men then held hands, as they had in the barracks a year earlier. This time they represented a much wider circle, arching through Bob Miles's organization in Michigan, the white trash neighborhoods of Philadelphia, the heart of Dixie, and the eclectic West Coast, where white racist programming ran on community cable TV. The oath Mathews read had changed very little from that first small meeting in the barracks, in the dark forest of Pend Oreille County.

Then came the most serious matter that was pending.

Randy Evans had seen an attorney in California over a worker's compensation claim stemming from an injury he had received working for a garbage company. In the office, he had overheard a secretary mention that "Dan Bauer" was on the phone. Although there didn't seem the remotest possibility of a connection between that phone call in teeming Southern California and Dan Bauer of Coeur d'Alene, who had been mysteriously aloof since winter, Evans mentioned the coincidence to Pierce.

Pierce was already annoyed with Bauer, who was responsible for his being arrested back in Union Gap, Washington, with phony fifty-dollar bills. When Gary Yarbrough returned to the panhandle from Boise after splitting the Ukiah loot in July, he turned over $110,000 to Bauer, $10,000 of it salary and the rest as a donation to Aryan Nations. But Pastor Butler turned down the money, and Pierce wanted an accounting from Bauer for it. Bauer proposed spending it on a project known around the Silent Brotherhood as "Reliance."

The Inner Circle held a meeting with Bauer in Duey's room at the Boisean Hotel, a funky little restored hostelry downtown.

Once on the carpet, Bauer gave a vigorous defense of the Reliance project. It turned out to be Mathews's own version of a Pentagon defense contracting boondoggle. Bauer said he knew two scientists who had been working on laser-beam and microwave weapons. The scientists' political leanings were sharply right, and Bauer proposed putting them on a Silent Brotherhood research grant to develop the weapons for the fight against ZOG.

Pierce argued with Mathews over the wasteful spending. Bauer countered by proposing a business front for the researchers, providing them with living expenses, false identification, and relocation money while they worked on the weapons. Pierce was outnumbered four to one. The Inner Circle thought it was a good idea.

When Bauer was finished, McBrearty ran him over the lie box and pronounced that he had passed. "Are you satisfied now, Brigham?" Mathews asked Pierce with complete faith in the voice stress analyzer.

"Frankly, Bob, I'm not," Pierce replied. "I don't think that test is effective at all. I don't like it, but I guess I'm outvoted."

High-powered microwave weapons in fact are under development in the United States and the Soviet Union. The weapons convert kinetic energy in electron beams into electromagnetic energy of microwave beams. But Bauer's contact turned out to be a writer capable of weaving a plausible story about these weapons of the future.

Pierce took his cadre back on the road, this time to the Klamath Mountains of Oregon. Mathews headed for Laramie, where his child was due on October 12. Duey returned to Bluecreek to prepare indoctrination material for his school. Parmenter went to the training camp to help cut wood for the cold season. Yarbrough went home to his ill daughter, intending to be on his own.

Robert and Sharon Merki took a short vacation to Jackson Hole and several other places and prepared for one of Identity's holy times, the Feast of Tabernacles.

THE PENNSYLVANIA LOTTERY paid off a jackpot for the FBI two days later. It was Monday, October 1. Tom Martinez sat in the hallway of the U.S. District Courthouse, in Philadelphia's Independence Hall neighborhood, waiting for his trial to start. He was near panic. Down the hall he saw the beer store owner waiting to go in and testify about Tom's two appearances at the store to buy lottery tickets with funny money.

Sue Martinez supported Tom, not with words but with her silent presence. She knew her husband was going through an inner terror she couldn't touch. She felt that when the crunch came, Tom would break like a dam, and everything he knew would come out in an unstoppable torrent.

Perry de Marco, Tom's attorney, had had a deadly serious discussion with him the day before, a sort of last talk before the trial. De Marco had been trying without success to get his client to open up. Now he had more bad news.

"Tom, there's a possibility they can really stick you with this," de Marco had told Martinez in his office. "They got your phone records, and you've called persons suspected of major counterfeiting activity out West. But more significantly, the FBI thinks your friends have been involved in robberies of armored cars in California and Washington.

"This suddenly has gotten a whole lot bigger, Tom."

Martinez had been hiding this terrible knowledge for months in order to protect his family and himself. But when de Marco said the government already had him tied to the incredible case the FBI was assembling out West, his wall of resistance crumbled.

Martinez was a street-corner racist who, when pushed to the limit, realized it wasn't truly in him. He wanted his family above all things. That's what the struggle was supposed to be about. But then he found that the struggle would cost him all of it.

He called de Marco over to the bench outside the courtroom Monday morning and asked him to summon the prosecutor, Assistant U.S. Attorney Bucky Mansuy.

Martinez wanted to talk. He desperately needed to talk.

Chapter 9

Judas Arrives on American Airlines

Across the dark, dry plains, Marie Craig looked out into the starry skies from the windows of the red-and-white Trailways bus. Spry for a septuagenarian, the petite gray-haired woman nevertheless found the trip tiring. She had watched the sun set over the treeless horizon from her window as the concrete of Interstate 80 rolled beneath her. The back road from Wilsonville to North Platte, Nebraska, covered 110 miles of grassland. Then it was 272 miles more to Laramie.

But it was worth it to Marie. A new life was coming. She was invited to attend the birth of her great-grandchild, Zillah's baby. It was Tuesday, October 2, 1984, one day after Tom Martinez broke down in Philadelphia, and Marie Craig wasn't the only one headed for Laramie that day. Martinez told the FBI that Mathews planned to attend the birth of his first natural child, which would be in Laramie. The FBI hadn't seen Mathews in months and wanted to pick up his tail.

Bob waited at the bus station until very late and greeted Marie with an embrace and a kiss on her soft cheek.

About 2 A.M., Zillah felt her water break. She was nine days early, but it was okay now that her grandma and Bob were there. She woke Bob to tell him. Early in the morning, Bob went into the kitchen. Marie was at the breakfast table.

"Well, she's in labor," Bob told her, grinning widely with anticipation.

"Thank God I made it here in time!" Marie said.

Zillah planned a natural home birth. Her boys would be there, her grandma and Bob, and they would take photographs as well. Two midwives arrived around 1 P.M., saw that Zillah was progressing slowly, then left for a few hours. Bob went out to run errands while Zillah got up and walked around the house to spur the labor.

When Bob returned about 4:00 the midwives were sitting on the front porch. He went to the kitchen, quartered several apples, and brought them outside on a plate for the two women. They talked about children and family for a while, then Bob went into the bedroom to see how Zillah was feeling. He saw his lover reclining on their brass-posted bed, and she reached for him to join her.

"Once we're calmed down from all this and you're well enough," Bob told her, "I've got it set for us to move. We're finally going to be like a real family." He pulled out some snapshots of a farmhouse near Boise and showed them to her. As she looked over the pictures and imagined life there with Bob, there was a knock on the door, and soon a delivery man brought in a bouquet of flowers.

"Who could that be from?" Bob asked coyly, but Zillah smiled. She knew Bob had done it. Bob always planned everything to the last detail.

Zillah started much stronger labor about 6 P.M., while Bob was out fetching a fast-food dinner. By the time he returned, she was calling for him to help with her back labor. Bob ran to the bedroom.

He sat on the bed while Dustin and Caleb watched. It was just before 7 P.M. when Bob watched with intense anticipation as the baby's head first appeared, then its shoulders. As the midwives helped the baby slip out of the womb and into the world, there was only one thing Bob wanted to know.

The baby was a girl.

Bob tried to disguise the disappointment in his eyes, but that was something he could never do. He had fervently wanted a son. Zillah saw the look on her lover's face and resolved not to address it now, not to let anything spoil the moment. The midwives handed the girl to Zillah, who brought the child to her breast.

"Your name," Zillah told the tiny bundle, "is Emerant."

Late that night, Bob climbed into bed and settled with his back to Zillah. Just give him room, Zillah thought. He'll grow to love her just as he would have loved a son, just as he loved Clint, she thought as she fell asleep. In the middle of the night, Zillah gathered Emerant from her cradle into their bed and nursed her a bit, then let the baby sleep between her and Bob.

The next thing Zillah knew, the room was light and the bed was bouncing. Still groggy, she was tempted to reach over with her foot and give Bob a shove to get him to stop shaking. Then she realized what he was doing.

Bob was on the edge of the bed holding Emerant, calling her "little princess" and rocking her so that the bed was bouncing. Zillah fought her initial urge and stayed quiet while Bob played with his daughter for ten more minutes. Afterward, Bob showered and dressed, then left the house about 11 A.M. for his morning schedule of errands and phone calls.

Zillah was nursing Emerant in the bedroom when Bob burst through the front door about noon.

"I've got to get out of here!" he yelled. "I'm under surveillance!"

The words pierced Zillah like a knife. She knew what it meant, but her mind rebelled. Then Bob flew into the bedroom and grabbed his suitcase.

"I'm being watched, Zillah! They found me! I was calling Ken Loff to check in, and when I looked across the way I saw a ZOG agent," Bob frantically recounted as he began throwing his clothes into the bag. "He had a camera!"

"Where are you going to go?" Zillah asked, clutching Emerant as she trailed Bob around the bedroom. He gathered his money and his papers, and loaded his gun.

"I don't know yet, Zillah, I don't know! I'll send for you, okay?"

"What will I do, Bob? What about the baby?" Zillah started to cry.

"Just stay here and wait!" Bob replied. "Just wait until you hear from me."

Grandma Craig took Emerant while Bob finished packing, so Zillah could say goodbye. Bob ran the suitcase to his car, then returned to the house.

"Zillah, I'll call as soon as I can," he said, embracing her. "I love you." They kissed briefly. Then Bob turned to Emerant, in Marie's arms, and leaned over to kiss her. "Goodbye, little princess," he said to Emerant, who barely opened her eyes. "I'm going out to make this world a better place for you."

As Bob darted down the walk, Zillah watched out the window and turned to Marie. "Oh, Grandma!," she moaned. "I'm never going to see him again." Marie Craig put her arm around her granddaughter's shoulder.

Just then Bob turned and bolted back to the house.

"Zillah!" he called. "I need you! Put on my jacket and my dad's old hat I got in the closet, and get in your car. I think the agents are out there. I want you to draw them off. Just drive around for about twenty minutes."

Sobbing, Zillah retrieved Bob's jacket and Johnny Mathews's hat from a closet. She put on the jacket over her maternity clothes, kissed Bob again, and walked to her car as quickly as her condition would allow. Zillah was shaking with fright as she put the keys in the ignition. The noon sun made it obvious the figure was not Bob Mathews. Yet when she drove off, an FBI car started after her.

Bob watched her go, then hurried to his car and left in the other direction. At Albertson's supermarket, he turned south on 3d Street before the FBI tail caught up. Bob bypassed the first freeway ramp and doubled back on 3d Street going north. He lost the tail going around the Albany County Courthouse, then roared toward the Interstate 80 ramp westbound toward Rawlins, 100 miles away.

Mathews thought he was clear, but about 15 miles out of Laramie he looked up and noticed a small plane keeping pace with him. "Damn," he thought. "The bastards must have had a plane on standby at the airport." Soon the car that had followed him in Laramie was in Mathews's rearview mirror.

Exits from the interstate in Wyoming are few and far between. Mathews had driven another 45 miles when he noticed a low bank of storm clouds gathering over the Snowy Range to the south. He decided to head for the hills and hole up. If there was to be a firefight with ZOG, he would make it a good one.

Mathews yanked his car off I-80 at the Elk Mountain exit onto a dirt road that went up the Medicine Bow River. He hit the clouds about 7,000 feet and the FBI lost him in the fog. He continued into the national forest, ending up in the tiny settlement of Encampment, Wyoming, where he stayed the next few days at a cabin owned by a friend.

Two days later, on Saturday, Sharon Merki called Zillah. Bob had contacted Sharon in Boise and wanted her to retrieve $10,000 he had left behind in his haste. Zillah rounded up the cash and stuffed it into the lining of a cloth baby carrier, the type that straps around the chest and holds the baby in front. Then she took the kids and Marie to a truck stop diner on the highway outside town.

The FBI tagged along, as the agents had since Thursday. But Mathews's plan hinged on the agents' unawareness that Sharon Merki was part of the scheme.

Sharon arrived and sat away from Zillah, who knew her from attending the Laporte church. After a few minutes, Sharon walked into the women's restroom. Zillah waited, figuring if she followed too closely the agents would take notice of Sharon. Finally Zillah got up and, as if to change the baby, went into the women's room with Emerant in the carrier. Before exchanging the money, Sharon told Zillah that Bob was hiding at Encampment and that he would send for her and the children as soon as he could figure out a safe way to spirit them out of Laramie.

Zillah pulled the cash out of the carrier's lining and handed it to Sharon, then rejoined her family. Sharon waited before leaving the restroom.

TOM MARTINEZ WASN'T the only associate of the Silent Brotherhood who was not so silent. Billy Soderquist, the National Alliance *wunderkind* and now an armed robber, had a girlfriend back in Salinas in whom he couldn't resist confiding.

It turned out that Soderquist's high school friend, Richie Kemp, had recruited a mutual friend from Salinas, Rick Steinbach. Steinbach already had a code name, Gigolo, and it was being arranged for him to start at half-salary as a recruit.

Mathews learned that Steinbach already knew something about his "action group." It appeared that Soderquist's girlfriend knew Steinbach too, and she had blabbed to him tht she was thinking of turning Billy and his friends over to the cops for the hefty reward money the insurance company for Brink's was offering.

Mathews, who had made it to a truck stop motel in Boise, called for a group meeting quickly to discuss these serious security matters—the surveillances and Soderquist's talking. The evening before October 11, most of the lieutenants in the Silent Brotherhood converged on Boise. Scutari had his wife, Michele, and their daughter Danielle, who had flown to Kalispell to live with Richard.

The next morning the group assembled at the 10th Street house of Jean Craig, who was running an errand for Bob. Duey, Merki, Silva, and Yarbrough were there in addition to several with whom Mathews had dinner the night before: Rader, Scutari, Parmenter, and McBrearty. All of the leaders were there except Pierce.

Mathews picked up a stack of papers and began to distribute them. Several of the leaders got copies to be distributed to their underlings. The six-page handouts were headed with the words "Bruders Schweigen Staff."

"That is the name for our organization, kinsmen," Mathews told the men. "It means 'Silent Brotherhood.' We have gone without a name long enough. This is what we are now. I hope that this name will become known throughout our racialist movement as the group that began the second American Revolution."

Scutari, who was now Mathews's closest adviser, said it didn't bother him whether they even had a name. "Names aren't important, actions are," he told Bob. "I don't care if we don't have a name. I'd just as soon we not be known at all."

Mathews walked them through the six pages, outlining the duties he expected his staff to fulfill. Mathews was in charge of overall coordination, recruitment, and liaison with "civil administrators," the racist leaders Mathews planned to have take charge of government once the revolution toppled the ZOG regime. He had them listed by code name, all united under him as he long had dreamed it would be. Some of those leaders had no idea Mathews was counting on them.

Mathews, code-named Carlos, was at the top. The country was divided into six regions. "Fox," the code name of the Michigan racist leader Bob Miles, was listed as the key civilian through which the other regions would report to Mathews. Miles was to be responsible for the Midwest district. Parmenter, code name Sandals, was listed as civil administrator for the Pacific Northwest. Under Miles were listed the following civilian authorities: "Bear," code name for Tom Metzger of the Fallbrook, California–based White Aryan Resistance, the West Coast; "Lone Star," Louis Beam's code name, the Western district; "Rounder," Frazier Glenn Miller of North Carolina's Knights, Southern and Southeastern United States; and "Eagle," William Pierce of the National Alliance, Northeastern United States.

The duties of staff members were less grandiose.

"Every staff member," Mathews said, "must see that each man in his command has memorized the Beartrap number and the current message center number, and check them periodically to see that they know it.

"Every staff member must make sure each man in his command has a minimum of $500 cash on his body at all times," Mathews continued. "And every staff member is responsible for keeping up the morale of his men at such a level that if they are separated from their units, they will continue to function and conduct themselves as true warriors on the attack!

"If you don't have any messages to leave, then don't call the message center," he continued. "We've had a lot of trouble with pay phones lately and we don't want to compromise the center. But if you do have a message for someone, call the center between 4 and 5 P.M., Mountain Standard Time. Then I will call right at 5, and between 5 and 6 Mountain Time I will call each staff member.

"Each of you *will be there* to receive my call, or have someone designated. We will have daily communications this way!"

On the sixth page, Mathews had a roster of the Silent Brotherhood, forty-two coded names. The last eleven were prospective members. The roster didn't include numerous "legals" who were assisting the gang in one way or another, some aware of the Silent Brotherhood's nature, others in complete ignorance of it. Each person was assigned a code number for message center purposes.

The message "have 1 contact 27" would mean "have
Carlos call Calvin," or "Mathews should call Randy
Evans."

Mathews's trusting soul was in evidence again. Tom
Martinez's code name, "Spider," was listed as a member,
although he hadn't taken the oath. Mathews already considered him a member, since Martinez had passed counterfeit money for the gang. Besides, Mathews was sure
he'd get him to run rather than go to prison.

McBrearty then explained the Beartrap system he'd set
up in Tulsa. He paid a retainer to a lawyer from Georgia
to come to the legal aid of anybody who was arrested.
The lawyer was an example of the Silent Brotherhood's
"legals."

Then McBrearty demonstrated how members should
code their phone lists. Each of the three components of
the phone number, including area code, was treated as a
unit. First, the numbers were altered one up, one down,
one up. Then the last digit in each of the three groups
was placed first. To decode, a member would retranspose
the first digit in all three groupings, then convert down,
up, down.

For example, the message center number in Boise was
208–343–2281. Using the up-down-up method, it became
399–434–3190. The last digit in each grouping then was
placed first, so the entire coded number looked like this:
939–443–0319.

The system then went on to code the days of the week
with even numbers. Sunday became 2, Monday 4, and so
on to Saturday, which was 14. Hours of the day were
assigned odd numbers. The nation's four continental time
zones were assigned numbers 1 through 4, west to east.

Rader sometimes used a pay phone outside 410 Main
Street in Ione with the number 509–442–9902. If Rader
wanted McBrearty to call him there on Wednesday, 6
P.M. Pacific time, the message would look like this: "Have
24 (McBrearty's code number) call 22 (Rader's code) at
871 (eight was Wednesday, seven was 6 P.M., one was
Pacific time zone), 069–353–1081."

It was a wonder anybody could remember it.

Rader said he'd have trouble checking in every day,
since he was working at the training camp, but he planned

to handle communications through an FM radio system. He had ordered three radio towers and two base stations, one for Ione and the other for the camp near Priest Lake. A tower would go at each base, and Rader was looking for a mountaintop midway between the two to set up a repeater tower.

Just then, Mathews saw Jean Craig come up the short walk to the front door with a small box. "Here's what I've been waiting to show you all," he said with pride as he opened the door for Jean, who was returning from Gem State Crystals.

"I just have a couple, Carlos," Jean told Mathews. "The rest will be ready very soon, he told me." She handed Mathews the box, which he opened. Out of it he pulled a medallion attached to a loop of silver chain. It was a shield with a battle ax raised above it, and the scroll just as Mathews had pictured it.

Emblazoned across the shield was the name "BRUDERS SCHWEIGEN."

Mathews passed one around the group. They all admired the craftsmanship.

"This is a truly significant symbol for our group," Mathews glowed as the men passed it around. "Fyrdung! The army of the folk!"

But the most serious matter remained for discussion. What should the group do about Bill Soderquist? He couldn't shut his mouth and couldn't keep from sucking cocaine up his nose. Soderquist was already on probation for leaving Ukiah and holing up in Salinas; then he violated probation by leaving training camp with some others, getting drunk in town, and, worst of all, blabbing to his girlfriend. Mathews asked for opinions.

"Technically, if we went by the book," said Scutari, "Billy and his girlfriend would be killed. Is that what we want?" The prospect of executing Soderquist wasn't pleasing to any of them. His mother was already beginning to phone Loff's wife from California to inquire about her son.

"I think I'd want to find out more about what happened," Duey responded. "Let's get Billy's side of this."

"This is a very serious thing here," Mathews reminded them. "We'll get Billy and this Steinbach guy down here for a talk, and we'll decide then."

Rader and Parmenter, unable to stay for the next day's "hearing," prepared to go to the airport. "You know, Big Boy,' Mathews bragged to Rader, "we're having official robes made up for those in the Inner Circle." The men sometimes called Rader "Big Boy" after the restaurant chain, because of the dog he had eaten.

When Soderquist got to Boise the next day, he was called on the carpet before Mathews and Scutari. They told him sternly that this would be his last chance. Mathews fined him $ 15,000—half of his bonus from the Ukiah robbery—and confined him to the camp for three months.

KEN LOFF LOOKED over the Bruders Schweigen documents Rader brought back to Ione. This Silent Brotherhood stuff was news to him. Loff had never even heard the group called "the Order" before, and he was a founding member. To him it was "the company." This new structure and German name worried him. He wondered what had happened to the dedicated group of idealistic men with whom he had held hands just over a year before. Why did something he wanted so much to happen, the great struggle for survival of the race, now frighten him to death?

Loff was so disturbed, he took his Sient Brotherhood papers outside and burned them when no one was around. Yet Loff continued to work by Rader's side, equipping the Aryan Academy with the best their stolen money could buy—more ATVs, snowmobiles, generators, and video cameras for surveillance.

Jackie Lee Norton, Rader's training assistant, led the men at camp in constructing a large shed and shower facility, cutting firewood, and setting up tents, in addition to placing machine gun nests on the hillsides flanking Big Meadows. There were plans to rim the camp, more than 110 acres, with barbed wire and to install farm gates across the dirt road.

On Saturday, October 13, Parmenter visited Janice in Cheney. After leaving, he noticed a car seeming to follow him. He doubled back to Cheney, then headed into Spokane to George Zaengle's house, where he knew Jimmy Dye would be.

"Hey, Mister May!" Parmenter called to Dye. "Let's

go up the training camp. I think the FBI was following me and I need to leave my car and get outta here."

"Shit!" Dye said as he got his keys for his Land Cruiser, which used to be red and now was gray. "So you bring 'em right here? I already had to have this sucker painted once 'cause the ZOG saw me in it at Kemp's house!"

As they headed toward the Idaho line on Interstate 90, Parmenter turned in his seat and saw the same car behind them that he had seen in Cheney.

"Fuckin' A," Parmenter groused. "They're on us again!" Dye drove up back roads into the panhandle from Post Falls to Sandpoint, where they stopped and waited. Satisfied that they had ditched the FBI, they headed to Priest River, 22 miles west, then turned north on the road to Priest Lake. They were nearly to the cutoff to the training camp when Dye again checked his mirrors and saw the FBI hanging behind him. They had nearly led the FBI straight to the camp!

Parmenter leaned in toward the windshield and looked into the partly cloudy sky. He saw a small plane about 1,000 feet up keeping pace with the Land Cruiser. "That's how they did it!" Parmenter yelled. "A plane! Carlos said they used a plane on him in Laramie! Drive by the road to camp and get back to Spokane!"

Parmenter contacted Mathews, who told him to dump both cars, Parmenter's and Dye's. They had been compromised. Then, Mathews instructed, go to Kalispell and clean out the homes they'd been using up there before the cops found them. It was time to regroup in Boise.

BRUCE PIERCE LEFT Boise following the Reliance Project meeting and led his would-be terrorists across the Oregon desert to Klamath Falls, on the edge of the Cascades. But shortly after arriving in the small town, Julie began having severe labor cramps, even though she only was six months along.

Bruce took her to a nearby emergency room, where an ultrasound examination determined she was having twins. But there was a serious problem. One twin was larger than the other, and a huge amount of amniotic fluid surrounded the larger one. The doctor recommended that Julie be rushed to the perinatal unit at Rogue Valley

Medical Center in Medford, 79 miles away. Bruce and Julie hurried to Medford, and the other members of Pierce's cell quickly followed.

At Rogue Valley, doctors stopped Julie's pre-term labor, but they made it clear to Bruce—who used the name Bill Smith at the hospital—that she faced the prospect of spending the rest of her pregnancy in the hospital.

Julie's babies suffered from twin-twin transfusion syndrome. The identical twins shared a placenta with some common blood vessels, but one twin was getting a large share of blood while the other was receiving little. The condition most often means death for both babies. Once the deprived child dies from the lack of nutrition, the shared placenta dooms the healthier one.

For the first two days, Pierce questioned the doctors over moral and ethical issues about the babies and the mother, concerned that every effort be made to save the babies. He was very specific that things had to go the way he outlined. Doctors at first were intimidated by Bruce's imposing presence. Until he assured them otherwise, his pro-life attitude made doctors assume he was Mormon.

Pierce and his crew liked Medford. With 40,000 people, it was big enough to satisfy their needs, yet it was near a wilderness area, and the California border was a short hop south. Pierce still had about $300,000, which he'd divided among his members while one of the wives kept a running account.

Soon after they hit Medford, Pierce was struck with an idea, which his men all liked. Instead of renting houses, they should adopt a truly mobile life-style in campers and travel trailers. "You know, we could blend in with all the West Coast snowbirds with our RVs plying the highways, heading south for the winter," Pierce told them. "We don't get tied down to a location." No houses meant no rent receipts and no inadvertent phone calls to hang them later.

Within days, they started spending $6,000 to $8,000 cash each for pickups and travel trailers, which they kept in rented spaces at a local campground.

After a week at Rogue Valley, monitoring of Julie's babies showed that the smaller one was becoming ill. Doctors advised Julie that they would have to take them now if either one were to have a chance. On October 10 Julie underwent an emergency caesarian. The outlook for the two babies, both girls, was dim.

The smaller twin, Becky, showed some improvement in the intensive care nursery after her initial struggle. The larger twin, Mary, lived only about ten hours, dying early the next day. She had dropsy, her body massively swollen with fluids. Bruce wanted to find a secluded mountaintop on which to bury Mary but got into a hassle with Jackson County authorities over the plan. Eventually he went to Memory Gardens, a large cemetery in Medford that had a practice of handling burials for children and indigents at low or no cost.

On October 22, Mary was buried in Memoy Gardens, while at Rogue Valley her sister, Becky, suffered a relapse. The final blow was encephalitis. Doctors were unable to drain the location in the tiny infant's brain. The doctor came to Bruce and Julie with his best advice, which was to allow the infant to die naturally. She was severely retarded and may never even raise her head, the doctor told the young couple. They agonized over losing another child.

Finally, after long discussion, they told the doctor they didn't want Becky to feel pain, but it might be best to remove the respirator. On October 27 Becky died in a room with Bruce and Julie after the doctor administered a sedative to the infant and turned off the life support system.

The next day, another tiny coffin with Becky's body was lowered next to Mary's at Memory Gardens. Bruce and Julie were the only ones there, and as Julie sobbed uncontrollably, Bruce read a few lines of scripture.

He ordered a headstone containing the phony name Pierce was using at the time, Smith. It became like many of the headstones from which grandmother Jean Craig and others in the Silent Brotherhood lifted the names of dead youngsters to create their own false identities. But no one will be able to sully Becky's and Mary's memories that way. In Oregon death certificates of children are cross-indexed with their birth certificates to prevent just such an abuse.

The only concession Pierce made to the infants' true

lineage was the initial "P" for both girls' middle names. Under the surname "Smith" carved into the stone, it read "Mary P." and "Becky P."

Across the stone was carved: "Our little girls in Jehovah's hands."

OCTOBER 18 DAWNED COOL over the Idaho panhandle. But by 9:30, the golden glow of the autumn sun warmed the clearing near the small town of Samuels, north of Sandpoint, where Gary Yarbrough had managed to keep the FBI surveillance at bay.

Yarbrough was inside the house when he first heard a truck engine echoing through the trees to the north, more than 100 yards from the main road.

Glancing out the window, Yarbrough caught sight of a green pickup entering the clearing on the dirt driveway that forked off Pack River Road. The truck had "U.S. Forest Service" on its door panels. To get this far, Yarbrough knew, the three men in the cab either couldn't read or were indifferent to the "no trespassing" signs he had posted near the gate at the edge of his driveway.

As the truck neared the house, it slowed while the three men peered into the windows of Yarbrough's hideaway. His blood boiled at the intrusion. Yarbrough grabbed a military fatigue jacket and a .45-caliber pistol, and ran out the side door into the woods behind his house, where the truck was headed out the back driveway. Yarbrough yelled, but the truck kept going.

Yarbrough reached the sawmill shed on the back of his rented land just in time to see one man get out of the passenger's seat to move the deadfall Yarbrough had placed across the driveway exit to keep out intruders. Yarbrough stepped out from behind the shed and cupped his pistol in both hands. Just then, the man turned and saw him. They were about 100 feet apart.

"Cra-ack!" the gun resounded in the tall timber. The man flinched and darted for the truck. Yarbrough, aiming over the cab, fired again. The man saw the puff of smoke from the muzzle. It looked as though Yarbrough was aiming directly at him.

"Cra-ack!" Another slug whizzed overhead, but the cartridge jammed in Yarbrough's ejector. As the man jumped into the truck, Yarbrough jogged back toward the house and tossed the weapon onto the front seat of his Jeep Cherokee.

The man outside the pickup was FBI Agent Michael Johnston. Agents John Gunn and James Wixon were inside. Johnston wasn't a man to walk away from a fight. A stout product of southern Idaho, he was a former football player and coach who summoned all the restraint he could muster not to return fire and drop Yarbrough where he stood. But he remembered what Wayne Manis told him shortly before Manis flew to Erie, Pennsylvania, to testify in an unrelated case in which he had worked undercover.

Get a Forest Service truck, Manis instructed, and drive by the house to get some idea of the layout. The last time Manis ventured onto the property, he had to eat dirt when Yarbrough drove by him. He had to get an eye on the man, but Manis told Johnston to keep it low key and not provoke a confrontation. The boss's orders were to remain in the "intelligence-gathering mode."

The agents were bending the Bill of Rights by going onto the property without a warrant, but they weren't entirely disappointed that Yarbrough shot at them. That gave them enough probable cause to get a search warrant and raid the house before Yarbrough could clean it out.

When Yarbrough cranked off those shots, Johnston knew the challenge couldn't go unanswered. He jumped back into the cab with Gunn and Wixon and went down to the Sandpoint police station, where he called Toby Harding, second-in-command in Butte, from Andy Anderson's desk in the detective bureau. Don Wofford, the New Jersey agent transferred to Butte for this case, argued they had to move quickly.

The FBI's elite Hostage Rescue Team was summoned from its base in Quantico, Virginia. It might be needed at Yarbrough's house. The agents began to map out a strategy for raiding the house at night. They knew only that Yarbrough had access to heavy firepower.

Once Wofford got to Sandpoint and debriefed Johnston, he began to assemble his paperwork for the search warrant. This was where Wofford excelled, keeping all the details catalogued and filed in his computer-like mind.

But another thing to consider was that the investigation was still secret, at least to the public. Wofford constructed a search warrant affidavit that would keep it that way. Nearly nine hours later, at 7 P.M., Wofford dialed U.S. Magistrate Mikel Williams in Boise to request a search warrant over the telephone, because driving to Coeur d'Alene for the nearest magistrate would take too long. Williams didn't ask why, if time was so important, the FBI had waited until evening to retaliate against someone who shot at an agent before 10 A.M. Then, concealing the true nature of the investigation, Wofford dictated an affidavit to the magistrate to the effect that the FBI had received a tip that Yarbrough's brother, Steven Ray Yarbrough, was living in the house at Samuels. Steven was wanted in Arizona on a federal warrant for unlawful flight to avoid prosecution on theft, robbery, and burglary charges.

"I am fully aware," Wofford dictated into Williams's recorder, "of all the details of an investigation currently being conducted in the Sandpoint, Idaho, area to locate and arrest an individual identified as Steven Ray Yarbrough."

The FBI, of course, had had Gary under constant surveillance since September 5 and knew Steven wasn't living with him. Wofford never mentioned the Ukiah armored car robbery or Gary Yarbrough's suspected role in it, the murder of Alan Berg, or any hint of the existence of a militant racist gang, of which the FBI already knew. If the affidavit became public, it would look like a simple fugitive hunt, and not one involving Gary Yarbrough at all.

Williams authorized the search warrant over the phone. Wofford told the strike force, now numbering thirty agents with the arrival of the HRT, it was a "go."

Agents assigned to the HRT are a breed unto themselves, looked upon with wariness even by some regular agents. The HRT troops tend to look like animals, and some even smell like animals. They go in and out without emotion, and about the only things they ever sign are ammunition vouchers.

The strike force met at Sandpoint to go over details of the operation. Police Chief Bill Keise and Detective Andy

Anderson were invited to accompany it. After a bit of arguing with the HRT leader over the plans, the brigade set out for Samuels just before 9 P.M. and began to filter through the timber around Yarbrough's clearing.

Yarbrough stepped out into the dark with a guest, a fellow named Danny, after hearing cars approach. Together they walked off the large front deck onto the lawn and proceeded away from the house. Yarbrough had a flashlight and a pistol. Suddenly, he saw headlights at the edge of the clearing.

"Who's there? Guys, is that you?" Yarbrough yelled, thinking Kemp or some of the others might be coming.

"This is the FBI!" an agent yelled through a bullhorn. "Stay where you are!"

Yarbrough tossed his flashlight to the ground, hit the dirt and rolled into a ditch that crossed the front of his land. Danny turned and ran to the house.

The agents, having seen a figure run back into the house, assumed it was Yarbrough and surrounded the house. Sizing up the situation, Yarbrough decided to blend in with the strike force. Lying on his belly in the ditch, he turned to face his own house, pointing his pistol at it as if he were one of the agents.

As the agents marshaled in the pitch-black yard, one pulled a car up on the driveway and parked it several yards from the ditch where Yarbrough lay motionless. Two agents, a man and woman, began to pull equipment out of the trunk. The female agent glanced over and saw the figure in the ditch.

"Who's that?" the agent asked, nudging her partner whose head was buried in the car trunk. "Is he with us?" Yarbrough didn't look over.

The male agent glanced over for a second, then went back to the trunk. "He's with HRT. Can't you tell?"

"I really think we ought to identify him," the woman persisted.

"C'mon, he's with us! Now gimme a hand with this equipment," her partner answered. Yarbrough collapsed in relief when the agents left to join the others.

Time wore on while agents took positions, and negotiations with Betty Yarbrough dragged. She denied her husband was in the house. As Gary lay in the ditch, he felt stronger and stronger urges to relieve himself. Finally, he did a push-up and urinated on the ground beneath him. Later, overcome by exhaustion, he fell asleep in the ditch. When he awakened, the agents had entered his house, and he saw his chance to escape.

Making it to the tree line, he disappeared down a trail. As he stole across the quiet forest floor, he realized he had left his gun in the ditch. But that didn't bother him as much as what else he was leaving behind. Mathews had wanted the MAC-10 they used on Berg to be cut up and buried. Instead, it still was sitting in a brown briefcase on Yarbrough's top floor.

When the FBI entered the house, it was like hitting the Comstock Lode. As the agents swarmed through the house, Anderson was invited to join them. Inside, he saw an open book on a bed. The book was Kenneth Goddard's *Balefire*, about a terrorist planning to strike at the Los Angeles Olympic Games. Certain sections were underlined in red.

Anderson watched as agents sorted and catalogued an alarming array of ordnance from the house, ranging from a cocked Barnett Commando crossbow to two MAC-10s with silencers. Pistols, shotguns, and assault rifles with thousands of rounds of ammunition in cases and clips were found next to camouflage netting, a gas mask, a grappling hook, and some line. There were brass knuckles and switchblade knives, ammo vests and police scanners. Anderson marveled at the sight.

"Come on in," Wofford called to him from a bedroom. "I want you to take a look at this." Inside the room was a walk-in closet and ladder leading through a small opening into the loft area. Anderson poked his head through the opening.

Along a wall, set on a mantle piece, was a 3-by-5-foot portrait of Adolf Hitler, draped in black crepe paper with a candle on either side. Close by was a picture of Jesus Christ. On the floor was a brown case with a .45-caliber MAC-10. In addition, there were seventy-five Atlas electric blasting caps, twenty-five nonelectric blasting caps, ninety-nine sticks of Gelmax dynamite, a 1½-pound block of C4 plastic explosive, 75 feet of safety fuse, and several high-explosive, smoke, and tear gas grenades.

At the other end of the long room, separated from the huge cache of arms and explosives by a hanging plastic sheet, was a child's bed.

Yarbrough had documents all over the house. Many of them had to do with the gang, including the Bruders Schweigen documents Mathews had given out in Boise. All were in code. The agents also found a hoard of information on local law enforcement officers including computer printouts with their names and addresses, vehicle license numbers, photos, and other information. The SWAT team leader's name was first on the list.

Anderson was stunned. The gang had done its homework. Cops are naturally paranoid, a professional asset if they want to stay alive long enough to see the kids grow up. Finding Yarbrough's computerized list was sobering. It made Anderson and the others want to bust this gang as quickly as possible.

Anderson already had enough motive, however. Between the drug trade and the neo-Nazis, his adopted home was becoming hostile territory. Anderson figured six out of every ten cars that went by had a loaded gun inside. In rural America, many people carry guns anyway. When people travel the long distances of the West, the only backup they have when trouble hits is themselves.

But the presence of druggies and right-wingers prompted people who never would consider owning a weapon to arm themselves. Sandpoint residents normally didn't have much to fear, but it wasn't a normal time in the panhandle, not when people stole out into the night to spraypaint swastikas and "Remember the 6 Million" on railroad overpasses. People normally apathetic about things outside the small spheres of their own lives were smacked in the face with reality.

It was irritating to people like Andy Anderson, who weren't racists and resented the reputation Aryan Nations brought to their region. When people began to find "running nigger" targets slipped under their windshield wipers in parking lots, they couldn't sit on the fence any more. They had to choose sides.

Wayne Manis got back late from testifying in Erie and learned about the raid. He was told that Wofford, Harding, and the HRT were up in Sandpoint right now.

Damn! Manis thought. He wanted to be in on it. He catnapped for two hours before rising to make the hour's drive to Sandpoint.

When he saw the two MAC-10s, a fleeting thought crossed Manis's mind that they might have found the Berg murder weapon. But Manis thought that nobody would be foolish enough to have kept that gun.

Gary Yarbrough hiked through the forest until he found a vacant house. Prying open a door, he entered and found a rifle. He took it and, on his way out, ripped a telephone from the wall to bring with him. The FBI now had the lineman's phone Yarbrough kept at his house. With it, he'd been able to contact the message center without using his home phone or a pay phone. He simply patched the lineman's receiver into a junction box and made all the calls he wanted.

Once when he left his house to make a call that way, an agent followed him down a wooded trail. Yarbrough came out on a deserted country road. He hiked down the road to a junction box, opened it and began hooking his receiver into the terminals when he spotted the man who had been following him emerging from the trailhead. The agent stopped cold, surprised that Yarbrough was right there.

While the agent watched, Yarbrough smoothly disconnected the receiver, shut the box and stood up. At that, the agent started walking toward him, and Yarbrough turned to approach him. Their gazes were fixed on each other, their hands in their pockets, as they closed. Without a word or nod, they casually strolled past one another on the deserted back road. As they passed, each turned to face the other, walking backward and not letting the other out of his sight.

Yarbrough reached the trailhead and split; the agent stopped to collect himself before heading back to base.

TWO DAYS BEFORE the FBI hit Yarbrough's house, Frank Silva was visiting with Robert Merki, who lived near him on the south side of Boise. Silva had brought some disturbing news. Silva's father-in-law had taken the train up from Los Angeles for a visit and told Frank that the FBI had been to his house asking what his son-in-law was doing now in Idaho.

Merki felt a choking sensation, wondering just how close the FBI noose was to him. On October 19, he found out. Merki's home telephone rang that morning, and he answered it to hear Gary Yarbrough's voice, sounding urgent.

"Noah! This is Sam! ZOG raided my house! I've been shot in the leg and I'm hurt," Gary lied to get them to hurry. "It's cold. You gotta get me some help!"

"You were what?" Merki said in terror. "Where are you?"

"I hooked up an old phone at a junction box along the road here," Yarbrough said. "Look, you gotta get a message to Carlos to come get me. The fuckin' ZOG got everything. I can't even get my car!"

Yarbrough told Merki he would hide near a restaurant outside Sandpoint and wait until help arrived. After he hung up, Merki caught his breath. He was angry that Yarbrough had called his house, which violated security rules. The group was concerned about government wiretaps and patterns on their phone bills. The fact that the message center wasn't manned until 4 P.M. didn't matter to Merki as much as it did to Yarbrough, who had more immediate needs.

Merki dialed the truck stop motel in Boise where Mathews was staying and told him what had happened up north. Mathews figured everybody in Boise was endangered because of the captured lists. He told Merki to move swiftly and get the printing press out of his garage. Merki asked Sharon to rent a U-Haul truck while he started to pack their belongings.

Mathews called his old friend Ken Loff in Ione.

"Hey, buddy!" Mathews sad with an exuberance that belied his purpose in calling. "Listen. I need your help. Sam's been raided by the ZOG."

Loff got a sinking feeling. "What happened?"

"The bastards shot him in the leg, but he'll be all right if we can get him out," Mathews answered. "Get up to the training camp and bring back Richie Kemp. Then get the army together."

Mathews next called Richard Scutari in Kalispell. He told him Yarbrough was shot and trapped in the middle of the manhunt. "I want you to go over to the training camp and take over until Rader gets there," Mathews ordered him. Richard hung up and turned to Michele, who had only recently moved to Montana.

"Things are busting loose," he told her. "I want you to take Danielle back to Florida. I don't know if you'll ever see me again."

Scutari got Barnhill and rode over to the Priest Lake training camp, where Scutari told the half-dozen men there he was taking over.

"If any of you don't like it," he told them, "let's step out in the road and I'll make you like it." Scutari thought the men at the camp were wimps.

Parmenter and Dye returned to Boise from Kalispell with their belongings stacked on a 1949 GMC flatbed truck. When Mathews told them of Yarbrough's situation, Parmenter suddenly realized the Silent Brotherhood's confrontation with ZOG was just around the corner. Mathews was pushing everyone farther along the course, only now people were beginning to have second thoughts.

Silva was helping Merki pack when Mathews, Parmenter, and Dye arrived. Sharon Merki's oldest and youngest children, Suzanne and Kurt Stewart, were helping too. It looked like a typical middle-class family making a move until five men lugged the heavy Multilith 1250 press out of the garage and into the U-Haul.

One other thing was out of place. Across the street, a man wearing a dark blue jacket and baseball cap was crouched behind a neighbor's woodpile, aiming a camera with a telephoto lens at the movers. Merki spotted him.

"There's a ZOG agent now!" Merki alerted Mathews. "He's taking our picture!"

"Everybody stay cool," Mathews advised. "Let's just finish up and get out."

When the house was nearly empty, Mathews left with Dye and Parmenter for Meridian, just west of Boise, to put the old flatbed truck, Dye's Land Cruiser, and their belongings in a storage lot. Then they went to the 10th Street house to warn Jean Craig that she could be under surveillance. After that, they left Boise.

Merki, meanwhile, left Sharon behind and dropped off Silva half a block from his house on Ona Street. Silva ran to his Mustang and followed Merki. He found the FBI on his tail. They paraded over the bridge into downtown Boise, Merki in the U-Haul, Silva in his Mustang, and the FBI behind them. Merki pulled into the lot at the Red Lion Riverside Inn and went into the bar with Silva to figure out what they would do next. The FBI agents came in and sat at a table nearby. It was a confusing situation, since both sides knew they were watching each other. Merki glanced over at the agents while he downed a stiff drink.

"What the hell are they up to?" Merki asked Silva, the strain of the day clearly showing. "Why aren't they arresting us?" Merki and Silva took turns getting up from their table and walking around, sometimes phoning Sharon Merki, just to watch the agents' reactions.

Suzanne Stewart came in and sat with her stepfather and Silva. Glancing around, she recognized one of the FBI agents from the pictures she'd been taking of Boise-area law enforcement agents. It looked like a standoff.

Mathews, halfway to Oregon by this time, checked with Sharon Merki and learned her husband and Silva were trapped in the Red Lion bar. He walked back to his car and grabbed Parmenter and Dye.

"We've got to go back to Boise and rescue Noah and Sterling," Mathews told them, his eyes as intense as they'd ever seen them. "The ZOG has them cornered at the Riverside. This is it, kinsmen! We'll wait until dark, then rush the lounge and bust them out! We'll show ZOG we won't run!"

Parmenter had to cool down Mathews. The last thing Parmenter wanted was to storm the Red Lion Inn, guns blazing against the FBI.

"Hold it, Carlos," Parmenter said, his hands on Mathews's shoulders. "Just let them slip out on their own. It's obvious the ZOG isn't going to arrest them. They had me and Jimmy the same way. They just wanna tail them to see where they're going. See if Silva can slip the tail."

That satisfied Mathews for the time, but he began to wonder about this army of his that never wanted to see action. He wanted it so badly he could taste it.

Merki and Silva managed to slip out to Silva's Mustang after about ninety minutes of consternation in the bar.

The car sprinted down 27th Street to State Street, then west for a few miles until they reached a pizza parlor. They stopped for dinner and to catch their breath. They had left the U-Haul, with all the incriminating counterfeiting evidence, in the Red Lion parking lot.

Silva made a few phone calls in an attempt to locate Mathews. When that failed, he and Merki drove north into the mountains to the sawmill town of Horseshoe Bend, where Silva finally reached Mathews. They arranged to meet at a restaurant across the border in Oregon and then drive to Baker, Oregon, for the night.

By the end of the day, the Silent Brotherhood's losses were significant. Besides all the documents lost at Yarbrough's house, the U-Haul was in FBI hands.

BY SUNDAY, MOST Silent Brotherhood members in the area had made it to the camp to regroup after the confusion triggered by the raid on Yarbrough's house.

Mathews's caravan rendezvoused Saturday morning with Randy Duey in Spokane, where they bought a van to replace the cars they had to dump in Boise. Duey was accompanied by two Canadian recruits, Jim and Edgar, who were going to live at Duey's indoctrination camp in Bluecreek. On Sunday morning they met Jean Craig and Shirley Silva, who also drove out of Boise, and went up to Bluecreek. Also arriving there were two of Sharon Merki's sons, Ian and Cooper Stewart.

Mathews instructed Duey in the protocol for greeting Syrian officials. Mathews still hoped for an audience to get funding from the Syrians for his own war against the Jews. He told Duey to greet a Syrian by clasping his hands on the man's shoulders instead of just shaking his hand. Mathews asked Duey to go to the Syrian Embassy in Washington.

Duey then showed Mathews the texts he had handwritten for his indoctrination course. There were three of them: "The Enemy's Organization," "The Purpose of the Aryan Soldier's Academy" and "On Being Underground."

Then the group, except for the women and Cooper Stewart, drove to the training camp, arriving about 8 P.M. It was the largest assembly of the Silent Brotherhood ever in one place, twenty men, all gathered in the huge mess tent Rader had erected.

Mathews felt a surge of pleasure when he saw their faces. He realized that in several months' time he'd expanded the Silent Brotherhood so that there were more than twice this number out and about, and more were coming. He believed now that within his reach was the capability of pulling off major feats of urban terrorism. He was ready to bare his teeth.

No one noticed it more than Ken Loff, who'd known Mathews longer than any of the others. This was the first time Loff had seen Mathews since that August meeting in Boise. In two months, it looked to him, Bob had aged ten years. He obviously had too much going at once. Loff thought he saw a death pall on his friend's face.

The men listened to Yarbrough recount the raid by the ZOG strike force. When he finished by saying ". . . and they got the Berg gun," a chill went through some of the men who'd not known of the killing.

Then Mathews and Rader stood up to discuss all the confrontations with the FBI and how to shake surveillance. They discussed errors they'd made and how to avoid them, Mathews using as an example his grievous mistake of leaving Barnhill's gun behind at Ukiah. Parmenter got up to talk about the surveillance on him and Jimmy Dye, and some mistakes he made that contributed to it.

Then, while Rader distributed some new equipment to the men, Mathews launched into his battle cry:

"Kinsmen! We must strike back at ZOG for what he has done to our comrade Gary! True to our oath, we must repay the ZOG bastards for what they have done! We have the kinsmen here to do it! We must march on Sandpoint and tak back what the devils have confiscated! We must raid their offices if necessary to reclaim what is ours!"

The men, not wanting to go on a commando raid just yet, glanced uneasily at one another. Loff thought Mathews had gone off the deep end. Scutari and Rader were upset that Mathews was saying such things in front of Ian Stewart and the two Canadians, men who weren't yet properly screened. Rader left the tent to stand guard, and Jackie Norton tagged along.

"You know, Jackie, it might be a good idea if we started lookin' for a way out of this group," Rader told Norton. "Bob's influencing these guys to overlook his own mistakes. He's pacifying them with words. But he ain't really in touch with these guys. He don't have enough contact with them."

"Why's he talking about goin' after the FBI?" Norton asked, still believing Rader had hired him for a legitimate job. "What can they do to us?"

"Open your eyes, Jackie!" Rader said with urgency. "This ain't the CSA. Bob's taken these guys way beyond that. Where do you think all this money's been comin' from? Some sugar daddy? He's been robbin' armored trucks!"

Norton suddenly felt panicky. He had moved his wife and children up here in the belief he was running another survivalist camp like the CSA. Even with all the loose lips in the Silent Brotherhood, nobody ever told Norton exactly where the money came from, and Norton never asked.

"Do you think we can leave without gettin' shot in the back?" Norton asked. Rader shrugged, then walked back to where Mathews was finishing his call to arms.

"Kinsmen, remember! Blood! Soil! Honor! Faith and race!" Mathews was shouting. "We will never be taken!"

Scutari and Rader called Mathews into Rader's trailer when he finished.

"I have no doubt, Bob, that we could march back to Gary's house or wherever they have all those documents and take them all back. We have the men and the firepower here. But they don't know we exist," Scutari assessed incorrectly. "Why let them know we exist? Our training camp is so close, why dirty our nest?"

Rader also jumped in to reason with Mathews that a sneak attack on the FBI would be the beginning of the end for the Silent Brotherhood. He persuaded Mathews that while he might be ready, his men lacked the confidence.

They read the scorn and disappointment on Mathews's face. He was armed and ready for battle and was having difficulty accepting the fact the others weren't.

Finally they decided to lie low and make adjustments

because of the information the FBI now had. Mathews told Rader to keep the men in camp, particularly Barnhill and Yarbrough, until they heard otherwise.

About midnight, Mathews left in the van with several people, including Scutari, while the others were to remain in camp until further notice.

Mathews and Scutari left for a trip to the south in the morning, stopping among other places in Birmingham, Alabama, to meet some Klansmen who were associated with Bill Riccio and Mike Norris, the Alabamians who had met in Boise on September 29.

Riccio still didn't want to go underground, but Norris not only was ready but had recruited another Klan friend, Mark Frank Jones, twenty-six. Like his friend Norris, Jones was intrigued when told about the stranger Carlos. After meeting Mathews, Jones too became convinced that an armed struggle by a white underground was the only avenue left to solve the country's racial problems.

"Why, this ZOG regime is so corrupt," Mathews told Jones, "we gotta remove it entirely, throw the baby out with the bath water."

Not everybody agreed, however, particularly in light of a letter mailed in mid-October by a trio of renegades at Pastor Butler's Aryan Nations. They had pilfered a copy of Butler's big mailing list and drafted a letter claiming there was an FBI sting operation going on to entrap right-wing leaders in criminal activity. Those three young men went on in November to stage a bank robbery of their own in Pacific Beach, Washington, netting $7,000.

Such suspicions caused several high-profile racists down South to refuse to meet with Mathews. Some who did meet walked away convinced, ironically because of his unusual depth of fervor, that Mathews was indeed an FBI plant.

When Mathews and Scutari checked into their motel in Birmingham, Mathews reflexively turned on the television set in the room to Cable News Network. Mathews was a news junkie. Whenever he hit a town, the first thing he did was buy one paper from every rack. When the screen lit up, an anchor was announcing some stunning news about mass evacuations being ordered in New York, Washington, and San Francisco, all amid urgent Soviet warnings of war with the United States.

"What!" Mathews yelled. "What is this?" Scutari joined him in front of the screen.

The anchor talked about some international incident that had provoked the Soviets into arming their missiles for launch. It appeared that World War III was about to begin. Mathews and Scutari sat on the bed nearly in shock.

"They can't do this!" Mathews yelled, wide-eyed. Since he first read the John Birch Society circular in his Sunday paper at age eleven, he had firmly believed this day wasn't just possible, it was inevitable.

"We're not ready yet!" Mathews yelled at the TV. "The commies can't do this now! We're not in place yet! Just a few more months! Our civil administrators aren't ready to emerge from the rubble!"

Scutari too was in awe at, what he thought was happening. He remembered those anxious days in 1973 on the North Sea oil platform, when the United States went on stage 3 nuclear alert during the Arab-Israeli war.

Mathews grabbed the telephone and dialed the Birmingham police dispatcher to see if there was some official word about this crisis. As he waited on hold, Scutari watched a crawl start across the TV screen. "This is a demonstration . . . ," it began. Mathews had tuned in just as CNN was demonstrating how its newsroom would operate in a nuclear crisis.

The Birmingham dispatcher came back on the line after discovering the same thing. "I'll bet you're watching CNN," the dispatcher told flustered Mathews.

Mathews and Scutari calmed down after learning they still had time to get their underground organized for post-Armageddon.

In central Nebraska's farm belt, meanwhile, more seeds of discontent bore fruit in violence that very week. It was a smaller, but real, sign of crisis.

Arthur Kirk, a farmer in deep financial trouble, tried to stop a foreclosure with legal tactics suggested by Roderick Elliott of the National Agricultural Press Association, the man whose newspaper had been squashed by Alan Berg.

On October 24, on Kirk's farm outside Cairo, Nebraska, deputies trying to serve legal papers found Kirk dressed in camouflage gear and a gas mask, with an assault rifle on his shoulder. Kirk pointed a revolver at a deputy's head and warned him to leave. The Nebraska State Patrol SWAT team was summoned, and telephone negotiations were attempted. But Kirk was clearly at the end of his rope.

"Why don't you let me try and make a living!" he screamed over the phone. "Damn fucking Jews destroyed everything I ever worked for! I worked my ass off for forty-nine God-damned years and I got nothing to show for it!

"Who's got the power of the world? Who runs this world? The fucking Jews! By God, I ain't puttin' up with their shit now!"

About 9:30 that night, Kirk made a charge at the police. Warned to stop, he fired instead and was shot by police. He fell dead in his backyard.

IT DIDN'T TAKE long for the mood at the training camp to disintegrate into intolerance. Bill Nash, the National Alliance recruit from Philadelphia, did the cooking, and it was nothing close to what mother used to make. Yarbrough was moody, not used to hiding out away from his wife and four daughters. Barnhill was getting on people's nerves with his know-it-all attitude, made worse by the fact that Andy could back up most anything he said. The men called him "Android."

Rader left once again with Loff, this time to spend $5,000 for camping gear at a military surplus show at Reno's MGM Grand Hotel. In his absence, the men bickered over conditions at the camp. It had started to snow, and the nights were becoming bitter cold. After a week, Rader returned on Halloween to hear reports that the men were approaching mutiny. Lying low so the heat could die down was one thing. Freezing their butts off was quite another. Valley Forge, my ass! These patriots started to yearn for a warm bed with a roof overhead.

Passing through Newport on his way back to camp, Rader stopped at a Safeway and bought the thickest cuts of steak he could find. Then he bought a few cases of beer. When he arrived at camp, he set up in his trailer and called in each man individually, asking him whether he wanted to remain at camp or leave. Only a few decided to stay.

That settled, Rader set up a campfire where the men held their last meal together, barbecued steaks and beer. Most of the men who left went to Richie Kemp's trailer in Ione. The next day Loff drove Yarbrough north of Sandpoint, dropping him off near Pack River Road so he could sneak back to his family.

From down south, Mathews called Loff's house and was startled when Barnhill answered the phone. "What the hell are you doing there?" Mathews asked him.

"There's no one left at the training camp," Barnhill replied. "Everybody was getting on each other's nerves there so Rader let most of us leave."

Mathews hung up and turned to Scutari. "Rader let the guys leave camp 'cause they didn't want to stay," he said in disbelief. Scutari blew his top.

"This is a military leader?" Scutari scoffed about Rader. "He can't even keep his men at camp?" They headed for the airport.

Ken Loff walked into his kitchen on the afternoon of November 4 to see Andy Barnhill standing there. "Carlos is here," Barnhill said told Loff. "He wants to see you in the basement bedroom." Loff went downstairs. Also waiting down there to see Mathews were the three young men from Salinas—Kemp, Soderquist, and their friend Rick Steinbach. Rader had also been summoned for a meeting.

"Hi, buddy!" Mathews said to Loff, smiling as he was that afternoon in 1976 when they met. "Got some business we need to transact. Andy's gonna leave us. He wants to be on his own over in Kalispell and I want you to give him $60,000."

"Sure, Bob," Loff replied. "How about you? Where are you setting up?"

"In Portland with Mr. Black and a few of the other guys," Mathews responded. "We're getting bigger every day, Ken. Everything we talked about all these years, it's really starting!" Ken recognized the familiar look in Bob's eye.

"That's great, Bob," Ken said. Mathews then reached into his case and pulled out a pendant. It was one of the Bruders Schweigen medallions Jean Craig had ordered.

"This is our symbol, Ken," Bob offered. "Please take it."

Loff looked it over, the shield and battle ax, the inscriptions. He ran his thumb over the intricate design of the scroll. Then, remembering how he'd burned the papers Rader brought back from Boise, he handed it back. "I don't want this," he said, unsure how Bob would take the rebuff.

"Fine," his friend answered. "That's okay. By the way, buddy, it's possible the ZOG might come by to question you about some of us, and, well, I was just wondering where your head was at. Can you handle that kind of pressure?"

Loff, suddenly terrified, sat straight up and thought for a minute.

"Yeah," he finally replied. "I think I'll be all right."

Rader arrived and told Mathews that the first few snowfalls of the season had sapped the men's spirit. Rader wanted to go to Arkansas or Missouri and buy an all-season camp. Mathews concurred, partly because he recognized the need to escape what the Silent Brotherhood members were calling "the killing zone."

The others went back to Kemp's trailer nearby, and soon Soderquist and Steinbach departed for Salinas.

Bob, driving Scutari's green Ford Bronco, then went down to Metaline Falls to pick up Debbie and his son, Clinton, who were going to Portland with him.

Una Mathews saw Bob coming down the gravel drive that led into Mathews Acres. She hadn't seen her son often since he began traveling so much. She saw Lee frequently, since he still taught at the school in town. But the antipathy between Bob and Lee had grown into downright loathing, and the brothers who'd been inseparable as youngsters in Arizona now didn't speak to each other.

Bob walked over to Una's house while Debbie packed. He had something to show his mother. He walked into her kitchen and greeted her with an embrace.

"Hey, Mom, I've got some great news for you," he said with a smile as big as she'd ever seen. Bob reached into his pocket and pulled out some photographs. "You have a new granddaughter!" Bob said. "I've got a daughter, in Wyoming."

Her son a father, with a mistress! Una knew how fiercely he wanted a child of his own flesh. "Siring," he called it, as though he still were running the Galloway ranch. In Portland, through a sperm bank, a surrogate mother now was carrying a child conceived with Bob's sperm. But a mistress?

Una looked at the pictures of baby Emerant while Bob raved about her. As he continued to talk about his battle for the future of his race, Una could see how serious he'd become. She always believed Bob was being figurative when he spoke in such terms. She never had the sixth sense Johnny had about their Robbie.

Bob talked a while about how he had rebounded from the loneliness of a year ago and how much pleasure he got from his new work, which Una assumed was in some sort of right-wing speakers' bureau. As he talked, Bob was framed by the living room window, from which there was a clear view across to the summit of Hooknose Mountain. Bob stared at the mountain for a minute, then turned to Una.

"You know, Mom," he finished, "I'm really not afraid to die for my race."

A chill went through Una. Suddenly she realized her son was involved in something very dangerous. She looked at Bob as he waited for her to respond. He was a handsome man by any standard, a loving son who had the world within his grasp when he started Mathews Acres. She remembered the letters filled with hope, the drawings of the flowers and the cabins. Now she was struck by despair and struggled momentarily before finding an appropriate response.

"What a waste," Una said, looking in hopelessness at her son.

Bob kissed her goodbye, and Una watched from her window as he drove with Debbie and Clinton out the gravel drive, disappearing into the trees.

THE MORNING WAS damp when Ken Loff went to his garden to dig up his special crop—$60,000 in crisp, consecutively numbered twenties and fifties. Taking the money out of the plastic container that sealed it from the dirt and moisture, Loff stuffed it into a brown paper bag and took it over to Richie Kemp's trailer, where Andy Barnhill waited for it.

Barnhill was trying to persuade Kemp to go to Kalispell with him, but Kemp was undecided. He liked Ione, liked being near Loff and his children. Yet he too was struck by the sudden urge to hide. He told Barnhill he'd think about it.

About noon, after Barnhill had left with the money, Loff invited Kemp to his house. On the short ride they saw a car headed toward Loff's farm. Inside were two men wearing suits. "Oh my God!" Loff said to Kemp. "It's the FBI! Bob warned me they'd be coming!" He turned and drove toward a pay phone to call Marlene.

"I guess they've made the decision for me," Kemp said. "I'm going to have to go to Montana with Andy." Loff called home, and Marlene, eight months pregnant with their fourth child, answered it. Ken asked if she could get rid of the agents. But before she answered, one of the agents asked for the phone.

"Mr. Loff?" he said. "I'm Agent Jim Davis from the Spokane FBI office. Is it possible for you to come home? There are some questions we'd like to ask you."

"Uh, well, okay," Loff stammered. "I can be there in fifteen minutes."

By the time Ken arrived, he'd already decided to lie as best as he could. There was no way he could tell the ZOG devils what he'd been doing the last year. Davis introduced himself and Agent John Sylvester, then began the interview.

"Mr. Loff," Davis said. "We're looking for some people associated with Aryan Nations and we understand that you had been there on several occasions."

Loff nodded. His children were baptized there, so he couldn't deny it.

"Have you seen Bruce Pierce lately?" Davis asked.

"Pierce? I don't believe I recall him," Loff said, not wanting to be associated with a counterfeiting fugitive.

"Oh, is that so?" David observed, taking notes. "And what about Andrew Barnhill? Do you know him?"

"Barnhill, you say?" Loff replied. "No, can't say that I know him either."

"Mr. Loff, you co-signed a note for Richard Kemp when he bought a Toyota Celica last year," Davis observed. "A Pend Oreille County deputy has observed Mr. Barnhill driving that car. Do you still say you don't know Andrew Barnhill."

Loff swallowed hard. He had just left Barnhill an hour earlier, after handing him $60,000 in stolen cash. "No, I don't," he replied. "Richie probably knows him and loaned him the car."

"Where is Mr. Kemp now?" Davis asked, unaware Kemp was within several miles.

"He may have gone back to Salinas to see his family."

"When was the last time you saw Robert Mathews?"

"Bob?" Loff mused. Bob had been in his basement just the night before. "Oh, I'd say six months ago."

"Six months?" Davis came back. "We have your phone records here, Ken, showing numerous calls to Mr. Mathews's home."

"Well, that's my wife. She calls Debbie all the time."

Loff wove an intricate web of lies for more than an hour before Davis and Sylvester gave up. Davis handed Loff his business card when he left.

"Think about everything that was said here, Mr. Loff," he said. "We'll be back in touch." Walking out to their car, Davis turned to Sylvester. "He's lying something terrible. He'll come around eventually."

Soon afterward, a shaken Loff drove to Rader's house. "You gotta get the rest of the money off my land soon as you can!" he pleaded. "Just get it off!"

Kemp sneaked back to Loff's house after dark and knocked on a window. Down in the basement, Loff told Kemp what he thought the FBI already knew. Marlene made Kemp some sandwiches before Kemp left Ione for good, headed to Kalispell.

Rader, concerned that the FBI might find the training camp as well, spent that night camped in deep snow after his truck became mired on the isolated back road to the training camp. In the morning he hiked into camp. George Zaengle, the city boy, was the only one there. It had been too cold for the few others.

"This is ridiculous," Rader said. "None of you guys wants to train! We gotta close this camp for the season." A heavy snow began falling again when they started striking the tents. Before long Denver Parmenter and Ian Stewart hiked in the front way across Big Meadows and helped out. They placed a large assortment of guns in a special plastic drum and buried it in their foxhole. They stored some equipment in the shed and left the large mess tent standing.

"Let's hope we have better luck at the next camp down south," Rader said. "You all lay low. I'll notify you by mail when and where to come."

Parmenter said he was headed for Colorado and could be reached by mail under the name Carl Schultz at general delivery in the ritzy ski resort of Vail. From his large library in the trailer, Rader fetched a copy of *The Road Back,* the terrorism manual studied religiously by survivalists, and loaned it to Parmenter for those cold nights by the fire.

The next day Rader brought Jackie Norton to Loff's farm to get the rest of the money. About $480,000 was stuffed into Norton's knapsack. Loff had disbursed $1 million since becoming the banker after the Ukiah robbery. After the men left, Loff uncovered $60,000 he had hidden in his attic. After dark, Marlene, her baby kicking inside the womb, held a flashlight for her husband while he buried that nest egg in 3-pound butter tubs under the carport.

THE MOST ACTIVE members of the Silent Brotherhood managed to get out of "the killing zone" by mid-November. Merki and his wife rendezvoused with Randy Duey and headed for Portland for a meeting with Mathews, who was in the process of renting a chain of safehouses there. At the meeting, Scutari gave out the next generation of security devices the Silent Brotherhood staff was to use.

One device was a radio frequency detector, worn on the body and down the sleeve. It vibrated if it picked up radio signals and could detect FBI informants wearing a transmitter. While meeting at the motel, one of the devices went off, prompting everybody to cast wary glances at each other. The culprit turned out to be a radio in the cab of a garbage truck making a pickup outside the motel room.

After the meeting Duey and the Merkis went in search of a haven of their own. After passing through the seaside resort of Astoria, Oregon, then up to Mount Vernon, Washington, they found some well-hidden houses for rent on Whidbey Island, a serpentine stretch of land at the head of Puget Sound northwest of Seattle.

Merki, no enthusiast for "roughing it" like the survivalists in the group, rented a modern vacation home on a sea-wall looking east over Saratoga Passage. It was in a private community called the Beachcombers Club, accessible down steep South Hidden Beach Drive. Merki told his landlady he and his wife were Dale and Molly Bradley and that he was a teacher on sabbatical to do some writing.

Duey found an older house on the water down a long forested driveway off North Bluff Road, about 2 miles north of the Merkis.

The two Canadians, Jim and Edgar, tagged along and found a large chalet-style house on the island's west shore near Greenbank. It was only 3 miles in a straight line southwest from Merki's place, at one of the narrowest points of the island. The house was in a clearing at the end of a 200-yard overgrown driveway, through the thick trees that lined Smugglers Cove Road.

At the same time in Oregon, Mathews found a house to rent in the tiny settlement of Government Camp, near Mount Hood east of Portland. Those with him, by now including the fugitive Gary Yarbrough, found houses in the nearby towns of Welches, Brightwood, and Rhododendron.

Bruce Pierce left behind the pain of Medford for the desert southwest, leading his "snowbirds" to a dusty town called Pahrump in the hot stretch between Las Vegas and Death Valley. They set up their travel trailers in a court there.

Only Ardie McBrearty, the mild-mannered tax protester, moved in the wrong direction, leaving Arkansas around the beginning of November to a place south of Oldtown, Idaho, close to Newport, Washington.

Around Thanksgiving, Scutari showed up at Rader's

house with a U-Haul attached to his Bronco, intending to tow his belongings from Kalispell to his new hideout near Mathews at Mount Hood. Mathews wanted him to bring as much of the remaining loot as Rader could spare. After some dickering, Rader agreed to get $200,000 for Mathews from what they'd dug up on Loff's farm.

Scutari spent Thanksgiving with his friend McBrearty, and the next day Rader and Norton showed up with the cash. While meeting in the basement, Norton voiced a concern that had been eating at him since the big meeting at the training camp: Mathews was going too far too fast. "He's going to get some people killed before long," Norton maintained. "He's goin' cuckoo."

"Don't you worry about Bob," Scutari said. "He's never been sharper. Once all this heat dies down, he'll only be more ready to go to Step 6."

Scutari headed out onto the snow-covered roads the next day, November 24, taking his belongings to Mount Hood. His wife and daughter were preparing to fly back from Florida after he'd sent them home in haste following the FBI raid on Yarbrough.

The FBI got an unexpected break around this time. Seattle Agent Norm Stephenson, biting around the edges of the Aryan Nations probe, checked out an address in western Washington linked to the three young men Pastor Butler accused of stealing his mailing list. They were the ones who had sent the nationwide letters warning of an FBI sting operation against right-wing leaders.

Inside the house, Stephenson found Eric Mackey, one of the three. They talked cordially for a while, and Stephenson said he'd be back. The next day, when Stephenson arrived, the house reeked of marijuana. He saw Mackey again and said, "I guess you know why I'm here." Stephenson was shocked when Mackey replied he did indeed know why.

"It's about the bank robbery we committed," Mackey blurted out. He described the Pacific Beach bank robbery of November 16, which netted Mackey and his friends, Eugene Kinerk and Kelly Carner, nearly $7,000. Stephenson was skeptical until Mackey led him to a spot in the woods where they had buried the clothing worn during the robbery. He arrested Mackey, and within days

Carner and Kinerk were also in custody. And they were willing to talk about what they'd heard of Bob Mathews's secret army.

AMERICAN AIRLINES FLIGHT 349 had been chasing daylight for six hours from Philadelphia before dipping into its landing approach along the Columbia River. Far ahead, the sun was dropping into the orange haze of the western horizon. Tom Martinez glanced out the window to the south, where Mount Hood thrust its mighty summit through a cloud cover, its snowcap luminescent in the horizontal light.

The jetliner encountered a steady rain on its descent and was still being buffeted as its wheels hit the runway at Portland International Airport. Martinez felt his stomach crawl into his throat. The night before, after picking at his Thanksgiving dinner, Martinez had talked with Mathews to firm up the details of this trip. Mathews made it clear Martinez should forget reporting for his sentencing on his counterfeiting plea on December 14 and join the Silent Brotherhood.

Instead, Martinez was betraying his friend to the FBI agents who had been his constant companions since October 1. He was the bait for finding Mathews's hiding place. He had only one condition. The FBI was not to harm his friend, just take up surveillance so Martinez could leave without blowing his cover. It was very difficult for Martinez, especially after the call from Mathews on the pay phone at the Allegheny Avenue Sunoco station the night before.

"Now listen, come prepared to stay—okay?—in case our discussion leads that way," Mathews pleaded during the call, unsuspecting that Libby Pierciey, a Philadelphia-based FBI agent who had been Martinez's shadow for the last seven weeks, was taping the coversation through the long-distance static.

" 'Cause I picked up some information and I guarantee you, they're going to nail it to you," Mathews said to frighten Martinez. "Have a good talk with Sue and bring enough stuff to be prepared to stay, okay? And, you know, be sure and bring pictures with you and the kids. I found out, that's the one thing that keeps me going." As the passengers unbuckled their seat belts and started milling in the aisle of the plane, tears welled in Martinez's eyes.

"You've gotta learn to trust me," Mathews had told him in a bitter irony, considering the situation, "because I guarantee you, I'm not gonna screw you."

Martinez knew Mathews loved him as a brother and had stuck with him through his legal predicament. Martinez gratefully spent the stolen loot on his lawyer's retainer, thereby committing another crime. Mathews was blind to any possibility of betrayal. But what gnawed deeper within Martinez was an even darker truth.

Yes, he admitted to himself, he might have considered joining Mathews and running from the feds. He might have burrowed into the racist underground.

Only one thing stood between him and that cataclysmic decision. He loved his wife and children. That love was his sole link to reality now. He didn't want their husband and father to be a murderer.

"Eighty-eight, take care of yourself," Martinez had ended the call with the neo-Nazi coded greeting that means "Heil Hitler." "H" is the eighth letter of the alphabet. Interestingly, "88" also is ham radio code for "hugs and kisses."

"Yeah, eighty-eight, take care," Mathews replied.

Martinez was under watch by FBI spies throughout the airport when he landed at 6 P.M. He knew Mathews wouldn't be at the gate, so he went right to the baggage claim area, where he spotted his friend. A smile of recognition crossed Bob's face, but Tom sensed a tension in his friend before they reached out and shook hands. Bob placed his free hand on Tom's shoulder, as was his habit.

"Hi, buddy, it's good to see you," Mathews said, his eyes sweeping the terminal for any sign that Tom had been followed. When they walked into the rainy night, Martinez noticed two men seated in a bus shelter. One kept glancing toward them, periodically bending down the newspaper that covered his face, just like a B-movie detective. Martinez prayed Mathews wouldn't notice.

When they approached Bob's car, Tom reached for the door handle but felt an arm brush past him to get it first. Startled, Tom turned and saw a wiry, red-haired man in a

Jeff cap. It was Gary Yarbrough, whom Martinez had never met.

"Hey, what do you want?" Martinez asked defiantly.

"That's okay, Tom," Mathews laughed. "He's one of us. His name is Reds, but you can call him Sam."

"Well, I hope he's not like the Son of Sam," Martinez made a nervous attempt at levity as he ducked into the front seat. Yarbrough climbed in back as Mathews started the car and checked his mirrors.

"There's a Volvo, a silver gray Volvo over there," he told Yarbrough as he pulled out into the steady drizzle. "See if it pulls out." As Bob rounded the drive in front of the terminal, Yarbrough looked over his shoulder.

"Yeah, he's comin'," he reported. The Volvo got closer, and Martinez began to tremble. Was his cover blown already? How could he get out of this death car?

He gasped with terror when something touched his leg. Looking down, he saw Mathews had placed a pistol on the seat next to him. Martinez's heart revved up so hard, he could almost hear it. Turning slightly, he watched Yarbrough pick up a machine gun from the floor and screw a silencer on the end of the barrel. Then Yarbrough set a hand grenade on the seat.

Martinez felt beads of cold sweat trickling down his collar. He knew Bob had been involved in violent crimes, but the point now was driven home vividly.

Mathews turned south out of the airport drive onto NE 82d Avenue. Soon he jerked the car down a dead-end alley and swung around so they faced the street. Mathews cut the lights and engine. The men stared ahead at the traffic passing on 82d. The only sound was the maddening, monotonous patter of the rain on the roof of the car. Minutes seemed like an eternity to Martinez. The Volvo didn't come.

The silent tension lasted about five minutes, until Mathews suddenly spun and slapped Martinez on the thigh, causing the Philadelphian to jump and gasp. "Spider!" Mathews said with his childlike lilt, "it's so good to see you!"

Mathews refired the engine and started back up 82d. Martinez soon saw the familiar green neon sign of a Holiday Inn ahead on the left. "I got me a room there,"

Tom tried to guide Bob, knowing the FBI had set up a listening post next to his room.

"Forget that," Mathews said. "We have a room for you at the motel where we're staying. It'll be better to be together."

"What if Sue tries to call?" Tom protested meekly. "I told her I'd be at the Holiday Inn."

"Cripes, Tom, call from the other place!" Mathews answered with resolution.

Mathews stopped at a parking lot where he saw a phone booth, saying he had to call Zillah. While Bob was gone, Yarbrough gave Martinez his embellished version of the Sandpoint shootout, making it sound like the Aryan version of the bridge at Concord. Martinez suddenly realized "Reds" was Gary Yarbrough.

"Damn phone system!" Mathews said as he got back to the car. "It's out of order! Let's get something to eat. You hungry, Spider?"

It was raining harder. The three men dashed into a diner, where Mathews ordered his favorite snack, hot apple pie and milk, for all.

About 8 P.M., with the rain slackening into a mist, they arrived at their motel. The Capri was an unremarkable L-shaped, two-level motel on the northeast corner of 82d and Halsey Street. The entrance off Halsey went past the white stone-façade office on the right into the parking lot, which otherwise was sealed off from the street by a white wooden fence and shrubbery. A swimming pool was tucked in the corner of the lot. The only exits from the lot were the narrow driveway past the office and an alleyway around the west side to the rear of the motel.

Mathews nosed his car into a spot near a dark green door with a white number 14 on it, on the short leg of the L a few rooms down from the office. Mathews already had a key and pushed the door open or Martinez.

"This is your room, Tom," Mathews said. "Reds and me got room 42, upstairs over there." Mathews pointed to a second-level room on the long leg of the L, which had a clear line of sight to Martinez's door. Yarbrough pulled out an electronic device and began running it over the walls. It was a bug detector that would pick up electrical impulses if a microphone were in the room.

Martinez sat in one of the chairs at a round table as Yarbrough moved around the perimeter.

Suddenly the beeper went off, alerting Yarbrough to possible danger.

"It's only the air freshener, Reds," Martinez quickly sought to calm him. "It's the fuckin' battery in the air freshener." Sure enough, the wall-mounted device was setting off the bug detector. Satisfied, Yarbrough plopped down on one of the beds and opened the Friday edition of the Portland *Oregonian*.

"Listen, Tom, I want to talk to you," Mathews said. "Come on up to my room."

Crossing the parking lot, Martinez saw three staircases leading to a second-level catwalk, one at each end and one in the center. Turning, he saw that the catwalk continued over his room, ending at a fourth staircase next to the office.

"I want to tell you what I set up for you, buddy," Mathews began once they had settled into Room 42. "You go back tomorrow, get everything ready to leave, and on Tuesday I'll call to give you a meeting place in Philadelphia. You'll hook up there with David Lane. Remember Dave?"

"Yeah, Bob, I remember him," Martinez replied, half listening and half figuring out how he could get out alone to notify the FBI where he was.

Then, as though Martinez had already taken the oath of the Silent Brotherhood, Mathews told him he'd be part of an assassination team to kill anti-Klan attorney Morris Dees. Mathews, still ignoring the "need-to-know" maxim he preached, might have been the least silent member of the entire brotherhood.

The way Bob spoke of freedom rather than prison, of fighting for his beliefs rather than watching ohers trample them, of throwing off the oppressive yoke smothering the working-class white male sounded so familiar to Tom. He had tossed those same lines to his acquaintances on street corners in Kensington while collecting $150 a week for the neo-Nazi cause. For an hour he listened and remembered his own days of fervor, of commitment.

Then Yarbrough came up to the room, carrying the machine gun and silencer. A shiver ran through Martinez's body as he watched Yarbrough put the gun on the counter, then pull off his shirt to reveal his scrawny rib cage. Yarbrough stretched out on a bed. His chest was covered with tattoos, and he was wearing his Bruders Schweigen medallion on a chain around his neck.

The harsh reality of Yarbrough terrified Martinez in a way Mathews' smooth talk could not. Seeing Yarbrough's gun made him realize the idealism he saw in Mathews three years ago had disintegrated into an awful, senseless violence.

Mathews decided Martinez should return to Philadelphia on an earlier flight, because the Silent Brotherhood was having a business meeting in Portland the next day. Bob called American Airlines and changed Tom's reservation. Then he dialed the front desk and requested a 7 A.M. wake-up call for Room 42. Martinez was getting desperate to let the FBI know where he was, and he needed an excuse to get out.

"Hey," Martinez broke in, "it's still early. Why not go out for some beers and see if we can find some women?"

"No way," Mathews sighed. "I'm bushed, buddy. You go on if you want. There's a bar where we saw some beautiful women the other night. You can go ahead and take the car." Mathews wrote some directions and tossed the keys to Martinez.

Yarbrough bolted upright. "That ain't such a great fuckin' idea, ya know," he advised Mathews. "There's stuff in the trunk."

"Oh, yeah, that's right," Mathews corrected himself. "Guess you'll have to walk somewhere nearby, buddy."

Standing for a moment on the catwalk as he left his friend's room, Martinez scanned the cars in the lot. There was nothing familiar. He figured the FBI had lost him. Rushing down to Room 14, he splashed some water on his face and grabbed a fresh shirt.

It was close to 10 P.M. when Martinez ventured into the chilly fog, crossing Halsey to the corner of 82d. He turned left across the bridge that spanned the commuter rail line and freeway into downtown and began looking for a telephone. Glancing over his shoulder, he saw a dark sedan pull out and start to follow him. A chill ran through him. There was no way to tell if it was the FBI or someone Mathews had sent to tail him. Martinez stopped at the first open diner.

Inside at the counter, a man approached Martinez after he had ordered and sat down next to him. The man studied the menu hanging on the wall behind the counter. Then, without taking his eyes off it, he said, "Libby sent me."

Martinez turned and looked at the man.

"Meet me around the corner," the man said, getting up to leave.

Waiting before he followed, Martinez spotted the dark sedan at the rear of the restaurant. Two agents inside motioned for him to get in the back seat.

One agent explained how they lost the tail leaving the airport, then scoured parking lots of nearly every motel in the area before finding Mathews's car. Then the other agent asked, "What's Mathews's plans?"

"They put in a 7 o'clock wake-up call," Martinez related, "so we can go to breakfast before taking me to the airport for a 9 o'clock flight home. They're in 42 and I'm in 14. They got some business goin' here tomorrow."

"Who's the second guy?" one agent asked.

"Gary Yarbrough," Martinez answered. Both agents suddenly flashed looks of alert at each other. The one in the passenger's seat dug into his jacket pocket for a mug shot of Yarbrough, which Martinez confirmed was the man with Mathews.

"Well, that puts a different slant on the whole thing," the agent said. Reaching for his cellular phone, the agent punched in a number and told the person on the other end what he just learned. Listening for a moment, he then placed the receiver in the cradle. "Okay, go on back to your room and stay there for further instructions," he said to Martinez.

"Nothing's going to happen, is it?" Martinez said. "Libby guaranteed me you'd just watch Bob, not hurt him, and nothing would happen while I was here."

"Don't worry about it," the agent answered. "We'll handle everything."

WAYNE MANIS'S HOME PHONE rang late Thanksgiving night. On the other end was Toby Harding, his supervisor in

Butte, asking Manis if he'd like to go to Portland on an operation to pick up Mathews. The informant in Philadelphia, Harding told Manis, had set up a meeting for Friday night.

"Let the Portland crew handle it," Manis replied, too tired to go.

Late on Friday night, Manis's sleep was broken by another phone call, this time from the head of the FBI's Portland SWAT team, Paul Hudson. Not only was Mathews in Portland, he told Manis, but the informant had also fingered Gary Yarbrough.

"Take 'em both down," Manis, on record as the case agent, advised Hudson. Now Manis was sorry he hadn't gone to Portland. It was going to break wide open. He had no qualms about doing it now, not since the FBI lab had finished testing one of the MAC-10s taken at Yarbrough's house. The firing pin had been checked against impressions on the shell casings found in Denver and in the meadow at Pierce's house in Troy. They matched perfectly.

It was the gun used to kill Alan Berg, the gun Manis assumed was rusting at the bottom of a clear blue mountain lake. Manis couldn't believe his luck.

About 4 A.M. Saturday twenty agents, including the SWAT team and a San Francisco contingent, had assembled at the Sheraton near the airport. Ted Gardner, special-agent-in-charge of the Portland field office, briefed them on the operation.

When Libby Pierciey learned of the plans to abandon the agreement and make arrests, she protested vigorously, but the Portland agents were determined that Yarbrough, who had shot at one of their own and had made the Bureau look silly, would not be permitted to slip away.

Saturday morning dawned with remnants of Friday's rain reflected in puddles on the Capri parking lot. Agent Art Hensel arrived at the manager's office at 5:45, flashing his badge to the night manager, Jerry Riedl. Hensel said the FBI wanted all the guests except those in Room 42 awakened and in the office before 7 A.M.

Within an hour the guests had been herded through the office into a small lounge, where fresh coffee was usually kept brewing. Hensel told them to go inside and sit on the floor. A large window in the lounge looked straight down the sidewalk in front of Room 14. The staircase from the catwalk passed right in front of the window. The drapes were pulled so Mathews wouldn't be able to see the guests huddled inside from his vantage point across the way.

Martinez awoke at 6:55. Slowly, he went to his window and pulled the curtain, looking toward Room 42. There was no sign of life. He hopped into the shower and let the spray chase the butterflies around in his stomach.

As he was drying off, his phone rang.

"Tom?" a woman's voice said. "This is Libby. There's been a change in plans. Lock your door and stay in your room. It's going down." She hung up. Martinez rushed to the window and peered out again. Still nothing from Room 42. He slumped back onto his bed, staring at the floor while trying to figure out why the FBI was breaking its word to him. He felt helpless to stop what he had started.

Around 8 o'clock, Martinez's phone rang. It was Yarbrough.

"You ready?" Gary asked simply. "We'll be right down."

Seconds after he hung up, Pierciey called again.

"What did he say to you?" she asked Tom.

"He said they're comin' down," Martinez replied.

"Okay. Stay put no matter what happens," she ordered before disconnecting.

Martinez hurried to the peephole in his door. Through the fisheye he saw Mathews on the catwalk outside Room 42, stretching in the cool morning air, inhaling expansively to take in the new day. He then went back inside. A long time passed until, about 8:40, the door suddenly opened and Mathews, wearing a parka, walked out and closed the door. He was carrying a clipboard with papers.

"The package is out and moving," Hensel, inside the office, radioed to the team. Out of the corner of his eye, Hensel saw a female FBI agent, Jonella Boicken, moving up the center staircase opposite where Mathews was headed.

Mathews walked along the catwalk, surveying the area

from his high ground for trouble. He turned right, crossing above Martinez's room. Then, as he neared the stairs that descended past the office window, he caught sight of a man hiding in the bushes across the parking lot. Suddenly the lot erupted with danger.

"Gary! Watch out!" he yelled back toward his room. As Mathews bolted down the staircase, Boicken fired a shot at him. Her bullet missed, smashing through the window into the lounge where all the guests were crouched on the floor. The slug ricocheted off the stone fireplace in the far corner of the room, punched a hole in the coffee urn on a table, and smacked Riedl in the shoulder.

Mathews ran past the office and out the driveway, which unexplainedly had been left unsealed by the assault team. He rounded the corner, going left down Halsey. Hensel jerked the office door open and started after him. Agent Kenneth Lovin, armed with a shotgun, ran down the sidewalk toward him from 82d.

"Mathews!" Hensel yelled. "Freeze, you bastard!" He pointed his pistol at the fleeing figure for a moment, but held his fire and resumed the chase.

The sidewalk ended at the back of the motel. Mathews and the agents took to the street to keep their footing. Hensel put on a burst of speed to try to catch up with Mathews, who had made the Y-shaped intersection at the end of the block and narrowly avoided being struck by cars as he scurried across the street.

Down the left side, Mathews skirted a two-story brick office building and sprinted down a narrow driveway, dropping his clipboard. Straight ahead, beyond the parking lot, he saw a modern two-story apartment house down an embankment. He raced down the hill, fighting a snagging ground cover of ivy, and came to a staircase under some thick trees in the rear yard of the apartments.

Quickly looking around the sloping yard, he spotted a concrete retaining wall topped by a red fence, ending abruptly at the property line. Darting down a short set of steps then through some more bramble, Mathews squeezed through the opening between the retaining wall and an adjacent wooden shed.

Badly winded, Mathews jerked his semi-automatic pistol from his waistband and crouched behind the wall to see how close the agents were behind him.

Yarbrough had heard Mathews shout and, judging that the cops must be in the parking lot, rushed into the bathroom, opened the rear window and climbed out. There was a thick tangle of bushes 15 feet below the window. As he clung to the sill, he heard footsteps stampeding toward him. He dropped into the bushes, but before he could regain balance, hands were grabbing him and pushing him roughly to the ground. As his arms were twisted behind his back and handcuffs snapped around his wrists, he looked up into the barrel of an Uzi.

Hensel and Lovin, fearing an ambush, took a wide turn around the office building and saw Mathews disappear down the steep hill at the rear of the lot. Then they spotted the clipboard Mathews had dropped. The top sheet headed "Bruders Schweigen Staff" included the coded lists of gang leaders and their assignments.

As they reached the hill, Hensel skidded through the same tangle of ivy vines that had snagged Mathews. He ran to the staircase and stopped to survey the scene, complicated by numerous possible hiding places and escape routes. He was starting down the steps from one landing to the next when he heard Lovin yell.

"Look out, Art!"

At that moment, Mathews peeked from behind the concrete wall about 20 feet away. Hensel froze, staring directly at Mathews. He could see no sign of fear. Relying on his training, Hensel flopped onto his back, feet in the air, just as Mathews fired. Time seemed to slow as the round came at him, and he watched it ricochet off his shin 2 inches below his knee. He found it curious that there appeared to be a smoke trail in the air from the bullet leading directly to him.

Turning to his side, Hensel squeezed off two quick shots, both of which went wide. Mathews fired again, and the slug slammed like a hammer on the bottom of Hensel's shoe. At almost the same time, Hensel heard the horrific roar of Lovin's shotgun and saw large pits explode into the concrete near Mathews' head.

Mathews was holding his weapon in his right hand when Lovin drew down on him. Mathews ducked behind the wall, but his gun hand was exposed. A number of the double-aught pellets slashed into his hand, and a searing pain exploded in his arm. But he knew he had to make a move or the agents would be on him in seconds.

The lot behind him was filled with a tangle of trees, landscape rocks, and loose poles. Mathews bolted through the lot to the street, crossed in mid-block, and vaulted a small backyard fence, headed for the next block. Lovin skidded down to Hensel, asking if he was all right. Hensel, oblivious to his wounds, said he was. Both agents crept cautiously down to the wall, but Mathews was gone.

Moving between houses in the quiet neighborhood, Mathews made it two blocks from the shooting scene, reaching Schuyler Street. Two workers were installing a burglar alarm in a house nearby. Mathews rushed over to them. "I need some help," Mathews said. "I kind of dinged up my hand." Blood was pouring down his fingers.

"Jump in the truck," one of the workers said. "I'll take you to a hospital."

"I was working on a buddy's car," Mathews explained as the worker drove him from the manhunt, "and my hand slipped off the wrench into the engine fan."

Hensel and Lovin ventured past the retaining wall but turned right, through a series of backyards instead of straight to the street. The owner of the corner house was eating breakfast when he saw the two men with guns stealing through his yard. Angered, he quickly retrieved a rifle and bolted toward his front door to head them off. But he screeched to a stop when he got there and saw the men's backs. Their jackets read "FBI" in huge, yellow letters.

"Fellas need some help?" he yelled.

"Yeah," said Hensel, the pain of his injured foot finally getting to him. He leaned against a utility pole at the corner. "Call the police."

The worker drove Mathews clear to Gresham, 10 miles east, looking for a hospital. As they passed a Union 76 service station, Mathews spotted a car with skis mounted on the roof. Mount Hood was the closest ski area.

"Hey, just drop me off here," Mathews told the worker. "I can make it from here." Mathews thanked the man, then sprinted over to the station's restroom, where he washed his mangled hand and wrapped several sheets of paper towels around it to try to stop the bleeding. Then he walked over to the pumps and asked the couple with the skis on their car whether they were headed for Mount Hood.

"Sure are," the man answered as he signed his credit card slip for his gasoline. He gave Mathews a ride to Brightwood, 25 miles away, and dropped him off near the Oregon Ark motel. From there, Mathews hiked to Country Club Road, where Frank Silva had rented a house just a week earlier.

Back at the Capri, agents found a treasure trove inside Room 42 and in the trunk of Mathews's car. In addition to various weapons and the grenade Yarbrough had left behind, they found coded documents relating to the Silent Brotherhood and $30,000 in currency, some of it bearing stamps indicating it had been in banks along the Brink's route through Ukiah. But what stopped them cold was a note pad with a hand-printed declaration of war by the "White American Revolutionary Army" against the "Zionist Occupation Government" and the "Jew-controlled media."

While the agents had their field day, Tom Martinez huddled inside Room 14, wondering if he'd been forgotten in the excitement. Peering through the curtains periodically, he watched television, radio, and newspaper crews trying to interview the cops. For four hours he kept dialing a "hello" number Pierciey had given him, a line to the FBI that was answered only, "Hello," without identifying it as the FBI. It was how he was supposed to get help. But no one answered.

Martinez's anger built at being double-crossed, making him a marked man. He overheard a maid outside his room talking to a member of the press. She was telling him that the man in Room 14 "was with the FBI."

That sent Martinez through the ceiling. On the first chance he got, he snuck out and hurried to a nearby restaurant. The people at the counter were engrossed in conversation about the shootout. He brushed past them to get to a phone booth. He looked up the main FBI number and asked for someone in authority. An agent came on and asked if he could help.

"Yeah," Martinez all but screamed. "This is Tom Martinez. You people get me the hell out of here!"

Some time later, one of Martinez's neighbors in Kensington watched with curiosity as Sue Martinez arrived home. The neighbor was aware that the young family had suddenly abandoned the house recently. The neighbor didn't know why. She watched as Sue went into the house, then after several minutes left again with an artificial Christmas tree.

Chapter 10

Blood, Soil, and Honor

Richard Scutari pulled his Bronco and U-Haul trailer into Brightwood about 1 P.M. Saturday. Never having driven on snow before, he'd had a few chilling moments on the road from *Kalispell*. And with $200,000 in stolen money as cargo, he had reason to be cautious. Parking on Country Club Road, he saw Frank Silva's pickup and Gary Yarbrough's car parked in front of Silva's rented house.

Stretching to relieve his driving cramps, Scutari started toward the front door when Silva rushed out, yelling, "Bob's been shot and Gary's in jail!"

Hurrying inside, Scutari saw Mathews seated in a large overstuffed chair, his bloody right hand wrapped in a bandage. Mathews gave a small shrug as if to say, "I'm sorry." Next to the chair were bloodied bandages Silva and his wife, Shirley, had been using to administer to the wound.

"What the hell happened?" Scutari exclaimed.

"The ZOG bastards got Gary," Mathews said dejectedly. He calmly recounted for Scutari the events at the Capri that morning.

"We better get out of here pronto," Scutari said as Mathews finished. "I say we head for Arizona or Texas."

"No," Mathews said. "We have safe houses on Whidbey Island across from Seattle. We have to go there to regroup."

Scutari jumped up and asked Silva to start loading the back of his pickup with anything they could find to make a blind for Mathews. The truck had a camper shell on the back, and they carried out blankets, sofa pillows, and small pieces of furniture to form a tunnel in which Mathews could hide. "We're too damn hot here," Scutari said as they worked. "We gotta get out of the Northwest."

They hurried back into the house to help Mathews out. Gently they laid him on a row of pillows and started packing blankets and furniture around him. They didn't know exactly where Duey's safehouses were, but once they were safely out of the manhunt they could contact Duey through the message center.

Before closing the tailgate, Scutari handed Mathews a fully loaded 9mm H&K-94 carbine, a round already chambered. "I'm going to be right behind you, pal. If they try to stop us, you know what to do," Scutari said. Mathews smiled and nodded. It was dark by the time the two trucks hit the road.

The FBI missed them by only minutes. Poring over documents left at the Capri, they found rental papers for houses near Mount Hood. By the time the agents got a strike force together, however, Mathews had slipped away. When agents finally arrived in Brightwood, trudging through knee-deep snow to get to the door of Silva's house, they found it deserted. All that was left behind was a pile of bloody bandages beside a chair. They ran a listing on the car in front with Idaho license plates and learned it was registered to a Gerry Olbu of Sandpoint, Idaho—Gary Yarbrough's alias.

It was after dark when Silva pulled his pickup into a motel parking lot off SE 128th Street outside Everett, Washington. It was 200 miles away from Portland, 20 miles north of downtown Seattle. Scutari registered them for the night, then helped Mathews to a second-floor room in the corner of the motel.

In the bathroom, Scutari held Mathews's hand over the washbasin and gingerly started unwrapping the bandages from his hand. Under the gauze was a matted, deep-red clump of paper towels that had become fused with Mathews's torn flesh. The wound reopened when Scutari started pulling the paper away.

Lovin's shotgun had been loaded with buckshot, and the pellets had grazed across the top of Mathews's hand, searing the skin and tearing out chunks of muscle, but no bones appeared to be broken. Looking at it, Mathews said, "I guess I'll be learning to do things with my left hand from now on."

Scutari was feeling queasier than Mathews. He prepared a blade to cut away the skin from the paper towels. He told his friend he'd have to hurt him to clean it, because he had nothing to kill the pain. "Don't worry about it, pal," Mathews replied. "Just do what you can." When Scutari sliced at the loose flesh, Mathews remained silent and still.

Later, with the wound bandaged properly, Scutari left the motel for a walk. His mind was clouded by the events of the past twenty-four hours. As he walked, one thing kept coming back to him: Martinez refused the voice stress test, and Martinez was at the Capri when the FBI moved in. In Scutari's mind, there was only one person who could have double-crossed Mathews.

ON SUNDAY MORNING, Randy Duey met Robert and Sharon Merki and walked down 82d Avenue to Elmer's Pancake House for breakfast. They had arrived in Portland Saturday for a meeting of the Silent Brotherhood, but, while they thought they were at the right motel, they couldn't find Mathews.

While waiting for their breakfast, Duey went out to a newspaper rack on the sidewalk and bought a copy of the Portland *Oregonian*. Back at the table, Duey glanced at a large front-page photo showing three Portland police SWAT eam members carrying shotguns and automatic rifles about to enter a home during a search in northeast Portland. Duey started to read the accompanying news story:

An FBI agent, a motel manager and a fleeing gunman were shot Saturday morning after two fugitives tried to escape from a northeast Portland motel. One man was arrested at the motel, but police were searching for the other man between Wood Village and Mount Hood Saturday night.

Duey skimmed to the seventh paragraph, then suddenly grasped the paper as though he'd been shot through the heart.

About the same time, a second man jumped from a second-floor window at the back of the motel and was captured there by agents, said Detective David W. Simpson, public information officer for the Portland Police Bureau. The man was identified as Gary Lee Yarbrough, 29, of northern Idaho.

"Oh, Jesus mercy!" Duey wailed.

"What is it?" the Merkis asked in tandem.

The article didn't identify the other suspect but said in an exchange of gunfire between the FBI agents and the man, ". . . witnesses said the suspect was believed to be injured in the hand."

Glancing back to the top of the article, Duey felt his breath being sucked out of him. He'd skimmed the second paragraph without it sinking in.

"Injured were Jerry Riedl, manager of the Capri Motel . . ."

"What's wrong? Robert Merki asked, seeing Duey go ashen. In a quavering voice, Duey told them what he'd just read. Then, his voice rising, he added:

"And that's not the worst. The shootout took place at the Capri Motel!"

"At *our* motel?" Robert asked incredulously. "No wonder Carlos wasn't there."

Badly shaken, the trio quickly paid their breakfast tab and rushed back to the Capri, grabbing their clothes and checking out immediately.

On the drive back to their hideouts on Whidbey Island, Duey stopped several times to call the message center. First he learned that Mathews had gone to the Seattle area. Once Duey arrived and found a phone at which he could be reached, that number was relayed, to Scutari, who told them to come to Everett.

It wasn't until after Duey and the Merkis rejoined Mathews in Everett and rehashed the events in Portland that the real irony of the motel struck them. After checking in Saturday afternoon, Sharon became nauseated by the odor of a newly installed carpet in her room. She complained, and the manager moved them to another room—42. From their door, they could look down to Duey's room—14. Both rooms, it seemed, had sudden vacancies earlier that day.

The discussion turned to the next move. Scutari and

Robert Merki were for heading south, Merki to Oklahoma, Scutari preferring the desert Southwest. Duey argued that they already had safehouses just across the
sound on Whidbey Island.

Mathews settled it. "I want to get over to Whidbey, at
least 'til things calm down. The Merkis and Duey left
immediately to get things ready on Whidbey."

THE BALEFUL MOAN of a distant ship's horn echoed across
the fog-blanketed waters of Puget Sound as Frank Silva
guided his pickup down the steep hill to the Mukilteo
ferry dock and pulled into the shortest of four lines of
cars. He cut the engine, cracked his window, and told his
young daughter to listen. They could hear the sharp cry
of gulls over the rush of the water washing the beach.

It was 9 A.M. Monday, November 26. When the Silvas
left Everett fifteen minutes earlier with Bob Mathews in
the back of their camper, Richard Scutari went in the
opposite direction to Spokane on family business. His
wife, Michele, had flown to Portland on Saturday to
rejoin him. When he called her from Everett, he asked
whether she realized what had happened to Mathews.

"Yes," Michele answered. "I'm looking at his picture
in the Sunday paper right now."

"Then you know it's dangerous and you better go
home," Richard advised.

"No, Richard. Not again," she replied. "This time I
want to be with you."

Scutari relented and told his wife to fly to Spokane. He
picked her up there, stored their belongings, and dumped
the U-Haul, which, without thinking ahead, he'd rented
in his own name. Then they rejoined Mathews on Whidbey Island.

The Mukilteo ferry, 6 miles southwest of Everett, carries auto traffic and pedestrians 3 miles across Possession
Sound to the dock at Columbia Beach, below the small
village of Clinton on the southeast tip of Whidbey Island.

Whidbey, 50 twisting miles long, is the second largest
island in the continental United States, after New York's
Long Island. There are only two exits from the serpentine
stretch of land to the mainland. One is the dramatic
bridge over narrow Deception Pass on the northern end

leading to Fidalgo Island, then to the mainland near Mount Vernon. The other is the Washington State Ferry system that departs every half hour for the twenty-minute crossing between Mukilteo and Clinton. The Keystone—Port Townsend ferry goes from Whidbey to the Olympic Peninsula.

Silva watched a multideck ferry, the *Kittitas*, emerge from the fog, its horn bellowing as it floated to rest at the dock. After the inbound traffic cleared the ramp, Silva started his truck and joined the outbound traffic rolling toward the collection gates in rows of two. He paid his fare and rolled over the gangway onto the car deck. Once snuggled between cars on the narrow outer deck, he sent Shirley upstairs to get coffee and hot chocolate while he stayed with his daughter on the car deck making sure nobody got nosey about their cargo.

Issuing several blasts from its horn, the *Kittitas* moved away from the dock with a muffled roar, slowly slicing across the cold silver surface of the sound and leaving a long string of white turbulence trailing behind. Slowly the land dropped away and the beacon from the small white lighthouse on Elliot Point next to the dock disappeared in the misty fog.

Whidbey is one of more than 600 islands along the Washington coast, testimony to an earlier ice age. Shaped like a giant sea serpent, it bulges at both ends but is only a mile or so across along its waist. On a clear day, the white cliffs of Whidbey are visible to someone looking north up Puget Sound from Seattle's West Point. The island has several natural harbors but few inviting beaches. Most of its coast is sheer cliffs with rocky outcroppings and narrow, rough beaches buffeted by strong winds. There are also some marshy areas and lagoons.

Almost at dead center and near its narrowest point is Coupeville, on tranquil Penn Cove. A charming, picturesque hamlet, it became the Island County seat in 1881 and boasts forty-eight structures on the National Register of Historic Places. Whidbey remained relatively secluded until 1962, when Seattle hosted the World's Fair and erected its landmark Space Needle. Whidbey was "discovered" by some as the perfect place for vacation homes.

They joined a growing cadre of present and retired Boeing employees who also liked the solitude of the island.

The southwestern neck of the island forms Admiralty Bay, where strong winds often blow in from the sound. The small village of Greenbank is located on that neck. Looking down from the bluffs, one sees thousands of bleached logs littering the water's edge. Bald eagles and ospreys ride the thermals searching for fish.

South of Admiralty Bay is Smugglers Cove. According to legend, it was the place where Chinese workers were smuggled onto the island at the turn of the century, and where bootleggers shipped booze to the mainland during Prohibition.

In 1976 Larry Moore, an American faculty member at the University of British Columbia, built a four-bedroom, two-story cedar chalet-style home in a cliffside clearing 2 miles north of the cove, 100 feet above the water. The main living space was on the second floor. It contained a living room, a kitchen, a bathroom, and two bedrooms. A sundeck ran the entire length of the front, facing the water, and an outside staircase descended on the side to the rear of the house. The bottom floor had sliding glass doors that opened onto a full porch shaded by the sundeck above. The main area on that floor was a large, open playroom. An interior staircase in the center led upstairs.

A circular drive skirted the rear of the house. On the southern rim of the drive, Moore had a two-car garage. A few steps west of the garage he built a small storage shed partially hidden behind a couple of bushy fir trees.

The chalet was about 200 yards off Smugglers Cove Road. The clearing, carpeted with wild grass, was enclosed on three sides by a dense forest of towering fir and spruce trees, with a tangle of brush, ferns, and deadfall logs covering the forest floor. To the west was a clear view of Puget Sound. On the steep cliff, a wooden staircase worked down to the narrow beach.

During the winter Moore rented the chalet through Loganberry Hill Realty. In November 1984, it was rented to two Canadian men named Jim and Edgar.

SHORTLY BEFORE 10 A.M., the blare of the *Kittitas's* horn rumbled over the dock near Clinton. Reversing its powerful engines, the ferry slowed in a swirl of white water and nudged into the unloading ramp. Within minutes, a line of cars was rolling off the ramp and up the sharply winding road leading into Clinton.

As Silva pulled into the mall town, he saw Duey and the Merkis waiting in a car. With a quick wave, Duey pulled out, and Silva dropped in behind him.

A narrow two-lane highway bisects the island lengthwise, south to north. Dense stands of tall Douglas fir, Sitka spruce, and Ponderosa pine form natural windbreaks for small patches of cultivated land and pastures on both sides.

The two vehicles traveled north for 20 miles to Greenbank, little more than a general store with gas pumps. A halfmile beyond Greenbank, they turned west on Smugglers Cove Road for a couple of miles until they reached the narrow drive hacked through the forest down to Moore's chalet.

The two Canadians came out to help the others get Mathews from the camper into the house. Mathews told everyone his cover story would be that he was a writer named McBride seeking solitude after a recent divorce. That way no one would question "his" children being at the house.

Scutari arrived on the island a day later with Michele and their daughter, Danielle. As they crossed on the ferry, Michele looked uneasily at her husband. "This is a lousy place to hide," she said, assessing the escape possibilities.

"Well, don't tell me. Tell Bob," he said. "That's what I've been saying."

Danielle was just shy of her second birthday. Silva's daughter was a bit older and enjoyed playing mommy with her. Mathews missed both his children, and it was worse now because his photographs had been lost to the FBI at the Capri. He took time to romp on the floor with the girls, favoring his injured hand.

At other times, Mathews was busy writing. Having lost the early draft of his "declaration of war" in Portland, he wasted little time reconstructing it. He scanned a copy of the National Alliance booklet *Attack,* looking for inspiration and a little plagiarism. Earlier, anonymity was a supreme requirement for his "action group." But now it was apparent that Mathews had to make a statement.

"The whole thing was," Mathews reasoned to Scutari, "we didn't want people to know who we were. There's no sense to that now. It's time to introduce ourselves and get the word out that we exist before we don't any more."

Mathews's fatalism made Scutari push harder to leave for the Southwest. Yet to Scutari, Mathews seemed more at peace on Whidbey than at any time in the six months he had known him. When it was time to work, he'd be in the playroom toiling over the declaration of war or discussing with Scutari their future goals and strategies. If ZOG was closing in on him, Mathews didn't seem to notice.

In fact, the gang went on as though losing Yarbrough had been a minor setback. Although the Merkis were itching to leave Whidbey, more of their family arrived. Sharon's sons, Ian and Cooper Stewart, came about three days after Mathews, with their grandmother, Ida Bauman, and a trailer filled with her belongings. Merki sent his stepsons to store the furniture near Seattle. His little place at the Beachcombers Club was getting crowded. Ida moved in along with Cooper. But with no other beds, Ian Stewart was sent to stay with Mathews at Smugglers Cove.

And away from Whidbey, it was business as usual. Rader went off to Tulsa the day after the shootout in Portland to scout real estate for the new training camp. With the help of an old CSA friend, he found a 160-acre parcel in the most rugged section of the Ozarks in Shannon County, Missouri, and bought it for $27,800.

At the same time, Jackie Norton made payroll for the three Philadelphians living in Spokane, taking $10,000 for each down to a meeting at a Wendy's restaurant on East Sprague Avenue. After the transaction, George Zaengle told Norton he needed some advice.

"I got me a big problem," Zaengle said. "Martinez has been callin' my wife to find out if he's hot with us. He wants to meet me and find out where everybody is. I'm afraid, 'cause I think he might've set Carlos up in Portland."

"If I was you," Norton replied, "I'd get myself out of Spokane, make a clean break, and set up shop somewhere else. Next time that Martinez calls, you tell him you been scared off by the FBI and you quit the group. Then change your phone number, or leave town."

BRUCE PIERCE, LIVING with his cadre at a trailer court in godforsaken Pahrump, Nevada, contacted the message center and heard sketchy details about Portland the day after it happened. By Tuesday, November 27, with Mathews safely settled on the island, the message center passed along a coded bulletin to Pierce, which he knew meant he should proceed immediately to Seattle.

No one at the message center knew exactly where Pierce and his cell were situated from the time they left Salmon in September. Each time they'd ask, Pierce would reply, "I'm all right; that's all you need to know."

Pierce borrowed Tom Bentley's car and asked Randy Evans to go with him to Seattle, a day and a half of nonstop driving. They arrived early Thursday, and Pierce contacted the message center again. He played telephone tag before finally being directed to a 7-Eleven store in Everett, where Mr. Black would meet him.

Richard Scutari, driving his Bronco, brought Frank Silva along to the meeting. The way they constantly glanced around jangled Pierce.

"What's goin' on?" Pierce asked Scutari.

"Follow us to the ferry and then come up to the passenger deck," Scutari said out his truck window. "And keep flippin' CB channels so we don't stay on one." Pierce and Evans thought paranoia had taken root in the Northwest.

After parking on the car deck, the group went one by one to the ferry's seating area. Pierce watched seagulls circle the Elliot Point lighthouse for a while before sauntering over to an empty seat next to Silva. As the ferry left the dock, Silva went through an abridged version of what he understood had happened at the Capri and how they thought it was a set-up with Martinez as the bird dog. Mathews, however, wasn't yet convinced, Silva said.

When the ferry's horn sounded, all four men made their way back to the car deck. Soon they were off the gangway and through Clinton. It took thirty minutes to reach the Smugglers Cove hideout. Pierce and Evans hurried up to the second floor, where they met Scutari's and Silva's wives and daughters. Then Mathews came up from the playroom, his face brightening when he saw Pierce. Mathews quickly strode across the room and embraced him.

Then, relaxing in the playroom, Mathews gave Pierce the unabridged account of the Portland shootout. He described the confused tangle of thoughts and emotions he had during the long, bumpy ride buried with a cocked-and-locked 9mm carbine underneath the load in Silva's pickup, then as he stood stoically while Scutari cut the torn flesh off his hand in Everett.

Pierce settled back in a couch while he listened. When Mathews finished, Pierce shook his head, almost in disbelief. "Well, frankly, I'm envious," he said to Mathews's surprise. "I mean it, Bob. You went through something, you conquered your fear, learned a lot and used your head. I think that's something, to prove your mettle." Mathews smiled broadly at the praise.

By this time, Mike Norris and Mark Jones, the two Alabama Klansmen who were recruited by Mathews and Scutari, had made it to the island as well. They went from Birmingham to Kalispell after the Portland shootout and waited for Scutari's call to reinforce the main group. Smugglers Cove was becoming crowded.

After dinner that evening, Scutari said he had to pick up a man from the Portland area who had joined the Silent Brotherhood when they were renting their safehouses at Mount Hood. He was known to the group as "Fred." Scutari, who wanted a well-armed militia with him, asked Pierce, Duey, and Silva to go along.

Fred had gone to his home the day of the Portland shootout. When he returned to Mount Hood, he found all the safehouses empty. He went to a mechanic's shop where Scutari had had work done on his Bronco and asked the attendant if he knew where his friends had gone.

No, the attendant answered, but the FBI had been around asking questions.

Panicked, Fred drove back home and loaded his belongings in his truck in an effort to escape. But the FBI was on his tail, forcing him to ditch his truck and run. It took several days for him to contact Scutari. When he did, Scutari told Fred to look in the Yellow Pages under "Motels" in Everett, count down a certain number of listings, then go to that motel and wait for another contact.

"When we come by, you leave the motel, walk two blocks, then turn right," Scutari instructed. "If we see you're not being followed, we'll pick you up."

On the way over to pick up Fred, Pierce talked in the back seat with Randy Duey, whom he hadn't seen in two months. Pierce had missed his friend and the stimulating discussions they used to have. "Randy," Pierce finally said, "I'd give anything to have you join my cell."

"Really?" Duey responded, flattered. "I'll think about it."

When Scutari reached the motel, Fred started walking. The four men in the Bronco, all heavily armed, followed slowly until they were satisfied that Fred was alone. Scutari then pulled up and motioned him to get into the Bronco.

On the ride back to the ferry, Fred told them about his experiences shaking the FBI in Portland and what he had learned about the manhunt.

"Oh, by the way," Fred said as Scutari drove toward Mukilteo, intent on being inconspicuous. "They know all about your Ford Bronco."

"What!" Scutari shouted. "Well, so much for being covert." Scutari stashed the vehicle in a garage on Whidbey and took to driving another car.

"I'VE GOT SOMETHING I want you to sign," Mathews said to Pierce as the men returned from the mainland. "It's not complete yet, but it's our declaration of war on ZOG." He handed Pierce some of the draft he had assembled.

Pierce glanced at it, then whistled. He liked what he saw.

"Yeah," Mathews said with a gleam in his eyes. "It was important for us to stay underground in the beginning. But now, we've been all over the Jews-media. It's time we introduce ourselves." Crossing his long legs,

Pierce went through the draft to the signature page, where he read:

> We, the following, being of sound mind and under no duress, do hereby sign this document of our own free will, stating forthrightly and without fear that we declare ourselves to be in full and unrelenting state of war with those forces seeking and consciously promoting the destruction of our faith and our race.
>
> Therefore, for Blood, Soil, and Honor, for the future of our children, and for our King, Jesus Christ, we commit ourselves to Battle. Amen.

"Robert Jay Mathews" already was scrawled in the lower left. "You don't have to sign your real name if you don't want to," Mathews said, handing a pen to Pierce. Pierce was insulted that Mathews might think he'd use a phony name on such a document. Pierce felt that now he was really doing Yahweh's will.

He took the pen from Mathews and, placing the sheet on the countertop partition by the kitchen, wrote, in bold cursive, "Bruce Carroll Pierce" directly below Bob's name. Bruce felt that, after the tension with Bob in months past, his gesture of signing below Bob's name rather than immediately to the right of it would signify his obeisance. Then he handed the pen to Duey.

One by one, others signed the sheet. Scutari followed Duey, then Randy Evans, Robert Merki, and his wife, who used her maiden name, Sharon K. Donohue. Frank Silva was next, adding a flourish under his signature.

Others added their names in the days following. Ian Stewart wrote "Andrew C. Stewart," although at the time he was using the alias "Bartlett Duane Udell." The Klansmen Norris and Jones signed it "Paul Anderson" and "Steve Brant." The recent arrival from Portland went last, writing "Fred Jhonson."

After the first group signed, Mathews called them downstairs. Pierce and Scutari knew what was coming, one more taking of the oath, essentially unchanged from the night in the barracks with the original nine.

They formed a circle in the playroom. As the men held hands, Richard placed his little girl in the center, and they recited: "I, as a free Aryan man, hereby swear an unrelenting oath upon the green graves of our sires, upon the children in the wombs of our wives, upon the throne of God almighty, sacred is His name, to join together in holy union with those brothers in this circle and to declare forthright that from this moment on I have no fear of death, no fear of foe; that I have a sacred duty to do whatever is necessary to deliver our people from the Jew and bring total victory to the Aryan race. . . ."

Pierce and Scutari felt tears welling in their eyes. Those words tightened their chests with a sense of mission. Each time they repeated them, they renewed their bond with one another. Looking down at Danielle, who stared at the men and smiled when one made a quick face at her, the words thundered into Scutari's mind. His daughter, he thought. It's all for her. Once he had given his word under such conditions, nothing could make him go back on it.

That night, Mathews asked Pierce to stay with him in the bunks downstairs. Pierce took the top bunk so Mathews wouldn't have to use his injured hand climbing up. After hitting the lights, the two friends talked for hours. They batted ideas back and forth, the things they would do after Bob recuperated.

"Before we hit the vault in San Francisco," Pierce told him, "get this. We're gonna re-rob the Ukiah route of Brink's. Ron King told me the company made no security changes after we hit them."

"You're kidding!" a surprised Mathews said. "The system's gonna fall easier than we thought."

"We have it all planned," Pierce added, "but for a different spot on the route, farther along so there'll be more money. We got the escape route and switch plan all set."

"I hope my hand's healed enough to join you," Mathews said. "What about Los Angeles?"

"We've done some reconnaissance on that, Bob, and let me tell you, that place looks real vulnerable," Pierce reported. "It's best to start with LA because our suspicion about New York is right. There are so many utility sources into New York, it would be a logistical nightmare to try knocking it out before we have some more people ready.

"But what we found is there's only three main power lines feeding the Los Angeles area from outside. Knocking them out'll be child's play. We coordinate those explosives with some of the main cable junctions, and power and phones will be out for weeks. We got a couple of LA storm troopers who've pledged to join us.

"Then we drop a tub of cyanide into the aqueduct. Hell, it'll probably be detected at the filtration plants, but either way, we're causin' problems. The niggers'll be in the streets in an hour, and the cops'll be shooting. I just hope the big quake doesn't get 'em before we do."

Mathews was impressed. He'd dreamed of a repeat of the urban riots of the 1960s and wanted to capitalize on the strife to recruit frightened whites. Mathews enjoyed planning and was sorry Pierce was leaving the next day. It had been a short visit, but Pierce and Evans had to rejoin their men in Pahrump.

"Bruce, I'm sure glad it's going well for you," he said, "because I'm having trouble everywhere else. It's good to see you making progress. It's all working."

ROBERT AND SHARON MERKI hadn't felt safe since the injured Mathews arrived on Whidbey. Mathews was the focus of an intensive ZOG manhunt, making everyone on the island with him a little paranoid. The Merkis desperately wanted to leave, and each time they went to Smugglers Cove to see Bob, they broached the subject.

What the master counterfeiter wanted was real currency to fund a propaganda unit in Oklahoma, using printed and computerized material. Once, after the Merkis left his house, Mathews turned to Scutari, at this point his closest confidant.

"Well, Black, what do you make of Noah's request?" he asked.

"What I'm hearing," Scutari analyzed, "is a guy who wants out of the Bruders Schweigen, or at least to get away from the front lines."

"Noah's been with us quite some time," Mathews responded with concern. "He knows a lot about what we've done."

"Maybe that's exactly the kind of person we should

send away," Scutari said. "We decrease the chance of him being caught and having to test his loyalty."

On November 30 the Canadians, Jim and Edgar, told Mathews they had business in Canada but they'd be back if he'd wait for them. Mathews gave them his word he'd be there at least until December 9, and they assured him they'd be back before that.

Although his right hand was recuperating nicely, Mathews was convinced he'd never regain full use of it. When he worked on the declaration of war, the notes were practically illegible. Shirley Silva typed it for him, and she had to ask frequently about words she couldn't read. Mathews polished the first two pages, which were his own thoughts. He intended it to be his best piece of writing. It began:

It is now a dark and dismal time in the history of our race. All about us lie the green graves of our sires, yet, in a land once ours, we have become a people dispossessed. . . .

While we allow Mexicans by the legions to invade our soil, we murder our babies in equal numbers. Were the men of the Alamo only a myth? Whether by force of arms or force of the groin, the result of this invasion is the same. Yet our people do not resist.

Our heroes and our culture have been insulted and degraded. The mongrel hordes clamor to sever us from our inheritance. Yet our people do not care.

Throughout this land our children are being coerced into accepting nonwhites for their idols, their companions, and worst of all their mates. A course which is taking us straight to oblivion. Yet our people do not see. . . .

All about us the land is dying. Our cities swarm with dusky hordes.

The water is rancid and the air is rank. Our farms are being seized by usurious leeches and our people are being forced off the land. The Capitalists and the Communists pick gleefully at our bones while the vile hook-nosed masters of usury orchestrate our destruction. What is to become of our children in a land such as this? Yet still our people sleep!

Mathews invoked the names of a trio of right-wing martyrs, starting with John Singer, a Mormon polygamist in Utah who pulled his children out of public schools and refused to submit to state standards for home schooling. Singer was shot to death by police at his home in 1979, while he was fleeing with a gun when they tried to arrest him. Mathews then named Gordon Kahl, the Posse Comitatus tax protester killed in June 1983. Finally, Mathews invoked Arthur Kirk, the Nebraska farmer killed by police less than six weeks earlier. He continued:

To these three kinsmen we say: "Rise, rise from your graves, white brothers! Rise and join us! We go to avenge your deaths. The Aryan yeomanry is awakening. A long forgotten wind is starting to blow. Do you hear the approaching thunder? It is that of the awakened Saxon. War is upon the land. The tyrant's blood will flow."

Mathews attached to the back of his dissertation an "Open Letter to Congress" he had found in National Alliance literature. It warned of revenge on Congress members for atrocities against the people, such as the Vietnam War, which it called a "betrayal of 55,000 Americans." It ended with the warning: "When the day comes, we will not ask whether you swung to the right or whether you swung to the left; we will simply swing you by your neck."

On December 1, Mathews asked Ian to get his brother, Cooper, and take the ferry into Seattle. Ian was happy to do whatever Bob wanted.

"I want you guys to go to the Seattle public library," Mathews said. "They got a directory there, *Editor & Publisher,* that lists all the newspapers in the country and their circulation. I want you to get me the mailing addresses of the three biggest newspapers in each of the fifty states."

After Ian left, Scutari looked at Bob. "What's that all about?" he asked.

"This declaration of war," Mathews answered. "We're going to share it with the world. Can you see the editors' faces when they open it up? They're gonna know we're serious." Mathews then handed the declaration, including the signature page, to Randy Duey and asked him to go to the mainland and have a thousand copies of the eight-page document made for distribution.

Mathews was so confident that the recent confrontations with ZOG would solidify the Silent Brotherhood, he made a list-ditch effort to get Andy Barnhill and Richie Kemp to rejoin for the war he'd just declared. Sitting at a tape recorder, Mathews dictated a message that would be mailed to Barnhill in Kalispell.

"This, unless you change your mind," Mathews said, "will be the last time I ever talk to you or Rich. I will never submit nor surrender. My conscience is clear. Andy, can you or Rich say the same? Goodbye, kinsmen."

BY THE END of that first week of hiding on Whidbey Island, the speculation about how ZOG had found him at the Capri Motel had eaten at Mathews too long. There was never a doubt in Scutari's mind: Martinez had to be the Judas. Mathews still clung to his trust in Martinez, but he was running out of other explanations.

"Well, let's find out for sure," Scutari said.

On Monday, December 3, they sent Sharon Merki to a pay phone with a recorder. Fastening a suction-cup mike to the receiver, she called the Capri and talked with the night manager, Jerry Riedl, who was recovering from his bullet wound. Sharon identified herself as "Lisa from *People* magazine" in Los Angeles and pretended to interview Riedl for an article on the ambush at his motel.

As Riedl gave his recollection of the events, Sharon steered him around to the "man in Room 14"—Tom Martinez. Wasn't there some suspicion that he was with Mathews and Yarbrough, she asked?

"The FBI wasn't concerned with the man in Room 14 at all," Riedl said.

Sharon's stomach wrenched when she realized what Riedl's answer meant. Riedl went on to explain that the man in 14 had to be an informant, because when the FBI arrived at the motel, they told him they knew the two men in Room 42 had left a 7 A.M. wake-up call. The only one who could have told them was the man in Room 14. He was the only other one who knew.

At that point, a truck passing by Sharon hit its air horn to alert a car about to pull out, and Riedl realized "Lisa" was calling from a telephone booth.

"Well, I gotta go now," the motel manager said quickly and hung up, wondering who in the world the woman really was.

Randy Duey returned from the copy shop with boxes containing the thousand copies of the declaration of war. In the playroom, Mathews helped him go through the boxes. At one point a worried look replaced his normal smile, and he started flipping through the reams of paper. He hadn't felt like this since he was in the woods west of Ukiah reaching for the gun that was no longer there.

"Randy?" Mathews called to Duey. "Randy! Where's the original?"

They scoured the boxes. The original declaration of war was missing. The copy shop operator must have read it, become alarmed, and kept it, they figured. Duey hadn't given an address, but their location in the Seattle area could be compromised. Mathews wondered how much time he'd have.

"This is it, Bob," Scutari pleaded. "You gotta leave now."

"I told Jim and Edgar I'd wait for them here because the message center is moving," Mathews argued. "If no one stays, we'll lose those two Canadian kinsmen who won't know how to contact us. I'll be all right." Scutari had asked his brother Frank to set up an answering machine in a rented office in Vero Beach, Florida, and pass messages. Frank agreed to help his younger brother.

When Sharon Merki returned with her tape, she urgently called the men down to the playroom. She had proof, she said, that Martinez was an FBI mole.

The group listened to the tape several times. For most, it erased any doubt about "Spider" Martinez, but not for Mathews. For a time, Bob clung to the slim chance his friend wasn't the traitor. He wouldn't bring himself to admit the obvious. It wasn't part of his script, which called for Tom to join him in the victorious struggle. Mathews always had gotten his way, ever since he was eleven.

But by the end of that day, Mathews had no choice but to accept it as true. He wrote about his disappointment to Zillah:

> It appears now that all of the problems we have suffered since the birth of our daughter arise from the direction of one vile traitor. Tom Martinez sold his soul to ZOG and betrayed all he believes in, his brothers and himself. What a low, miserable, wretched creature he has become!

He told Zillah he had planned to have her and the children picked up the Monday after Thanksgiving to live at Mount Hood. The shootout had prevented that.

> I felt no pain when I got shot and I have not felt any pain yet. At least not in my body. I feel an excruciating pain in my soul at the loss of Gary, the betrayal of Tom, and worst of all, at our lengthening separation. The only child from my loins and she has but only once felt my touch or seen my face. Standing strong and true can leave a man so lonely.

It was to be Mathews's biggest day of disillusionment.

That same day, while they were gathered around the tape recorder, one of Mathews's own followers went to another pay phone. A mist hung in the air around the phone booth as a quivering hand pushed a quarter into the slot. After a brief pause, the operator came on and asked for more change. Hearing the correct tones indicating that the caller had paid, the operator put through the call.

The answering voice said: "FBI Seattle."

There was a pause, then the person in the phone booth said, "You're looking for Robert Mathews? He's here on Whidbey Island. Some of the other people are here, living in three houses on the island. Tell Agent Stephenson.

"Would you like to talk to him?" the FBI receptionist asked.

"No. Just pass it on. They've got a lot of weapons and ammunition here. Mathews is in a house on Smugglers Cove Road, there's a bunch staying there."

The line then went dead.

*   *   *

ROBERT MERKI WAS more determined than ever to abandon the island after Sharon had made the tape with the Capri manager. That evening, he and his wife went out to dinner with Randy Duey in Coupeville. Afterward they dropped Duey at his house and drove the short distance to their place. They stopped at the bank of mailboxes at the entryway into the subdivision, and Sharon checked their box.

As she started back, she noticed a car had followed them around the curve on the steep hill leading into the area. The Beachcombers Club, a collection of fifteen houses along the seawall at the bottom of a 150-foot bluff, consisted of summer homes. Only two other houses were occupied in December. Sharon knew their cars, and the one stopped back at the curve didn't belong to either of them.

Returning to her car, she warned Robert. They watched in the rearview mirror as they eased down the narrow drive between the houses and the bluff. The drive deadended at the last house.

Turning the car by their house, Robert and Sharon looked back down the drive and saw that the other car had stopped at the mailboxes while a man got out and checked to see which box Sharon had opened. Then he got back in his car, which quickly turned and headed back up the hill.

Robert Merki threw his car into gear and took out after the other car, catching up to it as it crested the hill and started for the main road. Sharon jotted down the license number before it turned onto North Bluff Road. On Tuesday morning, Sharon checked the plate with the state motor vehicle department and was told the car was registered to the Whidbey Naval Air Station, a small landing strip just north on the road between Greenbank and Coupeville.

That frightened the Merkis even more, and they again asked Mathews to approve their Oklahoma propaganda shop. Mathews remembered Scutari's counsel and told Merki he'd give him $10,000. To show there were no hard feelings, he gave Robert and Sharon each a Bruders Schweigen medallion.

That afternoon the house at Smugglers Cove resembled the mailing room of some civic group, as the men and women gathered around a big table upstairs to stuff a thousand mailers. What set it apart was the document being mailed—a declaration of war to save the white race. As some stuffed the envelopes, others scribbled out addresses from the list Ian and Cooper obtained from *Editor & Publisher*. They readied other envelopes for people on their own mailing lists from the movement. Ian was still staying with Mathews, but his brother Cooper had left the island the day after the mission to the Seattle library.

Scutari stood at the sliding glass doors, using binoculars to scan the water. He zeroed in on a fishing boat with a cabin anchored out in Admiralty Inlet. The boat's windows were tinted so he couldn't see inside.

"What're you seein'?" Duey asked Scutari.

"He don't see nothin'," Mathews laughed. "He's been watching those boats every day. They're always out there."

"Yeah." Scutari said in a low grumble. "Maybe. That one boat's been out there since yesterday. I don't like it, Bob."

"What about the car from the naval station that followed us?" Merki chimed in from the table where he and several others were working. "And that guy who came to the door today asking if we wanted to buy firewood? I just have this bad feeling he was checking us out."

"That guy was a fed for sure, Bob," Scutari agreed. "My gut tells me that."

"No, I don't think so," Mathews replied. "We should be careful, but that guy could have been legit." Scutari, who had been right about Martinez, was unconvinced.

Later, Duey wrote a short letter to the manager of the Capri Motel to apologize for the recent "ruckus" there and for his friend's misrepresenting herself as a reporter from *People*. He enclosed $100 for the trouble.

Nor was Mathews finished writing yet. He composed a four-page "letter to the editor" for the *Newport Miner*, the Pend Oreille County newspaper that had printed so many of his earlier letters. This would be the most explicit one yet.

It detailed his experience in Metaline Falls after leaving the tax fight in Arizona, how the government harassed him and "tried to have me fired from my job" at the zinc mine when all he wanted was to clear his land and live peacefully. He told how he turned to reading and discovered a "wrongfully suppressed emotion buried deep within my soul, that of racial pride and consciousness."

The stronger my love for my people grew, the deeper became my hatred for those who would destroy my race, my heritage, and darken the future of my children.

By the time my son had arrived I realized that White America, indeed my entire race, was headed for oblivion unless white men rose and turned the tide. The more I came to love my son the more I realized that unless things changed radically, by the time he was my age, he would be a stranger in his own land, a blond-haired, blue-eyed Aryan in a country populated mainly by Mexicans, mulattoes, blacks, and Asians. His future was growing darker by the day.

Then he revealed what he had tried so hard—as had the FBI as well—to conceal from the world: "A secret war has been developing for the last year between the regime in Washington and an ever growing number of white people who are determined to regain what *our* forefathers discovered, explored, conquered, settled, built, and died for." The phrasing matched that of his National Alliance speech fifteen months earlier.

The FBI has been able to keep this war secret only because up until now we have been doing nothing more than growing and preparing. The government, however, seems determined to force the issue, so we have no choice left but to stand up and fight back. Hail Victory!

He included a warning for Martinez: "As for the traitor in Room 14, we will eventually find him. If it takes 10 years and we have to travel to the far ends of the earth we will find him. And true to our oath when we do find him, we will remove his head from his body." Then he had a warning for the FBI:

> *I am not going into hiding, rather I will press the FBI and let them know what it is like to become the hunted. Doing so it is only logical to assume that my days on this planet are rapidly drawing to a close. Even so, I have no fear. For the reality of life is death and the worst the enemy can do to me is shorten my tour of duty in this world. I will leave knowing that my family and friends love me and support me. I will leave knowing I have made the ultimate sacrifice to secure the future of my children.*
>
> *As always, for blood, soil, honor, for faith and for race,*

Robert Jay Mathews

What he didn't know was that, because of a phone call from one in his own midst, the FBI was already marshaling for battle on Whidbey Island.

EARLY IN THE EVENING on November 4, Wayne Manis sat on the bed in his Kalispell motel room going over last-minute preparations with Jean Nishimori, an agent from the Seattle FBI office. They had tracked Andy Barnhill to a bar where he and Richie Kemp had purchased a poker game, which is legal in Montana. Manis arranged to sit in on a game, and he was determined that the gambling impresarios would lose a great deal more than their money that night.

But on Tuesday, as Manis and Nishimori readied the net for Barnhill and Kemp, Manis got a call from Toby Harding, his supervisor in Butte.

"You gotta get to Whidbey Island immediately," Harding said. "We have Mathews under surveillance with about a dozen of his people and it's about to go down."

So, Manis thought to himself, Mathews went north out of Portland?

"There's a Bureau plane on its way to Kalispell to pick you up," Harding said. "It'll bring you to Butte. We already have your ticket for a Seattle flight leaving in less than three hours. You should just make it if you hurry."

The next morning, Wednesday, Agent Don Wofford ran an affidavit by a federal judge. Wofford felt there was enough probable cause to authorize a wiretap on Suzanne Stewart's phone in Boise. Sharon Merki's daughter had come into the investigation when Wayne Manis had watched Gary Yarbrough dial her number from a pay phone in Sandpoint on September 5. Agents in Boise had her under surveillance, just as she had watched them, since October 1. The judge approved the wiretap, giving the FBI a direct patch into the Silent Brotherhood's communications.

And in Seattle, Agent Norm Stephenson swore out a criminal complaint charging six men with the Northgate robbery in April: Mathews, Pierce, Barnhill, Duey, Yarbrough, and Parmenter. He missed only Richie Kemp. In his affidavit, Stephenson outlined the evidence, including photo identifications of Barnhill and Pierce by the people who sold the switch cars, a statement from a "source of information"—Tom Martinez—that Mathews had admitted the robbery, and details from searches at Barnhill's house in Laclede and Duey's Newport residence, which turned up newspaper articles about the Northgate robbery.

Magistrate Philip Sweigert signed the arrest warrants for all six, giving the FBI task force on Whidbey the grounds to attack.

Customers at Warren Caveness's general store in Greenbank were beginning to ask whether he'd been noticing an unusual amount of activity in the area in the last few days. It seemed there were an awful lot of men driving around like they were lost. Callers to the sheriff's office were told it had something to do with "a tactical exercise" at the naval air station.

A persistent drizzle hung in the air Thursday morning as people gathered for breakfast in the Smugglers Cove house. The banter around the table concerned abandoning the island that day. Scutari was leading a caravan including Silva and his family, Norris, and Jones to look for safehouses in the Southwest. Scutari wanted Mathews to go too, and for a moment it looked as though Mathews would.

Then he backed down, despite Scutari's protests. "I promised our two Canadian kinsmen I'd wait until after this weekend," Mathews insisted. He handed Scutari several envelopes to be mailed away from the Seattle area, so the postmark would be meaningless. Among them were letters to his mother, to Debbie, and to Zillah, all saying essentially the same thing, that he missed them and found it ironic that fighting for his family separated him from them.

"I'll drop 'em in the mailbox in Yakima," Scutari assured him.

"You taking the ferry over?" Mathews asked.

"Naw," Scutari answered. "We had one of the cars repaired up in Oak Harbor, and the dipshit forgot to put the dipstick back in. We gotta go way up there to get it, so we'll take the bridge over Deception Pass."

Piling into two Oldsmobiles and Silva's pickup, Scutari and his family, Silva and his family, and Norris and Jones circled out the dirt driveway and disappeared into the tall trees that shielded the property from the road. They made it as far as the main highway 2 miles away when Silva called on the CB asking Scutari to hold up. In the rush to leave, Shirley Silva had forgotten to hug Mathews. She suddenly felt a compelling need to return.

Mathews was surprised and flattered when the group came back just for that hug. Scutari made one last stab at getting Mathews to leave.

"I'll be all right, Black. Really," he said. Scutari looked into Mathews's normally brilliant eyes and saw a distant look that troubled him.

The group left again and headed north to retrieve the dipstick, thereby unwittingly eluding the FBI surveillance.

BILL DeLAPP WALKED out the front door of his large two-story woodframe house at the Beachcombers Club that same morning and stood looking over Saratoga Passage toward Camano Island. Sharon Merki suddenly came around the far side of her much smaller house next door. The Merkis' rental was a small one-and-a-half-floor chalet with a deck across the front and wrapping around the side. It was surrounded by a white picket fence and had a stylish staircase, also enclosed by the fence, leading down the seawall to the rough, pitch-colored beach.

Standing next to the railing, Sharon called out a neighborly, "Morning, Bill."

"Morning, Molly," DeLapp returned. Sharon had introduced herself as "Molly Bradley" when she moved in during November. Looking at her more closely, DeLapp noticed Sharon had brown hair today. A couple of days ago it was black. At first he wasn't sure it was "Molly," because he'd seen an older woman next door, Ida, and a young, attractive woman—Suzanne Stewart—who arrived once with a man. They were introduced as Molly's daughter and son-in-law.

"How you enjoying your sabbatical?" DeLapp called to Sharon.

"It's been perfect," she smiled. "We hate to be going."

"Oh, you leaving?" DeLapp asked.

"Afraid we have to," she answered, then walked around the side again.

DeLapp waited a moment, then went inside his house, where a woman sat in a chair reading a magazine. DeLapp told her, "She says they're getting ready to take off."

The woman got up, walked casually up the stairs and met a man at the top. "Bill says the Merkis are getting ready to go," she said.

DeLapp heard a two-way radio click on and the man upstairs saying, "We have received information the subjects at Beachcombers may be readying to leave."

"Keep an eye on them," a voice responded over the crackle of static. "If they pull out, notify us immediately."

DeLapp's houseguests had been there since Tuesday, after the Island County sheriff had called Bill up to Coupeville to meet the FBI. The agents told DeLapp his new neighbors were suspected counterfeiters. The FBI wanted to use DeLapp's house for a stakeout. He agreed, and a male and female agent—a couple to arouse less suspicion—were dispatched to his house. From DeLapp's second floor, they could see down into the Merkis' living room side window.

Six people remained under FBI watch on Whidbey Island on Thursday. Ian Stewart stayed with Bob at Smugglers Cove. The Merkis and the elderly Ida Bauman were at the Beachcombers Club. Duey was alone off North Bluff Road. The FBI, though, was unsure whether more people were in those three houses.

When Bob fell asleep that night, he had a vivid dream that his entire family was around him. It was like dreams he had had as a child, Mom and Dad up in the mountains on their family ranch, his brothers there too. Debbie was there with Clinton, and Zillah with her boys and little Emerant. In his dream, Bob could reach out and touch them all. Everything was as he felt it should have been.

Late that same night, the FBI began banging on doors of houses near the three hideouts, telling folks arrests were going to be made. Because there could be gunplay, residents would have to evacuate immediately. A steady stream of cars passed through the roadblocks that suddenly sprang up as residents headed for the safety of friends' or relatives' houses in other parts of the island.

The two-story metal building on the Whidbey Naval Air Station, situated in Smith Prairie on a big bend in the island, became the barracks for an increasing number of FBI agents mustering on the island. Wayne Manis arrived Wednesday after a short briefing in Seattle. Turning off the two-lane highway into the airfield, Manis saw a two-story farm house to the right of the driveway. The metal building was opposite on the left. Just beyond was a squat 25-foot control tower painted in wide orange, white, and red vertical stripes.

By Thursday night, 150 agents had been assigned to Whidbey. Alan Whitaker, special agent-in-charge of the Seattle FBI office, established the main command post in the metal building. The "on-site" command post was in the control tower.

Whitaker prepared a briefing for the assault teams on the morning operation. When Manis entered the main command post, he found Wofford, the bearded "Wolfman," who nodded and pointed to an empty seat. At the front of the room Manis saw a tall, prematurely balding man. He was Gene Wilson, Assistant U.S. Attorney in Seattle, who had come to observe the operation since this would be his case.

SWAT teams from FBI offices in Seattle, Portland, Butte, San Francisco, and Los Angeles were assembled in the room, along with the Hostage Rescue Team from Quantico and reserve agents. Denver and Salt Lake City teams were on standby.

"Some of the subjects were seen leaving the island today," Whitaker told the assembly. "Spotters are trying to reestablish surveillance on them." Pointing to aerial shots, Whitaker outlined the positions for each assault team. Manis, a member of the Butte division SWAT team, was assigned to the Merki house.

"We will be in position tonight, then at sunrise we'll announce our presence at all three houses. We hope we'll have a give-up situation, but you all know what to do if we don't. Tomorrow may be a very long day."

Shortly after 11 P.M. Thursday, the Butte SWAT team hopped out of the back of a van atop the bluff that pinned the Beachcombers Club against the water of Hidden Beach below. Manis and the others were dressed in full battle gear—flak vests and camouflage uniforms, with painted faces and automatic rifles. It reminded him of being in the Marine Corps. The night was pitch black, and they could hear the water slapping the seawall far below them. The rain, driven by a brisk breeze, cut through the extra layers of clothing.

Agent Gary Lincoln, team leader on the Merki house, had twelve agents at his disposal. He quickly set about deploying them. Pointing out the Merki house below, Lincoln put trained sniper Bill Buie on the steep bluff, where he'd have a clear field of fire. Steve "Stumpy" Fiddler was assigned to be Buie's spotter. Lincoln split the remaining agents into three teams, assigning one to cover the seawall from the south, the second to cover the opposite side at the entrance road in case anyone tried to make a break north. The third group would spend the night snug and warm in the DeLapp house, which had been evacuated earlier.

Buie and Fiddler checked their gear, then started the dangerous descent down the steep bluff, through bramble and high weeds, around scattered fir trees and over small rock outcroppings, until they found a secure position. The other agents went north and marched quietly down the curving road, hugging the hillside to take advantage of the darkness. When they reached South Hidden Beach

Drive, they moved quickly, silently, into their assigned positions. Manis went with the group that was to occupy the DeLapp house.

Once inside, Kelly Hemmert and Nelson Leavitt secured the bottom floor, then Lincoln led Manis and Jim Davis from Spokane, temporarily assigned to Butte SWAT, upstairs. "This is perfect," Lincoln said, looking through the large upstairs window. "You can see right into the Merki place."

The agents settled down to watch, the occasional chatter of the radio breaking the silence. It was six hours until light.

FRIDAY MORNING DAWNED overcast once again. A pair of binoculars scanned the trees near Smugglers Cove, coming to rest on a small gray bird, a finch of some sort. The lenses held steady on the bird for a minute, then swept to the left in search of the bird's mate. The woman holding the glasses detected movement and backtracked to a tree. Whatever was by the tree was large, possibly a deer. She saw nothing for a moment, then in the shadows she spotted it again.

Balancing her arms on her window sill to steady the powerful glasses, she made out a man's head. He was wearing a camouflage outfit. Probably a bird watcher like herself, trying to get close, she thought. Then she froze. In the glasses she could clearly see the man was holding a rifle with a large scope.

A mile and a half south of Mathews's house, Janet Ferguson was up early and opened her floor-to-ceiling drapes in her home on Lagoon Point. She loved the way the house looked out over Puget Sound. As she watched the texture of the silvery water in the morning fog, five men in camouflage uniforms carrying automatic weapons jogged up the beach past her home.

At 7 A.M., Manis heard the phone ringing in the Merki house next door. It rang twice, then there was silence.

"Okay, they've made the notifications," Lincoln said. "The suspects should be checking to see if they're surrounded. Be careful, but let our presence be known."

A second later, Robert Merki's horrified face appeared at the side window. When he looked up to the second floor, Manis rose and pointed his automatic rifle straight at Merki's head. Merki's face turned ashen, and he ducked out of sight.

Randy Duey had no telephone. When he heard his name being called over a bullhorn, he nearly panicked. It wasn't enough they had him surrounded, but they knew exactly who he was. But how did they know? What did they know? Did they know about Walter West? About Ukiah? How much trouble was he in?

Devoutly avoiding the windows where an agent might get a clear shot at him, Duey weighed his options: suicide, shooting it out, making a break for it and perhaps escaping. He felt certain of one thing. If he gave the ZOG bastards the slightest opening, they would gun him down. There was no due process for Aryan warriors, like Gordon Kahl and Arthur Kirk.

There was no escape for Duey to the east, facing the water. His only hope was to make it across 25 feet of yard and driveway behind the house and into the thick stand of trees. If he could get there, he might have a chance. He peeked through the rear window next to the back door.

Pulling back the bolt on his Uzi machine pistol for the umpteenth time, he made one last check that a round was in the chamber. Then, after checking his 9mm semi-automatic pistol, he put a gun in each hand, uttered a last prayer, and hurled himself through the door.

Before he had gone six steps, he began spotting figures behind the large fir trees next to the outbuildings and even lying flat on the ground in the center of the dirt driveway, all pointing automatic rifles at him. He made out their faces. They were white men. He had expected a horde of mongrels.

Quickly his nerve dropped like lead weights around his ankles and he staggered to a stop, unable to focus on the voice shouting to him through the bullhorn. It was over. Slowly the weapons slid from his hands and clattered at his feet. He first went to his knees, then flat on the ground.

The next three hours were the most frustrating of Manis's life. The Merkis refused to come out. Looking down into their house, Manis could see them scrambling about and throwing bundles of documents into the fire-place. A long column of gray smoke poured out of the chimney, and Manis saw incriminating evidence dissipat-ing into the drizzle. The SWAT team repeatedly called the command post asking permission to fire tear gas into the home, but each request was denied. Whitaker was trading some evidence for the safety of his men.

A little after 10 A.M., the FBI brought in a helicopter gunship and flew it over Merki's house. The large chop-per squatted down right above the little summer home, thumping the roof with shock waves. The chopper's pilot held his position for five minutes, hoping to terrify the Merkis into coming out. But the terror of the moment only drove the Merkis to step up their frantic burning.

About 11:15, Merki felt he had burned as much as he could. Fearing the FBI would storm the house, he eyed the substantial arsenal of firearms there. Merki judged the situation to be hopeless. He dialed the number the FBI had given him, and said they were coming out.

The agents in DeLapp's house scrambled downstairs and took up positions outside Merki's smaller house. Lincoln, standing on the front porch of the DeLapp house with a bullhorn, ordered Robert Merki to come out first. Once he was out, Sharon was to follow, and then the older woman. But Sharon messed it up by following her husband directly. Agents quickly moved in and snapped handcuffs on the pair. Then Ida Bauman came out, slightly bewildered by the situation.

It took several hours to search and inventory the house. Merki had failed to burn a significant quantity of evi-dence, including the surveillance photographs he had taken with Denver Parmenter at the Brink's depot in San Fran-cisco in August. It turned out most members of the Silent Brotherhood were pack rats.

When the search was completed, the FBI allowed Bill DeLapp and his wife back into their home. An agent would stay around, although they didn't expect any more trouble. An hour later, Suzanne Stewart and her hus-band, Eric Tornatzky, drove up unchallenged and walked around the house. Seeing DeLapp outside, Suzanne asked if he'd seen her folks. He said the FBI had raided the house and arrested them. Suzanne thanked him, casually walked back to her car, and drove off.

DeLapp was incensed. Grabbing the telephone, he called the sheriff's office demanding to talk to the FBI. He wanted to give them a large chunk of his mind.

WAYNE MANIS FIGURED two out of three would be easy. It was Mathews who concerned him. He wanted Mathews alive, and a chance to sweat him. Mathews was the central figure in his case, yet Manis had never spoken with him. But when Manis returned to the airfield command post, he wasn't surprised that the task force at Smugglers Cove had gotten nowhere all morning with Mathews.

Agent Wofford told Manis there were five SWAT teams and the Hostage Rescue Team surrounding Mathews. There was no chance of escape. A total of fifty-two agents were assigned to the Smugglers Cove assault. "Our biggest problem," Wofford assessed, "is we don't know for sure whether any women or children are in the house. There's no phone in the house and Mathews hasn't responded at all to the bullhorn."

Wofford stayed at the CP to interrogate the Merkis while Manis, still the case agent, was sent forward to Mathews's house.

Manis drove the 8 miles from the naval base to Smugglers Cove Road. A large crowd of people, including a growing number of newspaper and television reporters hungry for any rumors about what was happening, stood outside the Island County sheriff's roadblock. Volunteer deputies and firefighters manning the roadblock didn't know any more than those asking the questions.

When he reached Smugglers Cove Road, Manis started down the winding driveway toward the Moore house. Someone yelled from the thick timber, "Hey, T!" Turning, Manis saw Danny Colson, the agent who headed the Hostage Rescue Team.

Following a rope strung waist-high through the forest as a guide, Manis and Colson worked their way in a semicircle through the trees to the clearing to take up a position south of the house, next to the two-car garage. SWAT teams were stationed on three sides of the clearing. Los Angeles was on the south, Portland on the north. Butte, Seattle, and San Francisco covered in between.

"Duey and Merki confirm Mathews is in there, but they won't say if anyone else is with him," Manis told Colson.

Manis looked at the house. In the gray light of the overcast day, it seemed vacant. Manis liked three of the four sides, open ground that would give Mathews no escape. But 20 feet away on the west side, facing the water, was a bluff that could be reached in no time on the dead run. If the fog rolled in tonight as it had last night, it could tempt Mathews.

"We hear there's quite an arsenal inside," Colson added. "The Coast Guard shut off the inlet so no ships can pass out front. And the FAA at Sea-Tac is keeping small aircraft away. We hear Mathews may have LAWS rockets in there."

Manis looked at the house again. His spirits sank. "I got a bad feeling Mathews has developed a Hitler complex and this is his Berlin bunker," he said.

In fact, at that moment inside the house, Ian Stewart watched as Mathews wrote another letter with his bandaged hand. It was, in essence, a suicide note:

We all knew it would be like this, that it would be our own brothers who would first try to destroy our efforts to save our race and our terminally ill nation. Why are so many white men so eager to destroy their own kind for the benefit of the Jews and the mongrels?

I see three FBI agents hiding behind some trees to the north of the house. I could have easily killed them, I had their faces in my sights. They look like good racial stock yet all their talents are given to a government which is openly trying to mongrelize the very race these agents are part of. Why can't they see?

White men killing white men, Saxon killing Dane;
When will it end? The Aryans' bane?

I knew last night that today would be my last day in this life. When I went to bed I saw all my loved ones so clearly, as if they were there with me. All my memories flashed through my mind. I knew then that my tour of duty was up.

I have been a good soldier, a fearless warrior. I will die with honor and join my brothers in Valhalla. For blood, soil, and honor. For faith and for race. For the future of my children. For the green graves of my sires.

Robert Jay Mathews

BY MIDDAY IT WAS OBVIOUS to Alan Whitaker that the FBI had to make a different move. Mathews hadn't responded to their initiatives. Whitaker approved a plan to take Robert Merki from the Island County Jail in Coupeville to the scene to try to talk to Mathews. Merki, manacled around the wrists and ankles, was escorted around the garage and handed a bullhorn.

Triggering the mike, Merki called out, "Bob. It's me. Noah. If you can hear me, give me some sign." There was nothing for a moment, then the shade in the rear bedroom went up and down twice.

"Bob, if your answer is yes to what I have to say, raise the shade once. If it's no, do it twice. Okay?" The blind went up and down once.

"Bob, you've got to give up," Merki's amplified voice pierced the dampness. "This place is crawling with feds. This isn't the place to die. Come on out."

The shade went up and down twice.

"Bob, they could have rushed me, killed me and Sharon. But they didn't. If you surrender, you'll be treated fairly," Merki pleaded.

Mathews shouted something. As clearly as anyone could make it out, he was asking about Randy Duey. Mathews was not convinced Duey was unharmed, despite Merki's assurances. Whitaker arranged for a van to go to Coupeville and bring Duey from the Island County Jail. An hour later, Duey appeared by the garage, securely manacled and holding the bullhorn.

"Bob!" Duey pleaded. "It's Randy! Come out, please. We need you, Bob, to fight another day. The movement needs you."

Mathews poked his head past the side of the window to look back at Duey.

"Bob, when I came out of my house, I had my Uzi and

a pistol. I ran right into them and they easily could have killed me," Duey yelled. "I'll guarantee if you come out, they won't kill you." Still, Mathews refused to surrender.

"This isn't going to work," Colson said. "We need a two-way conversation with this guy. Ask him if he'll let us give him a field phone."

Duey relayed the request and the shade raised and lowered once. An HRT commando took the phone pack, paused at the edge of the woods for a moment, then made a dash for the rear door. Dropping it next to the door, he fled back to cover. A few seconds later the door opened a crack and a hand reached out, grabbed the phone, and slammed the door shut.

Within minutes, the forward CP had Mathews on the line. His terms of surrender were clear: "I want parts of eastern Washington, Idaho, and Montana set aside as an Aryan homeland, where my kinsmen will be free to live as they choose," he said. It was not an auspicious start to negotiations.

Throughout the day Mathews's mood swung from rational to suicidal. When darkness set in around dinnertime, the floodlights were turned on, bathing the house with an eerie, milky glow. Mathews told Merki his guns had night vision scopes through which he'd been reading the SWAT teams' name tags. "Hey, Noah," Mathews told Merki, "I can see Agent Fiddler out beside a tree in the back." Steve Fiddler was quickly notified to take a more secure position.

Tacticians at the command post debated whether to contact Debbie Mathews in Metaline Falls to see if she would come and talk with Bob. Ultimately they decided that Debbie might only use the opportunity to encourage her husband to become the next right-wing martyr.

All hope that Merki could talk Mathews out of the house faded around 8 P.M. as Mathews's position became rock-hard: "No, no, just do what you gotta do."

Inside the house, Mathews and Ian Stewart talked over their options. Mathews had made his choice. Stewart wavered, believing the FBI would kill him whether he stayed or left. As time dragged on, however, having heard his stepfather Robert Merki outside, Stewart decided to take his chances on surrendering.

Shortly before 11 P.M., Mathews rang the field phone to the forward command post. "I have a man in here who wishes to come out," he said. He hung up and handed Ian his last letter, which Ian slipped into his duffel bag along with $40,000 in cash he expected to keep. With a heavy sigh, Ian opened the door.

After some tense moments when the agents wondered what was in Ian's bag, the young man was taken down quickly and handcuffed. But he was uncooperative and misleading when asked whether anyone else was in the house with Mathews.

The SWAT teams prepared to spend the night in the woods. A half-hour after Stewart surrendered, while Manis and Colson were sitting behind the garage sipping coffee, the drone of the generators was split sharply by a gunshot inside the house, followed by a long, pitiful moan. Then the woods fell quiet again.

"He killed himself!" Colson bolted upright.

After a discussion of the situation at the command post, the consensus was that Mathews was probably dead. That meant the agents would have to enter the house, but Whitaker decided to wait until daylight just in case it was a ploy.

The damp, cold night passed slowly. Colson and Manis caught a little sleep while others pulled watch duty.

MANIS WENT OVER the attack plan with his colleagues on the Butte SWAT team in the morning while the Seattle team also readied itself. Those two squads drew the duty of storming the house. Seattle would enter first and clear the first floor. Butte then would storm the second floor.

About midmorning, forward agents requested permission to fire tear gas into the house, and commanders gave the okay. The first round of nauseating, eye-searing CS gas went through a window, exploding in a huge puff of white smoke in the playroom. It brought no response from Mathews. Manis figured that if Mathews was still alive, he was most likely to be wearing a gas mask.

By midday, a total of six canisters had saturated the house with noxious vapors, and still nothing moved inside. At 2 P.M., Whitaker ordered the assault teams to stand by to enter the house.

The eight-man Seattle team scurried up to the house and pressed against the cedar exterior. They brought with them Deputy Bill Flanders of the Island County sheriff's K-9 squad, handler of a ferocious German shepherd named Oman Vom Kaisertor. As they rounded the corner to the front of the house and broke out the glass in the sliding doors, the Butte team moved to the side of the house.

Manis, Buie, and "Stumpy" Fiddler stayed outside while Gary Lincoln, Kelly Hemmert, and Nelson Leavitt followed the Seattle team into the house. Manis found himself near a broken-out window, holding his assault rifle at the ready.

Oman the shepherd didn't last long. Spooked by the tear-gas residue, the dog loped back out through the window near Manis, pulling Flanders along. Amid the tension, Manis heard the dog barking and turned to see Oman nipping at his rear.

"Great," Manis thought. "Never send a German shepherd after a neo-Nazi."

They were at the most crucial point of the operation. They were in the house, and if Mathews was still alive, he'd be readying his response.

Mathews didn't wait long. Up on the second floor, he had heard the glass breaking. He steadied his machine gun and scanned the floor, visualizing the layout of the bottom level and imagining where the agents would be standing. He decided to start in the southwest corner and work his way across. Without hesitation, Mathews squeezed the trigger and held it tightly.

The agents recoiled instinctively as a stream of bullets punched through the ceiling above them, criss-crossing in a deadly "Z" pattern and striking the walls and floor. Several agents aimed upward and returned fire blindly through the ceiling, but Mathews had already moved out of the way.

Manis was flattened against the house with the dog still snarling at him. He didn't know which to fear most at the moment, the dog's fangs or Mathews's slugs. Manis looked through the window and saw Hemmert against a wall 20 feet away. The agents inside were catching their breath after the initial wave of bullets. Lincoln, across the playroom, motioned for Hemmert to move over as the Butte team got ready to storm the staircase.

Apparently Mathews had stopped only to slap in a fresh ammo clip.

Hemmert launched himself away from the wall. Just as he did, a second torrent of lead burst through the ceiling, blistering the wallboard where Hemmert had been standing only a second before. Manis watched chunks of the cedar exterior blasted away as the slugs pierced the house near him. Deciding where to stand had turned into a variation of Russian roulette.

"I'm taking the dog back to the woods," Flanders said quickly.

"Go ahead," said Manis. "We'll cover you." Suddenly an agent in the trees shouted, "Watch out, T! He's in the window above you!" Manis flinched as Mathews again fired blindly through the floor, the bullets splintering the cedar just above Manis's head.

Fiddler, Buie, and Manis ran to the rear corner of the house, slipping on the wet ground and caroming into each other. Fiddler was pushed out into the open and made a mad scramble to get back before Mathews could spot him.

Manis and Buie moved several yards from the house and took cover behind two small trees. Mathews opened fire again, splintering a plywood cover on a rear window of the house. The agents returned fire whenever they thought they knew where Mathews was standing. The intense firefight went on for fifteen minutes. Each time there was a lull, Manis wondered, "Is he hit? Is it finally over?" Then the shooting would start again.

Manis and Buie pulled back to the garage. Less than a minute later, the entry team was ordered to retreat. They broke out and ran for cover. Mathews held his fire as they ran. When the agents reassembled in the woods, they looked over each other carefully. They had been like the magician's assistant who climbs inside the box that is then pierced with a dozen swords. Although a hundred or more rounds had been fired at close quarters, no one was hit.

As it turned out, none of their bullets had hit Mathews, either.

*   *   *

As DUSK OF THE SECOND day darkened the clearing, Whitaker knew he couldn't wait much longer. He decided to try to unnerve Mathews with the same tactic used at the Merki house, the helicopter.

Soon, in the distance, the chopping sound of the gunship came in off the water. Like a huge dragonfly with a blinding searchlight, the noisy machine came at the house and hovered over it. In the searchlight's beam, the turbulence from the chopper's blades could be seen sucking shingles from the roof. The helicopter descended to within 3 feet of the roof.

Mathews started running through the upper floor and firing his machine gun through the roof at the helicopter. The pilot was ordered to back off.

As the chopper lifted, the Portland SWAT team north of the house sent a volley of shots into the second floor. Mathews responded by spraying the woods with automatic weapon fire. The shooting lasted fifteen seconds before the woods fell silent again except for the clatter of the retreating chopper.

Scrambling for a better position, Manis crawled into a swale encircled by the dirt drive behind the house. Before he had time to set up, a muzzle flash came right in his face from the second floor. Manis immediately returned fire, sending several slugs straight into the window. He was sure he had hit Mathews.

But a second later Manis heard Mathews shooting toward the Los Angeles team on the south side.

It was then that a decision was made that was likely to end the standoff. An order came down from the command post to lob M-79 Starburst flares into the playroom. In addition to illuminating the inside of the house, the FBI knew that the flares would probably set the house on fire. The FBI believed Mathews would have plenty of time to come out of the house before the fire got out of control. It was Mathews's choice. But one way or another, the impasse would be over.

The forward agents waited for an Island County fire company to arrive with a pumper truck. Manis was apprehensive that if a fire got out of control, the most valuable evidence in his entire case would go up in smoke.

Around 6:30 P.M., when the fire truck was ready, three flares were fired through an already broken window and ignited in a fiery explosion. Sure enough, a fire started. Everyone held position while watching the flames start to roar through the bottom floor. They could hear sporadic shooting on the second level. They kept their eyes glued to the exits from the house for any sign that Mathews was coming out. The heat exploded ammunition like popcorn inside the house, preventing the firefighters from coming near.

Steadily the fire grew, leaping from the bottom floor windows and licking up the sides of the house. Manis, in the swale 25 feet away, felt the heat singe his face. Soon the shooting stopped.

There was no sign that Mathews was coming out.

For twenty minutes the flames were intense, raging a couple of hundred feet into the sky and illuminating the foggy heavens in an eerie orange glow that could be seen by reporters at the roadblocks, by people on the island, and by residents on other islands in the sound. The roof collapsed and dropped into the first floor, and still the flames soared above the tops of the tallest trees.

An FBI spokesman later announced to reporters the tragic end to the seige, adding that the fire "was not started intentionally," although indeed, as the result of a calculated risk, it had been started knowingly.

By Sunday morning, about 8 A.M., the debris had cooled enough for agents to start sifting for evidence. Along one side of the burned-out house, a blackened bathtub that had fallen from the second floor rested at a tilted angle against the water heater. Next to it, apparently dumped out of the tub, searchers found the badly burned remnants of a human body.

Embedded in the chest cavity was a piece of molten gold. It was Mathews's Bruders Schweigen medallion.

HIDING IN A MOTEL ROOM in the tiny Pacific resort of Seaside, Oregon, Denver Parmenter opened the Sunday, December 9, edition of the Portland *Oregonian* and read the news that Mathews was dead, burned alive on Whidbey Island.

Parmenter had gone to Oregon to be near the battleground. He had heard about the Portland shootout after Thanksgiving by way of a phone call from his hiding place in Durango, Colorado, to Jim Dye. He immediately returned to the Vail ski resort and left a forwarding address to general delivery in Seaside so that Randall Rader still could reach him. Then he went to Boise to get the 1949 GMC flatbed he had left in storage and drove to Seaside to wait for Rader's letter.

But now the tether that held the Silent Brotherhood together was broken. Parmenter was confused. He, more than most others, had been a signpost for Mathews back in the summer of 1983. Mathews loved to debate tactics with Parmenter, a sharp political science student in college. And as they walked around Mathews Acres that summer, Parmenter had helped plant the seed of the Bruders Schweigen in Mathews's mind by displaying a willingness to advance to the next level of conflict outlined so graphically in their right-wing texts.

Now Parmenter's concern was avoiding capture. From the searches at Whidbey, Portland, and Sandpoint, the FBI had boxloads of coded documents, easy enough to crack. Cranking up the GMC flatbed, Parmenter instinctively drove to Spokane, but as he approached that city, he realized he couldn't go near his old hangouts without fear of capture. He couldn't contact Janice in Cheney or see his daughter. Lost, alone, and fearful, Parmenter traveled over familiar ground to Priest Lake.

The flatbed bucked and snorted up the narrow, curving road that led to the abandoned training camp. It was fast becoming impassable as snow continued to fall. The truck rolled to a quiet stop, nosing through a curtain of trees into Big Meadows, but he couldn't go farther. Parmenter climbed down from the truck, zipping his jacket as he alighted, and walked through shin-deep snow to the front of the truck, where he leaned against the beat-up chrome grill.

His eyes slowly scanned the landscape where the camp had been, nestled between the hills at the far end of the white-shrouded meadow. The mess tent had collapsed under weight of the snow. As Parmenter stared pensively, snowflakes began to build on the tall man's eyebrows and thick, black hair.

It had meant so much to him, the sense of belonging he had acquired here. He had lost his wife and child to this obsessive attachment. For years he felt like an outcast because of the strange set of beliefs he adopted. But when he found these men, he found acceptance. They had all pledged undying loyalty to each other and to the cause. They had tested that loyalty through a long winter, spring, and summer of daring robberies together.

He was immobilized by conflicting thoughts. Although young, articulate, and college-educated, he had followed Mathews as willingly as any of the others. Now, a year after quitting his job, after losing his family for what he felt would be a long and glorious struggle, he was overcome with a sense of total waste and failure.

The snow, floating softly like shredded pieces of tissue, muted the other sounds of the forest. The only sound Parmenter heard was his own breath, turning into hoary vapor in the frigid winter air.

Epilogue:

"Blood Will Flow"

Mathews's death was like breaking a trance. It signaled the end of the Silent Brotherhood as a viable group, although some tried to keep it going. Most simply ran for cover. It quickly became apparent that the "Silent Brotherhood" was neither, as "ZOG" mobilized even greater forces after Mathews's death than before.

It also was after Whidbey Island that the American public learned about the Silent Brotherhood, which authorities called "The Order," and about the links among the various crimes the gang had committed. The arrests and trials that followed Whidbey Island were well documented in the media.

Led in the effort by assistant U.S. Attorney Gene Wilson in Seattle, the Justice Department built a massive racketeering case against the gang, charging sixty-seven separate crimes. The case was aided by more than half of the people who had followed or helped Mathews, starting with Bill Soderquist. He was the only one to escape unpunished by virtue of total immunity, and the only cooperating witness to insist in court that he still held all of his racist, anti-Semitic views.

The list of those who turned over for the government includes major players as well as minor ones: Denver Parmenter, Randall Rader, Robert Merki, Ken Loff, Thomas Martinez, James Dye, Dan Bauer, Jackie Lee Norton, Mark Jones, and Charles Ostrout. On April 12, 1985, a federal grand jury in Seattle indicted twenty-four members on racketeering and conspiracy charges. By the time the trial began in September 1985, twelve had pleaded guilty. Ten were convicted on December 30, 1985, after sixteen weeks on trial. Richard Scutari, who was at large

450

and on the FBI's Ten Most-Wanted list during the trial, pleaded guilty after his capture in March 1986.

The twenty-fourth defendant was David Tate, the young man with the gun and the Bible. But he never answered the Seattle indictment. Instead, he is serving life without parole in a Missouri state prison for gunning down a State Trooper, Jimmie Linegar, who had stopped him on a lonely highway near Ridgedale, Missouri, for a routine traffic check on April 15, 1985.

One other lawman died during the case. Clifton Browning, an FBI agent based in Grand Junction, Colorado, was a spotter pilot on the Zillah Craig surveillance. While flying home from Laramie on December 8, 1984, his plane disappeared from radar in a snowstorm 10 miles south of Meeker, Colorado, about the same time Mathews was making his final stand on Whidbey Island. Browning's body was found in the wreckage the next day. His involvement in the case had never been revealed until now.

Federal agents mounted a full-scale assault on the CSA survivalist camp in the Ozarks in April 1985, and broke it apart. Jim Ellison, the CSA leader, was later convicted of racketeering and eventually turned government witness.

The Seattle trial was the largest of eight trials stemming from the case. In addition, others among the more than seventy-five people arrested reached agreements to plead guilty in proceedings before judges. The government batted 1.000, getting convictions or plea agreements for every suspect, until November 1987 in Denver. The first acquittals came then, as a federal jury voted not to convict Richard Scutari and Jean Craig of violating Alan Berg's civil rights. Bruce Pierce and David Lane were convicted by the same jury. State murder charges, at this point, have not been filed against any of them in Colorado.

In the spring of 1988, a federal jury in Fort Smith, Arkansas, handed the government its worst loss. Prosecutors had parlayed their investigation into a wide-ranging sedition indictment against ten people, including such leaders as Richard Butler, Bob Miles, and the Klansman Louis Beam. Pierce, Lane, Scutari, Ardie McBrearty, and Andy Barnhill were also among the defendants. Four

others were named in the indictment with plotting to kill
a federal judge and an FBI agent.

The jury acquitted thirteen of the fourteen defendants;
the last one, the gun dealer Robert Smalley, had been
acquitted by the judge earlier for lack of evidence.

Finally, Mathews's death meant not only the end of his
underground; it marked the end of his quest for another
"child of my loins." The surrogate mother impregnated
with his sperm in Portland had a miscarriage. And the
sperm bank, after discovering who its client was, discarded the remainder of Mathews's semen.

THE SILENT BROTHERHOOD aroused great controversy not
only among its opponents but among others in the radical
right. The gang was blamd for hurting the movement
with its crime rampage. Others praised it while backing
away from condoning the violence.

Richard Butler said the men of the Silent Brotherhood
"will become heroes to our grandchildren, like John Paul
Jones and Sam Adams." In the summer of 1985, white
teenage girls shouted and waved to a phalanx of Klansmen marching in Raleigh, North Carolina. The girls held
aloft a sign reading, "We Love the Order."

But it appeared that Mathews's goal of unifying the
radical right had mainly divided it. Bruce Pierce said in a
1986 *Rocky Mountain News* interview at the Leavenworth federal penitentiary:

> I've heard my own people, different people in
> the movement, say I hurt it. I've heard what they've
> said and I've gotten a couple of letters, and they've said,
> "What you've done is you've hurt us and you've
> brought too much attention down upon us, and re-
> ally what did you accomplish."
>
> That makes me defensive, but I realize a lot of
> people are going to feel that way. It's very easy to
> criticize the man in the arena of battle. In retro-
> spect, have I hurt the movement or not, it's irrelevant
> when you consider that it's all according to God's
> will.
>
> We had been making statements for years and I
> think we all recognized that it wasn't going to be

done by talking. Our own people in the movement had been talking for years. And we really by far would have preferred to do this on a discussion level. It just wasn't going to happen.

I don't think we had any idea that we could start and finish in 1984. But you have to begin and you have to make a stand. And if it be we were unsuccessful this time, that's not to say that in other times someone else won't be successful. Our actions were based upon our beliefs, and our beliefs were that in the end we wanted a separate nation.

So it became apparent that the far right was as fractured after Mathews as before. That had not changed, despite the money he spread around the movement hoping it would act like glue—some of which remains unrecovered.

What did change was the uneasy and unwritten code of the far right, that the survival training, the weapons stockpiles, and the preaching of racist and antigovernment messages were purely defensive. A group of people deeply dissatisfied with the American way of life had gone so far as to form a racist underground. That it was better organized in their imaginations than in the field is of little solace. They were not criminals, with very limited exceptions, but rather ordinary people. They didn't shave their heads and wear black leather jackets.

They simply emerged, under the catalytic Robert Mathews, from a fairly indeterminate pool of disturbed folk who wanted to protect their insular existence from threatening changes.

So the crushing of the Silent Brotherhood was an attack on a Hydra. A chronology of events shows not only the direct outgrowths but other developments adding to the tense atmosphere of race relations and survivalism in America.

At the July 1986 Aryan World Congress, medallions honoring imprisoned Silent Brotherhood members were sold for $7. The inscription read: "Should you fall, my friend, another friend will emerge from the shadows to take your place." Two months later, those friends did emerge.

A gang calling itself Bruders Schweigen Strike Force II surfaced, composed of five people with Aryan Nations ties. They carried out a string of bombings, including three in one day in Coeur d'Alene in September 1986 meant to divert police from a planned bank robbery. They were also involved in counterfeiting.

In May 1986, Americans swamped gun stores to buy the remaining legal machine guns before a law took effect banning their manufacture for public sale. The price of a MAC-10 jumped to $1,195. Registration applications, from those obeying the gun registration law, poured into Washington, D.C., by the tens of thousands. Before the law, the office generally received fewer than one hundred a day.

On August 31, 1986, a Connecticut Yankee was selected as Imperial Wizard of the Invisible Empire faction of the Ku Klux Klan. In early December 1986, the sheriff of Jefferson Parish, Louisiana, told his deputies to attack a crime wave by stopping blacks walking in white neighborhoods. Jefferson Parish officials that same month erected barriers across a street leading into the suburbs from New Orleans to try to cut crime. The city tore it down.

One of the patriarchs of the Identity movement, Colonel William Potter Gale, who was Richard Butler's foil in the 1960s under Wesley Swift, was indicted with seven others by a federal grand jury in Las Vegas on October 9, 1986. The indictment charged that they had conspired to mail death threats to IRS officials and a judge who interfered with the "Committee of the States" constitutionalist movement based at Gale's property near Yosemite. Gale was convicted and sentenced to a year in prison. He died in March 1988 before starting his sentence.

On December 15, 1986, FBI agents arrested six members of a survivalist group called the Arizona Patriots. Evidence showed the men were planning to rob an armored truck leaving the Laughlin, Nevada, gambling halls and to bomb the IRS center in Ogden, Utah. With a VCR plugged into a portable generator in their primitive encampment, they had watched the film *Red Dawn,* about guerrilla resistance to a communist invasion of America. Reporters skulking around the Patriots' ranch near Kingman found blueprints for the plant and switching yard at Glen Canyon Dam on the Colorado River, the piping system at Davis Dam farther downriver, and the power and lighting systems at the Fort Thompson substation on the Missouri River in South Dakota.

Five days afterward, a mob of white youths wielding bats and tree limbs chased three black men from a pizza parlor in Howard Beach, Queens, yelling, "Niggers, get out of the neighborhood!" One of the black men, Michael Griffith, was struck and killed by a car. Three white teens later were convicted of manslaughter and assault, receiving sentences ranging from five to thirty years. The assault riveted America's attention on racism. It was more pandemic than generally assumed, and it didn't have to be organized to be deadly.

A federal grand jury indicted five associates of Frazier Glenn Miller's White Patriots Party on January 8, 1987, for conspiring to obtain military weapons from Fort Bragg. Two were convicted, two pleaded guilty, and one, Anthony Wydra, 19, was acquitted. Wydra later did some legal legwork for Bruce Pierce and told him he had found some exculpatory evidence. Before he could tell Pierce what it was, Wydra was shot and killed on January 7, 1989, while driving a car near Camp Lejeune, North Carolina, by a Marine sergeant in the back seat. Investigators ruled it the result of a drunken accident. Prison officials claimed Wydra actually was working on a plan to assist Pierce and several others to break out of Leavenworth. They then transferred Pierce, Scutari, and Evans to Marion Penitentiary, the nation's tightest prison.

On January 24, 1987, twenty thousand civil rights marchers walked through the all-white county of Forsyth, Georgia, to protest a rock-throwing incident by four hundred Klansmen and their supporters the week before. County leaders agreed to form a biracial commission to study integration. On February 7, 1987, about a hundred Klansmen marched in College Park, Georgia, after city leaders tried to prevent the demonstration. The Klan was protesting the murder of a fifteen-year-old white boy, shot in the back while walking home from church. Four black youths were charged with the murder. Such crimes, the Klan countercharged, are hardly ever called "racist."

Five days later a federal jury in Mobile, Alabama, voted $7 million in damages against United Klans of America to the mother of Michael Donald, a nineteen-year-old black man who was beaten, slashed, and hanged by Klansmen in Mobile in March 1981. Donald had been pulled at random off the streets because the Klansmen were angered over the killing of a white policeman in Montgomery by a black assailant. United Klans signed over its 7,000-square-foot headquarters building in Tuscaloosa to Donald's mother, Beulah Mae Donald. She died on September 17, 1988.

Mrs. Donald's attorney was Morris Dees, Mathews's target after Alan Berg.

In March 1987, a farmer near Oxford, Ohio, who was fighting the Federal Land Bank's forthcoming sale of his farm, reached the end of his rope. No one would listen to his claim that the government was unfairly foreclosing on his land. He went with his plight to the local media, which dismissed him because they had already done the "struggling farmer" story.

Then, by chance, the farmer got a call from the local Ku Klux Klan. The caller said he'd read about the fore-closure sale in the public notices and asked if he could use some help. The farmer got plenty of news coverage on a weekend in March when he allowed the Klan to stage a rally on his farm.

"They were the only group that decided to try to help me," the perplexed farmer said. "At this point in time, with the illegal foreclosure, I'm trying to get publicity any way I can. They said they needed somebody who had the guts to stand up and fight the system, and they offered to give whatever help they can. I'm not a Klan member and I doubt I ever will be. But you never know."

A New York state affirmative action training manual was recalled on April 24, 1987, after complaints of reverse racism. Authored by a black woman, the manual stated: "All white individuals in our society are racists. Even if a white is totally free from all conscious racial prejudices, he remains a racist for he receives benefits distributed by a White racist society through its institutions . . . In the United States at present only whites can be racist, since whites dominate and control the institutions that create and enforce American cultural norms and values."

Throughout 1987 and 1988, complaints of racism on America's college campuses were heard with increasing frequency. In one such incident in February 1988, five white University of Massachusetts students and a nonstudent beat two black men who went to a party with a white woman. It prompted a six-day takeover of an administration building by minority students.

Three Portland, Oregon, teens were arrested on March 10, 1988, on assault and intimidation charges after the beating of a 27-year-old Oriental man. The youths were members of the Aryan Youth Movement, headed by Tom Metzger's son, John Metzger, who was involved in the free-for-all fight between skinheads, black guests and audience members on Geraldo Rivera's televison show.

Secret Service agents arrested a Washington, Missouri, couple on May 13, 1988, on a charge of conspiring to kill Jesse Jackson, the first serious black contender for the presidency. In a secretly taped conversation, the thirty-year-old male suspect told an informant he was a member of both the CSA and "the Order." The man, in fact, was neither. He was simply bragging.

In August 1988, a group of blacks in Chicago urged a blacks-only convention to select a single candidate for mayor after the death of Harold Washington. While some black politicians thought it was too divisive, one noted that whites stick together: "We, as black people, should think of black people first. Politically, economically, socially, nothing in the city or the country matters as much as race."

Ethiopian student Mulugeta Seraw, 27, was beaten to death with a baseball bat during a street fight in Portland, Oregon, on November 13, 1988. Three skinheads, members of East Side White Pride, later pleaded guilty to assault, intimidation, and harassment. Following the killing, the number of incidents of ehinic intimidation in Portland increased dramatically.

Former Klan Imperial Wizard David Duke won a special election for a Louisiana House seat and, on February 22, 1989, was sworn in after efforts to bar him from office failed. His district is not rural backwater; it is suburban

New Orleans. He began a race for the U.S. Senate in 1990.

The Anti-Defamation League issued a report in January 1989 showing that anti-Semitic incidents in the United States hit a five-year high in 1988, the tenth year of the survey. The highest year was 1982, just before the Silent Brotherhood organized. The ADL also warned of a marked rise in the number of racist skinheads, to whom murders of minorities in several states were attributed.

Daniel Johnson, head of the League of Pace Amendment Advocates, moved from California to Wyoming in time to run for Secretary of Defense Dick Cheney's vacated U.S. House seat in March 1989. The Pace Amendment would expel most non-whites from the country. Johnson, a white separatist, was aided in his campaign by a contingent of skinheads who later were found in possession of an illegal sawed-off shotgun. Johnson later lost the election.

On August 23, 1989, a mob of 30 mostly white youths in the Bensonhurst section of Brooklyn, having heard some blacks were coming to their turf for a fight, came across four black youths who were looking for a used car for sale. In the altercation that followed, Yusuf Hawkins, a 16-year-old black, was shot and killed. Seven whites were charged with his murder and one with assault. One member of the attacking mob was black.

On December 16, 1989, U.S. Appeals Judge Robert Vance opened a package he received in the mail at his Mountain Brook, Alabama, home, and was killed when a bomb packed with nails inside blew up. Two days later, in Savannah, Georgia, black city alderman and attorney Robert Robinson opened a similar package. He too was killed. That same day, another bomb was received at the llth Circuit Court of Appeals in Atlanta, on which Vance had served, and was defused. The following day, a fourth bomb from the same source was received by the Jacksonville, Florida, office of the National Association for the Advancement of Colored People, and was defused. A week later, a letter claiming responsibility for the bombings was sent to an Atlanta television station. Confirmed by the FBI as having come from the person who sent the bombs, the letter warned of retaliation against judges, lawyers, and NAACP officials "anytime a black man rapes a white woman." It said the bombs were "in reprisal for atrocities committed on Julie Love," a 27-year-old white pre-school teacher who disappeared in July 1988. Her remains were found a year later in an inner-city Atlanta neighborhood. She had been robbed, raped, and beaten to death. Two black men, one of whom pleaded guilty, were charged in the case.

Julie Love grew up in Judge Vance's hometown.

On January 21, 1990 the ADL issued its eleventh annual survey of anti-Semitic incidents in the United States. It showed the highest number of incidents of any year, up 42 percent since 1986. The most serious incident was the stabbing death of a Holocaust survivor in Brooklyn who protested swastikas that had been painted on his door.

Had Bob Mathews remained in Metaline Falls to pursue an honest life and rear his family, he would have been out of work. The Portland Lehigh Cement Company plant was sold to a Canadian corporation which, in May 1990, closed it for good, throwing 65 people out of work. For many, it was the only job they had ever had. LaFarge, the Canadian company, planned to demolish the buildings and concrete towers to ground level, removing all traces of the plant and its once-prominent place in the economics of the Pend Oreille Valley.

DEBBIE MATHEWS BROUGHT three-year-old Clinton out into the wet grass of their front yard. She carried her husband's cremated remains in a sealed box under her arm. When Una Mathews saw her daughter-in-law and grandson from her nearby house, she went outside and walked slowly toward them. The raindrops in the long grass glistened like diamonds and soaked their shoes as they made their way across the yard.

They met by the small apple tree Bob had planted shortly after they had moved to Mathews Acres. The tree, alive with white blossoms, was a housewarming gift from a neighbor. It was Memorial Day 1985, twenty-four weeks after Whidbey Island, and the skies were heavy with steel-gray clouds. Close by was the barracks, where some furnishings remained, notably Bill Soderquist's Nazi book collection.

Debbie used a trowel to carve out a patch of turf, then hollow out a square hole at the base of the apple tree. Gingerly, she scooped the dirt from around the roots, then let Clinton dig a bit, until the hole was a foot deep.

Debbie went back to her house and started a tape player. Leaving the front door open so they could hear it, she came back just as bagpipes began playing "Scotland the Brave." Debbie fell to her knees, kissed the small box and placed it into the ground.

Una Mathews looked toward the horizon as Debbie filled the hole. Across the valley, the Selkirk Mountains stood dark green against the gray sky. Turning, Una caught sight again of the naked summit of Hooknose. When Debbie finished replacing the turf, the ground looked as if it had never been disturbed.

"I'm going home," Una said softly to Debbie, then walked away.

Much later, Una moved off Mathews Acres into town, leaving the clearing in the Lead King Hills for a capacious apartment on Grand View Street in a building owned by Sheriff Tony Bamonte, still a family friend. Her son Lee, embittered by the notoriety his younger brother had brought to Metaline Falls and his family, still lived quietly up the street with his wife, son, and daughter.

Debbie later took computer classes at Selkirk High and bought a television and VCR for Clint. Una babysat with him often. Una liked Metaline Falls and decided to remain. But the months and years after 1984 were difficult as she tried to sort out the terrible ambivalence of her situation, the turbulent feelings of love and hate that sometimes overwhelmed her when she thought of her youngest son.

Eventually, Una came across a poem that helped express what was in her soul. She found it in the beginning of *The Mayor of Casterbridge* by Thomas Hardy: "This should have been a noble creature; He hath all the energy which would have made a goodly frame of glorious elements, had they been wisely mingled."

Her Robbie now was buried up on that land in the mountains where, since he was a child, he'd dreamed of having a place for his entire family. But her husband Johnny was buried in that four-plot the Masons donated back in Marfa, Texas, next to Una's mom and dad. How relieved Una was that Johnny hadn't lived to see what Robbie had done.

When she dies, Una told Lee, bury her next to Johnny on the west Texas plains, where in the 1950s, with her three young boys and her loving husband, America seemed so much simpler, the future was full of promise, and dreams were the stuff of life.

The Aftermath

Andrew Virgil Barnhill. Arrested January 7, 1985, while overseeing a legal poker game he and Richie Kemp had purchased in a bar in Kalispell, Montana, he stood trial in Seattle while his parents sat in the courtroom for nearly all of the four months for support. He was sentenced to forty years for racketeering, conspiracy, armored car robbery, and transporting stolen money. In 1987 he was indicted on sedition charges in Arkansas. Acting as his own attorney, he was found not guilty after telling the jury he had already been convicted for his role in the Silent Brotherhood. "Please don't convict me of those same robberies again," he said.

Daniel R. Bauer. A charter member of the Silent Brotherhood, he pleaded guilty in Boise to being an accessory and receiving stolen money. He was sentenced on January 6, 1986, to five years. He was released in February 1989, to the Hayden Lake area, where he resumed the contracting business.

Louis Beam. The firebrand speechmaker was indicted for sedition in 1987 and made the Ten Most-Wanted list before his arrest in Mexico. But in 1988, a federal jury in Arkansas aquitted him, whereupon he marched outside the Fort Smith federal courthouse and saluted the Confederate Memorial. In 1989, Beam formed a group called New Right to boost the formation of a whites-only nation, and resumed his public speaking as one of the foremost figures in the racist movement. He runs a computer consulting business in Austin, Texas, and publishes a quarterly called *The Seditionist*.

Thomas Bentley. Arrested on April 25, 1985, during the FBI siege of the CSA compound, the former principal of the Aryan Nations Academy was indicted in Seattle for racketeering. On the trial's opening day he pleaded guilty and was sentenced to seven and a half years. By 1990, he had been sent to a halfway house in Seattle to prepare for release.

Larry Broadbent. The Kootenai County undersheriff who made a career of tracking Aryan Nations members lost his job when voters elected a new sheriff in 1988. He stayed in Coeur d'Alene and went back to classes at North Idaho College.

Jefferson Dwayne Butler. The men who introduced Bruce Pierce to Identity was arrested April 22, 1985, during the CSA siege and was charged with possession of an explosive device. He served about a year in prison and after release went to live in Benton, Arkansas.

Richard G. Butler. The patriarch of Aryan Nations was indicted in April 1987 on a sedition charge, the government alleging the Silent Brotherhood plot was hatched at Butler's 1983 congress. While in custody he had chest pains and underwent quadruple heart bypass surgery, fully recovering his health. The Fort Smith jury found him not guilty, and returned to Hayden Lake to carry on his Identity ministry. In competition with Tom Metzger, he has been trying with mixed success to organize racist skinheads. He wants them to listen to Beethoven, he said. But all they play is Skrewdriver. His congresses are still held every July.

Donald Clarke. Robbie Mathews's friend from the Sons of Liberty, who fled to a white mercenary outfit in Rhodesia in 1975, was located by British Intelligence in a South African mine four years later. Extradited to the United States under indictment for conspiring to kill FBI Agent Charles Middleton, Clarke dealt his way free by trading his information on Arizona's right-wing extremists, including Robbie. In exchange, he was allowed to leave the U.S. forever. Clarke went to Europe, where he was reported to have died in a Jeep accident in West Germany in 1981.

Marvin Cooley. The Mesa, Arizona, tax protester whose group influenced Robbie Mathews and catapulted the young man into more extreme groups continued to advocate pleading the Fifth Amendment on income tax returns. In August 1989, he was sentenced to two years in prison, his second stretch, for not paying income tax on $100,000 he earned through lecturing and selling pamphlets against the income tax.

Jean Craig. She stood trial in Seattle for racketeering and conspiracy and was sentenced to forty years. In April 1987 she was indicted in Denver for violating Alan Berg's civil rights. After a trial, the jury acquitted her in November 1987. Curiously, the Seattle jury had found that she had indeed participated in the Berg murder.

Zillah Craig. After two years of resisting the FBI's questioning, she prayed for divine guidance. The next time she walked into an FBI interview, she didn't know which way the Lord was going to lead her until she opened her mouth. Out came all the secrets Bob Mathews had asked her to keep. She testified in Denver against her mother and in the Fort Smith sedition trial. She is now rearing her three children, including Bob Mathews's daughter, while living under an assumed name in a midsize American city.

Elden "Bud" Cutler. A security chief at Aryan Nations, he tried to contract the killing of Thomas Martinez prior to the Seattle trial. He was arrested in August 1985 in a Coeur d'Alene resort hotel after handing the money for the killing to an undercover agent. He was sentenced on March 21, 1986, to twelve years.

Morris Dees. The Montgomery civil rights attorney took his courtroom tactics to the West Coast in 1989. Hoping to do to Tom Metzger and his entourage of racist skinheads what he had done to United Klans, Dees filed suit in Portland, Oregon, in December 1989 seeking damages from Metzger, his son John Metzger, and several other skinheads in the 1988 beating death of Ethiopian student Mulugeta Seraw. The suit claims the skinheads were organized by the Metzgers.

Randy Duey. Arrested on Whidbey Island, the former postal clerk remained silent and stood trial in Seattle for racketeering, conspiracy, robbery, and other charges. He received a sentence of one hundred years.

James Dye. The Marine veteran was arrested in Spokane on January 3, 1985. He tried to lead the FBI to the grave of Walter West but never could find the spot. He testified in Seattle under a plea agreement and was sentenced to twenty years.

"Edgar". The Canadian recruit into the Silent Brotherhood never made it back to Whidbey Island with his friend, Jim. Authorities believe they have confined their activities since then to Canada.

Roderick Elliott. The Colorado publisher who suspended his agricultural newspaper after his controversial appearance on Alan Berg's radio program was indicted for theft in February 1985. He was charged with taking a quarter-million dollars in loans from farmers and friends, including Francis Farrell, and not repaying them. He was found guilty on most counts in May 1986 and sentenced to eight years. He was paroled to a Denver suburb in January 1990, and resumed giving advice to farmers fighting foreclosures.

James Ellison. "King James of the Ozarks" abdicated to the FBI during its seige of his CSA encampment in April 1985. He was convicted in Fort Smith in 1985 of racketeering and received twenty years. He also pleaded guilty to weapons offenses. After a year in prison he agreed to cooperate with the FBI against other right-wing leaders in an effort to reduce his sentence. He was the star witness in the Fort Smith sedition trial in February 1988, but all fourteen defendants were acquitted. The first of his two wives later divorced him. He is expected to be released in 1991.

Randy Evans. The Klansman from Rosamond, California, was arrested on April 25, 1985, at the seige of the CSA, where he had been hiding. He remained silent, stood trial in Seattle, and was sentenced to forty years. "Christ is King, gentlemen," he said to reporters at the trial.

Dan Gayman. The Identity minister from Schell City, Missouri, testified for the government at the Fort Smith sedition trial and turned over the $10,000 that Richard Scutari had given him after the Ukiah robbery. He also turned over $5,000 Mathews had sent to him through a contact in Denver. He still operates his church.

Mark Frank Jones. Arrested on January 10, 1985, in Northport, Alabama, following his return from Whidbey Island, he cooperated with the government and testified in trials in Salt Lake City and Seattle. Code-named "Goober Smoocher" by the Silent Brotherhood, he was given a new identity and relocated by the government.

Richard Kemp. Arrested on January 7, 1985, in the same poker game as Andy Barnhill, the former high school basketball star stood trial in Seattle and was sentenced to sixty years for racketeering, conspiracy, and armored car robbery. Before handing down the sentence, U.S. District Judge Walter McGovern noted he had just driven through Salinas, California, Kemp's hometown, on a vacation. Looking around, he imagined the young man there. "I thought to myself, 'What a terrible waste.' "

Kathy Kilty. Zillah Craig's friend disrupted the 1983 Aryan World Congress when she grabbed a man's ceremonial sword and tried to cut off his head. Observers thought she was demon-possessed, and she was subdued and taken to a Coeur d'Alene hospital. It turned out that she had Wilson's Disease and had suffered a seizure. Her mother brought her home to Wisconsin, where she evntually recovered. David Lane considered her an alibi witness for the day he was in Philadelphia with Tom Martinez. Lane said he was on a cross-country bus going to visit her. But before she could say anything about it, Kilty was struck and killed by a truck riding her bike on a Wisconsin road.

Eugene Kinerk. One of the three young Aryan Nations followers who robbed the bank in Pacific Beach, Washington, he pleaded guilty to that crime. He committed suicide in the Ada County Jail, Boise, on February 23, 1985, after being returned from testifying before the federal grand jury in Seattle. In his last note, he wrote: "I cooperated to hurt those who would kill."

Ronald Allen King. The Brink's supervisor in San Francisco who was helping the Silent Brotherhood after the Ukiah robbery was indicted in Seattle and pleaded guilty just before the scheduled trial date. He was sentenced to five years.

David Lane. Captured in March 1985 in Winston-Salem after Ken Loff helped the FBI track him by phone, Lane went on trial in Seattle and was given forty years for racketeering and conspiracy. He was convicted in federal court in Denver in November 1987 of violating Alan Berg's civil rights by killing him. The judge gave him another 150 years, consecutively, with no parole until the first fifty years are served. At his first sentencing in Seattle, Lane told U.S. District Judge Walter McGovern: "I have given all that I have to assure there will be future generations of white children. If the final victory be yours, then God have mercy on the last generation of white children."

Kenneth Loff. After the FBI returned to his farm on January 30 and excavated at the rabbit cages, Loff realized he needed a lawyer. He got one who cut a deal under which Loff would get five years off his sentence for each suspect he turned in. He was responsible for the captures of Randall Rader and David Lane. Loff pleaded guilty to conspiracy and was given five years. After his release, he left the Pacific Northwest and returned to New York.

Wayne Manis. After working on the Bruders Schweigen Strike Force II case, Manis asked the FBI to take him off Aryan Nations matters. He has since been able to turn some attention to his avocation of big game hunting, and in April 1990 bagged a 8-foot grizzly out of Nome, Alaska.

Thomas Martinez. Six days after Whidbey Island, Martinez appeared in federal court in Philadelphia on his counterfeiting charge. He was sentenced to three years on probation. After he testified at the Seattle trial, the FBI authorized a $25,000 payment to him for his services. In conjunction with the Anit-Defamation League, he has lectured young people against racism.

Ardie McBrearty. Arrested at his home in Gentry, Arkansas, on April 3, 1985, he was the only defendant to testify at the Seattle trial. He insisted he was no racist and had been misled by Mathews, which so upset some of the co-defendants that they fed information to the prosecution for cross-examination. He was convicted of racketeering and conspiracy and received forty years. He was indicted for sedition in Fort Smith but, acting as his own attorney, won an acquittal with the others. In his closing statement he told the jury the government was too willing to create conspiracies where they don't necessarily exist: "When Little Bo Peep can't find her sheep, the government says, 'I know where they are, let's look in her freezer!' "

Robert Merki. He reached a plea agreement under the Seattle indictment and, after testifying against the others, was sentenced to thirty years—ten of them for the old counterfeiting case before he met Mathews. At one point he told authorities he knew the idnetities of people in imminent danger of being assassinated, and would reveal them for a shorter sentence. Prosecutors refused to deal with him.

Sharon Merki. Under a plea agreement, she received twenty-five years, five of them stemming from her involvement in the 1982 counterfeiting episode.

Tom Metzger. Considered by many anti-racist to be the top organizer of racist skinheads in the nation, Metzger was sued in 1989 by Morris Dees in Portland, Oregon, over the Mulugeta Seraw killing by skinheads affiliated with Metzger's group. Through his White Aryan Resistance and the Aryan Youth Movement, led by his son John, Metzger emerged in the late 1980s as the nation's leading racist figure.

Robert Miles. The racist leader from Michigan was indicted in Fort Smith for sedition. He hired a Jewish attorney from Detroit, who became unofficial leader of the fourteen defense attorneys, and was acquitted. He returned to his farm in Cohoctah but, with his wife in declining health, in 1989 ceased publishing his newsletter, *From the Mountain*

Frazier Glenn Miller. After the North Carolina Klan leader was barred from paramilitary organizing by a civil judgment, obtained by Dees he was cited for contempt. He then went underground and issued his own declaration of war against ZOG. He was captured in May 1987 and pleaded guilty to mailing threats. He testified against the defendants in Fort Smith and returned the remaining stolen money Mathews had given him. He was sentenced to five years.

Col. Gordon "Jack" Mohr. Still working out of his

base in Bay St. Louis, Mississippi, the Identity preacher remains one of the most popular speakers and personalities in the movement.

William A. Nash. Arrested back home in Philadelphia, he pleaded guilty to a minor role in the Seattle racketeering indictment. A judge in Spokane gave him five years on probation after he served six months in jail.

Michael Stanley Norris. The Alabama Klansman who was acquitted in the 1981 "Bayou of Pigs" case was arrested with Mark Jones in Northport, Alabama, on January 10, 1985, and charged with harboring a fugitive, Richard Scutari during their escape from Whidbey Island. Jones, Robert Merki, and the Klansman Bill Riccio testified against him in a trial in Salt Lake City. After his release from federal prison, he returned to Tuscaloosa, Alabama, to run a grocery store.

Jackie Lee Norton. Randall Rader's training assistant was arrested in March 1985 in West Plains, Missouri, after Rader began cooperating with the FBI. He was named in the Seattle indictment, pleaded guilty to a minor role, and was given five years' probation after serving six months in jail. He returned to his southern Missouri home.

Charles E. Ostrout. Arrested in February 1985 at his home in tiny Lookout, California, the former Brink's manager who fingered the Ukiah route for Mathews was indicted for racketeering in San Francisco, apart from the defendants in Seattle. He testified against the others and was sentenced to five years.

Denver Parmenter. Arrested in Seaside, Oregon, ten days after Whidbey Island, the Inner Circle member became the star witness against the others at the Seattle trial, spending a week on the stand. He was sentenced to twenty years. He later testified in Denver and Fort Smith. He won a sentence reduction to ten years with testimony from prosecutors that Parmenter was the most rehabilitated of all the defendants. He was expected to be released sometime in 1990 under a new identity.

Pete Peters. The Identity pastor, who ran the Colorado church where Mathews and Lane met the Merkis, the Craigs, and others, became an up-and-coming force in the movement. Considered on the moderate end of the Identity spectrum,, he has spread his influence through speeches around the country, radio sermons, and Bible camps. His wife, Cheri, made a video on the Silent Brotherhood and the Fort Smith sedition trial, and the couple has fought obscenity, pornography, and homosexual rights in their county.

Bruce Carroll Pierce. Captured March 26, 1985, at a Rossville, Georgia, mail drop, Pierce was tabbed by authorities as the successor to Mathews. He left his cadre earlier after Tom Bentley had a vision that Pierce was a traitor. He became the lead defendant in Seattle and was sentenced to one hundred years. He was convicted in November 1987 in Denver of violating Alan Berg's civil rights by killing him, and was sentenced to another 150 years, consecutively. That made a total of 252 years, counting his previous counterfeiting conviction. He didn't ask the judges for mercy: "I'm not going to waste my time or yours," he told Judge Walter McGovern in Seattle. "I am sorry for the pain and grief I've caused my dear wife and my family. Whatever happens to me, I'd like to bring honor to my family and kinsmen, and glory to God." He was indicted in the Fort Smith sedition case but was acquitted. His son Jeremy returned to Kentucky to live with his mother. Julie divorced him and moved to the Spokane area, where she has custody of Kristi.

Gregory Pierce. Bruce's brother, who moved to Montana with him in 1979, he went on the road with him while Bruce was a fugitive late in 1984. He was arrested on February 22, 1985, in Belen, New Mexico, after he and Bruce went to a storage lot to retrieve a car that had been left there. Bruce narrowly escaped. Greg was charged with being an accessory after the Ukiah robbery, but the charge was later dropped.

William Pierce. After Whidbey Island, the author of *The Turner Diaries* said he did not believe America was ripe for that kind of revolution and expressed regret that his disciple Mathews had followed that line. Instead, Pierce took the National Alliance within the system. Purchasing a sufficient amount of stock in AT&T, the Alliance was able to force a question phasing out the corportation's affirmative action program before stockholders at the April 1988 annual meeting in Denver.

More that ninety-one percent of outstanding shares voted against it, no surprise. The shock was that, despite public protest linking it to the Silent Brotherhood and in the city where Alan Berg was murdered, the National Allaince initiative won nearly nine percent of outstanding AT&T shares. Later that year, the National Alliance sent recruitment fliers to homeowners in Yonkers, New York, where city officials were defying a court order to build subsidized low-income housing.

Randall Rader. Arrested at the Spokane airport after a tip from Ken Loff to the FBI, Rader soon became a key witness not only against the Silent Brotherhood but also against former CSA comrades, including James Ellison. He was responsible directly for at least six arrests, and indirectly for up to a dozen more. He entered the federal Witness Protection Program and on January 23, 1986, was given a suspended sentence and six years on probation by a federal judge in Spokane. The leniency to someone who was a key member of the group outraged the investigators and prosecutors who had worked on the case. He has since opened a small business and is self-supporting.

Wiliam Riccio. In a settlement of a 10-year-old case, the Klansman who resisted Mathews's recruiting pitch was sentenced in January 1989 to two years in prision for obstruction of justice stemming from a May 1979 attack by a KKK contingent on black protesters in Decatur, Alabama. "I guess I was hardheaded for a long time," Riccio told the judge. "I will not let this court down if given the opportunity to prove I am a changed person." Riccio served a year and was released.

Dennis Schleuter. The Fort Collins, Colorado, man who agreed to run the Silent Brotherhood's message center was unable to locate the group after he got out of his 20-day jail sentence. The raid on Yarbrough's house had scattered the group so Schleuter simply went home.

Frank Scutari. Richard's older brother, who was a school counselor and contractor in Stuart, Florida, agreed late in 1984 to run a message center in a Vero Beach office for his brother. On February 20, 1985, FBI agents and Martin County deputies staged a mini-commando raid on

Frank Scutari's home. He was later sentenced to three years for being an accessory after a crime.

Richard Scutari. The last of the Silent Brotherhood to be captured, he went to trade school in Tulsa and became a brake mechanic in San Antonio while his comrades were on trial in Seattle. His wife surrendered in Florida in January 1986, and three months later Richard was captured in Texas. He pleaded guilty in Seattle to all but the Berg killing and got forty years for racketeering and conspiracy, and twenty for the Ukiah robbery. In Denver, he was acquitted on charges he had violated Alan Berg's civil rights, and in the Fort Smith sedition trial, acting as his own attorney, he again was acquitted. Michele divorced him and testified against him at Fort Smith, something the judge there later decided he shouldn't have allowed. As Scutari cross-examined his ex-wife, his final question was difficult for both: "One last question, would you please forgive me for the pain I caused you and tell my baby I miss her?" Michele's answer: "I don't know that I want her to know that I've even seen you." He wrote an open letter to the 1986 Aryan Congress in which he called for other right-wing extremists to "learn from our mistakes, succeed where we failed. The Bruders Schweigen has shown you the way." The FBI mused over how different the Silent Brotherhood might have been had Scutari been among the original nine.

Frank Lee Silva. Arrested at a campground in northwest Arkansas just before the CSA seige, he stood trial in Seattle with his wife and daughter watching from the spectators' seats. He was sentenced to forty years for racketeering and conspiracy.

Robert Smalley. The Fort Smith gun dealer was convicted of falsifying records on guns he supplied to Randall Rader. He was sentenced to five years and was released early. Then he was indicted in the Fort Smith sedition case. He contended he'd already been convicted and punished for the same offenses. His case never got to a jury. U.S. District Judge Morris Arnold directed he be acquitted after the government rested its case.

Richard Snell. The former Jim Ellison disciple was charged in 1987 with sedition and conspiring to kill a federal judge and FBI agent. He was acquitted with the others at Fort Smith in 1988, and was immediately returned to death row in the Arkansas state prison, to await execution for killing the Texarkana pawnbroker.

Bill Soderquist. The bright young man who followed Mathews from the National Alliance into the Silent Brotherhood walked out of the Seattle courtroom in 1985 free and clear after implicating the defendants in various crimes and declaring under cross-examination that the Holocaust was a hoax.

Norm Stephenson. After the Seattle trial, the FBI transferred him to Arkansas where he worked on the sedition case and helped turn Jim Ellison over to the government's side. Afterward he was stationed at the Harrison, Arkansas, FBI office.

Ian Stewart. The last man to see Bob Mathews alive in the house on Whidbey Island, he was sentenced to six months in prison and five years probation.

Suzanne Stewart. The FBI placed a tap on her phone in Boise on December 5, 1984, three days before Mathews's death. On January 18, 1985, the FBI raided her house. It took her a while to notice the agents, exhibiting a macabre sense of humor, were wearing blue softball caps with the bright white letters "ZOG" stitched on them. A pre-med student at Boise State University, she pleaded guilty to conspiracy to rob armored cars and was sentenced on August 1, 1985, to ten years. She was later released and was reported to have returned to her studies for medical school.

David Tate. Certain a Missouri state trooper was about to arrest him as a fugitive while on a routine traffic stop near Ridgedale on April 15, 1985, the day the Seattle indictment was released, Tate burst out his van firing a MAC-11 machine pistol. He killed Trooper Jimmie Linegar and injured another, Allan Hines. He remained on the loose in the rugged Ozarks for nearly six days before being captured without a struggle in a Forsyth, Missouri, city park. He was sentenced to life without parole in the Missouri state prison.

Bill tenBensel. The veteran FBI agent took retirement and started his own private investigations firm in Santa Rosa, California.

Bob Tucker. He remained with the FBI after working

on the Brinkrob case, but transferred from the San Rafael office to Salt Lake city, Utah, his office of preference.

Jim Wallington. Four days after his arrest on April 22, 1985, during the seige of the CSA camp, the former member of Bruce Pierce's traveling cadre was released on his own recognizance on a charge of possession of an unregistered machine gun. That was the last authorities saw of him. As of spring 1990, he was still a fugitive.

Allen Whitaker. The agent-in-charge at the Whidby Island seige was transferred from Seattle to the Birmingham, Alabama, office. In December 1989, he headed up the investigation into the spate of mail bombings that killed Judge Vance in Birmingham and Robert Robinson in Savannah, Georgia.

Gary Lee Yarbrough. He remained silent after his arrest at the Capri Motel and was convicted in Boise in February 1985 of assaulting FBI agent Mike Johnston during the FBI's drive-by of his home. He pleaded guilty to weapons offenses as well and was sentenced to twenty-five years. An appeals court later knocked ten years off that. In the Seattle racketeering trial, Yarbrough was sentenced to sixty years. He asked Judge McGovern for only one favor, to be allowed to hug his children. "What we did wasn't out of racial hatred," he told McGovern. "It was love of my own kind, my country, my faith, and my culture. I won't plead to this court for any leniency because I know I won't receive any.

"Our system is breeding a generation that will destroy itself. The blood will flow, and it grieves me."

George Zaengle. Arrested in Bloomsburg, Pennsylvania, on April 3, 1985, he pleaded guilty in the Seattle case and was sentenced in Spokane to five years on probation.

Bibliography

Beam, Louis R. Jr. *Essays of a Klansman*. AKIA Publications, Hayden Lake, Idaho, 1982.

Beam, Louis R. Jr. *Understanding the Struggle, or Why We Have to Kill the Bastards*. Aryan Nations, Hayden Lake, Idaho, undated.

Betrayal: 100 Facts. CSA Enterprises, Pontiac, Mo., 1982.

Coates, James. *Armed and Dangerous: The Rise of the Survivalist Right*. Hill & Wang, New York, 1987.

Corcoran, James. *Bitter Harvest: Gordon Kahl and the Rise of the Posse Comitatus in the Heartland*. Viking, New York, 1990.

Extremism on the Right: A Handbook. Anti-Defamation League of B'nai B'rith, New York, 1983.

Finch, Phillip. *God, Guts, and Guns*. Seaview/Putnam, New York, 1983.

Gibbons, Floyd Phillips. *The Red Napoleon*. Southern Illinois University Press, Carbondale, 1976 (reprint of 1929 ed. published by J. Cape & H. Smith, New York).

Hate Groups in America. Anti-Defamation League of B'nai B'rith, New York, 1982.

Jones, J. Harry Jr. *The Minutemen*. Doubleday, Garden City, New York., 1968.

Lane, David. *Life Law*. Church of Jesus Christ Christian-Aryan Nations, Hayden Lake, Idaho, 1987.

Macaba. *The Road Back*. The Noontide Press, Torrance, Calif., 1973.

Macdonald, Andrew. *The Turner Diaries*. National Alliance, Arlington, Va., 1978.

Martin, Len. *Why They Wanted to Get Gordon Kahl*. Pro-American Press, Detroit Lakes, Minn., 1983.

Miles, Robert. *The Secret Army: Wenn Alle Bruder Schweigen*. Followers of the Way, Fowlerville, Mich., 1985.

474

MOHR, JACK. *Know Your Enemies!* Destiny Publishers, Merrimac, Mass. 1982.

Prepare War. CSA Enterprises, Pontiac, Mo., 1981.

SIMPSON, WILLIAM GAYLEY. *Which Way Western Man?* National Alliance, Arlington, Va., 1978.

SINGULAR, STEPHEN. *Talked to Death: The Life and Murder of Alan Berg.* Beech Tree Books, New York, 1987.

The Spotlight. Liberty Lobby Inc., Washington, D.C., assorted editions.

They Don't All Wear Sheets. Center for Democratic Renewal, Atlanta, 1987.

The Thunderbolt. The Thunderbolt Inc., Marietta, Ga., assorted editions.

Witchcraft and the Illuminati. Zarephath-Horeb, Pontiac, Mo., 1981.

Acknowledgments

When the authors set out to investigate the dichotomous life of Robert Jay Mathews, little was known about the man who had formed the Silent Brotherhood. Even less was understood. Through the willing assistance of many people, the authors were able to reconstruct the disturbing picture of Mathews's life and, more importantly, the role it played in the emergence of a more vocal, more militant radical right. For that assistance, from sources both inside and outside the Silent Brotherhood, the authors wish to express their deep gratitude.

Una Mathews graciously provided the key links in the chain and the leads for filling in the gaps in her son's early life, despite all the difficulty it gave her to discuss it. Richard Robertson, city editor of the *Arizona Republic* in Phoenix, went to extra lengths to assist the authors. Given very vague parameters, he succeeded in finding leads on major episodes of Mathews's life. That material enabled the authors to identify and locate sources who knew Mathews fourteen to twenty years earlier, including FBI Agent Charles Middleton, Dr. Bruce Rogers of the Birch Society, and the TV journalist Ted Knight.

Invaluable help for this book came from within the Silent Brotherhood itself. The authors talked extensively with Bruce Pierce, now at the federal penitentiary in Marion, Illinois, and Zillah Craig. Other members of the Silent Brotherhood contributed to interviews with varying degrees of input. The authors thank them for their unusual frankness. The right-wing leaders Richard Butler and Robert Miles were highly cooperative. Debbie Mathews kindly allowed the authors to interview her and tour the "barracks" and her property.

Many of the government investigators and prosecutors

who worked on the case considered it to be the most significant of their careers. The authors thank them for sharing their recollections and rendering assistance with research. Chief among these people are Wayne Manis of the FBI and Gene Wilson of the U.S. Attorney's office in Seattle; also, FBI agents Reg Powell, Bob Tucker, Bill tenBensel, and Norm Stephenson; federal prosecutors Peter Robinson and Bob Ward; local law enforcement officers Andy Anderson (Sandpoint, Idaho), Tony Bamonte (Pend Oreille County, Washington), Larry Broadbent (Kootenai County, Idaho), and Dan Molloy, Tom Haney, and John Wyckoff (Denver), plus Denver District Attorney Norm Early and his deputy Dave Heckenbach.

The authors also recognize the help rendered by three defense attorneys, David Chappel in Seattle, and Lee Foreman and Mary Kane in Denver; and our colleagues, John Accola, *Rocky Mountain News;* Bill Morlin, *Spokane Chronicle* and *Spokesman-Review;* James Coates, *Chicago Tribune;* and Kitty Caparella, *Philadelphia Daily News.*

Julian Bach, the authors' literary agent, provided guidance through the development of the book. And from the start, the authors' editor at the Free Press, Joyce Seltzer, grasped precisely what was signified by this sad episode in political terrorism. We also thank Jeff Long for his insight, and J. P. McLaughlin for his friendly editing.

Far too numerous to acknowledge individually are those people, numbering in the hundreds, whose insights or actual participation in the events of this book were shared with the authors while they were covering the events as a news story. They range from police detectives and storage yard owners to Klansmen and other far-right activists.

The authors do not contend that all the dialogue quoted in this book represents the actual words spoken at the time except in instances when those words were recorded, such as Mathews's National Alliance speech, Alan Berg's radio program, and David Lane's conversation in the Owl Cafe. The accuracy and context of reconstructed conversations are dependent on sworn testimony in several trials and on admissions to the authors by the persons being quoted.

K. F. and G. G.

Index

479